IN THE FUTURE OF YESTERDAY

RÜDIGER GÖRNER

In the Future of Yesterday
A Life of Stefan Zweig

First published by Haus Publishing in 2024
4 Cinnamon Row
London SW11 3TW
www.hauspublishing.com

Copyright © Rüdiger Görner, 2024

The right of the author to be identified as the author of this work has been asserted in accordance with the Copyright, Designs and Patents Act 1988
A CIP catalogue record for this book is available from the British Library

ISBN: 978-1-914979-10-1
eISBN: 978-1-914979-11-8

Typeset in Garamond by MacGuru Ltd
Printed in the UK by Clays Ltd (Elcograf S.p.A.)

All rights reserved.

A note from the author: All translations are my own unless stated otherwise – like with all of Zweig's essays, which have not appeared in English translation to date.

Remembering Anthea Bell and Donald A. Prater

Contents

Preliminaries, or How to Approach Stefan Zweig:
   A Writer from the Past for Our Time   1
Portrait of a Writer as a Young Man, or Early (Poetic)
   Orientations in Vienna and Elsewhere   17
The Virtue of Restlessness   39
Early Days for Fiction   63
Keeping Up with 'Life'   81
Jeremiah in the First World War   99
Tracing Demons, or How to Approach Greatness   125
Towards European Transnationalism   159
The Torch of Eros, or The Confusion of a Reluctant Modernist   177
Political Ridge Walks   193
Life Amidst Crises: Stefan Zweig at and around Fifty   205
The Uprooting of an Austrian, or Fascist Trauma and Early Exile   219
How to Become an Alien and Experiencing England   233
Autographs, Collections, and Other Approaches to
   World Literature   253
Zweig, the Transatlantic Explorer   265
Pity about Pity   285
Clarissa, Montaigne, Balzac: A Fragmentary Trio   297
Austria in Brazil: Arriving at the Final Address   313
Chess with Time, or Yesterday's Checkmate   331
Notes on Zweig's Legacy   341
Words of Thanks   357

Notes   359
Bibliography   381

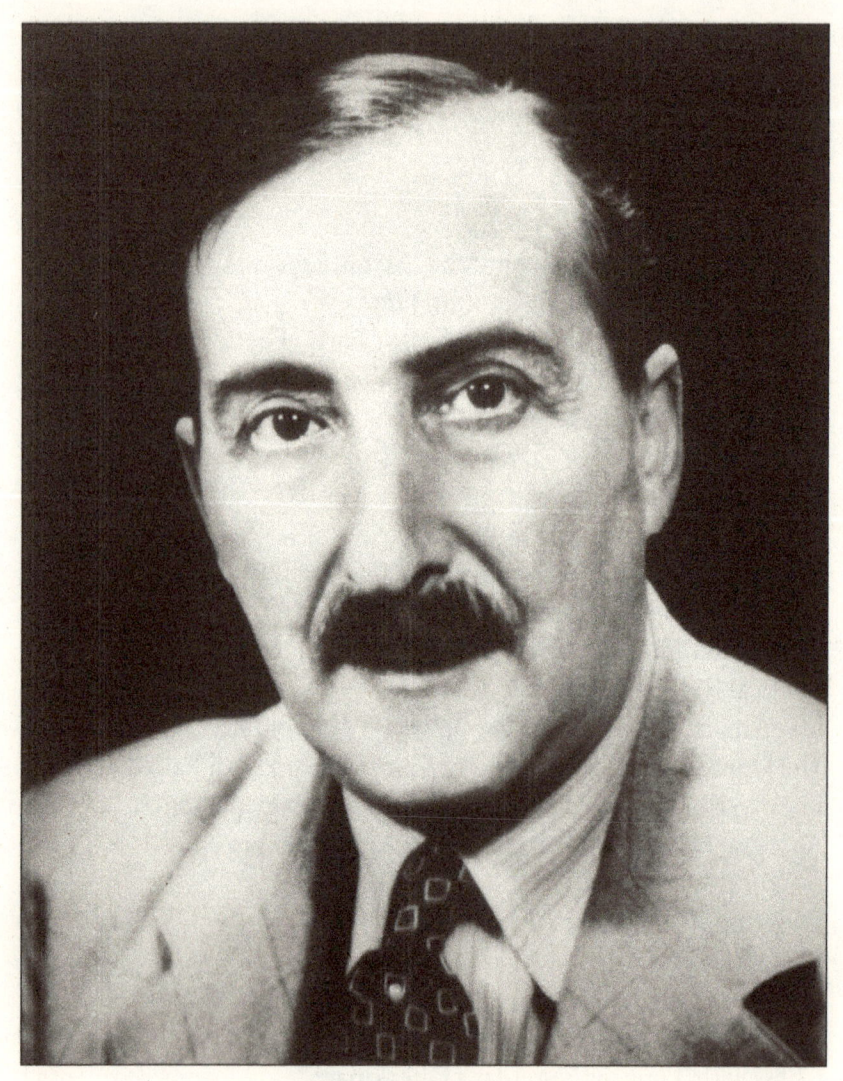

Stefan Zweig (1881–1942)
Heirs of Stefan Zweig

Preliminaries, or How to Approach Stefan Zweig: A Writer from the Past for Our Time

Contradictions, ambiguities, and uncertainties condition the modern world. Back in 1863, Charles Baudelaire spoke of modernity as something that consisted of transitory and fugitive elements. In 1928, Virginia Woolf's elusive narrator in *Orlando*, which she explicitly called 'a biography', names one of those elements 'the shock of time'[1] and asks with disarming candour, 'For what more terrifying revelation can there be than that it is the present moment?', only to answer her own question: 'That we survive the shock at all is only possible because the past shelters us on one side, the future on another. But we have no time now for reflections; Orlando was terribly late already.'[2] Somewhere between the transitory fugitiveness and the sheltering past, we find the fluctuating locations of Stefan Zweig's restless life yet firmly anchored work. But anchored in what? In diverse values of Europe's cultural riches, which he perceived from early on through a Viennese lens. To be sure, he did not share the view that the present moment was in principle of 'terrifying' quality.

In fact, he cherished the present, the instant; he gave it his full attention, even though the present is the most transient and fugitive of all time denominations. Zweig would have underwritten T. S. Eliot's verses from his *Four Quartets* – 'Time present and time past / Are both perhaps present in time future / And time future contained in time past' – had Eliot not published his quartets in Surrey one year after Zweig took his own life in Petrópolis. Zweig would likely have taken issue with the following lines from Eliot's late poetic masterpiece: 'If all time is eternally present / All time is unredeemable'.[3] He may have argued that 'all time' requires qualifiers. The notion of an 'eternal presence' also might have disturbed him, even though the very best of his works generate just that: a sense of perpetuity, not of the present but of the past. To a certain extent, his fiction and essayistic prose declared past events, phenomena, and people to be part of our present-day experience. For it is indeed uncanny that, when reading Stefan Zweig today, one often feels like they are encountering the work of a contemporary, such is the psychological finesse of his fiction and the sincerity of his stance as a European humanist; for he was a decidedly European citizen of the world in the republic of letters, if ever there was one. Regardless of the difference in time and preferred subject matter, the immediacy and urgency of Zweig's writings continue to speak to us directly – notwithstanding his tendency, particularly in his earlier writings, to indulge in rhetorical pathos. But in this pathos, for instance in his essay on Dostoevsky, one senses the presence of the word's original meaning: human suffering. Compassion is a hallmark of his life's work; however, he does not speak to us as a finger-wagging moralist but as a psychologically astute witness of his time.

'I am somehow an anticipated echo', Zweig wrote in his diary on Friday 13 September 1912.[4] But an echo of what? And why an anticipated sound? At the time, he may have felt that he had already struck a chord with a future yet unknown. One could argue that before Zweig became an advocate of the 'world of yesterday', he believed to be in league with the future, an impression that was perhaps strongest in him in the 1920s and essentially connected with his vision for Europe.

With the ever-delusional benefit of hindsight, almost any course of life looks as if it had followed a consequential path. However, the opposite is true. Sudden changes of circumstances undermine a seemingly functional causality in life. Introducing a sense of stringent linearity into a biography is a sure recipe for turning a life into fiction; for little could be less linear than life in its ordinary or exceptional aspects. The seemingly straight lines of life are all too often intercepted by the unexpected and bent into curves or loops. Life at its most vulnerable but also its most exciting is as irregular as it can get; with Stefan Zweig this was most certainly the case, regardless of the appearance he gave as an exceptionally well-off representative of the guild of *hommes de lettres*.

Surprises and disappointments, hopes and frustrations, tedium and dread are our daily bread, in Zweig's case combined with an early feeling of being haunted – first by himself, later by Hitlerism and worldwide totalitarian strictures. Like any biographical approach, this one, too, cannot provide any more than perspectives on a life. Any other assumption would border on the illusionary. In Zweig's case, life was bursting with productivity to the very end. The question behind his seemingly tireless activity is: can we reconstruct what it was that drove this extraordinary writer and advocate of humanism? In trying to find an answer to this and to the following questions, we will have to break up chronologies and modify matters of causality as we understand when and how Zweig took to fictive inventions as imaginary interventions into ordinary reality. What role did imagination play in his world, which he had, at times, hoped to protect against external influences, only to find that this was impossible and that in fact he needed these influences as triggers for his imagination? If anything, Zweig was deeply preoccupied with the creative process and the mystery or secret behind it. In times most precarious, with world peace at a precipice, in January and February 1939 Zweig spoke about this very subject, combined with thoughts on 'The Historiography of Tomorrow' on a lecture tour through some fifteen US-American cities – such was the importance he attributed to the problem of human creativity in relation to preserving its origins.

Today, Zweig comes across as a traditionalist and modernist at the same time, whose life and work raise questions that concern us with an undiminished intensity. The following questions mattered to Zweig from the very beginning of his literary career: what is the place of emotions in an increasingly functional and thus sterile world? Can a male writer truly understand female psychology and are such categories appropriate at all? How can we engage with the great literature of the past and with 'greatness' as such? What is the function of cultural values and how are we dealing with their loss – for example, values that conditioned Vienna around 1900? What is the political status of humanism? Should it result in pacifist attitudes? And finally, are we in charge of ourselves in a world of increasing alienation?

But the principal question that rests with any biographer of Stefan Zweig reads: how to begin writing about a life, the richness of which would have been sufficient for several? How to adequately write some four hundred pages about an author whose productivity dwarfed that of most of his fellow writers? Zweig, by nature a rather shy and intensely private person, was brimming with artistic imagination and poetic sentiment coupled with, at times, public engagement and programmatic commitment to the idea of Europe. It is only consequential for this biography to portray the development of Zweig's role as a public figure, too. After all, his life coincided with a time in which politics began to dominate the intellectual agenda, as evidenced in 1911 by W. B. Yeats in his essay 'Synge and the Ireland of His Time'. In it, Yeats considers how the artist can retain intellectual independence and how a writer should, or should not, react to the political and social contexts of their time, 'retaining integrity while responding to the flux of contemporary history.' At the same time, 'the writer must also guard against 'unmeaning pedantries and silences', seeking and preserving the necessary 'salt and savour' in language and finding an anchorage in 'rich personal experience, patience of study, and delicacy of sense.'[5] It appears that such questions about the impact of time present on the creative process are timeless; they applied to Yeats just as much as to Stefan Zweig, as well as to all writers before, during, and after the First World War.

The timelessness of humanism

Part and parcel of Zweig's public engagement was the incessance of his letter writing, which made him a supreme networker in the name of humanism. In this respect he reminds one of Erasmus, on whom he wrote engagingly when fascism in Europe was rife (1934), and of the Swiss polymath of the Enlightenment, Johann Caspar Lavater, whose appetite for being in constant exchange with others was second to none even in the letter-dominated culture of the eighteenth century.

At first sight, the life of Stefan Zweig rarely resembled any of his stories. One could argue that he wrote until his life matched them, which he accomplished with his final fiction, *Chess,* completed at the end of January 1942 and with copies typed and dispatched by his second wife, Lotte Altmann, shortly before their joint suicide. By then, the game was over, but differently from his work on Balzac and Montaigne, *Chess*, much like *The World of Yesterday*, was 'written out of despair' as he put it in a letter in May 1940, adding: 'Perhaps it is more important in our time to have a testimony than a work of art.'

To state the obvious, no biography on Zweig can equal the vivaciousness, rhetorical flow, and flair of his own 'memoirs of a European', *The World of Yesterday* (1942); and it would be all too obvious to simply follow Zweig's own interpretation of his life. This book will do so only occasionally; its main sources are Zweig's letters, his diaries, and some of his characteristic works, thus pursuing a more generic method of composition. Likewise, it endeavours to offer, at least up to a point, insights into his private life, which Zweig himself virtually excluded from his memoirs, in which neither his first nor second wife, nor many of his personal friends, featured. But the first tender and sensitive, then determined and resolute, Friderike von Winternitz and the more reserved Lotte Altmann, the latter described by a protégé of Zweig's as a 'bright creature with melancholic eyes', need to be duly considered in any biographical account of Stefan Zweig, as they were the two women in his life that truly mattered to him.[6] Interestingly, it needed the instigation of Friderike for Zweig to add to the manuscript of *The World of Yesterday* an extensive intimate afterthought, which he called 'Eros Matutinus': in the morning, or dawn, of Eros. Yet except for one paragraph, in which he admits that he found the alleged 'innocence' of young ladies around 1900 alluring, this chapter reads more like a rather abstract cultural history of eroticism and sexuality in Vienna's *fin de siècle* than an account of his own countless erotic adventures. To a certain extent his sexual drive fuelled his creative one, before the latter absorbed the former.

As guarded as he was about his private life, Zweig otherwise came across as open-minded and worldly to the point of cosmopolitan.

He was a curious, restless European right from the start, and a literary explorer who went beyond the European horizon from his early travels on. Or is cosmopolitanism, as Erich Maria Remarque put it in a televised interview in 1962, something one must learn?[7] Strangely, Zweig's and Remarque's paths rarely crossed despite sharing so much: most importantly, their pacifist beliefs.

Secrets and demons

Research on Zweig is gratifyingly extensive. Its biographical branch offers a whole range of perspectives, to which this book naturally owes a great deal. There is the first half-biography, half-monograph on Stefan Zweig by Erwin Rieger (1928); Friderike's not always reliable account of her second husband (1948); Elizabeth Allday's 'critical biography' (1972) and, in the same year, Donald A. Prater's subtle biography *European of Yesterday* (the title of its 1981 German version reads *The Life of an Impatient One*); Dominique Bona's most important biography in French (*Stefan Zweig: L'ami blesse*, 1996); Oliver Matuschek's major exploration of Zweig's *Three Lives* (2011) and, republished in the same year, Serge Niémetz's biography *Stefan Zweig: Le voyageur et ses mondes*, which centres on the various 'worlds' Zweig inhabited in literary and geographical terms; there is George Prochnik's distinctly narrative approach to Zweig's last phase of life with the dramatic title *The Impossible Exile: Stefan Zweig and the End of the World* (2014); and not to forget, Ulrich Weinzierl's intimate – at times voyeuristic – but illuminating, if not revelatory biographical essay in three parts, *Stefan Zweig's Burning Secret* (2015). The latter even identifies the date when Zweig had, for the first time, intercourse with his future wife, Friderike, namely on the 26 November 1912 in a hotel in Lübeck, two days before his thirty-first birthday. However, even a seemingly strange piece of biographical information like this one makes sense when Weinzierl informs us that, ten years later, Friderike congratulated her now husband on this date and not on the 28 November, his actual birthday, for which Zweig reproached her. The point is, however, as his biographic investigator correctly claims, that to Friderike this first physical union between the two meant more to her than to him. Incidentally, a similar date is not known for the first encounter with Lotte Altmann but we learn from this biographer a great deal about Zweig's '*Angstlust*', his (bi-)sexual orientation, and his occasional indulgence in exhibitionism.

Chronology is a relentless taskmaster, fit for stifling one's imagination. Admittedly it seems appropriate to begin a biography with a precise date and, in so doing, foster the illusion that facts really determine what is significant about a life. Many a biography sets in with a date of birth and the person's ancestry. Depending on the reliability of sources, dates of this kind of information are non-negotiable. But differently from describing the historical setting as such, the grammatical tense in which the biography is written can be negotiated. Some biographies are written in the present tense only.[8] We could follow this example given Zweig's concern with the present moment; even when he wrote, as he did so often, about historical events and personalities, he brought them into the contemporary world by way of his style of writing. So, perhaps, we, too, need to switch here and there between the past and present tense to highlight the phenomenon of Zweig's take on time.

There is an inevitable draw to the way in which Zweig ended his life and work, for it is problematically tempting to see this life through the lens of the decision to take his own, along with that of his second wife, in Petrópolis on 22 February 1942.[9] This is made only the more tempting given that there was a recognisable history or trace of suicidal moments in Zweig's life. By the same token, it would be equally misleading to compare Zweig's final action with, say, Heinrich von Kleist's and Henriette Vogel's death pact in November 1811. Both female partners suffered from severe long-term illness and Kleist was an object of intense fascination for Zweig, who gave an account of him, together with Friedrich Hölderlin and Friedrich Nietzsche, in one of his essays on the demonic in these writers, constituting one of his most popular essayistic trilogies (1925). *The Struggle with the Daemon* informed, for better or worse, generations of readers' opinions of these three ill-fated masters of the German tongue. Interestingly, the young Kleist was obsessed with working out a plan for how to lead his life, which did not come to anything. The young Zweig was the complete opposite, as he rejected from early on any thought of a properly structured life. Yet both arrived, albeit at different stages of their lives, at a point of futility and self-abandonment. For different reasons, they both led a life of discontinuities, full of coincidences and variety.[10]

Where did it come from, the alluring seductiveness of Zweig's essayistic and novelistic style, his rhetorical panache and compelling plots that made him one of the most popular German-language authors worldwide, with print runs that surpassed, at times, those of Thomas Mann? From a crossover of creative appropriation of literary models and sheer ingenuity; from an acquired taste for historical events (rather than developments) and a sense of verbal intimacy that he exercised in countless letters; and from a readiness for the unexpected and a feeling for tradition. Zweig's life was rich in crossovers of a similar kind, energised by an insatiable vitality blended with unsettling restlessness. Even in retrospect, portraying this extraordinary life and the extent of its (early) franticness can still have a bewildering effect on the biographer. One cannot but sympathise with those of his friends who found it difficult to keep up with him.

The man of moments

This said, it would arguably be more appropriate to organise this biography along the lines of an even more successful collection of Zweig's essays, or historical miniatures, known as *Decisive Moments in History* (1927, with the first English edition coming in 1940); it is also known under the titles *The Tide of Fortune*, or *Stellar Moments of Humankind*, which is closer to the German original *Sternstunden der Menschheit*. Zweig kept enlarging the number of essays for re-editions of this collection until the final number of fourteen was reached. The thematic outreach in his collection could not have been greater, demonstrating the sheer scope of Zweig's historical interests and the power of his narrative accomplishment, which provides the main quality that holds these essays together.

One needs to be sure about the scale of such 'decisive moments' to appreciate Zweig's achievement: 'The World Minute of Waterloo'; (Goethe writes) 'The Elegy of Marienbad'; 'The Discovery of Eldorado'; 'Heroic Moment' (the mock execution of Fyodor Dostoevsky); 'The Fight for the South Pole'; 'Escape to Immortality' (Vasco Núñez de Balboa discovers the Pacific Ocean); 'Conquest of Byzantium' (by the Ottomans); 'Resurrection of Georg Friedrich Händel'; 'The Genius of a Single Night' (Rouget de Lisle writes *La Marsellaise*); 'The First Word Across the Ocean' (Cyrus W. Field establishes the first trans-oceanic cable); 'The Flight to God' (an additional act to Leo Tolstoy's *The Light Shines in the Darkness*); 'The Sealed Train' (Lenin boards a train commissioned by the central powers to start the Russian Revolution); '*Cicero*', or 'The Head on the Rostrum'; and, added to the collection in 1940, 'Wilson's Failure'. The latter offered a revaluation of the word 'failure' in the sense that the story is written in praise of Wilson's famous 'Fourteen Points' for establishing peace in Europe. That they were betrayed during the peace negotiations in Versailles by France and Britain is one of – not only in Zweig's opinion – the major political tragedies of the twentieth century.

So, what if neither the date of Zweig's death, 22 February 1942, nor that of his birth in Vienna, 28 November 1881, were our starting point – which, then, could be another decisive date in the sea of possible options between those demarcations of a lifetime that might be telling and symbolic enough to serve as a suitable starting point for us? For such an approach I suggest 8 July 1917. It is the day when the *Neue Freie Presse*, the leading Austrian newspaper since the attempted revolution of 1848, published an extensive review by Stefan Zweig of Henri Barbusse's novelistic anti-war documentary – docufiction we would say these days – under the title *Le feu*. To be sure, this was not a mere review but a declaration of solidarity with this hitherto next-to-unknown French writer and his pacifist stance. It included Zweig's standpoint versus the human fiasco of the First World War and encapsulated his perspective on the future, of Europe in particular, which he was to unfold in the aftermath of this devastating catastrophe. But what made 8 July 1917 special was the fact that an article of this kind, and so prominently placed, was published at all at that time.

Zweig's argument reads as follows: Barbusse has written a book about the war, which has turned out to be a passionate plea for peace. What Émile Zola's novel *Nana* had achieved in times of peace, namely, to enlighten the general public about the corrupted social conditions in France, Barbusse has managed to achieve with *Le feu* using the sheer explosiveness of 'fiction'.[11] Zweig points out that the protagonist in *Le feu* is not only a witness of an entirely torn world, but that he testifies to hitherto unknown destruction as a collective consisting of seventeen soldiers who speak about their suffering with one voice, though with seventeen identifiable idioms, including the Paris vernacular, the *argot*. The author, Barbusse himself, functions, or so Zweig believed, like the horn of a gramophone for the variants within this voice. He enables suffering to speak. But there is one phrase that conditions the entire book as the reviewer suggests: '*On ne peut pas se figurer!*'[12] One really cannot imagine what one is faced with 'out there' in the trenches.

The appeal that comes from this graphic prose is unambiguous: neither Germany nor her enemies need to be defeated but war itself, the true enemy of the people. Zweig presents his readers with the key phrases of Barbusse's *Le feu* in French, which, in 1917, could have been called an act of literary treason: this voice of despair knows that these soldiers are merely '*machines à oublier*', machines of oblivion, like most of his readers.[13] But if this is so, all suffering would have been in vain: '*Tant de malheur est perdu!*', or 'so much misery is lost!'[14] Barbusse even predicted that there would be '*tourists des tranchées*', 'tourists of the trenches', first in the shape of war correspondents then as tourists of the trenches and battlefields – to the very day one of the most despicable facets of the tourist industry, and one which now stretches from Vietnam to the Middle East.[15]

Writing a biography of Stefan Zweig means to write about the life of a writer, who was to considerable extent a biographer himself. To be precise, Zweig's novelistic, historiographical, or essayistic writings are biographically conditioned in the sense that they aim to give accounts of life as a driving force, regardless of circumstances. Through his biographical work, Zweig wanted to honour the preciousness and dignity of life at a time when life was declared cheap on battlefields and in ministries of war. Zweig's motto for his biography of *Marie Antoinette* (1932), taken from Shakespeare's *The Second Part of Henry IV* (Act III, Scene 1), is telling: 'There is a history in all men's lives, / Figuring the nature of the times deceased ...' It is this very 'history' that Zweig attempted to tease out in his *Mary Stuart* (1935), *Magellan* (1938), and *Balzac* (posthumously, 1946); a history with a distinctly personal touch, which can mean different things. In *Mary Stuart*, Zweig's initial interest was the question of the legitimacy of her execution as he explained in *The World of Yesterday*; with Magellan it was his 'long-desired journey to South America' that triggered his interest in this Portuguese explorer and unmatched navigator; whilst with *Balzac* – an almost lifelong preoccupation of Zweig's – he found the writer's 'self-transformation' and 'sovereign re-shaping through acts of will' intriguing and rewarding enough to devote his energies to him, an exceptional writer who undertook his self-ennoblement in a distinctly bourgeois culture by calling himself *de* Balzac. With Balzac Zweig encountered a writer who constantly reinvented himself.

Empathy, which is regaining more attention again in today's revaluation of emotional values, was one hallmark of Zweig's approach to people he encountered and personalities he wrote about.[16] His was a highly developed intuition for the protagonists of his fiction and biographies as well as the culture in which they operated, and which had shaped them and which they helped to shape.

In an age of mass culture and ruthless populisms, Zweig insisted on the value of individualism. In doing so he continued the nineteenth-century tradition of 'the great men', extending it, but in his fiction only, to the great females of various social setups. Through his biographies, or rather, biographical narratives, Zweig made Nietzsche's *Second Untimely Meditation* timely: they demonstrate the 'use and abuse of history for life' in that they demonstrate just how much a writer needs to extract 'life' from history to make it tangible and intelligible.

Modes of writing lives

Zweig wrote his major biographies at a time when this literary genre was as popular as it is, once again, today. In his time, particularly in the 1920s and 1930s, the choice of historical personalities indicated alternatives to ideologically conditioned leadership figures, except for his 'portrait of a politician', *Joseph Fouché* (1930). In many ways, his Fouché is the timeless prototype of a manipulative survivor in any political system. This master of intrigue and chameleon-like adaptivity was seen by Zweig as 'a gambler-in-chief at the great roulette board of human destiny', perfectly recognisable in the political settings and dictatorships of Zweig's time.

With writing biographies of a more popular kind, Zweig found himself in good company. In the footsteps of the Russian *homme de lettres*, Dimitry Merezhkovsky, and his biographies on Tolstoy and Dostoevsky as well as Leonardo da Vinci and Jesus (much admired by a whole range of his contemporaries – Thomas Mann, Sigmund Freud, Henri Bergson, Rudolf Steiner, Tomáš Masaryk – but also by the notorious ideologue of National Socialism, Alfred Rosenberg), Zweig's main 'competitors' as popular biographers, Jacob Wassermann and Emil Ludwig, engaged in a particularly lively style of life-writing. With Zweig, the pinnacle of this art form was reached, arguably in conjunction with Klaus Mann's biographical novel on Tchaikovsky, *Symphonie Pathétique* (1935, American edition published 1948 and dedicated to Christopher Isherwood). Their way of 'biographising' crucially contributed to what is known as literary historiography, as opposed to its scholarly version. But there is little sense in such distinctions since *every* form of verbal representation of a historical reality contains elements of fiction.

Thoughts on how best to write a biography are part and parcel of this literary discipline. Would the ideal biography present a day-to-day account of a life? Or should the biographer provide a pathfinder through the labyrinth of the life in question? How prominent should the narrative element be? How 'intellectual' can a biography afford to be without alienating readers who also expect some entertaining insights into the life of a more or less well-known personality? On that note, there is the passionate dog-lover Zweig, or the man who preferred to celebrate his birthdays in 1923 and in the following year without his wife, for instance in Berlin's queer establishments, bars, and clubs. There is his paranoia about ageing, particularly in the 1920s, and his eagerness to escape, often to Paris, for work and amorous reasons. Not to forget his inclination to overfill his appointment diary and become trapped by all the work he had accepted, which he found burdensome but enjoyable at the same time. There is something eminently likeable about this old-fashioned elegant Austrian beau, who excelled during receptions whilst at the same time seeking solitude for his work, but then complaining about loneliness, which could temporarily be cured by the presence of his dog(s), or frantic travelling. There was plenty of stuff his 'life' was made of, not to forget Marcelle, his Parisian lover whilst Friderike, the estranged wife of the civil servant Felix von Winternitz and mother of their two daughters, Alexia Elisabeth (Alix) and Susanne Benediktine (Suse), courted him in Vienna (far less so the other way round!). Marcelle was 'with child' from him but terminated her pregnancy – whether on Zweig's instigation or not cannot be known. On the one hand, Zweig comes across as an erotic adventurer; on the other hand, he admitted to himself in his diary in late February 1913:

> The erotic appals me for it takes hold of me rather than me taking hold of her. I quiver of my own virtuosity. I speak at a theatre reception with a lady, a sculptress, quite intensely, and lo and behold I find myself in my bed with her at four o'clock in the morning. The way she stares at me as if all that would not be true, this awakening of a woman with a person whom she only knows physically – but for that matter extensively. (Tb, 41)

In short, it is only consequential to consider aspects of Zweig's sexuality given that he was an author who praised Freud's 'courage' in a letter to the founding father of psychoanalysis on 8 September 1926, arguing that autobiography, in particular, cannot be but bolder and clearer henceforth 'in this respect'. This said, in his own autobiography *The World of Yesterday*, he remained 'buttoned up': guarded and anxious to portray the time he lived in rather than analyse himself in front of all his readers.

Any life-writing must include the life of a person's œuvre or achievement of whatever kind that made him or her eligible, or worthy, of a biography. With Zweig, the colourfulness of his life matched the multifacetedness of his works and vice versa. This the biography's structure needs to reflect. In his own major biographies, Zweig was at pains to provide evocative narratives that would offer opportunities for the reader to identify with their protagonists – one of the reasons for their lasting popularity. For instance, the opening chapter of his *Magellan* does not only point to what was crucial to this early sixteenth-century seafarer and explorer but also offered the quintessential demand for any biographer: *navigare necesse est* – it is necessary to navigate in life, which is after all as inexhaustible as an ocean.[17]

In Zweig's own rich life there is plenty for any biographer to 'navigate' and to negotiate. In a letter of 18 July 1930 written to her husband from Flims in Switzerland, where she recuperated from domestic traumas (partly of her own making) back in Salzburg, Friderike claimed

> [...] that nobody knows you in truth more than I and that one day the most shallow and idiotic things will be written about you. This said, you only allow very few people to get closer to you as you are closed as regards your own persona (understandably so). Your written work represents, after all, only a third of yourself, and nobody has figured out its essence for the interpretation of the other two thirds.[18]

For our endeavour, though, the way in which Friderike understood her husband cannot be but a questionable element given her manipulative character and her readiness to shape Zweig's aftermath according to her measure. What concerns us more is the creative interplay between aspects of Zweig's life and work.[19] To a large extent, we will mainly be focusing on the biography of his writings and the development they signify, the position he obtained in his time through his extraordinary literary achievements, and his striving for the supremacy of humaneness in an age of ideological perversions (in its variants) with seemingly unlimited duration.

Portrait of the writer as a young man
Kunst Salon Pictzner

Portrait of a Writer as a Young Man, or Early (Poetic) Orientations in Vienna and Elsewhere

What is it about our fascination with the figure of the young poet? Is it that we hope to witness the becoming of a genius, or at least of a human with extraordinary qualities? Ironically, the one truly exceptional novelistic product of this urban legend called 'Vienna' that continues to stand out is Robert Musil's fragmentary masterpiece, *The Man Without Qualities*. At any rate, the protagonist, Ulrich, is not a 'young poet' but a meanderer in the emotional and cultural labyrinth of Vienna's pre-First World War years.

But reflections on the image of 'the young poet', this iconic figure of new beginnings at the time of an ageing culture that suffered from its own deceiving fertility, were rife in literary modernism, ranging from James Joyce to Rainer Maria Rilke, from Robert Walser to, later, Virginia Woolf. Focusing on a writer as a young man is still not out of fashion as we continue to be intrigued how and why it was that a great talent sets his own agenda in motion and follows his own creative instinct.[1] This fascination with youth was coupled with a whole artistic movement, the *Jugendstil*, with its Viennese variant. Its equivalent in literature was the aspiring writers of *Junges Wien*. In the visual arts, mainly between 1908 and 1911, Viennese Expressionism branched out of *Jugendstil*, abandoning any restraint – as epitomised by Egon Schiele, for a while Oskar Kokoschka,[2] Richard Gerstl,[3] and, often forgotten or overlooked in this visual context, Arnold Schoenberg, whose paintings matched his musical compositions.[4]

All that happened in the capital of a tired empire; yet, a cradle for unprecedented innovation in the arts, philosophy, and the science of unpicking the unconscious. It is Vienna during exactly this early period of Stefan Zweig's life, brimming with creativity to an extent and intensity almost unfathomable from today's perspective, that keeps haunting our imagination. Schiele was very much the 'perfect symbol of the Viennese antithesis', as William Boyd put it, 'namely that this small, safe, solid, beautiful, bourgeois capital city should have housed in the early years of the 20th century such a contrapuntal, boiling ferment of modernism'.[5] As the capital of the Austro-Hungarian Empire, its new denomination since 1867 following Austria's defeat against Prussia in 1866, Vienna was home to eleven officially recognised languages. In that respect it was the centre of multilingualism, consisting of German, Hungarian, Czech, Slovak, Polish, Ukrainian, Slovenian, Croatian, Serbian, Romanian, and Italian. The most important non-recognised minority language, though, was Yiddish. With that in mind, one feels inclined to paraphrase the famous opening sentence of Ludwig Wittgenstein's *Tractatus Logico-Philosophicus*: Whereof one cannot speak even when having so many languages available, thereof one must rightfully be silent.[6]

Our protagonist, Stefan Zweig, was a highly gifted young man but by his own recognition not a 'genius', if the measure for such a person is, say, the teenage Hugo von Hofmannsthal, whom the entirety of the young literati admired. The circle around Hofmannsthal – Arthur Schnitzler, Richard Beer-Hoffmann, and Felix Salten – liked sitting together in their favoured Viennese coffeehouses, then the very residences of intellectual sophistication. But none of them were able to produce such immaculate poems like young Hofmannsthal, himself only to admit in later years that the best a poet can hope for is that some five poems of his might survive in people's collective cultural memory.

The young Zweig did not belong to any such 'circle', but Hofmannsthal, six years Zweig's senior, was one of our writer's early role models, together with Paul Verlaine and Karl Emil Franzos, a populist writer from Eastern Galicia and editor of influential periodicals, such as the *Wiener Illustrierte Zeitung* and *Deutsche Dichtung*, which appeared in Berlin. However, the dominant influence on the young Stefan Zweig was the urban space of Vienna in its totality with all its social contradictions. There, on 28 November 1881, he was born into the Jewish family of a wealthy textile industrialist, Moritz Zweig, and his wife, Ida Brettauer, the daughter of a Jewish banking family. Their, and his, Judaism was 'through accident of birth', as Zweig later put it. One could call the Zweigs' Judaism 'assimilated', or mainly 'cultural' rather than religious. However, Stefan was to retain both, a refined sense of 'textures' as the fabric of literary texts, and a cultural concern with Judaism as reflected in several literary transformations of Jewish themes – for instance, in his novella *Buchmendel* and, most importantly, his drama *Jeremiah*, not to speak of his friendly relationship with Theodor Herzl, the founding father of Zionism. But this did not turn Stefan Zweig into a Zionist himself; he remained sceptical, if not averse, towards anything ideology-like. In rejecting 'isms' of all kinds, Zweig followed another of his early idols, Friedrich Nietzsche.

Given the privileged circumstances of his background, Stefan Zweig did not depend on income from his writings. The relationship with his more practically minded brother Alfred was by and large trouble-free. Two years Stefan's senior, Alfred's interests were never in conflict with the artistic and intellectual ambition of his brother. In fact, he continued the family textile business after his father's death in 1926 until his emigration to New York in 1938, where he died at the age of ninety-seven in 1977. Every so often, Stefan would emphasise in early letters that his family was well-heeled and although he made a point of standing on his own feet, its wealth provided him with a soft cushion. By comparison, the (upper-)middle class in Vienna represented 'a society at leisure'; cultural life in this city of some two million people by 1910 was marked by a high degree of sophistication, which involved deep learning and engagement in often-intense debates on music, literature, and the visual arts, as well as architecture, and their leading protagonists' push towards modernism.[7]

One gains the impression that he plunged himself into the world of the 'coffee-house literati' and was open to influences of all kinds. But this assumption was at least partly deceptive; Zweig often preferred to be on his own, or in the company of only very few close (mostly male and homosexually inclined) friends. At any rate, Zweig was eagerly looking for intellectual nourishment and found more in this Viennese atmosphere of plentifulness than anyone could possibly digest – it provided him with substance on which he could draw for the rest of his life. At the same time, he was eager to find something else, which was more difficult in this hyper-stimulating atmosphere: his own voice. The polyphony of voices belonging to what became known as *Junges Wien* was bewildering, but soon the young Zweig would look for inspiration elsewhere and far beyond the cultivated confinement of Vienna; he was to find it in the works and personality of Émile Verhaeren and the poetry of Walt Whitman.

Tales from the Vienna culture hub

Next to no story about Vienna around 1900 has remained untold. In the square of Europe's main centres, Paris, Berlin, and London, Vienna was the one most absorbed by traditionalism; yet, in the arts in general, tradition was blending with innovation. But even the secession movement felt somehow close to the establishment. When, in 1908, a major art and craft exhibition was held to mark the sixtieth anniversary of the reign of Emperor Franz Joseph I, the leader of the secessionists, Gustav Klimt, organised it, even though some of his art had been denounced as 'pornographic'. Musical life in Vienna was on its way to experiencing a 'scandal concert' conducted by Arnold Schönberg with pieces by composers of the Second Viennese School (Webern, Zemlinsky, Berg, and Schönberg himself), but it took place in the very temple of classical music, the Great Hall of the Musikverein. In architecture, Adolf Loos and the most urbane of architects at the time, Otto Wagner, were ready to kill off ornamental style in a house built next to the Royal City Palace, the Hofburg, with its dominant Baroque features and other historicist buildings in its immediate vicinity. This ornament-free design of a house on the Michaelerplatz caused what can only be described as persistent public outrage.

Vienna was still the emblematic capital of the nineteenth century's 'golden autumn', to use the proverbial title of Hilde Spiel's investigation into the *fin de siècle* in the metropolis of the Austro-Hungarian Empire.[8] All major building projects had been accomplished. The Ringstrasse, one of the nineteenth century's major architectural achievements, comparable to the avenue projects of Baron Haussmann in Paris, provided the space for a perpetual *corso* of those who wanted to be seen. In aesthetic terms, though, it perpetuated the historicist style, suggesting through the ring structure the eternal recurrence of the same. At any rate, the conception of the Ringstrasse provided a counterimage to a dead-end road. Or was this circling in perpetuity along the 'Ring' a different kind of dead end, albeit one in constant motion, illustrated by the circling trams biting their own tails? But regardless of its urban charm, Vienna was lacking in buzz, a quality Zweig was seeking and finally found in Berlin and, especially, Paris.

In Austria, after the loss of her political influence following defeat against Prussia in 1866, public wealth was chiefly directed towards the arts, while expenditure for the military decreased in real terms until 1912. As Zweig was to testify later, it was more important to see Gustav Mahler, the director of the Vienna Opera House from 1897–1908, on the streets of Vienna than a parade of the emperor's horse-guards. Vienna appeared to be the location for never-ending festivities. Life seemed but one extended waltz. It should not be forgotten that officers in the Imperial Army would only receive their commission if they could present their credentials in ballroom dancing. Vienna was yet the undisputed heart of European musical culture. But in terms of infrastructure and accommodation of the rapid growth of its population, 'traffic' became a major issue of public debate. Any demolition of old buildings in the inner quarters of the city caused a storm of occasionally favourable but mostly negative reactions. The slogan of the critics of urban innovation was: 'Vienna must not become New York!'[9] What traditionalists feared most was 'Americanisation', which was associated with a disfiguring of the 'artistic physiognomy of our city', as Josef August Lux put it in the *Neues Wiener Tagblatt* of March 1909.[10] The type of house that Loos had built in the centre of Vienna's old quarters should 'belong to the Broadway in New York', the enraged

Hugo Wittmann wrote in 1910.[11] More liberally minded publicists like Otto Stoessl argued, in Karl Kraus's periodical *Die Fackel* (*The Torch*), that Loos had counteracted mediocrity in architecture and contributed to genuine plurality of styles in the arts.[12] In this case, too, 'beauty' was very much in the eye of the beholder. On 11 December 1911 Loos explained in a public lecture the aesthetic rationale of his 'house at the Michaelerplatz' with 'sciopticon-projected images' – as the poster announcing the event pointed out, the old magic lantern medium had turned modern.[13]

Cracks in the social make-up of Vienna were visible to those who wanted to see them, hardly surprising given its main feature as the melting pot of the *Vielvölkerstaat*, the state of many peoples, a hyper-lively urban conglomerate suggesting, to more progressive minds, plurality as a way, if not condition, of life. Yet, the dominant cultural force came from a minority within this city and its empire, the German-speaking Austrians. Social tensions, scantily papered over, were an inevitable consequence, exacerbated by a rapidly increased number of 'unknown underdogs', whose one common denominator was hostility against Jews.

Anti-Semitism was rife, if not disproportionally prevalent by Western European levels of this poisonous vice, and personified by the mayor of Vienna, Karl Lueger, whose appointment was rejected three times by the emperor, clearly embarrassed by the fact that a racist of this kind should govern his cherished capital. Matters were not helped by hostile feelings amongst the assimilated Jewry towards the Eastern European Jews, mainly from the Austrian Crownland of Galicia and the Bukovina, who were looked down upon as an 'underclass' in social and cultural terms. Anything that irritated, from the compositions of the Second Viennese School to psychoanalysis, was in public opinion associated with 'Jewish' decadence. The Jewish intelligentsia was a thorn in the flesh, particularly of the Austro-German nationalists in Vienna. One of them was the 'embittered, paranoid vagrant' Adolf Hitler, some eight years Stefan Zweig's junior.[14] George Steiner was not alone in assuming that

[...] their eyes *must* have met. In a streetcar, on the Ringstrasse, on the Opernring, or in some of the cafés. Perhaps one of the numerous street photographers, under their black linen hoods, took a candid shot of them passing each other unaware. Mahler, Freud, Schoenberg, Karl Kraus, Adolf Hitler.[15]

He may have added Stefan Zweig, who would later remark that from his Salzburg residence on the Kapuzinerberg he was able to see Hitler's Berghof on the Obersalzberg across the border into Bavaria – proximities too close for comfort.

In search of direction

In this hotbed of unmatched artistic and intellectual talent but also malicious tongue-wagging, Zweig was striving for orientation. One important document from this early period is his essay 'Das Land ohne Patriotismus' ('The Country without Patriotism') of about 1909, which remained unpublished at the time. In view of Zweig's later emphatically non-ideological stance one could easily expect to have found in this text an early manifestation of his distaste for nationalistic sentiments. Not so. Zweig writes from the perspective of someone who has returned to Austria after several months of being abroad. Surprisingly, he does not notice any buzz or vibrant activity in the emperor's metropolis; instead, he believes that the wheel of time moves more slowly back there. Life seems hampered by sheer aversion to progress. Nothing has changed since he left. A sense of inertia and receptiveness prevails as the newspapers are still full of skirmishes and tensions between the nations within the Empire. Patchwork is the order of the day, without any vision:

> The civil servants, whom one meets, are tired and sullen; the artists merely ironic; the craftsman only concerned with themselves; the worker like the entire proletariat burdened by daily worries. A tragic pessimism dominates the world of business; moaning and dissatisfaction from all sides.[16]

This is not what we normally associate with the temple of culture and sophistication on the banks of the river Danube around 1900; it flatly contradicts our conception of pre-war Vienna as a haven of blissful cultural activity. But the young Zweig went one significant step further. He bemoaned the absence of a national common denominator in this empire and any sense of community that could transgress regional particularisations. 'Even the poets', he argued, 'are non-political' and not interested in Austria.[17] Liberalism failed to maintain its 1848 momentum, which pointed towards the formation of a 'genuinely liberal Austrian state'. The socialist movement, too, had succumbed to regional particularisation. To be sure, Zweig in 1909 referred to 'Austria' as the name for the overarching political edifice that had failed to generate its own 'nationalism' and pride in its achievements. He could not identify any 'unifying conception' that would underpin the Austrian supra-nation other than the aged emperor and his 'quasi-mythical power'. Zweig concluded his point by saying that other nations were looking towards the future whilst 'we' in Austria seemed to look backwards to find self-assurance; he called this 'a dangerous sign'.[18]

But this is not where his argument ends, for Zweig came up with a magical cut, as it were, suggesting a belief in beauty as a politically and socially applicable notion and quality. He saw, in the sheer beauty generated by the 'harmony of contrasts' in the country's minute coastal and vast continental landscapes, a remedy for social ills. What he had in mind is epitomised, for instance, by Salzburg, which he singled out as a 'miracle' – being an 'Italian town amid a mountainous region', together with 'the mystique of Prague and the unique beauty of Vienna', not to speak of the 'wild forests of the Bukovina'. From this he derived the belief that 'beauty is the best' this state had to offer as 'everything else in this country speaks against its existence save this ultimately highest quality.'[19]

It is just possible that Zweig had come across a chapter on the 'future of Vienna' by the widely admired Hermann Bahr, which he had published in 1906. In political terms, Bahr's text was harsher than Zweig's approach and his reference to 'beauty', which he acknowledges, is distinctly ironic: 'We [Austrians] are history, a beautiful reminiscence'. He regarded Prague as the place of the future as Vienna could not but sink into oblivion: 'Let us die in beauty', Bahr's conclusion reads.[20] His verdict was uncompromising: 'Some people outside of Austria think that the Austrian state is disintegrating. But this cannot be the case. For there is no such thing as an Austrian state'.[21] He then quoted the philosopher and orientalist, Paul de Lagarde, who had claimed in the mid-nineteenth century that Austria 'has no soul'. Bahr compared the Austrian Empire with the English East India Company, transposed onto Europe's central and (south-)eastern parts. His analysis could not have been harsher: 'In reality, it is a clique of families that oversees this Empire. It is in fact still the case that a few thousand people are subjecting themselves to a dynasty and for that they are rewarded by being allowed to govern.'[22] What should happen, according to Bahr, is that this perverted power must be crushed in order to create a genuine state. By the standards of 1906 this was nothing short of revolutionary and, in Bahr's case, may have been inspired by the first wave of revolutionary events in Russia.

With Zweig's non-ironic plea for the supremacy of 'beauty' as a socially and politically binding factor he literally took a leaf out of his first volume of poetry, *Silberne Saiten* (*Silver Strings*, 1901), dedicated to his 'dear parents'; nothing short of a celebration of verbal beauty, consonance, and harmony. With his poems, all too often underrated, he almost shamelessly professed his desire to 'aestheticise' his experience of life, taking literally Nietzsche's claim in *The Birth of Tragedy from the Spirit of Music* (1872) that existence was only justified through art. Unsurprisingly, then, music features prominently in these poems.

Given his privileged upbringing and opting for 'beauty' it is noteworthy that Zweig never lost sight of the socially disadvantaged. This is not reflected in his poetry but in some of his early prose. Whilst his poetry was a reservoir for pure verbal beauty in terms of pleasing metaphors and resounding rhymes and verbal rhythms, he seemed to have experimented with a social motif in what must have been one of his first novellas, only known from a letter he wrote to Karl Emil Franzos in

April 1899, written one year before finishing grammar school. In it, he asked the editor of the periodical *Deutsche Dichtung* whether a novella under the title *Peter der Dichter* (*Peter the Poet*) would be welcome. He then gave a brief sketch of its simplistic content: 'A worker grows into a poet, is proclaimed as a fashionable author but cannot maintain his position in "respectable society" and falls back into the working class he originally came from.'[23] A year later he recommended to an editor of folk poetry the extension of his anthology to European folk poetry in translation, to which he suggested the inclusion of poetry by the Italian poetess Ada Negri, whose working-class background had in fact helped her to gain some prominence in Italy (I, 17). She may well have been on Zweig's mind when, in later years, he wrote his novella *The Post Office Girl*, set in 1926 in provincial Austria, where the dull life of Christine, the twenty-eight-year-old protagonist, is briefly disturbed when a rich aunt whisks her to the Swiss Alps and exposes her to a society overflowing with wealth. But all too soon, Christine is cast out from this setup and gets together with a war veteran, as disaffected and disillusioned as herself. The gap between the rich and poor in post-First World War Austria sparked, to a certain extent, a continuation of Zweig's interest in the psychology of disappointment that originated in these early drafts.

During these early stages of Zweig's literary explorations and whilst preparing himself for his final examinations at the Maximilian Grammar School in Vienna's ninth district, he considered writing a 'Jewish novella', which he offered to Franzos and not to a Jewish paper for it would not contain any reference to a 'national mission' for the (Eastern European) Jewry; in other words, no reference to Zionism. The novella was to be called *In the Snow* and was about a Jewish community in the Middle Ages that escape from a looming pogrom, only to be caught in a horrific blizzard 'that redeems them from all suffering'. Zweig wrote to Franzos that he wanted to generate 'compassion, which we all have for our [Jewish] ancestors, or rather, should have' (I, 20). Regarding the publication of his 'Jewish novella', Zweig must eventually have changed his mind, since one year after Franzos had rejected it on stylistic grounds Zweig published it in the Viennese periodical *Die Welt*, the main journalistic medium of the Zionist movement there and then.

Equally interesting though is Zweig's reaction to Franzos's rejection, for he agreed wholeheartedly with it. What he had to say to Franzos in a letter written in early July 1900 says as much about the novella as his view of himself. It contains stunning self-criticism amounting to nothing short of a 'confession':

> I know quite well that this novella like most of my things are done in haste and fleetingly but – I don't know how one should call this quirk – I am unable to change anything after the final word is written. Usually, I do not even check them in terms of orthography or punctuation. It is a careless and obstinate way of working but I am completely clear about one thing: that it will prevent me from ever producing anything great. I don't know the art of being conscientious and hard-working. [...] At best, I have a bit of talent for producing sketches or poetry, but this is by no means anything original but still influenced from what I read when I was a boy. (I, 20–1)

Quite an admission for a young writer addressing his idol and hoping for his support. By now, though, a range of features of this young man have become apparent: through all this self-criticism shines a truly self-confident nineteen-year-old. He was socially aware, in need of orientation, interested in his Jewish origin, and concerned with translations as a crucial means of mediating between cultures. His suggestion to the German writer and editor, Ludwig Jacobowski, to extend his anthology of folk songs literally speaks volumes. This project could, however, not be realised, as Jacobowski died prematurely at only thirty-two years of age in 1900. In his letter to this important representative of early naturalism in Germany, Zweig argued that it was a 'necessity to translate' since one could only provide fresh inspiration to a people through offering it translations from foreign literatures (I, 18). According to the young Zweig, folk songs should not entrench nationalistic sentiments but make peoples share the – alleged – very best of their poetic substance.

In terms of his development at this early stage, Zweig's exchange with his contemporary, the journalist Leonhard Adelt, who was to become a close friend of his, is revealing. In a December 1901 letter he admitted to Adelt that he was not learning enough for his studies of literary history and 'exact philosophy' as the Austrian academic terminology had it at the time. Interestingly, Zweig did not mention philosophy but centred on his attitude towards literature. Studying it analytically, he argued, would 'destroy' the immediacy of its appreciation. He even spoke of an 'ossification' of literature through studying it academically; instead, Zweig opted for living life to the full. He disclosed that he could easily live the life of a dandy based on the wealth of his parents, but that he resisted the dependency on them that would go with it. He emphasised that he had a room of his own and only spent the nights back in the family home in Rathausgasse 17. One such room of his own was in Schwarzspanierstrasse 20, door 6, where he would keep electrifying spiritual company with Beethoven given that the composer's final address had been next door. In *The World of Yesterday* Zweig remembers the heaps of petitions students wrote against the decision by the Vienna City Council to pull down this very house where Beethoven died. Zweig aspired to lead a free life with 'frequent changes of location', resisting bourgeois philistine expectations for a professional career (I, 27–9). Once he came of age, or so he believed, there would be no stopping him. For the time being, though, he pursued his studies working towards a thesis on the philosophy of Hippolyte Taine (1828–93), which he successfully submitted and defended in 1904. Zweig's choice of topic seemed surprising, if not strange, for there was little in his previous preoccupations that could have connected him with Taine's sociological positivism or indeed his critiquing of historicism. Nor would Taine's proximity to Émile Zola have been to Zweig's liking, who preferred Verlaine and French symbolism over Zola's social realism, if not naturalism, in literary writing. Yet, the comments he made in his letter to Adelt about literature provided a hint for his choice: working on Taine would prevent him from getting any deeper into 'literary history'; besides, Taine was praised by Nietzsche, whom Zweig and his Viennese contemporaries began to discover around that time.[24] But, perhaps, what mattered most to the young Zweig was Taine's being a *French* thinker, by then already his preferred culture. But in one major respect, Zweig took issue with Taine's belief that 'all human decision-making is determined by hereditary, social environment and historical situation'. Instead, he believed 'people need to be understood more as individuals' and in terms of their psychological make-up.[25]

To a certain extent, Ernest Renan would have suited Zweig better if only for the latter's stance on nationhood, which as we have seen already preoccupied Zweig from early on. In fact, but probably unbeknown to Zweig, Charles Péguy, then editor of the *Cahier de la Quinzaine*, embarked on a fundamental critique of Taine and Renan's conception of history in the very year when Zweig submitted his thesis on Taine.[26] However, Renan's already famous definition of the nation as the result of a 'daily plebiscite' and his notion of a nation as 'a soul, a spiritual principle' in charge of 'a rich legacy of memories' and the will to live together comes close to Zweig's early conception of nationhood. Indeed, he could have transferred Renan's question – why it is that Switzerland, 'which has three languages, two religions, and three of four races is a nation, while Tuscany, for instance, which is so homogeneous, is not' – to the Austro-Hungarian Empire.[27] Renan's position of 1882 would have struck a chord with Zweig, but it would not take long in the Austrian Empire for this 'rich legacy of [collective] memories' to fragment exactly in line with the ethnological 'homogeneity' of its respective parts, leading what has been termed a 'Balkanization of memory'.[28]

Orientation was everything to Zweig in those early years. In 1902 for instance, he read Flaubert's letters, in which he detected a perfect harmony of 'temperament, tuning and artistry of style' (I, 32), as well as Selma Lagerlöf, Victor Hugo, Walter Pater, Ivan Turgenev, Jacob Wassermann, Émile Verhaeren, and, time and again, Nietzsche together with Rainer Maria Rilke. It appears that he wrote as much as he read and never tired of listing his achievements: essays on Nietzsche and Victor Hugo, a novella (*The Love of Erika Ewald*), and anthologies with translations by various German-language poets of the poems of Baudelaire and Verlaine, not to speak of the waves of correspondence Zweig had to master already by then. Of all the letters written at this time, the one to Richard Dehmel stands out. Then, Dehmel was regarded as one of the most important poetic voices in the German language. The young Arnold Schönberg based his first major composition, his string sextet in one movement, Op. 4 (1899), on Dehmel's poem 'Verklärte Nacht' ('Transfigured Night'). It is a measure of Zweig's self-assurance that he dared, quite rightly, point out to this eminent poet, twenty-two years his senior, a misleading inaccuracy in Dehmel's version of Verlaine's poem 'A Rider's Destiny'.

In those weeks and months of 1902 Zweig visited Berlin and Paris whilst continuously wrestling with his emancipation from home, with its domineering materialism that he found increasingly nauseating. He knew that in Berlin he would lead a more independent life, which he indeed practised when he studied there for one semester in 1902/3. There, he met intellectuals like the critic and brilliant essayist Felix Poppenberg, whose dandyism and love for beauty some compared with that of Oscar Wilde and Herman Bang. Incidentally, Poppenberg, like Bang, committed suicide in the first year of the First World War as he realised that the Age of Beauty had come to a catastrophic end. In early 1903, however, Zweig found himself drawn back to the gentler thrills of Vienna. He enjoyed the carnival, the dancing, and the glitz, but remained conscious of the poverty at the edge of the city. His friend Adelt heard of allusions to harmless amorous adventures, whereby he admitted: 'It is no longer the woman that provides me with highest happiness for I have this sudden fear of all ecstatic emotions because I always am afraid of the petty sentiments behind them' (I, 27). Consequently, he did not allow even Wagner's *Tristan and Isolde* in the Hofoper to enthuse him. Zweig's behavioural pattern was by then well established: life and art are inextricably intertwined, but he emphasised time and again in these early years that he was not prepared to sacrifice 'life', and experiencing it to the full, for the sake of achieving the exceptional in the art of writing.

Yet, it was through literature, in this case through the art of translation, that Zweig would enter new friendships, most importantly with the Belgian poet Émile Verhaeren and the Swedish pedagogue, writer and women's-rights campaigner, Ellen Key. Likewise, Hermann Hesse became the addressee of very personal letters and a confidant in matters of writing before the two met in person.[29] This happened in June 1905 when Zweig visited the eminently successful writer, who was enjoying a demonstratively basic living with his wife, Maria Bernoulli, in the rural setting of Gaienhofen at the Lake of Constance.

Zweig's ethos of friendship was part and parcel of his seeking orientation in life.[30] In his first letter to Hesse in early February 1903, he conceded that he did not rate himself highly as a poet but that his use to the world may have consisted in his virtue of being 'a friend to his friends', an allusion to Schiller's 'Ode to Joy'. It was again in a letter to Hesse where he emphasised his role as someone who aligned himself in Vienna with a few 'silent ones in the country', like the poet Camill Hoffmann, Franz Carl Ginzkey, and French–Turkish poet Yahya Kemal Beyatli. It is significant that he should refer to Beyatli, who symbolised for him the contact with 'foreigners'. Zweig told Hesse that it was a mere myth to assume that the Viennese literary world is but 'one large table in a Coffee House', around which the literati sat day by day. Speaking for himself, Zweig stressed that he knew neither Arthur Schnitzler, Hermann Bahr, Hugo von Hofmannsthal, nor Peter Altenberg well personally, let alone intimately (I, 57). Zweig's ambition to find his own way and his desire to assert himself and his restlessness, which would become a feature of his life, are reflected in his frequently moving house within Vienna from one address, or rather 'room of his own' to another – in search for a quiet setting for his studies. Buchfeldgasse 2 in the eighth district was his next destination before moving in the same district into his first own flat in Kochgasse 8 in February 1907. To a certain extent, these moves were preludes to Zweig's extended traveling that reached a first climax in 1904/5.

What were the directions his own writing took at this time? Given his literary preferences, poetry should have been the main direction. But the writer of essayistic and novelistic prose in him grew stronger by the year. And, almost to his own surprise, the dramatist in him emerged almost from nowhere. His very first drama in verses about

– in his words – the 'ugliest and most vicious of all Greeks before Troy' (I, 104), Thersites, was accepted for performance at the Berlin Schauspielhaus, the foremost theatre in the German capital city. At the same time, Zweig turned out to be a highly accomplished translator of mainly French poetry, by Verhaeren in particular, but also some Keats and William Morris.[31]

Zweig became arguably more critical of his own poetry the more he translated Verhaeren and the closer he felt to Rilke's poetry, who soon turned into another important role model for Zweig.[32] In *The World of Yesterday* he even suggested that barely four weeks after the publication of *Silver Strings* he could no longer understand where he had taken the courage from to do so. He regarded these verses as 'unauthentic in their sentimentality' even though he credited them for their remarkable craftsmanship in terms of forms and sheer artistry.[33] Even though a volume with some of his novellas saw the light of day in 1904 under the title *Die Liebe der Erika Ewald* (*The Love of Erika Ewald*) it was through his translations that he felt on more solid ground. The mediation of great art had become his vocation, or so he thought. He pretended to have no ambitions of his own (I, 104) but was genuinely happy when he succeeded in suggesting projects to others, for example Verhaeren's translations of, and biography on, one of the key figures of literary naturalism, Johannes Schlaf. It made him 'proud to find' that his suggestions were taken up (I, 103). Schlaf must have shared Zweig's belief that Verhaeren was giving to Europe what Walt Whitman was presenting America with: an unconditional affirmation of the present time and the future. Small wonder that Schlaf also became Whitman's main translator into German for a while. Later, Schlaf's reputation suffered from his drifting into racist ideology, one main reason why Zweig did not mention him in *The World of Yesterday*. The very same happened to Zweig with a much closer friend at the time, Erwin Guido Kolbenheyer, who was to become a propagator of the racist *völkisch* movement, supported National Socialism from the outset, and, because of it, became an embarrassment to his former friend Zweig.

Émile Verhaeren, Zweig's first literary father figure

After the *Belle Époque*, European culture needed rejuvenation – or so Zweig believed, together with most representatives of *Junges Wien*. Inspiration for this new impulse was partly home-grown, partly imported from abroad – from France, but increasingly from Belgium, which only came into being as a state in 1830 with England as the guarantor of her neutrality. 'Newness' was a matter of opening up towards the Francophone world with Paris and Brussels as its hubs. The Arts and Crafts movement was in full swing in England with its chief protagonist, William Morris, in Belgium with Henry van de Velde. Art Nouveau, Art Deco, and *Jugendstil* enriched the options for architecture and were perceived as precursors to a more radical modernism with Constantin Meunier, Félicien Rops, George Minne, and Théo van Rysselberghe, but especially Fernand Khnopff providing new styles of painting. In literature, this was complemented by Charles van Lerberghe and Camille Lemonnier but most importantly by Émile Verhaeren. The extent of the cultural interchange and transfer activities between Brussels and Vienna around 1900 has only relatively recently attracted more attention.[34] Zweig's role as an early and tireless propagator of Verhaeren's poetry and plays was pivotal in this context.[35] In fact, Zweig had familiarised himself with Verhaeren's poetry already in his last years at grammar school. But even before he translated *Les apparus dans mon chemin* (*Appearances on my Path*), which was published in 1904 under the title *Ausgewählte Gedichte*, Zweig released his translations of poems by Camille Lemonnier and Charles van Lerberghe. What interested Zweig most – especially in Lemonnier's poetry – was 'the pantheist and vitalist attitude' these poems reflected, as well as 'his Flemish patriotic ideas'.[36] It was Verhaeren's vitalism that impressed Zweig and his Berlin publisher Schuster & Löffler, with whom his first collection of poetry, *Silver Strings*, had appeared.

Vitalism as poetically propagated by Verhaeren, Lemonnier, Walt Whitman, and in Germany by Richard Dehmel, Johannes Schlaf, and Paul Zech, was perceived as an antidote to Viennese aestheticism, which Zweig professed to have found nauseating precisely because of its apparent lifelessness. To Zweig's mind and taste, its artfulness or artistry bordered on artificiality. When Verhaeren gave a lecture in Vienna in 1912, mainly organised by Zweig, he was deeply disappointed to find that the city's literary establishment had snubbed the event. To Romain Rolland he wrote that the atmosphere in Vienna 'is too ironic, too critical, too close to the Jewish spirit. It is lacking in generous enthusiasm and consists ultimately only of some cliques who envy each other.'[37]

Several things are noteworthy here. Firstly, Zweig's sympathy for Flemish patriotism putting a question mark behind the assumption that he had been an internationalist from early on; secondly, his associating Jewish intellectualism with being too ironic and critical despite his own Jewish background (this argument, though, was not at all uncommon at the time and was to enter radical right-wing anti-Semitic rhetoric leading to denunciation of 'Jewish' critics altogether); and thirdly the elegance and sheer aesthetic appeal of Zweig's own translations of Verhaeren contradicted his intention to present the Belgian poet as an anti-aestheticist.

This said, the fragility of human existence concerned Zweig from the start. For instance, what fascinated him about the mythological Thersites, as described in detail by Homer in the second book of the Iliad, was the study of a character whose soul became paradoxically, or consequentially, more refined by his suffering from being unspeakably ugly. Still, Zweig believed that his work was on shaky grounds. He confided in Ellen Key in February 1906 that he had become oversensitive to the 'fragility in my works' (I, 115). This does not mean that he had lost faith in his own abilities, but he had grown aware of just how relative so-called achievements are in the arts, and literature in particular, if they cannot claim to be genuine with the prospect of attaining lasting value. Not so much this remarkably accomplished drama in verses, *Thersites*, published in 1907, was the case in mind but Zweig's first volume of poetry *Silver Strings*. The 'fragility' was not immediately evident but rather hidden behind the façade of verbal finesse. These early poems offer few surprises in the formation of metaphors, or in stylistic terms; they are conventional in terms of rhyme structure and the rather monotonous rhythms. There are next to no indications of experimentation or expressiveness that risk something. The rhymes are almost too smooth for words and their own good. The desire to create something 'beautiful' dominates these poems. Moments of sadness are inevitably resolved in glimmers of hope and vaguely defined yearnings. However, this aesthetic pronouncement in poetic form appears deliberately to be too beautiful to be true. Beneath the surface of 'silver strings' at night that are made to vibrate and resound by the moonlight, as the title poem puts it, loneliness looms, often only indicated by deletions marked with three dots. Some poems indicate that their subject feels trapped, like the rose in a vase that does not know whether it is dead or still alive.

These are the poems of a doubtlessly gifted adolescent; the measure of their quality is the type of poetry written around 1900, not yet affected by the dithyrambic raptures of Nietzsche's verse but, instead, ever so aware of the need to create 'pure' art. To a certain extent they represent the kind of aestheticism that Zweig criticised in others: 'Some tears tremble into my nights / No dream closes my sore eyes ... / Oh, how much I crave your lips / For their bell-pure and soft "you"!' Thus reads the first stanza of the poem 'From Charged Nights'.[38] Even some ten years later, the writing of poetry remained, according to Zweig's own admission, his main artistic challenge, simply because he rated the lyrical poet as the most sublime of artists. His diary entry of 11 September 1912 sounds appropriately ambiguous: 'In the evening attempt to writing a poem, half successful, a few stanzas of banal profundity, which I think is darkened and beautified by the rhythm' (Tb, 11).

For Zweig, poetry was the laurel-wreath-bearing hero in the art of literature. But his 'hero' was suffering. Perhaps, therefore, he continued to nurture his own poetry, leading to a new collection in 1917 (*Die frühen Kränze*, or *The Early Wreaths*), an edition of his *Collected Poems* (1924), and a selection of his poetry in 1931. The only known poem Zweig wrote after 1931 is what he called 'Last Poem' – a poetic 'thank you' of a sixty-year-old, as the subtitle reads – a poetic farewell, slightly reminiscent of his 'prologue and epilogue' to Shakespeare's *The Tempest*, which he had published in 1925 but began working on in

1912. His final poem closes with the lines: 'One never loves life more dearly / Than in the shadow of resignation' (*'Nie liebt man das Leben teurer / Als im Schatten des Verzichts.'*)[39]

From early on, Zweig was sceptical about what his time cherished most: the heroic. Long before his interest in writing biographical essays, let alone full-scale biographies, he felt attracted to tragic figures, if not anti-heroes in a time of heroism; Zweig's *Thersites* is the non-hero *per se* on stage. As it happened, this preference was coupled with his ambiguous feelings towards the theatre as an institution since it promoted, in his view, actors as cult figures, thus contributing to the shallowness of cultural life altogether. At the same time, he was particular about the performance of his dramas. When the great star of the Berlin Schauspielhaus, Adalbert Matkowsky (who was to play the role of Thersites), fell ill, Zweig withdrew his drama and gave it to the court theatres in Dresden and Kassel where it was first performed on 26 November 1908; he felt that not any old actor should be entrusted with the part.[40]

The example of Hofmannsthal's tragedy *Elektra*, first performed in 1903 with Gertrud Eysoldt in the title role and produced by Max Reinhardt, may have inspired Zweig to concern himself with dramatising particular aspects of Greek mythology. It was the moral victory of the defeated over the enigmatically powerful Achilles that must have intrigued Zweig.[41] His Thersites was fooled by the woman of his heart, Teleia, who instrumentalised his affection for her to make Achilles jealous. Unfulfilled love, already a motif in some of his early poems, was to become a main theme in Zweig's works to come.

The lasting legacy of *Junges Wien* in Zweig was, as said, his lifelong adoration for the young, male and female, manifesting itself in his enthusiasm and practical support for gifted young writers with homoerotic dispositions – from minor writers like (the deeply troubled) Ernst Rieger, Hans Müller-Einigen, Georg Busse-Palma, and Erich Ebermeyer to the highly gifted Klaus Mann.[42] Paradoxically, the post-Nietzschean affirmation of life, bordering on a cult-like attitude towards health and vitality, led in the case of many to drug addiction (in Zweig's circle, Ernst Rieger and Klaus Mann) and suicide including, eventually, Zweig himself. By the same token, Zweig's obsession with youth and youthfulness resulted in his phobia of age, later coupled with an acute awareness that the bell was tolling for the ageing culture he was brought up in.

The young Zweig was evidently aware of his seductive effect he had on males and females, meaning his sheer power over the emotions of others.[43] One of those who fell under his spell during his brief study period in Berlin in 1902–3 was Hans Müller-Einigen, later (notoriously) known for his patriotic dramas and his libretti for operettas. He remembered this first encounter, and Zweig's eyes in particular, in his memoirs *Jugend in Wien*, published in Bern in 1945, that is to say three years after Zweig's suicide. According to Müller-Einigen Zweig's eyes seemed to have consisted of deep-black but soft ink:

> When these eyes fixated you, sucked you in, at the same time lurking and wooing, then they seemed to ask after hidden and secret things, to which nobody would admit ... One finds this unspoken luring and threatening tenderness of the superior Being only in Vienna.[44]

The 'secret' kept burning in his friends, and mostly in Zweig himself. But clearly, it was he who had struck the match first. Again, in a Nietzschean vein, one could say that the result was a flame that, at times, threatened to consume him.

Man of the world
Albert Harlingue/Roger-Viollet

The Virtue of Restlessness

Travelling became an integral part of the young Stefan Zweig's 'orientation'. Experiencing 'foreignness' belonged to his conception of development. Towards the end of his second stay in Paris, where he spent half a year from autumn 1904 until spring 1905, Zweig quoted in a letter to Hesse (I, 99) two lines from the poem 'In der Fremde' ('In Foreign Lands') by his revered nineteenth-century icon of Austrian literature, Franz Grillparzer: *'Ein Wandrer, der zwei Fremden / Und keine Heimat hat.'* ('A wanderer who counts two foreign countries his own / but no homeland.') These verses anticipate Nietzsche's poem 'Vereinsamt' ('Lonesome'), written in 1884 and published ten years later by his sister in the *Magazin für Litteratur*. The final line of this outburst of emotional desolation that features crows, a lonely wanderer in winter, and bitter self-mocking reads: *'Weh dem, der keine Heimat hat'* ('Pity the one who cannot call anywhere his home'). To a certain extent, both (Grillparzer's and Nietzsche's) poems echo Franz Schubert's song cycle *Die Winterreise* after Wilhelm Müller's lyrical composition, with the message that the uprooted one will never find roots again. Perhaps this feeling was deep down in Zweig, too, despite his 'secure' background, when he decided that Grillparzer's lines should also feature as a motto in his programmatic poem 'Fahrten' ('Journeys'). By the same token one could argue that because of his secure background he could afford to be restless.

However, whilst Zweig's poem begins with the confession 'I am too tired to travel', it proclaims that home is wherever fancy takes him to, in whatever country where he finds himself as a guest. Being able to move from place to place had a liberating effect on the ever-restless Zweig. At any rate, it is not difficult to see why Zweig was so fond of Grillparzer's poem. It indicates fatigue and exhaustion from travelling, and the second stanza could have been written by Zweig himself. It opens with the rhetorical question, 'Will you, thus, return home?' The reply is clear: 'Oh no! Going home is about the last thing! / There the vitality of life is dying / Of sheer tedium.' Travel became 'unquestionably the fulcrum' of Zweig's entire adult life. Eventually, travel for Zweig meant no longer merely parting from home for a while 'but it had become a home in itself'.[1]

Anyhow, these were not the sentiments of an *artiste-flâneur* in the making, even though Paris was to become something of a 'home' to Zweig. But he was clearly too restless to merely stroll for hours through Les Halles or along the endless boulevards. When he actually did explore some of the boulevards in Paris he felt he 'no longer belonged to himself', such was the distraction that all the things along and off the boulevards provided him with, most notably these alluring looks from some French ladies 'that have the capacity not only to awaken dreamers but the dead', as he informed Hesse in a letter from Paris in 1905 (I, 99).

'Leisure' is not a quality that we normally connect with Zweig, but he is reported to have suffered from stretches of tedium and boredom, particularly early in his life when he was unsure of the routes to take. Perhaps he was aware of Seneca's famous definition of '*otium*', or leisure, suggesting that without any intellectual activity leisure is death and a grave for any living human being.[2]

Zweig would have already then subscribed to what Franz Hessel, Berlin's most known *flaneur*, had to say about the 'difficult art of promenading' ('Von der schwierigen Kunst spazieren zu gehen', 1932):

> When you are promenading make sure that you want to arrive somewhere. Perhaps then you have a chance of going off your way in a pleasant manner. But every *Abweg*, or course off the beaten track, necessitates having a way, or path, in the first place.[3]

Aimless drifting for long was not Zweig's thing. Also, his first major excursion to Brussels in 1902 had but one aim: meeting his idol, the poet Émile Verhaeren.

Taster tours and first English flavours

It was between July 1904 and September 1905 when the extent of Zweig's journeying amounted to a taste of things to come. First, he visited the Marienbad Spa, where his parents were taking their customary cure in characteristic style with their own servants and maids, followed by a stay in Ostend (where he met his brother Albert), thereafter in Heyst, Blankenberge, Bruges, Berlin, Paris, Avignon, Arles, Seville, and places in Algiers. After a short while back in Vienna he ventured off to the South Tyrol and Florence. Some fruits of these journeys were pastiches in prose, impressionistic essays on places and their psycho-topology, as one could term them. For he viewed these places as organisms with a soul of their own. Thus, their actual 'analysis' in pseudo-psychological terms was appropriate, given that he associated their respective 'soul' with that of humans. It is the perception of 'organic' entities that fascinated Zweig, mainly because he occasionally feared that he could never produce such an organism of literary works and, one day, must sell great heaps of fragments and scrap papers full of drafts and plans; or so he told his closest friend, at the time Franz Carl Ginzkey (I, 98). This is also why he admired Verhaeren's œuvre so much: precisely because it offered such 'an organic unity with prospects towards the future and times past' (I, 93).

For Zweig, places had anthropomorphic features. For instance, he regarded the 'physiognomy of Ostend' to be the exact mirror of its visitors. And in Seville he mused that the 'faces of towns' can be 'like men, sad and old, smiling and young, menacing and slender, lithe and worn'.[4] To Zweig's ears, there was even a town-specific musicality to an urban atmosphere such as in Seville, which he compared with that of Salzburg. 1905 was the first time that he singled out Salzburg as the measure for beauty in townscapes against which he would hold, in the final years of his life, Bath and Petrópolis, with favourable results for both.

His impressions of Ostend focused on the contrast between the elegance and sumptuousness of this then haven for Europe's real and bogus aristocracy and the poverty and destitution among the ordinary people there, harbour workers and fishermen, let alone the desertedness of the town after the high season is over. In Avignon he emphasised the harmony between town and surroundings with reference to the Fontaine de Vaucluse 'beyond its walls, immortalised by those two great figures of love, Laura and Petrarch.' Zweig exercised his ability to characterise nature and its sheer poetry when he described this particular setting:

> If the source itself is not particularly memorable, its romanticism is not entirely unworthy of Petrarch, who made it unforgettable: in a green ravine, clasped between rocks, the water suddenly leaps like a white flame to descend in a roaring cascade down the valley, clear, transparent, a truly invigorated spring.[5]

It was through travelling that Zweig learnt to see and to transform what he had seen into interpretative writing. This he achieved impressively in his essay on Hyde Park, written a few weeks after his first arrival in London in spring 1906 where he was to spend some four months. He took lodgings in 84, Kensington Gardens Square within walking distance from the park. Perhaps he succeeded so admirably in writing this essay because he found it difficult to get accustomed to his new uncongenial surroundings. He informed Ellen Key that he found the few English people he had met relatively closed up and rather cold, withdrawn, and not very cordial (I, 117). More problematic still was the climate and its paralyzing atmosphere, which had killed all his 'courage for work' (I, 118). In his essay he was more explicit:

> And the air bears sound unwillingly; light, colour and groping glances tint in a peculiar way this heavy London atmosphere, which is saturated with sea salt, made yellow by the mists and grey by the smoke of countless chimneys. It veils shapes, makes them rounded and obscure, dims the distance and causes the sky close by to incline prematurely into the outline of the horizon's shadow.[6]

The seemingly perpetual greyness in and over London got to him. Had anyone told him at the time that this place, still full of Dickensian gloom, would in some twenty-five years become the first major haven of his exile, he would have shrugged this suggestion off as utter fiction and a most unpleasant thought. But then, the unimaginable is often only too likely to turn into reality.

What 'saved' Zweig there and then in London were trips to Oxford, which he termed 'one half of England's brain with Cambridge being the other', and places in Scotland. London he perceived as the ever-restless pulsating heart of this 'huge organism' called England and her Empire.[7] Although the London atmosphere made him suffer, he did not go as far as Karl Philip Moritz who in 1782 had reason to call the city a large urban 'dungeon', from which he, too, successfully escaped into the pastoral English countryside.[8]

Zweig felt that what helped him most were encounters with William Butler Yeats, the symbolist poet Arthur Symons, and the art historian Archibald G. B. Russell. Zweig grew so fond of Yeats's poetry that he attempted a translation of his poetic play *The Shadowy Waters* with a view to offer to it the German stage, though the project did not come to anything. But both Yeats and Russell, in particular, introduced Zweig to the art of William Blake. It was in 1906 when Russell published an edition of Blake's letters; when Zweig translated his friend's study on Blake's visionary art philosophy into German; and when Zweig acquired an original pencil drawing by Blake, his 'King John'. Zweig was to attribute such importance to this drawing that he would later argue to recognise the spirit and very 'genius of England' in this drawing, something he had tried to find in her 'streets and cities' in vain.[9]

As it happened, the essay 'Hyde Park' was his entry ticket to the culture of London. When it was published in the *Neue Freie Presse* in Vienna on 8 June 1906 it was met with considerable resonance, but Zweig's claim that the *Daily Mail* and several other English newspapers had reprinted extracts was more a case of wishful thinking on his part; the kind of tall story that he was perfectly capable of releasing when he felt it would befit him. As is commonly known since the days

King John, an early favourite of Zweig
William Blake

of Plato, being cavalier with the truth is a writer's prerogative. After all, the author of *The Decay of Lying* had only died six years prior to Zweig's stay in London.

Curiously, on his travels at the time Zweig avoided Switzerland. In fact, he must have been one of the very few travellers who positively 'hated, despised' this Alpine paradise in Europe's midst. As he wrote to Eugenie Hirschfeld just before his departure from London in August 1906, he felt disgusted by the 'over-urbanised, picture-book-like' country, full of Englishmen and Berliners (I, 127). This outburst proves that Zweig was perfectly capable of coming up with peculiar prejudices and expressions of stunning irritation. Raging tempers were not at all alien to this otherwise demonstratively calm poet–traveller.

Back in Vienna he confided to Ellen Key that he could not but 'always swing back' to this city. But he was aware that this sense of belonging has its shortcomings, for it makes one lose something 'wonderful: that abroad one cannot feel properly at home'. He professed that 'proximity and distance' should ideally be on a par with each other (I, 133). During the year he spent in Vienna in his new flat in Kochgasse 8, from September 1906 until September 1907, Zweig read avidly and worked on his study on Verhaeren. Shakespeare – or in his at times shaky spelling, 'Shacespeare' – and Balzac were his company together with works by Max Brod (Kafka's friend) and, time and again, Rilke. *Père Goriot* and the *Illusions Perdues* by Balzac were his favourites, and it is a believable claim, made to Max Brod, that he knew *The Tempest* 'almost by heart' while reading *Romeo and Juliet* as well as *Titus Andronicus*, like a reminiscence of his time in London (I, 153).

World views

During this year in Vienna Zweig wrote precious little in his letters about the cultural life in this city. He seemed more in tune with people elsewhere, including the Berlin poet Richard Dehmel – the earlier slight disagreement, if not irritation, over nuances of the latter's translation of Verhaeren well buried. In a letter to him, Zweig argued that the standing of poetry amongst literary critics suffered from 'theatre paralysis' and the privileging of stage productions in the review sections of the papers. But the depth of poetry – once again his example was Verhaeren – would provide a more profound reflection of what he called *Weltanschauung unserer Zeit*, the view of the world in our time. By *Weltanschauung* Zweig did not mean 'ideology' but a particular perception of the world, more in the sense of the word *Weltbetrachtung*, the seeing of the world, as he put it in a letter to Rilke in August 1907 (I, 156). Unbeknown to Zweig, in an early Rilke novella called *Ewald Tragy* (probably written in 1898, published posthumously), his addressee had mocked this obsession with *Weltanschauung* at the time, as one day Tragy 'awakes in the morning with a new *Weltanschauung* in his mind'.[10] Perhaps Rilke may have seen in Zweig's remark a case of unwitting irony.

Once again, in the autumn of 1907 the *Reiselust* (or wanderlust) got the better of Zweig and he ventured to Rome via Genoa, Corsica, and Sardinia. Detours were part of Zweig's travel repertoire. He asked his friend, the half-Italian art historian and art dealer Benno Geiger, for recommendations of where to stay in Rome. It had to be a *proper* and clean pension for he was terrified of vermin of any kind. Besides, he urged him to write a letter of introduction to Filippo Tommaso Marinetti. This is significant given that he intended to meet a writer who, in complete contrast to Zweig himself, must have been known to him as someone who was already severely critical of literary and artistic traditions. He felt 'sympathetic' with what he had heard of Marinetti's activities (I, 159), which were to lead the Italian to publish his 'Futurist Manifesto' in *Le Figaro* on 20 February 1909. This simply shows the vital interest Zweig had in wanting to be aware of the artistic currents and trends of his time. The meeting with Marinetti did not come to anything but he proudly reported that he stayed in a very pleasant English pension in the Via Emilia with a 'delightful balcony overlooking a little garden', for which he paid the trifle of eight lira per day 'without alcohol and coffee' (I, 160). It is, however, not Rome's alleged *dolce vita* he was after but a place to read Goethe's novel *Wilhelm Meister* at long last. It was only in this special setting that he could fully appreciate the wonders of this extraordinary novel, as he put it. In other words, while he felt that he continued to be in a prolonged phase of personal and cultural development he took to *the* German classic of a *Bildungsroman*, a novel about exemplary education and cultural self-formation.

A year later, in autumn 1908, Zweig found himself preparing for his passage to India, which soon became to him 'more important than anything else' (I, 172). But before embarking on this voyage he reflected on the meaning of his study on Verhaeren and his own development to date. His book on the Belgian poet was to be 'more than a mere biography' but a *Weltanschauungsbuch* (a book on how to view the world), an exemplary presentation of an exemplary man, as Ellen Key learned from him in August 1908 (I, 173). And when the editor of the prestigious weekly for German culture, *Morgen* (*Tomorrow*), Herwarth Walden, invited him to supply an autobiographical note, he singled out his travels as the most formative influence on his own development. From these journeys, or so Zweig wrote, a 'strong cosmopolitan feeling' emerged, which he obviously regarded, for good measure, as his main capital (I, 175–6). *Tomorrow* brought together a stunning array of co-editors: Richard Strauss for music, Werner Sombart for social politics, the eminent Danish literary critic and scholar Georg Brandes for literature, Richard Muther for the arts, and Hugo von Hofmannsthal for poetry. It seemed that, before setting off on his five-month Indian venture, Zweig had arrived – in terms of early literary recognition.

Zweig's passage to India

His itinerary included, as usual, some meandering but this time with a purpose. He had to go to Berlin and Leipzig first, then to Dresden and Kassel for the first performances of his play *Thersites*, then back to Vienna, but in transit only, and to Trieste thereafter from where he would embark to the Red Sea, followed by a sea voyage to Bombay. Until May 1909, Zweig joked, he would be untraceable even for the police. Already, from Calcutta he proudly announced to Victor

Fleischer his route through India with precise dates: back and forth from Calcutta to Darjeeling in the Himalayas, to Rangoon, Madras, and Colombo on Ceylon ('For how long I will stay in Ceylon will depend on Ceylon itself' (I, 186)) – and back to Vienna. Zweig had become a world traveller and, from the perspective of his family, a bit of a prodigal son.

Little had prepared Zweig for India except the strongest possible recommendation from Walther Rathenau, the son of the founder of AEG; then one of its board members, later its director, he was an intellectual and writer in support of Zionist ideals during the First World War. He acted as advisor for supplies with raw materials to the German Ministry of War; in 1921 he became Germany's first Jewish foreign secretary. But in June 1922 he was assassinated by a right-wing radical as a punishment for having 'fulfilled', or complied with, all the demands of the allied enemies of Germany. There was even a term for such 'traitors' of German interests: *Erfüllungspolitiker*. However, all of that was in the far distance when Zweig met Rathenau through the editor of the weekly journal *Die Zukunft*, Maximilian Harden.[11] Like Zweig, Rathenau was a contributor to Harden's journal except he published his articles under a pseudonym.

Zweig and Rathenau saw eye to eye in more than one way. Both shared a profound mistrust of the over-mechanisation of life; in Rathenau's case this was not without irony given his position as one of the main industrialists in the *Kaiserreich*. In his review of Rathenau's major intellectual work 'Zur Kritik der Zeit' ('Critiquing our Time') for the *Neue Freie Presse*, Zweig characterised him as an 'amphibic creature between merchant and artist, man of action and thinker.' He credited Rathenau with a strong sense for 'what was real' and a distinctly visionary imagination.[12]

Zweig travelled to India in the company of a Viennese journalist and minor writer, Hermann Bessemer, who turned out to be not an ideal travel companion as their interests diverged quite drastically.[13] It was the colourfulness of Indian life, its openness and rich fabric, that impressed Zweig most. Retrospectively, in *The World of Yesterday*, he would emphasise the poverty and deprivation he had seen and how the class structure of Indian society appalled him. The obsession with 'purity' among higher-ranking castes had demonstrated to him the madness of racial theories. But the most important literary 'product' of his journey to India was his poem 'Taj Mahal', later published in his collection *Neue Fahrten* (*New Voyages*) with the subtitle 'Funerary monument for Muntaz Mahals in Delhi':

> If reflected in a pond
> it seems like a toy
> as its white shapes are scaled down.
> Tender and ivory-like
> it lies on display as if under frosted glass;
> (one is almost fearful to break it).
>
> And then a glance, and look, it is a building!
> rising, glaring, flawless and stony
> it ascends, gleamingly detaching its surfaces
> from the greenness of leaves, rising in ever purer
> movements up into the shining blue,
>
> up into the light, and radiating with the glittering sun
> as if from its breast those past hearts
> would breathe in the cool crypta
> (the great prince and the beloved spouse).
>
> But in the evening, it seems a dream. Like a tear,
> that turned into marble it shines the sorrow
> over the vanished Beloved into darkness.[14]

For his roughly half-year Indian venture Zweig had prepared himself well through reading and writing about current literature on the sub-continent – from Ernst Haeckel's *Indische Reisebriefe* (*Letters from an Indian Journey*, which was already in its fifth edition by 1908) to Pierre Loti's *Indien (ohne die Engländer)*, published in Berlin and Paris in 1905. The very title of the latter, *Indian (without the English)*, indicated what was to become Zweig's main concern, namely, to dissociate the 'real' India from its Western influence. Like so many young German-speaking literati at the time – the other prominent examples being Hermann Hesse and Max Dauthendey – Zweig sought to find uncorrupted 'authenticity' in India, *Urkultur*, preferably without any colonial traces. In so doing he connected with the romantic notion of an Indo-Germanic ideal, but he remained free from any racist perversions of this conception, which became common currency in radical right-wing circles.[15]

The desired 'authenticity' in Indian culture Zweig saw in Benares (Varanasi), as his detailed and as ever impressionistic travelogue on 'The City of a Thousand Temples' demonstrated. The mystique of purification as an integral element of the Hindu religion impressed him. Expiation as a main feature of religious practices and ceremonies found genuine resonance in Zweig. At the same time, he was fascinated by the colourful spectacle that unfolded before his eyes, rated by him as a 'performance'.[16] Consequently, he compared the wide steps down to the river Ganges to an 'amphitheatre', with nature, the pyres, boats decorated with flowers, and the towers of Benares as the stage setting. The presence of worship and death, the sacred moment of dying in public – Zweig observed an old man who was brought to the banks of the sacred river to meet his end – suggested to him the unity of life and death. The act of expiation in the river occurs, after all, with swimming corpses all around those seeking atonement and propitiation. Knowing what we know now about Zweig's complex sexuality and moral dilemmas it would be plausible to read into his extended description of these acts of expiation as an attempt to expiate himself.

Zweig's impression of a particularly colourful residence, Gwalior, is of a different kind. He felt that it showed him the India of the future, with the maharaja being fully anglicised; opening his palace to tourists and allowing his domain to lose its authenticity. But there was another uncorruptible feature which Zweig pointed out – in line with his by then (1908) firmly established interest in sudden occurrences. In this case, it was the landscape itself that presented him with an example of this quality; for the rock formation on which the palace of Gwalior rests, 'suddenly springs from the yellow clay' of the flat land. He called this 'suddenness' in the topography of the Gwalior area 'indescribable' in its effect on the visitor (AR, 107). The rock formation represented to him a sublime paradox, spontaneity in the state of petrification. In retrospect, in the summer of 1909 Zweig reflected on politics in India, and the *Neue Freie Presse* published his writings as its leader column on 13 July under the title 'Die indische Gefahr für England' ('The Indian Danger for England'). Zweig argued that England should always be aware of a potential uprising of the subcontinent, for the English there behaved like a 'cast above all casts' having seemingly forgotten the catastrophe of the 1857 revolt. He also pointed to the fact that 'India' as such did not exist (yet) but consisted as a 'conglomerate of different races'. The Indians would not 'clench their fists' but 'organised resistance' would inevitably and irresistibly develop 'together with an increasingly determined will of the people that is being suppressed' (AR, 284). Notwithstanding all obvious differences, Zweig's readers could have interpreted this analysis as an analogy of the situation in the Habsburg Empire, where the German-speaking Austrians formed an elitist 'cast' above the 'conglomerate' of different peoples. Be it as it may, Zweig's political observations, rare as they had been, were surprisingly astute but possibly supported by comments he picked up from the German military attaché in Japan, Karl Haushofer, whom Zweig met on his journey to India.[17] Coincidence had it that in the autumn of the same year, the young Mahatma Gandhi developed the conception of *Hind Swaraj* (self-rule in India) onboard the ship that brought him back from England to South Africa.

After his return from India, the ever-restless Zweig wanted to remain 'in hiding' in his Viennese apartment to gather himself and sort himself out. It appears that Zweig must have found it difficult at times to keep up with himself. No sooner was he back from India, where he had seen 'everything' from the Himalayas to Ceylon, he found himself making plans for further trips. In two years' time, he would write from Vienna once again to Ellen Key; he wanted to travel to Japan and China, and back via Russia. By now, as a consequence of all his travelling, he felt like a stranger in his hometown, bereft of a sense of belonging. Instead, he regarded 'the world as my home' (I, 188). Again, he was driven by 'restlessness, lack of inner peace' as he told friend and journalist, Leonard Adelt. He could not work out whether he should once more 'escape' into 'distant lands' or 'retreat' into his work, adding the following: 'I will not tell you anything about India, nothing about what it was that urged me to go, and nothing about what it means to me now. I hardly know myself where I stand' (I, 189). But deep down he knew that this had been a journey 'in order to move away from myself' (I, 190).

Time and again, Zweig was looking for retreats. They did not have to be as far afield as the Himalayas. St Blasien in the southern part of the Black Forest also did the trick of steadying his nerves, at least for a short while. One of the reasons for this restlessness was Zweig's dissatisfaction with his own literary work, as he conceded to his fellow contender in respect of translating poetry from the French, Paul Zech:

> I don't like my novellas any longer [...] like so many of us in Vienna, I have begun too early with writing and we now have to work in earnest on ourselves and must not be deluded by our all too easy successes of our first slick attempts [at producing literary texts]. (I, 207)

Towards the Americas

By mid-February 1911 Zweig found himself as a 'first-class passenger' on his next transatlantic adventure, this time to the Americas; starting in New York, to Boston and places in Canada, then down south right to the Panama Canal. Not much is known about the details of this journey as Zweig was particularly guarded in respect of his whereabouts. But there are four essayistic pieces that give us an idea of what he found noteworthy: 'With the French in Canada', 'The Rhythm of New York', 'Parsifal in New York', and, most substantially, 'The Hour between two Oceans. The Panama Canal'. When reading these travelogues, one gains the impression that Zweig was measuring his descriptive capacity against the extraordinariness of what he encountered. Take for instance this one sentence about a winter's evening in Boston that seemed at first to offer nothing but greyness: 'But then, in an instant, illuminated adverts were twitching, screaming words ran with breakneck speed up the front of houses, only to cascade headlong downwards and climbing up again' (AR, 129). Words in electric motion are followed by the perpetual movement in a train through the seemingly endless snowy plains of North America towards the Canadian border, straight to Quebec. There he encountered a reservoir of French speakers, an island made of words spoken in 'peculiar French', which moved Zweig as much as pockets of German speakers all over America. But his French bias is obvious as he commended the Quebecois for their resistance against Anglophone 'infiltration'. He sided, as so often, with a minority, arguing that, ironically, the original colonialists, the French Canadians, would soon share the fate of the Native North Americans.

But it was Zweig's essay on 'The Rhythm of New York' in which he excelled in terms of his ability to combine figurative speech with non-literal meaning. He singles out the 'rhythm' of urbane living as the major hallmark of this metropolitan phenomenon, with its multilingual culture and the forcefulness of its tart beauty. He detected a rhythm in New York that amounted to a violation, if not 'rape' of nature (AR, 135). It was a precise moment and location when Zweig physically felt this rhythm and energy, which he describes as if they were urbanised versions of Walt Whitman's vitalist poetry. This occurred, according to Zweig, when he stood on Brooklyn Bridge, which he compares to a 'nerve' that connects New York with Brooklyn (AR, 137). It also appeared to him like an excursion into a mountainous, if not Alpine, region, with the skyscrapers to his left and right like jagged heaps of stone. He repeatedly saw in these building complexes overhanging rock formations with ridges and abysses. The constancy of movement in this mega-city, however, reminded him of the sea and streams, leading him to the thought that New York with its high-rise buildings had become an 'imitation' of Alpine regions and a seascape. In New York, he recognised the capital of restlessness that penetrated every aspect of life. Typically, in its midst, Zweig identified what he made out as the epitome of German high culture: a performance of Wagner's *Parsifal* in the Metropolitan Opera House. As so often, Zweig was the man of the moment, for he attended a performance conducted by the Frankfurt-born Alfred Hertz, who gained prominence as a Wagner conductor. Some of his performances were experimentally recorded by Lionel Mapleson. Yet, Zweig wrote rather condescendingly about what seemed to have been an inadequate production, wondering, too, whether a good conductor can afford to be podgy, if not fat (Zweig would not have known that Hertz suffered from polio, which forced him to walk with a cane). He was bemused by the fact that the audience used torches during the performance so to be able to read the libretto, indulging in eating ice cream during the intervals. It was then in the foyer where he overheard conversations of mostly Germans who had come from afar to attend this performance, since this music, Zweig mused, was their 'real home'. He was touched that during all this 'Yankee toing and froing', this most 'emphatic of symbols' of German culture dominated the scene (AR, 137).

Undoubtedly, Zweig had the gift of the moment as his final travelogue of 1911 about the Panama Canal also confirms. He saw it in the making three years prior to the opening, on the day when the First World War broke out. Once again, Zweig likens a connecting construction – in this case a canal and not a bridge – to a nerve strand connecting the two halves of an entire continent and of two oceans. Our restless traveller hails the drama of planning and construction. Through his reflections he sought to add to this dramatisation, for example by speaking of the 'intoxication', or even frenzy, of accomplishing this extraordinary project. He did not forget to mention the thousands of workers that perished since the first attempts were made to realise this gigantic undertaking but felt that he bore witness to 'a transformation of the world' (AR, 147–57). Zweig felt confirmed in his belief that the building of this canal would contribute to a 'revaluation' – and he deliberately used one of Nietzsche's favourite concepts, *Umwertung* – of time and space. Through this project the age of technology would honour the excitement of speed, 'which fills our century so heroically' (AR, 157). Zweig's enthusiasm for what he saw at the Culebra Cut, the system of locks and hydraulic wonders, knew no bounds. He felt privileged to have seen this newest wonder of the technical world in progress. Clearly, Zweig's fascination with the creative process was not limited to artistic production. It was also rooted in his profound interest in technological progress, as he demonstrated in this essay-like reportage on the Panama Canal. In *Decisive Moments in History* he revisited this area and project, which went back to the visionary initiative of Emperor Charles V in the early sixteenth century: 'Vasco Núñez de Balboa discovers the Pacific Ocean' by going across the American continent at the very land isthmus where the future canal would be built some four centuries later.

On his voyage back from New York Zweig must have read James Creelman's biography of Porfirio Díaz, the eighty-year-old re-elected president of Mexico who, in his younger years, had fought against the brother of Emperor Franz Joseph, the ill-fated Emperor Maximilian I of Mexico. By the time Zweig visited Mexico the country had experienced the beginning of a new rebellion that turned into a full-scale revolution (1910–20), mainly because the presidential elections were rigged and conflicting groups violently opposed each other. In addition, US-American interests were at stake, mainly in connection with the controlling of the Panama Canal and US companies' eagerness to exploit Mexico's rich mineral resources, gold included.

Having seen the impressive work in progress on the Panama Canal, Zweig clearly gathered enough impressions of the Central American region for him to explore the political reality, especially in Mexico. Onboard ship he began writing his second extended political article (after his piece on the assumed revolutionary mood in India): 'Politische Eindrücke von einer mexikanischen Reise' ('Political Impressions from a Mexican Journey') with the telling subtitle 'Die imperialistische Politik Amerikas' ('The imperialist politics of America') adding, instead of his name, 'from an Austrian'. Again, it was designed for the *Neue Freie Presse* in Vienna, which published the provocative text on 26 April 1911 (as it happened, Porfirio Díaz resigned as president two weeks later, opening the way to the no less corrupt Francisco I Madero, who had powerful allies in the commercial and banking world in New York).

Zweig's article is noteworthy for it displays sharp political judgement and grasp of detail, not without his now characteristic eye for drama in (contemporary) history. Meanwhile, a drama of a different kind unfolded in one of the cabins of this steamer. The fatally ill Gustav Mahler, accompanied by his wife Alma and his mother-in-law, was on his way back to Europe, too. And there was the young composer Ferruccio Busoni, with whom Zweig conversed amicably when he was not working on his political article, and from whom he heard details about Mahler's condition; for it was Busoni who, as one of very few fellow passengers, had access to Mahler on his last journey. We can pass over the fact that, after their arrival in Cherbourg, Zweig was too keen for his own good and everyone else's taste, as he wanted to get more than a mere glimpse of the ailing composer. For our purposes, it is more essential to have a closer look at Zweig's article than to examine his over-eager curiosity in Mahler's fate.[18] His tribute to Mahler appeared in the shape of an article, 'Gustav Mahlers Wiederkehr' ('Gustav Mahler's Return'), and a large-scale poem entitled 'The Conductor'. Interestingly, the poem remembers not the composer but the artist in charge of an orchestra. This is one of a whole series of 'character poems' that includes lyrical explorations of the sculptor (Rodin), the singer, the painter, the pilot, the dreamer, even the emperor, not to forget the repenter. These poems read like exercises in lyrical character casting, vaguely reminiscent of Rilke's earlier poetry. But let us now turn to his impressions of the situation in Mexico in spring 1911.

First, Zweig could see in Porfirio Díaz a potential object of literary exploration, given the Mexican's colourful life, which included a narrow escape from execution. Zweig saw in him a political equivalent to Casanova and the Comte de Rochefort, who famously featured in Alexandre Dumas's *The Three Musketeers*; in short a hazarder in Mexican politics. Second, he wanted to interest his readers in Austria in transatlantic affairs, arguing that their political awareness is too Eurocentric. Third, even though he belittled the 'permanent state of revolution' in countries in Central America, he nonetheless acknowledged that the comedy-like guerrillas had acquired considerable determination and skill turning themselves into a proper army. Fourth, he turned to the attitude of US citizens in need of some excitement, who visited in high numbers as tourists, 'with their Kodak cameras' at hand, battle grounds in Mexico. But when, by March, the US government gave order to mobilise some twenty thousand soldiers and sent them to the Mexican border the situation became less touristic. Zweig's speculations about the reasons for the revolutionary situation in Mexico were not entirely wrong when he assumed that the US had masterminded the whole affair in the first place. Wall Street capitalism had no qualms about showing its ugly face, as Zweig, together with others, correctly assumed. Capitalist interventionism, thinly disguised as an investment strategy for Mexico, did not even shy away from sending provocateurs into Mexico to create a reason for US military intervention. But this only sharpened Mexican resilience and a strengthening of what had hardly existed before: Mexican patriotism against US expansionism. Zweig assumed that the 'annexation of Mexico is a likely part of the US agenda for the future', at the very least the plan to make the country fully dependent on US capital.[19]

It seemed that during, and in consequence of, his journey to India and the Americas Zweig had lost his political virginity. This remarkable article demonstrated a high degree of political awareness on Zweig's part and showed that he already understood more about political psychology than he is normally credited for. But when it came to assessing political developments closer to home a sense of naivety again prevailed. This was to become most apparent in his first comments surrounding the outbreak of the First World War.

Travelling into the War, almost

But first, and after weeks of hospitalisation in connection with an inflammation of the pleura – the loss of working time annoyed him greatly – Zweig was to retrace his steps in old Europe, from Merano to Antwerp, from Liège to Ostend. Whilst he rediscovered Merano, the pearl of the South Tyrol, as a town and landscape of harmonic transition from the Northern to the Southern hemisphere (AR, 161–9), he would experience Ostend – literally days before the outbreak of the war – as a dream-like setting: offshore but frighteningly disturbed by the news of the outside world.[20] It was in Ostend where he met his French lover Marcelle for the last time and where he inhaled with the sea air the splendor that would sink back into the past only too soon. But the piece on Merano stands out in terms of the sheer beauty of his description and choice of metaphors. He speaks of the silhouettes of this landscape turning into lines of a melody with its transitions being pure music. Zweig compares this very landscape with a 'huge sun dial' (AR, 166) and notices a 'miraculous simultaneity of contrasts' in this 'Merano world', consisting of a landscape with which one enters a dialogue and indeed a friendship (AR, 168). In his praise for this landscape and its irresistible attractions upon the visitor, Zweig does not over-indulge but keeps it measured and thus convincing.

Given circumstances, we also encounter Zweig as an armchair traveller, for instance when he writes from Vienna about Liège, Leuven, or Antwerp after the outbreak of the war. News of sieges or attacks on places he knew in peacetime triggered reflections on their character. For example, he compares – somewhat surprisingly given the coal mining industry there – Liège with Salzburg, which became Zweig's measure for all townscapes in terms of its layout, its function as a religious centre, and its citadel on a domineering hill. But with reference to modern Liège, he criticises the 'longing of provincial towns for having boulevards like in Brussels and Paris' and calls it 'the pointless will to metropolitan airs and graces' that fails to recognise its own 'measure' (AR, 173). News of the German bombardment of Leuven with the destruction of its most precious university library enraged the world of culture. It caused a rift between Zweig and his, by then, friend Romain Rolland, and even Émile Verhaeren – both fundamental Germanophiles, who were appalled by this act of brutality – because on first hearing about this destruction Zweig responded with disbelief, assuming it was an act of 'enemy propaganda'. But his short and moving article on Leuven, published in the *Neue Freie Presse* on 30 August

1914, attempted to 'allow the memory of Leuven', to rebuild it and to restore its former beauty. By then, Zweig had begun to instrumentalise memory to recuperate and aestheticise loss. Furthermore, he found excuses in history for the siege of Antwerp by German troops in his article published only one month later in the same newspaper, recommending his readers to consult one of Friedrich Schiller's masterpieces in historiography, 'Belagerung von Antwerpen durch den Prinzen von Parma in den Jahren 1584 und 1585' ('The Siege of Antwerp by the Prince of Parma in the Years 1584 and 1585'), and to consider Napoleon's occupation of Antwerp in order to see the German siege of 1914 in perspective.[21] To Zweig, Antwerp was mainly the city of Peter Paul Rubens, thus connecting it with his translation of Verhaeren's study on this great artist. He reminded his readers of the strong presence of German-speaking merchants in Antwerp throughout the ages and of Emperor Charles V's early engagement in turning the city into a commercial powerhouse. Zweig said all this with the intention of condoning Germany's military action to turn Antwerp into a commercial and naval vantage point – in fact, not dissimilar to Napoleon's strategy against England, which had attempted to take hold of Antwerp herself.

As we have seen, travel literally under any circumstances had turned into a leitmotif in Zweig's life, but this was travel prose with a difference. This 'difference' became even more apparent when Zweig had to travel on an official mission to Galicia in summer 1915 to inspect the state of this *Kronland* of the Habsburg monarchy after the expulsion of the Russian army. He visited Grodek and Lemberg (now Lviv), Tarnow, Przemyśl, and Gorlice, saw the endless fields devastated by military action but was keen to emphasise the 'recuperation' of Galicia, by then liberated from the czarist troops. He noticed no Galician patriotism, but Austrian flags everywhere coupled with a sense of relief among the people that the Russians had been defeated for the time being – with the crucial help of the German ally, and Bavarian troops in particular.

Embellishing the appearance of former zones of horror, like the scene of the first major battle in Galicia back in 1914 near Grodek, is one thing ('Like sprouting blood, red poppies are flowering over smashed former military positions and barbed wire' with former trenches 'smoothed over into peaceful field paths' (AR, 193)); trying to find a new language to express the unsaid is quite another. And here are some of them: a grave cross Zweig calls the 'cross flower of the war'; moments of decision turn into 'molecules of coincidence'. But even then, when Zweig was sent to Galicia on an official mission it was with 'impatience' that he waited for his departure and, quite paradoxically, the same impatience extended in his mind the entire journey.

Sometimes it can be irritating or, literally, disarming to read Zweig's albeit few travel-related texts written in this period, which radiate, even in 1917, a sense of surprising relaxation whilst mass movements of thousands of soldiers across Europe occurred. Incidentally, the latter has been identified as one of the main reasons for the rapid spread of the influenza (or 'Spanish flu') of 1918, the worst pandemic since the days of the Black Death, causing anything between sixty and one hundred million deaths.[22] But in an article Zweig, by then already a correspondent of the *Neue Freie Presse* in Zurich, recommended reading a book with the title *The Art of Travelling at Home* for mental relief from the traumas of war; it was about the history of steamboat trips up and down the Danube. It is as if Zweig was already then talking about the yesterday of a world that was in a state of rapid disintegration. Without mentioning the war once, Zweig called for seeing the Danube River what it really is: the mainstream of Central Europe and a 'peaceful mediator' between 'Orient and Occident' (AR, 217). It is a conception which in our time no one has entertained more fascinatingly than Claudio Magris, who declared, by implication, this river to be the artery of the European consciousness.[23]

1920s: A rare moment of relaxation
Heirs of Stefan Zweig

Early Days for Fiction

Separating the lyrical poet from the essayist, the author of fiction from the dramatist, the translator from the writer of travelogues is, in Stefan Zweig's case, as problematic as it can get. In terms of subject matter and style of writing they were closely interlinked but, at the same time, Zweig's ambition of expressing himself in all genres of literary production was evident from early on in his career. As seen, he was in his early twenties when he published his first volumes of poetry and prose and was around 1900 evidently concerned with making his mark, or at least with putting his markers down, in the vibrant world of literary publishing. Whether they admitted to it or not, writers then aspired not only to playing a leading role in cultural life but obtaining the position of a spiritual leader, too. No one at that time fulfilled this role with more self-styled accomplishment than the poet Stefan George. In the German-speaking world George soon turned into a role model for young writers, but for Stefan Zweig not necessarily so. It speaks in his favour that he endeavoured to find his own place, keeping so-called 'circles' at arm's length, and looking for inspiration often, if not mainly, outside of the German-language culture.

Imagination was everything for the young Stefan Zweig. What mattered to him most was the creative impulse. Poetry and prose lent themselves to his urge to express himself as if they were twins, albeit not identical ones. Rather, one emerged from the other at the same time. Instants triggered his desire to cast the moment in a literary form. One could picture Zweig in his teens reciting Schiller's poem 'Die Gunst des Augenblicks' ('The Grace of the Moment'), whereby the German word for 'instant' really means 'blink of an eye'; it indicates a flash or split second. Schiller's poem suggests that 'the mightiest of all

/ rulers is the instant'. Furthermore, the poem establishes a connection between creation and emotion, a sentiment close to Zweig's heart – or better, the conception of creation: 'As quickly as the mind gives birth / to a work it needs to be felt.' But Schiller's poem ends on a muted note: 'Thus each beautiful gift / is as fleeting as the flash's glance, / and quickly night will lock / it up in its darkish grave.'[1] Given their fugitiveness, if not volatility, ideas need to be grasped in an instant and endowed with form. Even though this was contrary to Schiller's own way of working, these lines capture precisely (early) Zweig's method of writing – but as we have seen already, not always to his advantage. Haste is, after all, a notoriously problematic ally for artists of whatever denomination.

First attempts of narrating female psychology

Extrapolating from the temperature of the moment resulted in Zweig's concern with *Stimmungen*, or moods, which he endeavoured to capture predominantly in novellas. The novella became his preferred medium of fiction, whereby he did not necessarily follow to the letter Goethe's famous definition of the mode as the depiction of 'an unheard-of occurrence'. Zweig's conception of the *Stimmungsnovelle* entailed the creation of lyrical moments or sentiments in prose. To a certain extent, they were from the very beginning also designed as psychological case studies of particular intensity. The reader of these novellas is driven along by an almost irresistible suggestiveness and buildup of emotional tension. Even in weaker texts this feature of Zweig's narrative artistry is strongly present.

What interested Zweig the novelist most was the psyche of female, womanly patterns of behaviour in response to the social constraints that women were subjected to. Zweig's female protagonists are no saints, but victims of the role assigned to them by a male-dominated society. Zweig's understanding of 'the female character' in his fiction and biographies is astounding. It was the result of the intensity of his empathy and ability to enter his female protagonists' minds and hearts. In this context, we can define empathy as an activated form of sympathy or compassion; it means a working involvement with the needs of the Other.

In one of his first successful attempts at writing a novella, *Praterfrühling* (*Spring in the Prater*, 1900) the emphasis is on the experience of love as a social equaliser, at least for a short while, as both protagonists, Lizzie and Hans, belong to different social strata of society. Lizzie lives in a luxurious but randomly furnished apartment in Vienna's First District overlooking the elegant Graben whilst Hans's lodgings in the student quarter of the Eighth District are modest to the point of shabby. Beautiful Lizzie is the lover of many an upper-class 'gentleman', whose appearance in the *corso* on Derby Day is spoilt by her tailoress failing to turn up in time to deliver her new dress. Instead, she goes through her wardrobe and comes across a long-forgotten garment, a simple dress that she wore when she fell in love for the first time. In an 'instant', she decides to wear it and join the Derby as an ordinary visitor. It is there that she meets the unassuming Hans. They are instantly attracted to each other and spend the night together in the student's downmarket abode. But it appears that for Lizzie this experience is only an imitation of her first love, generated by her wearing this old dress. Thus, the next day, she again receives her classy lovers, if not 'clients', even though she retains a child-like smile when remembering the encounter with Hans the day before. Two levels of remembrance compete in her, mediated only by her simple dress. Alluding to Gottfried Keller's famous novella *Kleider machen Leute* (*Clothes Make the Man*, 1874) one could call Zweig's early taster of his narrative skills 'clothes generate sentiments'.

This female perspective is effectively complemented by observations of two children at the threshold of adolescence in the novella *Die Gouvernante* (*The Governess*, 1907/11). They lose their innocence simply by watching the suffering of their idolised governess, who is with child following a relationship with a cousin of theirs who fails to own up to his responsibility. Once the governess is found out, challenged, and angrily dismissed by the sisters' mother, she leaves the house head over heels, in utter distress and desolation. The narrator, who delegates much of his storytelling to the two sisters, portrays her as a victim of bourgeois hypocrisy. Letters are then found in her room by the master of the house indicating that she will take her own life. But no one explains what has happened to the two young sisters. They are left in the dark to speculate why their adored governess is so inconsolably upset. They catch only snippets of the accusation their mother throws at her. But through their assumptions and speculations they mature in their judgement quite rapidly:

> An unconscious sense of femininity has made them revere their Fräulein even more since they found out about her baby. They both keep thinking about it, and no longer with mere childish curiosity, but deeply moved and sympathetic.[2]

The consequences of this situation for the governess are fatal and for the two sisters profound:

> They know all about it now. They know that they have been told lies [...] They do not love their parents any more, they don't believe in them. They know that they can never trust anyone, the whole monstrous weight of life will weigh down on their slender shoulders.[3]

They realise that 'their childhood came to an end' by now and are overcome by anguish:

> They are afraid of the life ahead of them, after the first terrifying glimpse that they had of it today. They are afraid of the life ahead of them into which they will now pass, dark and menacing like a gloomy forest through which they must go.[4]

At this point the 'atmospheric' transition occurs, a feature of many a novella by Zweig: 'Their confused fears become dimmer, almost dreamlike, their sobbing is softer and softer'.[5] The rest is – falling asleep.

This story resembles a counterpoint to the vitalism Zweig had associated himself with, mostly in connection with his work on Verhaeren. Given the prominence he allowed the motif of *Angst* to obtain, one cannot but identify a foreshadowing of this existential theme that would take centre stage only a few years later (1912) in what was to become one of his most well-known stories of the same title, *Angst (Fear)*. But *The Governess* also revealed a weakness in Zweig's novelistic compositions: his tendency to drive a particular point or motif. Bluntly put, to overdo it when it came to repeating a sentiment or thought, as evidenced by the passage just quoted.

Yet, as these early traces of Zweig's narrative ingenuity already demonstrate, the stylistic effect of his stories owed everything to the 'suggestive dynamics' of his figurative and colourful imagination.[6] With reference to his concern for the female perspective one could take this point one step further and speak of this writer's imaginative comprehension that enabled him to enter the female psyche to this extraordinary extent.

It is the unexpected turn; the introduction of an uncanny motif; a rupture in style or character that distinguishes a genuinely artistic creation from trashy literature. In some of the best of his lesser-known early works of fiction, Zweig manages to integrate nearly all of these features into his narratives, saturated with a stunning richness of multifaceted life experiences. He does so with particular accomplishment in his story *Die Wunder des Lebens* (*The Miracles of Life*, 1903). It takes us back to the Antwerp of the mid-sixteenth century and introduces an aged artist, who receives a commission from his wealthy merchant friend to complement an altar piece with a second painting of Madonna with the Child. It should match the first Madonna painting created by a famous Venetian artist. In search for a model the aged artist finds Esther, a shy and withdrawn fifteen-year-old Jewish girl, who lives with her foster father, an innkeeper, who does not really understand her (emotional) needs. It takes a great deal of persuasion for her to sit for the artist, a devout Catholic, who even organises for a baby from a migrant mother to be brought to the studio and to be held by Esther. She only gradually overcomes her initial aversion to the nakedness of the baby in her arms but soon grows fond of it. With exquisite subtlety the narrator depicts the tender affection of the artist for his young model, who only very occasionally reciprocates. Eventually, Esther feels more at home in the studio than in her living quarters above the inn, mainly because of the baby whom she can hold and comfort. There is a moment of sudden tension when the aged artist oversteps his mark, suggesting that by becoming his Madonna with the Child, she would leave her Jewishness behind and enter the 'true' Christian faith, a thought Esther reacts to with horror. When the painting is finished the baby is gone, taken back by her real mother who has to leave Antwerp again, which upsets Esther profoundly as she had begun to regard this baby as her own. But the artist tells the distraught Esther that she can see 'her' baby as often as she likes, for his Madonna with the Child painting will now be part of the altar in the main church. So, in order to see 'her baby' the Jewish girl needs to enter a sphere that she had learnt to detest, given that she narrowly escaped a pogrom herself as a child. Often, she is in raptures when she is in front of what is her portrait, not because she sees herself, looking like the Venetian Madonna's sister, but 'her child'; this makes her forget the clerical surroundings. But when on the 'feast day of St Mary' Protestant zealots take to the streets of Antwerp on an anti-Catholic rampage of looting they find in the main cathedral the terrified Esther. First, they recognise her in the painting which stuns them into silence for a while. 'A terrible idea flashed through her head – they were going to murder the picture' and with it 'her own living child'. Then, a woman in the background shouts: 'It's only the Jew girl from the tavern'. The zealots now feel their own awe-inspired silence has humiliated them. Their rage returns but Esther tries to stand her ground, defending 'the picture as if it really were her own warm life'. But then she is fatally struck by a dagger and sinks to the ground: 'The picture of the Madonna and Child, and the picture of the Madonna of the Wounded Heart both fell under a single furious blow from an axe.'[7]

One could argue that Zweig wrote stories of this kind to escape the difficulties in, and with, his own life and, at the same time and paradoxically so, confront them through the way he composed his fiction. And that it came across as neatly 'composed' from the very beginning was confirmed to him much later by his critical friend, Joseph Roth, in one his first surviving letters to him of 24 January 1928.[8] It is a story whose first half is dominated by 'as if' constructions. This suggests issues of plausibility and credibility. But the more the story develops, the clearer it becomes that it succeeds in convincing itself – and prospective readers – of the likelihood of these unusual, if not extraordinary occurrences. In rare moments, Zweig's narrator mentions something self-revealing, or autobiographical by default. When the narrator describes the ageing artist's sentiments he alludes to a particular deficiency of the latter: 'In a life full of busy work – perhaps he had in fact worked *too* hard, failing to keep an enquiring eye on his true self – a change had come over the painter since he set eyes on the young Italian's picture.'[9] It is notable how the age gap between the artist and Esther is bridged by a subtle late, or in the girl's case, early (re-)awakening of a faintly erotic attraction for the other, a motif quite prominent in Zweig's early fiction. The relationship between the two is held in a delicate balance:

> The difference between the sexes meant nothing to the two of them; such thoughts were now extinguished in him and merely cast the evening light of memory into his life, and as for the girl, her dim sense of her own femininity had not fully awoken and was expressed only as vague, restless longing that had no aim as yet.[10]

Specialising in lost causes

Does the autobiographical psychology behind comments like these really suggest that Zweig was hiding behind them, camouflaging his own interest in underage girls, or in faint non-sexual erotic fantasies? This question is far from rhetorical as it simply cannot have a conclusive answer. The problem of the age gap between lovers clearly concerned Zweig to the very end of his life, as one of his last novellas,

Die spät bezahlte Schuld (*The Debt*, 1941) demonstrates.[11] In fact, one would be forgiven for counting *The Debt* amongst Zweig's early novellas, such is the youthfulness of this prose piece in the way it captures the sentiments of a juvenile enthusiast, or 'follower' in our sense of the word, whose adoration of an once-known actor knows hardly any bounds. In fact, the protagonist, Margaret, a mature woman and wife of a surgeon, writes a letter of 'confession' to her old schoolfriend Ellen, who had also been a fervent admirer of this actor, Sturz, whose career on the Innsbruck stage had ended abruptly when his affair with the wife of the theatre director was discovered. The long and short of it is that unbeknown to her friend Ellen, young Margaret had paid Sturz a visit shortly before his departure, putting herself at his disposal. But Sturz acted in a gentlemanly manner and did not take advantage of his 'innocent' fan. This act of chivalry impresses Margaret even more with the benefit of hindsight, and when she goes to a village above Bozen (Bolzano, in the South Tyrol) for a short period of recuperation she encounters Sturz – the name meaning 'abrupt fall' – as an old, dishevelled man. He has lived in poverty following a mild stroke and his real identity is unknown to the locals, who treat him badly. But Margaret recognises in this ruin of a man the former star of the Innsbruck stage because of his still-striking voice and manner of speech. Addressing him with the title he never had, *Herr Hofschauspieler* (court actor), in front of all the locals in the inn where she is staying, she displays to his amazement detailed knowledge of his former parts and reviews he had received. In so doing, she restores his honour, makes the locals treat him with dignity, and repays her 'debt' to him without disclosing to him that she is the girl who had once visited him. She pretends that all she knows about him is due to her husband, who had followed Sturz's career in so much detail.

So, the final happiness for the aged actor is based on half-truth, but for Margaret the main thing is to make Sturz forget his old-age misery to the point that he even entertains the faint hope that he might recover and find himself on stage again. Nurturing illusions can in some cases obtain the quality of a medicine. Margaret's sentimental journey represents the small world of her very own 'yesterday', ridden with memories of overwrought emotions. And yet, it shows that Zweig in 1941 reconnected with his own past, even to the point of imitating the style of his early prose.

But what does 'early prose' in Zweig's case really mean? It comes across as psychologically exploratory but never stylistically experimental; it is emotionally charged, expressive but not expressionistic; it radiates youthfulness but combines it with surprising maturity in terms of compositional finesse and insight into human nature. Equally stunning is the extent of his experience of life given his rather sheltered upbringing. Not all of it could have originated in mere imagination. 'Real' experiences must have supported his fiction at this stage already. Whether we are biographically minded in our interpretations of text or not, what W. H. Auden had to say about 'The Composer' (December 1938) in all genres of the arts rings true, even for young Zweig: 'Rummaging into his living, the poet fetches / The images out that hurt and connect, / From Life to Art by painstaking adaption, / Relying on us to cover the rift.'[12] Zweig's insights into the psychology of both sexes, and indeed that of children, speak in favour of this author having done just what Auden was to state. In *Der Stern über dem Walde* (*The Star Above the Forest*, 1904) it is the psyche of a gallant waiter in a hotel somewhere on the Riviera. Attending to a breathtakingly beautiful Polish countess, he is so taken with her that he fetishises things which were on her table, such as glasses from which she drank, which he surreptitiously takes up to his room. The countess, however, takes no notice of him. Head over heels in illusionary, if not masochistic, love with her, the waiter cannot bear her leaving. Thus, on the day of her departure he decides 'with strange certainty' to throw himself under the very train which she had boarded, to 'bleed to death beneath her feet.'[13] But it is clear to him, too, 'that he was dying for her sake, and she would never know.'[14] What follows is painfully realistic and poetical at once:

> He flung himself down on the rails with a brusque movement. At first he felt the pleasantly cool sensation of the strips of iron against his temples for a moment. His injuries were already such

that he could not move. Very quietly, the rhythmic chugging of the approaching engine came through the breathless air from afar. [...] The train rattled closer and closer. Then he opened his eyes once more. Above him was a silent, blue-black sky, with the tops of a few trees swaying in front of it. And above the forest stood a shining, white star. [...] Then he closed his eyes. The rails were trembling and swaying, closer and closer came the rattling of the express train, making the forest echo as if great bells were hammering out a rhythm [...] One more deafening, rushing, whirring sound, a whirlwind of noise, then a shrill scream, the terrifyingly animal scream of the steam whistle, and the screech and groan of brakes applied in vain ...[15]

At this moment of the novella its narrative perspective changes – from the victim of hopeless love to the unattainable countess in her compartment. But the shock of this moment affects her with sudden vigour. She cannot help but notice the frantic commotion outside of the halted train: 'words are flying back and forth, different voices: a suicide ... under the wheels ... dead ... yes, out here in the open ....' Then she sees a single star shining above the forest. 'Looking at it, she abruptly feels such grief as she has never known before. A fiery grief, full of a longing that has not been part of her own life ....'[16] It is as if her emotions are literally beside herself but with no consequence thereafter as the train slowly rattles on. Passages like this one illustrate the extent and quality of Zweig's narrative prowess. One needs to bear them in mind when explaining just why he became so successful a writer. The foundations he had laid with his first two collections of novellas appropriately recurred to 'initial experiences' – of love, emotional failure, and mortal danger – as the title of his second collection (*Erste Erlebnisse*, or *Initial Experiences*, 1911) signalled. The other danger, which Zweig did not always manage to avoid, was overindulgence in narrative effects. But these first attempts at finding his own narrative voice also demonstrated that he could successfully work through such occasional shortcomings.

By 1911 literary success was in the air for Zweig, but it was not yet clear how lasting it would be. The main leitmotifs of his fiction, however, were clearly visible; suicide was one of them, strikingly prominent, if not omnipresent. Likewise, the experience of suddenness occurred in almost every text. Another prevailing motif was the fate of Jews, poignantly epitomised by the novella *Im Schnee* (*In the Snow*, 1901), in which a small Jewish community in 'a small medieval German town close to the Polish border' live in fear of flagellants who are out to harm them. On hearing of their imminent arrival, the Jews leave their quarter and town as fugitives under freezing conditions. They manage to escape the henchmen but not the bitter cold, in which they perish. No matter whether Jews are portrayed in Zweig's early stories as individuals like Esther in *The Miracles of Life*, or as groups as in this story, their fate seems inescapable. The same is true for an utterly disillusioned schoolboy in the story *Ein Verbummelter* (*Idling Away*, 1901), who rebels against the teacher that makes him repeat the year twice. Following his rebellion against what he regards as utter humiliation with words 'that struck like lightning', he leaves the school and rushes through the town towards a bridge, from which he jumps to find his end.[17]

Living in 'burning secrets'

When it came to selecting his early prose Zweig, at the time barely twenty-three years of age, was discerning. His first collection of prose consisted only of four novellas: the title story *The Love of Erika Ewald*; *The Star Above the Forest*; *Die Wanderung* (*The Wandering*, 1902); and *The Miracles of Life*. With Erika Ewald, a piano teacher who falls in love with a virtuoso violinist, Zweig created a female figure for whom 'love' is deeply ambiguous. First, her feelings for the violinist are purely spiritual and she rejects his physical advances; when they later develop into physical desire, she is snubbed by him. In a moving moment, Erika stands in front of a mirror, stark naked, remarking to herself what a pity it is that this attractive body should fail to be loved. It is at this moment when Erika renounces love altogether.

With his novella, or 'legend', *The Wandering*, Zweig takes his readers two thousand years back, into biblical times, to a young man who has heard rumours of the Messiah having arrived in Jerusalem. He makes his way to the city in search of the redeemer. When he arrives, he is told that Pontius Pilate has condemned three criminals to die on the cross. So, the young man walks towards Calvary but cannot get close enough to the three crosses to see the convicted properly; instead he turns around and keeps searching for the Messiah.

In all of Zweig's early prose, lost causes dominate, and a sense of futility prevails. Likewise, the problem of identity is an overriding theme in all these early novellas, quite dramatically so in *Das Kreuz* (*The Cross*, 1906). It tells the story of a colonel in the Napoleonic army in Catalonia in 1810 who becomes the only survivor of an ambush by Catalonian partisans. Stripped naked, he manages to hide in the woods; later he finds a dead Spaniard whose clothes he puts on, making his way somehow to the next village in hope of finding shelter and food there. But his French accent betrays him and he meets nothing but closed doors. Eventually, he hears an approaching French squadron which he greets enthusiastically, forgetting about his Spanish clothes. The French mistake him for a Spanish rebel and kill him. Zweig, as narrator, sees history as paved with fateful moments, which may or may not reflect his outlook on time altogether. The reader is supposed to gain the impression that time is studded with such moments of sudden occurrences or indeed momentous decisions. At any rate, Zweig was to refer to time – in unmistakably Nietzschean terms – as the 'greatest transformer of all values', words with which he introduced his speech on the Austrian feminist and pacifist Bertha von Suttner in 1917.[18]

By 1910 Zweig's accomplishments as a writer of novelistic prose were such that he could take on genuinely historical subject matter and turn it into fiction. This happened with the novella *Geschichte eines Untergangs* (the English title *Twilight* rather misses the point – *Story of a Decline* would certainly come closer).[19] It is the story of the mistress of Louis XV's short-lived prime minister, the Duke of Bourbon, Jeanne Agnès Berthelot de Plemont, Marquise de Prie (1698–1727).

One could argue that with this story about *the* power woman of the *ancient régime* just before Madame de Pompadour, Zweig rehearsed his approach to biographical narration, of which he was to become a master. It is not so much that his novellas were autobiographical; rather, he was trying out possibilities of blending document and fiction, historical knowledge and imagination. Zweig considered the fictionalisation of facts for the sake of emulating himself into the psyche of his – preferably female – historical protagonists.

Following her fall from grace and unparalleled influence, Madame de Prie is banned from court by the king and exiled to her country estate in Normandy, Courbépine. Already, 'on the third day' after her arrival in exile, 'she lost control of her impatience and it turned violent. The solitude oppressed her; she needed people, or at least news of people, of the court, the natural home of her whole being with all its ramifications, of her friends, something to excite or merely touch her.'[20] Getting more and more restless in her *palais*-like country house, she lies to herself about her situation. She tells herself that this exile is only for a short while and that her friends at court, including Voltaire, who had once dedicated a play to her, would crave for her to return and influence the king accordingly. But she lives from one disappointment to another whilst continuing to 'betray time'. Her relationship with her secretary turns into her utter humiliation but regardless she concentrates all her energies on organising a final banquet and ball in celebration of her end. From her point of view, this festivity should be appreciated like a 'work of art'. She premeditates her death and counts on the assumption that turning Courbépine for once into a mini-Versailles in the province would cause such a sensation that through there and then dying in such style she would become immortal. The festivity takes place, but it is only followed by dread and emptiness. When she finally takes her own life, and this news reaches Paris and Versailles, all her 'friends' who had attended the spectacular feast at Courbépine have forgotten her. Were it not for the poetically exquisite ending one could regard this story as an example of hedonism turning into nihilism. But Zweig, or rather, his narrator, true to form, concludes as follows:

And nothing was left of the strange end of Madame de Prie, her real life and the ingeniously devised deception of her death but a few dry lines in some book of memoirs or other, conveying to their reader as little of the passionate emotions of her life as a pressed flower allows one to guess at the fragrant marvel of its long-forgotten spring.[21]

There really was not more to say other than to wait for Zweig to take up the monumental challenge of writing about Marie Antoinette. With this novella, the the stage was set for what was to happen some fifty years after Madame de Prie.

But emotionalised historiography was not Zweig's only novelistic call before 1914; another was what might be termed psychography. It was in this 'genre' where he delivered his first masterpiece as a writer of fiction, *Das brennende Geheimnis* (*The Burning Secret*, 1911). It appeared as the third of 'Four Stories from the Land of Childhood' published in book form in November 1911 under the umbrella title *Erstes Erlebnis* (*First Experience*). And another 'first': *First Experience* was the first book that appeared with Insel Verlag, through which close partnerships were established with Anton Kippenberg, who was Rilke's publisher, too, and with Samuel Fischer as well as Kurt Wolff, both iconic names for presenting modern literature in Germany. Such was the resonance of this particular story that it appeared in a single edition in 1914, reaching 170,000 copies by 1932. A year later, a film version was released with a star cast but, as Zweig remembers in *The World of Yesterday*, following the burning of the Reichstag the film was banned because people connected the title, 'Burning Secret', with the sinister circumstances of this spectacular occurrence, with which the Nazis gave themselves a pretext for sweeping measures against their opponents.[22]

It is a measure for the continuing resonance of this story that the publicist Ulrich Weinzierl gave his biographical sketches of our subject the title *Stefan Zweigs brennendes Geheimnis* (*Stefan Zweig's Burning Secret*), thus using the title to allude to Zweig's own 'secret': his homosexual and exhibitionist inclinations. And there is, of course, Andrew Birkin's star-studded film version of 1988, with Klaus Maria Brandauer as the baron, Faye Dunaway as Mathilde, and David Eberts as Edgar. As indicated before, the biographical suggestion is that Zweig would have chosen this title for reasons that had to do with his very own 'burning secret', mainly his intimate life, erotic and sexual preferences, and 'virtuosity' that made him shudder to quote the February 1913 entry into his diary again (Tb, 41).

This novella offers a study in the development of a child's psyche at the threshold of puberty coupled with the fateful attraction between two adults. The art of entering a relationship is examined from the viewpoint of an unattached, erotically adventurous aristocrat, who always needs 'sensuous attraction' to 'stimulate his energy to its full force';[23] of an elegant lady, mother of one child, who begins 'to regret having stayed faithful to a husband she never really loved';[24] and of a boy of about twelve, Edgar, 'with a face of mingled pallor and uncertainty' and besides 'shy, awkward, nervous [...] with fidgety movements and dark, darting eyes', convalescing after some prolonged illness.[25] His father stays back in Vienna to look after his business. To a certain extent, the baron and Edgar have features and characteristics of Zweig himself – the child in him and the lusting 'huntsman scenting prey'. Edgar's 'dark, darting eyes' could, perhaps in a more mature age, resemble these '*Blickinjectionen*' (injection-like looks) Zweig was, in the eyes of others, capable of.[26]

The setting of the novella is a grand hotel in the mountainous area of Semmering near Vienna, and was well known by Zweig as a frequent visitor of this area. In the story, the baron soon realises that through this boy he can get closer to his 'prey': the type of a lady 'he liked very much, one of those rather voluptuous Jewish women just before the age of over-maturity, and obviously passionate, but with enough experience to conceal her temperament behind a façade of elegant melancholy.[27] The boy and the baron quickly befriend each other but by degrees, as the relationship between the baron and Edgar's mother unfolds, the boy realises that he is being used by the baron for him to get closer to his mother until both are merely annoyed by the presence of Edgar. He disturbs their intimacy. A final escalation is inevitable when Edgar mistakes certain noises between the two lovers on the dark corridor of the hotel for his mother's cries for help and attacks the baron. When his mother later wants to force her son to write a letter of apology to the baron after his sudden departure, Edgar lashes out and hits her. Once he realises what he has done he escapes on his own, taking the train to Baden near Vienna, where his grandmother lives. The train journey signifies a final transition from his privileged childhood innocence to an observer of workers with whom he shares, for the first time in his life, a third-class compartment. Before he enters his grandmother's house, where the reunion with his, by then, worried family takes place, Edgar walks aimlessly through the dark park and woods of Baden with noises that are as strange to him as the noise in the dark hotel corridor. It is lovers' ground, clearly intimately known by the narrator and, more than likely, by Zweig himself, who frequented this part of the spa town as often as the wooded areas near Schönbrunn and elsewhere. It is the zone where certain 'passers-by' can have 'dangerous effects on children', as Zweig recorded in his diary (Tb, 35).

But the actual 'burning secret' of the story is the one between Edgar and his mother. For when his father suddenly turns up for the final reunion and prompts him for the reasons for his running away from the hotel his mother gives Edgar a sign to suggest that he should not reveal the real reason to his father. Edgar understands and solely blames himself. Through this 'burning secret' a new 'alliance' between mother and son is established, confirming, though, that her marriage is based on a lie.

The concision and the focus on the particular as implied in the form of the novella made it easier for Zweig to avoid confronting the all too prosaic in his prose. He could, at least initially, still connect the lyrical with his narratives, thus demonstrating how art can interfere with life in a meaningful way even though his own life was catching up with him. Whilst his Edgar could at the end of the 'burning secret' still afford to begin 'to dream the deeper dream of his own life', Zweig himself was soon about to face harsher realities. But for the time being, matters of the heart took over.

Signing a copy of *Marie Antoinette*
ullstein bild – RDB

Keeping Up with 'Life'

'My life dances between memories and expectations like a spectre being a dread to myself', Zweig noted in his diary on 17 October 1912, barely one month after his first private meeting with Friderike von Winternitz in her house in Döbling, one of Vienna's elegant districts. In between, he recorded 'some lighter affairs, nothing clever'. But he credited a recently employed 'new servant' for making his life more regular. 'Dread', however, would become a main feature of his emotional set-up, coming, at times, close to feelings of disgust at himself. This is in stark contrast to the façade of elegance he liked to sport otherwise, as reflected by the large number of photographic portraits of his from this time.

In and around 1912 he frequented once again his favourite coffeehouses, such as the Griensteidl and the Herrenhof; spoke of 'episodic encounters', probably with males and females; wished he were in the South Tyrol, preferably in Merano; attended rehearsals of his new play *Haus am Meer* (*The House at the Sea*) in the Burgtheater; received (male) visitors, mostly fellow writers like Franz Theodor Csokor, Jacob Wassermann, and Paul Zifferer, having 'eclipsed eroticisms' for a (short) while; and continued to translate Verhaeren (Tb, 16–23). In fact, it was a copy of his translation of Verhaeren's *Hymns to Life* (1912) that was given to Friderike by a friend of hers prior to her meeting Zweig, whom she first spotted in a restaurant in Vienna.[1] It was her who took the initiative. Friderike had published a volume of stories under her maiden name Fritzi Burger on the 'psychology of maidens'. The title of the collection was taken from Nietzsche's *Also sprach Zarathustra* (*Thus Spoke Zarathustra*): 'Love is the danger for the loneliest.'[2] In the original, the context of his quotation is Zarathustra's self-mockery but, as so often, combined with a fundamental, if not existential statement: love can delude people once they *realise* just how lonely they are. The protagonist in Friderike's novella suffers from being misunderstood by her family and friends, but once her senses and intellect have awoken she believes in the strength of her love and art – stating, however, that art must not be compromised by feelings.

By the time Friderike invited Zweig into her home, the youngest of her two daughters was two years old. In his diary entry about this first encounter Zweig waxes lyrical, calling Friderike 'a truly sensitive woman' and adding that 'she is probably the most tender being that one could imagine but with an energy of emotional honesty that makes her great. The way she said how tragic it is that one can only have children by a male was bold and noble.' Zweig emphasises that he resisted the temptation 'to make use of her softness erotically'. Then he speaks of the 'marvellous tenderness' in her almost 'musical movements' when she held her sickly youngest child in her arms. He concludes his diary entry as follows: 'She seems to be in a state between the girl-like longing for beauty and motherly calmness, whereby her husband is like a clapper that does not reach either side of the bell' (Tb, 15–16).

Ideally, one would now like to know how this encounter, which obviously had left a deep impression on Zweig, continued to 'work' *in* him. His final word in the diary that day reads: 'Dull brooding in the evening. Café, this unnecessary finale I want to wean myself off.' In German his phrase is '*dumpf im Übersinnen*', a strange expression as it implies both reflection and a surplus of sensuality; it is a feeling that was to stay with him for quite some time. We need to bear in mind that he once again took to keeping a diary in September 1912 after his Paris and London diaries were stolen, a fact to which he referred as the 'most horrible thing' that could have happened to him, given that these two years had been the 'most intensive' of his life to date. One can also assume, as some biographers have done, that they contained references to his sexual practices.[3] Regardless, Zweig himself gives us a clear reason why he, in principle an unreliable diarist, took to writing a diary again, which tells us something about his central concern from early on, namely, to support his memory. A diary would enable him to read about past occurrences and the 'faces' of the people he met. He realised that, otherwise, he could not 'own' this past nor relive it. After all, he believed so much in his life to be 'floating' and he clearly wanted to enable himself to hold on to some record of inward and outward experiences (Tb, 9).

To a certain extent, his motivation to write a diary, albeit a fragmentary one, as it turned out to be, was one element in his attempt to come to a less fraught relationship with time; for the one thing that plagued him from early on was, as mentioned before, the anxiety of ageing. On the one hand he was keen to see developments gaining in momentum; 'acceleration' was not only the title of one of Johann Strauss's waltzes (1860) but, to a certain extent, the motto for the way in which Zweig operated, too. On the other hand, the rapid passing of time concerned him and his preoccupation with 'youth' was just the other side of the coin called 'fear of getting old'.

A measure for the successes of his personal exchanges with friends and the quality of their conversations was whether he could discuss matters of sex with them – which he always recorded in his diary entries. One month after his first encounter with Friderike von Winternitz, Zweig noted: 'Oscar A.H. Schmitz with me, good conversation as always *since* it is sexual' (Tb, 9, my emphasis). Schmitz, a gifted author and self-styled dandy who saw himself initially in the footsteps of Stefan George and Hugo von Hofmannsthal, gained some notoriety with his prose *Hashish* (1902). Zweig had reviewed it, calling it one of the 'smartest and stylistically most outstanding collection of novellas in the last years'.[4]

It is revealing just how concerned Zweig was at the beginning of his relationship with his future wife to keep it removed from erotic, let alone sexual, connotations. As it happened, she courted him and not the other way round, and her intentions may well have been different ones. Initially at least, Zweig liked to see in this married mother of two daughters a friend, confidante, and fellow writer. A friendship of this quality would provide him with some stability and an alternative to casual sex. One is reminded of Klaus Mann's remark: 'Love is risk, danger; Friendship is security. The sexual fixation, the addiction to be with a particular human body, a particular mouth, a particular embrace causes pain of such cruelty that we cannot bear it without the comfort of friendship.'[5] Zweig, in the years up to the First World War, continued to seek friendship as a counterbalance to his sexual cravings.

In his way, Zweig did in fact live his life to the full, in intellectual and physical terms that is. Therefore, it was only consequential that Friderike received his translations of Verhaeren's cycle *Hymns to Life*, which contained a poem that celebrated the 'present day', exclaiming 'The moment is ours'.[6]

The rhythm of being

In his letters between 1911 and 1914 one concept gained a distinct prominence: 'rhythm'. In October 1911 he mentions his plan to collect some of his articles, as diverse as on the Panama Canal, the World Exhibition, New York, the cable car to the Jungfrau Mountain, and pieces on modern factories, in a volume to be called *About the Rhythm of Our Time* – as strange a mixture as the bewilderingly varied phenomena of that period itself. The musical meaning of rhythm gained currency in Zweig's world in this pre-war period. There was his connection with Hermann Bahr and his wife, the acclaimed Wagner singer Anna Bahr-Mildenburg, who according to Ethel Smyth, the English composer and former student of Johannes Brahms who at the time felt more at home in the German-speaking lands than back in England, was 'the most superb of Isoldes' ever.[7] Following a visit in London, Bahr brought with him a novella by Maurice Baring, *Fête Galante*; he had been in contact with Smyth, who showed an interest in turning this story into a one-act opera, but needed a librettist to accomplish this. Bahr 'naturally' thought of Zweig as the 'only one who could do this sort of thing' (I, 519). Zweig considered but refused, suggesting his friend Felix Braun instead with the astute argument that this text would lend itself more to a 'musical pantomime'. Smyth eventually composed this work as a 'dance-dream' in 1921/2 based on her own libretto.

It is worth mentioning this episode because it illustrates the kind of connections that conditioned Zweig's life then and in the decades to come. Time and again, he was the stretch and pivot point between people and their concerns, and between literature and music.

The other 'rhythm' with lasting effect was Zweig's friendship with Romain Rolland, which began with their February 1911 encounter in Paris just prior to Zweig's embarking for the Americas. Three features defined their friendship from the outset: their fundamental humanism, belief in a Europe beyond nations, and the significance of music. In fact, it was the ten-volume novel by Rolland, *Jean-Christophe*, a legendary achievement in the field of novelistic approaches to music, that brought both authors together – to be precise, Zweig's involvement in getting this epic novel translated into German. By 1912, the then Frankfurt publisher Rütten & Loening had agreed to accept the publication of *Jean-Christophe* in a translation by Otto Grauthoff, incidentally a close friend of Thomas Mann.

When the final volume of Rolland's epic appeared in autumn 1912, Zweig celebrated this event – and an event it was – with the publication of an (open-)letter-and-review hybrid in the *Berliner Tageblatt*. Zweig clearly felt that Rolland's achievement warranted a special form of reflection about the sheer scale of this novelistic undertaking and, most importantly, its meaning. In his essayistic open letter Zweig argues that the completion of *Jean-Christophe* was not only a literary but an 'ethical achievement'; for in those 'restless' and troubled times when everyone wanted to achieve quick successes, 'impatiently looking up from work to its effect' or impact, Rolland (or so his fervent admirer argues) remained unperturbed by such considerations, beavering away 'almost during his entire youth' with this gigantic novelistic project. Moreover, Zweig argues, 'you have made it your task in the midst of a chauvinist France to turn an imaginary German musician, a Beethoven redivivus, into a genuine hero of genius and attitude without turning him into a comical figure as this happens so often with a German in French novels even those by Balzac.'[8] Zweig suggests in the open letter to his German readership that this French author had promoted music to the status of a novelistic protagonist that managed to 'bind all contrasts together', including the Franco-German antagonisms. In this sense, *Jean-Christophe* is imbued by, and represents, the ethos of pacifism and transnational sentiments, as well as humanist aesthetics, in the name of music. Apart from anything else, Zweig was quick to recognise what Rolland had hoped to achieve with this novel: nothing less than a literary manifestation of the European spirit. Zweig's letter did a great deal to introduce Rolland to German readers at a time when Germany's intervention in Morocco to counteract French colonial expansion in Northern Africa (1911) caused massive friction between the two countries, and the war on the Balkans (1912–13) foreshadowed what was to come in August 1914.

Interestingly, Friderike von Winternitz was integrated into Zweig's friendship with Rolland from the very beginning. In April 1912 she would sign a postcard Zweig sent to Rolland from Florence and a year later Zweig enclosed a sonnet by Friderike in a letter to the revered French writer ('You have comforted us with your work. / You who sings from the heart of things / Penetrating the darkness of the soul, / You never looked at us as if we were a game or beast' (RR/SZ, I, 39, 60)). Later, Rolland would often take sides with Friderike when tensions between her and Zweig became an issue.

In summer 1912 he spent a few weeks in Paris in the occasional company of Rilke, Verhaeren, Rolland, and the latter's friend from student days at the École Normale Supérieure, and fellow writer, André Suarès. He stayed in the Rue Beaujolais in a hotel of the same name but when he returned to Paris in early March 1913 and was looking for accommodation, he seemed to have forgotten this place as his diary entry shows. Be it as it may, for the first night on 3 March 1913 he stayed in the Hôtel Voltaire, which turned out to be too noisy (like most of Paris by then) as Zweig complained about the 'terrible traffic and petrol fumes'. But then he found 'a small hôtel Beaujolais' (Tb, 42), which overlooked the gardens of the Palais Royal. As we have heard earlier, Zweig's diaries written during his previous stay in Paris were stolen and it really appears that this shock obliterated much of his memory of his stay in summer 1912, including of the very same hotel where he found himself again in spring 1913. But it was then that he experienced a truly fulfilling time in the French metropolis, again with the same friends but not to forget Marcelle, of whom Friderike, back in Vienna, knew. But she accepted this parallelism of affection, realising that there was a price to pay for a relationship with 'her' emotionally volatile Stefan Zweig.

Before Zweig made his way to Paris yet again, he had joined a high-profile literary society event, the celebrations for Gerhart Hauptmann's fiftieth anniversary. They took place in Berlin and, two days later, in Vienna, where Hauptmann gave a reading from his unpublished drama *The Bow of Ulysses* at the Musikvereinssaal in front of the city's *crème de la crème*. At a banquet thereafter, he was feted by Felix Salten as the main *souverain* of German letters, even if the speech by the Austrian education minister, Max Hussarek von Henlein, was – according to Arthur Schnitzler – unspeakable in terms of dullness and stupidity. Hofmannsthal had prepared a eulogy too, but was hurt by the fact that Salten was given preference over him. Zweig was also present and introduced to Hauptmann for a second time. He clearly was so impressed with Zweig that he spontaneously invited him to his estate in Silesia, Agnetendorf (Jagniątków). Like Schnitzler, Zweig was attracted by Hauptmann's mere appearance – the older he got the more he turned into a Goethe lookalike. Zweig spoke of Hauptmann's attractiveness, commenting on the receding hair that 'set free his imposing forehead and facial features.' His comments on Hauptmann's 'performance' give an indication just of how much attention Zweig paid to gestures. He read with great 'inwardness', whilst 'his hand was swinging incessantly as if pulling up every sentence by doing so, clenching and lifting it as if he wanted to support his otherwise rather weak voice' (Tb, 30).[9] With the content of Hauptmann's reading though, Zweig was clearly less impressed than with him as a person and performer.

But a great deal more happened that late autumn and winter of 1912–13, before Paris provided him with variations *à la française* of his by now established themes of life: work on an essay on Rolland, translation of Verhaeren's monograph on Rubens, constant interference from Eros that also led to misunderstandings, for instance between him and a rather persistent lady from Baden near Vienna who had expected more from him, as the way in which he had looked at her seemed to have been over-promising. There was a short trip to Dresden for a symphonic concert conducted by the great Ernst von Schuch, and to spend time with his then close friend, the poet and essayist Camill Hoffmann. He also went to the much-disliked city of Munich for a joint reading with the sharp critic of the Wilhelminian bourgeoisie, Frank Wedekind, not to forget the 'hot celebration' of Friderike's birthday there on 4 December, 'whereby the cards of the perversion were put more openly than ever on the table' (Tb, 32). It is left to the imagination of the reader what kind of 'perversion' Zweig was referring to here. The short Munich episode is again noteworthy for Zweig's account of Wedekind's appearance and style of recitation:

> His face is very calm, narrow lips, which he permanently moistens whilst speaking, the word spoken harshly but quietly, a certain sedateness in his demeanor that indicates inner irritability. The eyes grey, the hair grey, a bit spookily English, half preacher half fool, very curious, E.T.A. Hoffmann-like. (Tb, 33)

Zweig then took up any opportunity for pen-portraying. It was as if he exercised this ability, which came in handy when he embarked on larger-scale essays on writers, let alone his later biographies. Furthermore, these impressionistic sketches of people evidence Zweig's keen interest in the personality of others – be they his compatriots or historical figures. He did not 'read' a person's features along the lines of physiognomy, but he attributed to them a graphic psychology – hence our initial characterisation of Zweig as a psychograph.

With Paris already in mind, Zweig found himself on a short whirlwind tour to Prague, again Dresden, and Leipzig, then back to Vienna, where he attended a performance of Wedekind's 'scandalous' play *Pandora's Box* and Kleist's *The Prince of Homburg*. Before doing so, he promenaded in the Schönbornpark recording a particular 'adventure':

The worst of it, I did not feel anything. Where another than myself would have collapsed given the extent of the pressure, and where my whole life, my entire existence was at stake and already lost, I was overcome by a certain helplessness and by calm thereafter.

Whilst thereafter, watching the performance of Kleist's drama, he was able to 'forget *everything*' (Tb, 41). It seems fair to assume that this opaque note points to yet another act of exhibitionism, even though it happened on an evening in February with not the most benign temperatures for revealing oneself.

Paris at that point meant whirlwind activities on Zweig's part. This time, the diary entries provide a comprehensive picture of his activities, meetings with next to everyone among the literati there: eminent translators like Henri Guilbeaux and Léon Bazalgette, writers like Jean-Richard Bloch, Paul Fort, André Suarès, and Charles Vildrac, and the exiled Russian poet Konstantin D. Balmont. As it happened, Rilke and Verhaeren were in town, too. Together with Romain Rolland, Zweig invited them to a *déjeuner*. They talked about Tolstoy (Rolland), animals (Rilke, who had just returned from Ronda in Spain; specifically, cats), and on the origins of French painting (Verhaeren). They all signed a postcard to their publisher back in Leipzig, Anton Kippenberg. In the next couple of weeks his encounters with Rilke were to be more cordial than they ever would be in the years to come. With Verhaeren he visited Marie Antoinette's small theatre in the Trianon, her pavilion and the Fermières, impressions which would feature in his large-scale biography of France's unfortunate queen of Habsburg origin.

But before seeing all these friends and acquaintances, and only three days after his arrival in Paris, Zweig went by himself to the Musée Carnavalet, once the palatial home of the great *femme de lettres* Madame de Sévigné, where he viewed the collection of famous death masks. It was as if he wanted to be in dialogue with these dead faces. That of the young Duke of Reichstadt, Napoleon's only child with his second wife, Marie Louise of Austria, impressed him most given his distinctly Habsburgian features, in particular 'the heavy lower lip'. Flaubert's face looked uncomfortably 'bourgeois' to him, and Victor Hugo's face had almost been 'dissolved' by death (Tb, 44).

In real life, there was a young Italian composer, Gian Francesco Malipiero, who attracted him for a moment, only to find himself in the evening of the same day (9 March 1913) in the company of a certain Marcelle and Suzanne. In his previous diary entry, he refers to meeting a 'very nice girl' in the Métro but with whom 'nothing serious happened thereafter'; he adds: 'I am not lusting in that sense but am simply curious perhaps because I am too often only by myself.' He speaks of 'indifferent adventures', which he never continued. After exchanging addresses, he would not, however, follow things up by letter (Tb, 44).

The labour of love

But with this 'nice girl', matters were different; it is likely that it was Marcelle, for only two nights later they were intimate with each other. Zweig records 'full triumphs of true ecstasy' (Tb, 47). In between engagements of all sorts, Zweig was working on his novella *Fear*, which did not reflect in any way his present circumstances; not that it should have done. In fact, one could argue that it represented a complete contrast to the bliss he had experienced in Paris during these weeks and months.

Zweig's diary entries of his time in Paris are bursting with 'life'. We find him in dance clubs, bars, in the Café des Lilas with countless young talents; in bed with Marcelle working on a poem ('The Sleepless Ones'); in Notre-Dame with Marcelle admiring the Rosetta; in the Père Lachaise cemetery, again with Marcelle; revising his translation of Verhaeren's monograph on Rubens, which his publisher, Kippenberg, heavily criticised; and enjoying yet another wild night with Marcelle, whose rapturous ecstasy indicated to him that she 'was conceiving', as indeed she was (Tb, 59). In the midst of all this, he visited Rilke in his top-floor studio apartment in 17, Rue Campagne-Première, an island of contemplation that Zweig describes in detail. Rilke told him that 'Paris offered to him the highest degree of solitude'; he confirmed that

El Greco and Cézanne were essential influences on his work, conceding, though, that he found it almost impossible to write since having completed his novel *Malte Laurids Brigge*, which had come out in 1910 (Tb, 53).

At the end of this Rilke afternoon on 18 March Zweig moved on to Verhaeren, where he met the equally famous Belgian painter Théo van Rysselberghe. The calm in this tempest of life was not only the atmosphere in Rilke's apartment but also moments when he thought of Friderike, who stayed in Merano at the time wondering, or not, what was going on in Paris. Zweig's letters to her of that time are lost but not a poem he sent to her, which contains the following lines: 'Quiet thoughts approach / me in my lonesome dark hours / thoughts of you, you in the distance' (SZ/FZ, 30). But one could also interpret the phrase 'you, you in the distance' as 'you, the distant one'. Unless he wrote to her about it, she would not have expected him to be on board the airship *Dupuy de Lôme*, from where he sent a postcard to Rolland. In short, there was very little that Zweig left out in terms of experience. He even recommended that Rilke visit the Robinson Park near Meudon by train from the Gare de Luxembourg, a journey 'not much longer than one by the Métro', strange as it may be to imagine Rilke ever using the Métro. The 'caravans of the *grisettes*' would be quite a sight on a Sunday, as Zweig smugly added. (In fact, Rilke confirmed to him that he knew the park, with or without the *grisettes*, which he must have visited when he stayed with Rodin in Meudon.)

Zweig compares Marcelle and Friderike directly in his diary of 29 March, 1913 – that is, after the moment he was convinced that Marcelle had conceived following her orgasmic convulsions: 'How similar these figures are, she [Marcelle] and F. [Friderike], what beautiful serious shapes surround my fate that tends to evade when facing such greatness knowing about its flexibility (hat in hand) instead of embracing it forcefully.' In the next sentence, without any transition, he reports to himself that in the same night he was considering a new novella 'in the series of ill deeds done to women' (Tb, 60). Given his own private situation it clearly did not occur to him that he himself was about to commit an 'ill deed' of this very kind.

Marcelle's pregnancy, according to Zweig's diary records, gave their 'provisional' relationship an unexpected gravitas and meaning. Zweig's imminent departure from Paris on 23 April resulted in a 'stormy and beautiful' final night. He noted his lover's 'physical suffering' but, to his relief, she managed to 'smile it off'. He took with him a renewed 'will to work', which included the completion of his short but significant novella *Mondscheingasse*, or *Moonbeam Alley*. The mere prospect of the people back in Vienna positively disgusted him, or so he claimed in his diary, a strong sentiment which he hoped would drive him into the kind of solitude that his work required. Contrary to Marcelle, he left Paris '*froh und leicht*' – relieved and light in mood – thanking this city for what it had provided him with (Tb, 68). To call this attitude selfish would not be off the mark. In the early days of April, Zweig received a letter from Friderike, which she had written from Merano, where she enjoyed the early spring. One can only speculate how she must have felt about her by now beloved Stefan allegedly having a great time in Paris without her. She concludes her letter ominously enough with an emphasis on tolerance: 'Tell me as little as you like' (SZ/FZ, 32).

At any rate, Zweig had by now become a dedicated collector – of autographs and 'encounters'. His main 'trophy' in terms of autographs was the manuscript of Rilke's *Cornet*, which the revered poet sent him at the end of his stay in Paris. When he returned to Paris one year later he would pay his first visit to a trader of antiquities, acquiring a page written by Racine. By the mid-1930s Zweig had brought together a collection of autographs that was almost second to none. This interest of his was intrinsically linked to his reflections on the creative process as such. But it was already in that year (1913) that Zweig would write about the collecting of autographs 'as a work of art' – one could argue as a *meta*-art or a creation consisting of creations.

On the way back from Paris to Vienna (and to Friderike), Zweig was not in a hurry. He interrupted his journey in Salzburg and visited Hermann Bahr, who resided in a palatial apartment on the first floor of Arenberg Castle. He admired Bahr as a raconteur of stories about the people he knew, ranging from the legendary actor Josef Kainz to

Cosima Wagner, from Hofmannsthal to Gustav Mahler, from Hendrik Ibsen to Hugo Wolf, followed 'by long and good debates on erotics' (Tb, 70). Perhaps Zweig needed a fresh impression of Bahr in preparation for a lecture on him, which he was to give in the largest lecture hall of Vienna University two weeks after his return from Paris. To a certain extent, Bahr was the Rabindranath Tagore of literary modernism in Austria, revered by students and fellow writers as a sage and a bit of a prophet.

Soon, though, Zweig found himself back on his walks through the park of Schönbrunn 'in habitual thoughts that take hold of me rather strongly', as he noted in his diary, adding: 'Disappointment mingles with succeeding' (Tb, 71). Was he falling back into bad habits in the woods of Schönbrunn and elsewhere, or was he talking about the progress with his novella *Moonbeam Alley*? It was only a week after his return from Paris that Friderike visited him. He described her as 'sweet and tender' but he wished that the sensual side in her would be 'absent', calling it 'disturbing'. But he was pleased to have her around, since she seemed to have helped him to find new 'clarity' – about himself (Tb, 71). It was just four days later when he received Marcelle's letter from hospital, probably after her abortion, after which he referred to his aforementioned wavering between 'shame and utter shamelessness' (Tb, 71). At any rate, his novella *Moonbeam Alley* was done and Friderike applauded it.

Down *Moonbeam Alley*

Judging from the letter Friderike had written to him in mid-June 1913 after having read this 'inflammatory' novella, she was not at all disturbed by its sordid and seedy atmosphere. It was so fundamentally different from her own writings at the time, in particular her novel *Der Ruf der Heimat* (*The Calling of the Homeland*), which appeared later, on Zweig's recommendation with his former publisher Schuster & Loeffler, in Berlin and Leipzig. Zweig reviewed it in the *Berliner Tagblatt*, calling it 'this beautiful first novel by a woman' full of 'inner clarity'. In truth, only the title and occasional references to it in the narrative could be called 'beautiful' in a conventional meaning of the word. Otherwise, it offered social drama and depravation as well as the disintegration of two individuals, with all the psychological torment that goes with it.

The setting of Zweig's novella is a 'small French seaport' into which a traveller, the narrator, is drawn having missed the 'night train to Germany'. But he is also drawn into a conflict there between a couple, turning into a matter of life and death. In occurs in a run-down inn in a moonlit alley, part of this 'sensually unregulated world where instinct still has free rein, brutal and unbridled'. The narrator compares it with the street labyrinths in other seaports like 'Hamburg and Colombo and Havana'. Interestingly, in her letter about this novella, Friderike identified the alley in question with the 'Niedergasse' in Hamburg, which they both saw during their joint visit to Germany's 'Gate to the World'.

But it is the psychology in this story that is so striking, more astonishing still the economy of narration. *Moonbeam Alley* comes across as a condensed prelude to a tragedy that might, or might not, unfold after the end of the story. Yet, this 'condensation' contains everything we need to know about this tormented couple. What tears them apart binds them together at the same time. We learn that the once-affluent husband of Françoise had humiliated her over the years by making her beg him for even the smallest purchase. Now, the tables are reversed, as she humiliates him by throwing herself at any stranger, including the narrator, in front of her husband, to whom she refers only as the 'miser'. She makes him jealous and a local laughing-stock, to the point that he can hardly articulate anything. He is lost for words, or rather, words escape him when he wants to assert himself. Eventually he manages to confide in the narrator, imploring him to speak with his wife Françoise on his behalf. But the narrator, incapable of stepping in, can only respond with a persistent feeling of 'dread' at such human fate. 'I knew that he wanted to talk to me, but in my daze, where the curiosity of my heart mingled uncertainty with physical numbness, I did nothing to encourage or discourage him.' Even though emotionally highly charged, the narrator appears indifferent but by default, condemned to be a mere observer, psychologically incapacitated and therefore unable to intervene.

Just before he finally leaves this place, the narrator goes back to the alley where he sees the emotionally and physically wrecked husband of Françoise lurking outside the inn, where he is waiting until the next lover leaves her. And once again, 'dread' and the 'cowardly fear of getting involved' take hold of the narrator as he realises what is going on. He sees the man quickly opening his hand, exposing 'a glint of metal in it. From a distance, I couldn't tell whether the moonlight showed money or a knife gleaming there in his fingers ....'.[10] Friderike's comment betrays not only 'close' but 'deep reading' when she said: 'You have never shed light so deeply into the heart of passion as with this novella'. It is as if one awakes from a violent but, at the same time, elevating dream' (SZ/FZ, 35). From her point of view, *Moonbeam Alley* was nothing short of revealing about the psyche of her 'dear one'.

Keeping up with the pace of his own life, then, remained one of Zweig's main challenges right up to the outbreak of the First World War, when the pace of history overtook him – to his utter bewilderment. The months between finishing *Moonbeam Alley* in June 1913 and August 1914 were, once again, packed with restless activity but, like so many others, he was seemingly oblivious to the mounting political and military danger. Zweig was working on an extended essay on Dostoevsky and he travelled again during most of the autumn – to Merano, Genoa, Palermo, and back to Vienna via Naples and Rome. Meanwhile, his 'lamb', Friderike, had come to the decision that she should get a divorce from her estranged husband whilst, early in 1914, Zweig was lecturing on Dostoevsky in Berlin, Hamburg, and Mannheim following a couple of days, again, in Salzburg with Hermann Bahr.

Paris was on the cards once more in March 1914. Friderike, his 'lamb', behaved 'courageously' as she testified to herself in a letter Zweig received back in his Parisian Hôtel Beaujolais, meaning that she did not make a fuss before his departure. She described the agonising negotiations with her husband over the divorce, whereby he suddenly behaved like the male protagonist in Zweig's *Moonbeam Alley* towards his wife Françoise, in the sense that it was now Felix von Winterberg who wanted to demonstrate Friderike's dependency on him. But she concluded her letter by apologising for bothering him with all these issues, given 'that you will doubtlessly be falling in love over there'. In following letters she made it plain to him that she wanted to join him in Paris, too; not anywhere but in his very hotel, regardless of Marcelle, as her whole body and soul were longing for him. She offered herself to him as his secretary, to help him with the volume of Verlaine translations and free him for his own 'real' work. Then she emphasised that her longing was in truth more spiritual than carnal. 'I do not even envision the lust of being in your arms' (SZ/FZ, 47), she tellingly added. By 15 April Friderike was in Paris with him for the final fortnight of his stay, a quasi-*ménage à trois* with Marcelle. Zweig's diary does not offer any insights into what happened during this time; it breaks off when the excitement of this short 'threesome' existence began. Before, he was busy with masterminding the Verlaine translations, spending time with Rolland and Verhaeren, visiting Flaubert's Rouen with his Belgian friend, moving in the gay circles around André Gide with his friend, the dramatist Henri Ghéon, and enjoying every moment with Marcelle.

In the Bibliothèque Nationale he made a discovery: the poems by the Romantic writer Marceline Desbordes-Valmore (1786–1859), whose works, 'Pauvres Fleurs' ('Poor Flowers', 1839), 'Les Pleurs' ('The Tears', 1833), and 'Bouquets et prières' ('Bouquets and Prayers', 1843), as well as her prose, *L'Atelier d'un peintre* (*A Painter's Studio*, 1833), was admired by Baudelaire and indeed Verlaine. He worked with the translator Gisela Etzel-Kühn towards a book on this Romantic poetess, who was by then unknown in Germany. The biographical essay that emerged from this period of research would amount to one of the very few studies on female writers in Zweig's œuvre.[11]

Lord of the manor at Kapuzinerberg 5, Salzburg,
with spaniel Kaspar in attendance
Heirs of Stefan Zweig

Jeremiah in the First World War

By the time Stefan Zweig reached Vienna in the evening of 31 July 1914, Europe had arrived at a point of no return. Contrary to the cliché of popular exuberance at the prospect of war, his diary records an atmosphere of general low-spiritedness, worry, anxiety, and consternation. Rumours of all sorts were rife, including the 'news' that the French president, Raymond Poincaré, had been assassinated.

Right to the last minute, while still in Ostend before leaving Belgium on the last train close to the outbreak of the First World War, Zweig did not believe that war in Europe would be declared. He correctly did not use the term 'war broke out' as if it were a natural disaster, since war is after all a man-made wilful act of aggression – unleashed not by the people, but by politicians and so-called 'leaders', misleaders rather, as they drive their people into a collective abyss.

At first, Zweig's pacifist beliefs were on shaky ground and were tested, if not severely challenged, by his patriotic feelings, which were at first clearly stronger for Germany than Austria. He quickly realised that Austria would be lost without Germany behind her and that the Wilhelminian Empire would have to bear the brunt of military action.

The rapid devaluation of the Austrian currency concerned him as much as the will of his fellow Viennese to continue to amuse themselves as if nothing had happened disgusted him. Unfit for military service on health grounds, Zweig had offered his services to the Ministry of War to work for its press department. In fact, he was moved to the War Archive in Vienna on 1 December 1914, where he worked on the documentation of the war – alongside writers like Franz Theodor Csokor, Alfred Polgar, the Shaw translator Siegfried Trebitsch, and later Franz Werfel and Rainer Maria Rilke – known amongst these protagonists of war-recording as hero fashioning. The archive resided in the Seventh District in Vienna in the barracks at Stiftsgasse 2, in room 535 to be precise. The list of works Zweig contributed to during the first year of his time in the War Archive makes for an interesting read. In addition to proofreading various texts, he produced several recommendations for officers and the Red Cross; an introduction to a study on the work of the Red Cross; a compilation of source material on the war; an introduction to a monograph on the first year of the war; and an extended article on caring for refugees.

He was in correspondence with Insel Verlag over anthologies of war poetry whereby he made the point of focusing more specifically on Austrian writers, as they should not, in his opinion, have merely been subsumed under 'German poets'. The more information he received about the atrocious conditions on the Eastern front, the more urgently he felt the need to draw attention to that suffering. In so doing he hoped to readdress the balance, since most of the German-language press concentrated on reports about the Western front after the early German 'successes' against the Russian army in and around East Prussia. Yet, when reading Zweig's diary entries during the first half-year of the war, one gains the impression that he wanted to mutate to a German rather than an Austrian patriot. Any 'good news' from Germany he recorded as stabilising anchors for himself, given the difficulties the Austro-Hungarian army met in Galicia and in the Balkans, especially in Serbia.

In his initial enthusiasm for German patriotism he went completely overboard in his praise for the poet Richard Dehmel, who supported the German war effort not only through his poetry but as a volunteer and lieutenant. Zweig wrote to Dehmel's wife on 28 August, as it happened Goethe's birthday, stating that he regarded her husband as identical 'with the entire German people' (II, 16).

On the day England declared war on Germany (4 August 1914) following the German invasion of Belgium, Zweig expressed a truly particular wish in a letter to his publisher, Anton Kippenberg, in Leipzig: in case anything happened to him, Insel Verlag were to produce an affordable selection of his collected works, including some hitherto unpublished material. This request confirms the high opinion Zweig seemed to have had of his literary achievements to date.

Whatever the war would lead to, Zweig had his literary work firmly in mind before his duties in the War Archive began to absorb more and more of his time. For instance, the last we hear in his diary of Marcelle, now firmly cut off from him in Paris, refers to a plan for a book in which he hoped to describe her and his own 'fate in an intensified way' (Tb, 87). This project was later to accompany him into exile and be turned into his fragmentary novel *Clarissa*. Four days after he had contemplated this novelistic undertaking he wrote the article 'The Sleepless World', in which he imagined clocks wandering through the night – suggesting that we would all have to relearn the grammar of time in order to get through the dread of the present, to transfer the past into the future. The neat pun here lies in the ambiguity of the German word *Grauen*, which can mean both 'dread' and 'dawn'.[1]

'Dread' was once again the right word to describe the by now undisputed destruction of major parts of the Belgian town of Leuven, including the famous library of the Catholic university in the last days of August 1914 and the shelling of Reims Cathedral three months later by German troops. This prompted a fierce letter by Romain Rolland to the German writer and dramatist Gerhart Hauptmann, who had publicly supported the German cause. But Zweig still disputed the validity of the enemies' claim that this had been a spiteful German attack without any military purpose; his stance threatened to cause a serious discord between him and Rolland. But even though Zweig's relationship with Rolland, who at the time worked for the Red Cross in Geneva to ensure postal communication with prisoners of war, was strained it appeared fully restored when Zweig realised just how much of his prestige Rolland had put at risk by uncompromisingly retaining his pacifist stance.

Matters with Émile Verhaeren were more complicated. Following the German invasion of Belgium, Verhaeren emigrated to London where he found lodgings at 18 Matheson Road, Kensington. From there he published, much to England's delight, vitriolic hate poems and pamphlets about Germany. On 13 March 1915 Zweig noted in his diary, following the publication of yet another such pamphlet by his once-closest non-German friend, Verhaeren, whose high pre-war standing in Germany owed next to everything to Zweig's initiatives, 'I am determined to finish things with him' (Tb, 147). His attitude remained unchanged until news reached him of Verhaeren's death in an accident at Rouen station on 27 November 1916, the very location where both friends had seen each other for the last time when they parted in June 1914. Incidentally, irony had it that the English translation of Zweig's monograph on Verhaeren, translated by Jethro Bithell, was now sought after as the only such study on the Belgian writer in English.

By contrast, his relationship with Rolland improved rapidly. Even though he felt, still, in December 1915 that he had 'to contradict him' in his letters vehemently, he was full of admiration for his French friend's 'sense of justice' (II, 97). They shared a profound distaste of war propaganda on both sides and supported Hermann Hesse, who had appealed to the poets in the world *not* to lend their voices to the warmongering of their governments. Such was Zweig's admiration for Rolland that he translated one of his articles ('Notre prochain, l'ennemi', or 'Hate of the enemy versus love thy neighbour') and even managed to get it published in the *Neue Freie Presse* some three months later on 25 March 1915.

Privacy in the Age of War

'My nerves are like worn strings', Zweig admitted to himself in his diary on 2 May 1915. The evening before he had spent time with a certain 'Eva C.', which did him 'a lot of good' (Tb, 165). Perhaps this unidentified 'Eva' was one of the 'women' Friderike referred to in some of her letters written to Zweig at the time. Apparently, he confessed to Friderike that he would 'creep with some women through whatever lanes' so not to encounter her, a confession that quite understandably hurt her (SZ/FZ, 60). Some of his jokes she found equally hurtful – likewise the cynical remarks he was obviously capable of, judging from

Friderike's comments. Still, in spring 1915 she noticed his erratic behaviour, sometimes leaving her, suddenly pretending that he had to work. She wanted to believe him but suspected that he was, yet again, off to some women. As this episode shows, the war only caused to a certain extent a change of pattern in Zweig's private habits. Cathartic it eventually became, but only by degrees. It is fair to assume, however, that Zweig remained in a state of inner uproar for quite some time with the war, his work in the archive, his unresolved future with Friderike, and perhaps also what he had left behind in Paris in terms of likely emotional damage in Marcelle.

Yet Friderike, too, seemed to have had a 'bad conscience' in respect of her own behaviour. The likely explanation can be found in one of the first surviving letters Zweig had written to her in August 1918, in which he referred to an unidentified 'youngster', whom she might be meeting in Zurich (SZ/FZ, 77). She once told Zweig that her favourite song was Cherubino's aria from Mozart's *Le Nozze di Figaro* (*The Marriage of Figaro*), '*Non so piu cosa son, cosa faccio*':

> I do not know anymore what I am, what I do,
> one moment I'm on fire, the next moment I am cold as ice,
> every woman changes my color,
> every woman makes me tremble.
> [...] and if I do not have anyone near to hear me
> I speak of love to myself! (SZ/FZ, 61)

It is difficult to imagine that Zweig would have missed the (bitter) irony of this reference.

At the time Zweig wrote this letter, Friderike stayed in the Swiss mountain village of Amden, off the Walensee, with her two daughters Suse and Alix, following their joint appearance at a conference of the Association for Perpetual Peace in Bern in mid-April 1918. There, Zweig had spoken about Bertha von Suttner, the Austrian Nobel Peace Prize winner, and their brief time together in the Hôtel Belvoir in Rüschlikon near Zurich. Due to his connections, Zweig had been released from his duties in the War Archive and was allowed to settle in Switzerland as a permanent correspondent of the *Neue Freie Presse* following negotiations with the editor back in Vienna, which Friderike led on Zweig's behalf; moreover, his anti-war drama *Jeremiah* was first performed in Zurich on 27 February 1918 to much acclaim.

As a divorcée, Friderike's own situation back in 1915 was not easy. Given the legal stipulations in Austria until the end of 1918, she was not able to remarry. For the time being she had two addresses: in Lange Gasse 49, near Zweig's flat in Kochgasse 8, and in Baden near Vienna in Mozartstrasse 25. Wishing to respect Zweig's 'freedom' she denied herself too much physical contact with her 'dear one'. But from autumn 1916 they travelled together more frequently; the volatile attraction turned into a major commitment when they spent three weeks together in Salzburg in October of that year. There, they spotted the former hunting lodge of the archbishops of Salzburg on the Kapuzinerberg, a baroque *palais*-like villa, which was to become their future place of residence. Zweig purchased this treasure of real estate, surrounded by eight thousand square metres of garden and forest, for ninety thousand Kronen in cash! Then, in autumn 1917, both travelled extensively in Switzerland together, visiting Romain Rolland in November in Villeneuve at Lake Geneva, where he stayed in the Hôtel Byron. In Geneva they met the French poet Pierre Jean Jouve, a pacifist and a close associate of Rolland's, and the Flemish graphic artist Frans Masereel; they also came to see the headquarters of the International Red Cross. It was clearly under the influence of these encounters that Zweig drew up a 'will of conscience' on his thirty-sixth birthday (28 November 1917) stating that he would never serve the military again in any capacity. In fact, in summer 1918 he published an essay in the Swiss periodical *Die Friedens-Warte* under the provocative title 'Confession to Defeatism', and it indeed provoked a fierce response from the Austro-Hungarian Embassy in Bern.

In his diary, Rolland gave an elaborate account of Zweig's visit in Villeneuve on 20 November for about one week. It was, as Rolland meticulously noted, 'the 1212th day of the war'. Rolland observed that by now Zweig showed 'a certain pride of being Austrian rather than German', as the Austrians appeared more 'human and liberal' compared with the Germans. He struck Rolland as an 'independent' human being with 'an assured sense of decency'. His further characterisation of Zweig is noteworthy given that there are few and far between of him at the time:

> Stefan Zweig has kept his youthful looks; he does not look older than thirty-five years of age. This face with its long nose causes at first the impression of Semitic cunningness, to which one's sympathy responds with some caution; his slightly heavy, tough and (when speaking in French) monotonous way of speech is not attractive. But when one does engage in conversation with him one recognises the straightness and the nobility of his character. [...] He endeavours to keep his soul unblemished in this war and to keep his moral independence against the immense official machinery intact that constricts us all. And even though he lives under less favourable circumstances than I do he succeeded in doing so. [...] To him this war was a filter for the souls.[2]

Given Rolland's famously tolerant own standards the opening remark contains an unmistakably anti-Semitic undertone. But the second half of the quote sets the record straight in the sense that he saw in Zweig a kindred spirit equally critical of warfare as he was.

In private terms, not all was well between Stefan and Friderike. In fact, 'work' caused a major discord, if not open rift. Zweig had agreed to preface and revise a new translation into German of Jean-Jacques Rousseau's novel *Émile ou De l'éducation* (*Émile, or On Education*). The latter task he entrusted Friderike with. She procrastinated with it and came up with her comments on the translation, which she finally deemed unacceptable, at the last minute. Zweig could not contain his displeasure, or rather, anger about the slack way she had handled this task. He pointed out to her that she had years ago applied to be his helper, and even learnt stenography for that purpose, only to admit to him that she found all that work too tedious (SZ/FZ, 76–9).

Whatever happened exactly there and then is impossible to reconstruct but it is a fact that Friderike, in the first years of their togetherness, never tired in emphasising just how connected she felt with Zweig through his work – to a certain extent it was a surrogate for what she thought to be too weak a physical bond between them. On the penultimate day of 1914 she told him, 'You are often so far away – but in your work I always hold you close to my heart – you often roll relentlessly such alien worlds between me and yourself, [but] your work arches golden bridges for me from you to my home. It is a home in the clouds and yet also in your heart, in your unfaithful faithful heart' (SZ/FZ, 59). These thoughts would reappear in a moving novella (*Compulsion*) which belonged to Zweig's 'works of the war', to be considered shortly.

The cause of Judaism and the case of Jeremiah

In Zweig's agonising over the reality and consequences of the war, one theme stands out – besides his increasing disenchantment with patriotism and move towards pacifism. It was intrinsically linked with his own problem of identity, namely Judaism.[3] In literary terms, we have already encountered this concern in the short novella *In the Snow*, depicting the fate of Jews in the Middle Ages driven by terror into death. But it was during the First World War that he worked on what he saw as a defining contribution to the conception of Judaism, his 'drama of prophecy', *Jeremiah* (1917).[4] Of equal significance are Zweig's letters on the subject, written at the time to Ernst Hardt, Abraham Schwadron (later, Avraham Sharon), Joseph Luitpold Stern, and Martin Buber in particular. There is little doubt that Zweig's work on his *Jeremiah* tragedy was also influenced by Franz Werfel's fierce anti-war version of Euripides's tragedy *The Trojan Women*, which he wrote in 1913 and first performed – somewhat surprisingly – in the middle of the First World War on 22 April 1916 in the Lessing Theatre in Berlin, an event that did not escape Zweig's attention (II, 106).[5] It is therefore not only Judaism that needs to be considered when looking at *Jeremiah*, but the challenges of identity together with the crisis of prophecy. It is telling that Zweig abandoned his original plan to write a series of essays on various Old Testament prophets for Martin Buber's new periodical *Der Jude*, probably because he felt that *Jeremiah* did contain all the relevant features of that crisis of prophetism.[6]

However, as seen already, Zweig's upbringing owed very little to Jewish orthodoxy and it was mainly through his affiliation with Theodor Herzl – the founder of the World Zionist Organization – that he felt reminded of his own Jewish origins. His friendship with Ephraim Mose Lilien brought him close to the Young Jewish Movement, working towards what was known as the Jewish Renaissance, but Zweig always stopped short of joining any such groupings. Thus any 'Judeocentric' approach to Zweig is just as ill-conceived as any other one-reason-only explanation of his complex and multi-layered personality. By the same token, portraying Zweig as nothing but a 'true European' would fail to acknowledge this other dimension in him: his concern for the Jewish faith. But any of his 'sides' should not be discussed at the expense of the other, as they complemented each other.

Before considering the aforementioned letters as contexts to Zweig's *Jeremiah*, one needs to realise that his diaries of this very period (May 1915 to February 1916) display far less sympathy with Jews. Especially on his inspection tour through Galicia, which he undertook as a newly promoted sergeant-major (which he commented on with irony), Zweig's depreciative comments on Jewish life in this large province hardly differ from the resentments against the Eastern European Jewry amongst many of his fellow assimilated Jewish and non-Jewish Viennese. Even before he went to Galicia, he noted that rabbis in Austria had issued over two thousand forged certificates for candidates allegedly becoming rabbis to be exempt from military service. He added: 'Such things compromise the achievements of tens of thousands of Jews serving at the front' (Tb, 183). In Tarnow he visited a ghetto and commented 'dirty and every hut as black as a coffin' (Tb, 192). In another Galician town he noted just how dirty the hotel was he had to stay in, owned by a 'pockmarked impertinent Jew' (Tb, 196). In short, sympathy for these Galician Jews are hard to find in these diary entries.

By contrast, similarly to his drama *Jeremiah*, Zweig's letters on Jewish identity address the *idea* of Judaism. Whilst sporadically working on *Jeremiah*, which he claimed to be a tragedy that he had 'always wanted to write' (Tb, 172), he read Ernst Hardt's three-act drama *König Salomo* (*King Solomon*),[7] sent to him by the author. In his response Zweig praised the depiction of aged King David and Hardt's capturing of the sheer 'might' of the Old Testament and its Judaist world, which he associated with 'hatred, strength, cleverness and sensuality' (II, 91). In a letter to another fellow writer, Abraham Schwadron, he remarked that in their part of Poland, the Germans based their administration on support from Jews, whilst the Austrians entrusted (Christian) Poles with that task. In his letters to Martin Buber, Zweig's stance towards his own Jewishness loses all ambiguity. He stated that he would not choose 'Judaism to be the dungeon for his feelings', arguing that Jews do not come across as self-assured and carefree. To him, however, Judaism was not 'burdensome; it does not enthuse me; nor does it torture me; nor does it set me apart from others; I feel it like I feel my heartbeat when I think of it and like I do not feel it when I do not think of it', adding quite cunningly, 'If you do not want more from me then I am yours', in reference to future contributions to Buber's periodical (II, 107–8).

But only three months later, again in a letter to Schwadron, Zweig admitted in view of the war that 'Judaism is now facing the most fundamental crisis since the inquisition.' Reason being, according to Zweig's 'prophetic' judgement, that those nations who could not speak up for themselves would blame the Jews for what was happening. He called for 'vigilance' against such prejudice (II, 113–14).

In the following three letters, written to Martin Buber during the first half of 1917, Zweig remained unambiguously clear about his position towards Judaism, notwithstanding some poignant nuances in his attitude: 'I have never felt freer through the Judaism within me than now in this time of national madness'. However, he spelt out very directly where he differed from Buber: 'I never wanted Judaism to become a nation and thus lower [...] itself to the present-day realities.' His point was that he 'loved the diaspora', affirming 'the meaning of its idealism as its cosmopolitan calling' (II, 130). Some five months later Zweig reaffirmed this judgement, emphasising that it was because of the war that he was able to sharpen his attitude towards Judaism (II, 142–3). Moreover, the 'history of the Jewish spirit' represented to Zweig 'a permanent revolt against reality', as he put it in his last letter to Buber during this period (II, 147). He also explained to Schwadron around the same time that the 'greatness of the Jewish people' rested on their spiritual 'home' being the 'eternal Jerusalem'; returning to 'the real Palestine' would however pull this spirit down and risk the transnational appeal of its ethos, which could have held the other nations together (II, 145–6). This was idealism squared, which Zweig shared with many of his assimilated fellow Jews at the time; they were in majority adamant critics of Zionism and the re-establishing of a Jewish nation-state. Interestingly, Zweig's comments coincided with the negotiations that led to the Balfour Declaration of 9 November 1917, which introduced the very concept of a 'national home for the Jewish people' but without any representation of the local population in Palestine.[8]

But what about Zweig's emotionally charged drama *Jeremiah*, the eponymous protagonist of which he said, in a diary entry dated 7 January 1915, that he had 'experienced' (Tb, 244) as one would a real person? His prophet is a highly complex character, traumatised by his own visions and tortured by his dreams. He seems at odds with reality and even describes himself as a 'fool at the mercy of my own delusions'.[9] The relationship between Jeremiah and his (nameless) mother is one of the most moving aspects of this poetic drama; her *raison d'être* is to be the mother of a prophet, even to the point of dreaming her son's dreams until she realises that they were the most genuine 'reality' in his (and her) life. Jeremiah refers to his mother as his 'lover', while she believes she is 'inhaling him through her senses'.[10] This is not to suggest an incestuous relationship, but the closest possible spiritual affinity between mother and son one would find expressed in physical metaphors.

This said, any form of physical passion is lost on Zweig's Jeremiah, who regards himself as an instrument of divine pronouncements. He feels a stranger in his own home, which is painful for his mother to observe. In turn 'she feels how death is growing within' herself, comparing it to a 'shadowy clock whose hands are about to move full circle.'[11] Ultimately, it is the prophet's mother who, in her mind, sees the fall of Jerusalem. At this stage her son is not ready to adopt this vision, but he understands that he must leave the 'sunken world of his mother' behind.

Later, the main problem for the king of Judah and his people is whether someone who appears to be a demented prophet can be taken seriously at all. Jeremiah comes across as an unorthodox prophet who proclaims decidedly dogmatic ideas. He predicts the destruction of the temple and Jerusalem as a punishment for the people of Judah, who have set up altars in the streets of Jerusalem 'to burn incense to Baal.' Nebuchadnezzar, the king of Babylon, attempts to estrange Jeremiah from his rival, the king of Judah, and appoints him court magician. But eventually, all attention is focused on the prophet's 'pure spirit,' which enables him to lead the people of Judah back to self-enlightenment and prepare them for the inevitable. He asks them not to look back but into the future. 'Those who prefer to rest', he says, 'have a homeland. But the entire world belongs to those who know how to migrate.'[12]

The most significant moment in this play is when the people of Jerusalem leave their city and the prophet abandons his elevated position, which includes his pronounced individualism, and loses himself in the vast crowds of emigrating Jews. The way in which Zweig describes this moment as part of the final stage direction (in 1917!) now reads like a premonition or eerie prophecy of what the European Jewry was to be subjected to only two decades later:

> Their emigration resembled the solemn celebration of an act of sacrifice. None of them pushed forward, none stayed behind; row after row passed by without any hurry and disappeared [...] It seemed as if an infinity emerged from darkness and entered the space beyond.[13]

One hears the murmur of voices knowing that one is that of the prophet Jeremiah, though now he has nothing more to say. But by succumbing to their destiny, the people of Judah, as some of the

Chaldeans remarked, radiate a peculiar strength. These Jews are literally going *into* the world and thus abandon themselves. This is Zweig's very message – that by doing so they immunise themselves against the bacteria called 'nationalism'.

From Zweig's point of view, it was no contradiction that only a few months prior to writing *Jeremiah*, which celebrated the moral victory of emigrating Jews over the soldiers of Babel, he published an essay, 'The Tower of Babel', in which he praised the edifice for the ambition it symbolised – namely, what is humanly possible if all peoples work together towards a common goal. Biblical myth has it that the multitude of languages spoken by those who wanted to stretch themselves to limitlessness ultimately destroyed this ambition. Zweig suggested that the act of creation, in no matter which language, needs to prevail; according to him, creativity would stimulate peaceful competition, even if by then Zweig saw Europe as a Babylonic ruin that was desperately waiting to be restored or rebuilt. In his darkest moments yet to come, he even began to doubt his most cherished object of political imagination: Europe. On 19 October 1918, that is, weeks before the end of the First World War, Zweig noted in his diary, 'But what is Europe? A fiction, which one should wean oneself off from like all summaries [*Zusammenfassungen*]' (Tb, 331). Europe, a 'summary', but of what? Of one's political illusions, or so he seemed to have felt at the time – albeit for a short while.

Zweig's *Jeremiah* is not only an impressive document of the author's increasingly pacifist stance amid a world war but also expresses his own struggle with his Jewish identity. Furthermore, it explores the significance of religious thought in a secular world dominated by power politics. This is an idea rarely found in Zweig's œuvre. Until *Jeremiah*, art had adopted the place of a quasi-religious belief in Zweig's works. However, it appears that Jeremiah's fate as a testimony of a genuine believer in God seemed to have reminded Zweig of the ancient foundations of humanism.

Zweig once remarked that all those who silently suffered hardship during the war would find their anguish expressed in *Jeremiah*, and he added in a letter written to Hermann Bahr in early September

1917 that this play was his 'escape' and 'confession box' (II, 152). But his character drama is also an essay on the clash of cultural values, the twisting of words, and the emergence of ambiguities to replace assumed certainties in life. The question as to whether the Jeremiah of this drama is capable of development at all or whether his character traits are set from the very beginning is in fact part and parcel of this character study, presented by Zweig in the shape of nine dramatic 'pictures'. They represent nine different perspectives about what can be called 'real' and what remains wishful thinking. One key feature of this drama and its pronounced perspectivism is the way in which Jeremiah and the other main protagonists deal with deception or alleged 'truths' that constitute the precarious 'reality' for Jerusalem during the eleven months of its siege (598–7 BCE) by the king of Babylon, Nebuchadnezzar II.

Zweig's drama shows how alleged delusion can turn into reason, suspicions and assumptions into facts, and divine intervention into turmoil. 'Lord … it is hard to be your messenger!', Jeremiah exclaims at the end of the fifth and most moving scene, the final encounter between the cursed prophet and his dying mother.[14] As mentioned, she is not granted a proper name in the play; her *raison d'être* rests exclusively with her son Jeremiah. The scene encapsulates some of the main motifs in this play as mentioned above: homecoming and expulsion, and the power of dreams, delusion, and self-deception.

In this play Zweig turns Jeremiah's inclination to lament into an ability to reconcile himself and his people with their fate. He can now convince his people that they should, like he himself, love their hardship as a sign from Yahweh. Zweig's Jeremiah can eventually abandon his self-doubt and devote himself to helping build up the inner strength of his suffering fellow emigrants. As problematic as this seems if viewed against the backdrop of the Shoah it suggests the putting into practice of the Nietzschean principle *amor fati*, love thy fate.

What matters here is Zweig's concern with the moral superiority of the defeated – not any defeated individual, but a Jewish one.[15] Predictably, Rolland expressed special enthusiasm for this drama in his review in Buber's periodical *Der Jude*, claiming that Zweig's *Jeremiah* was one of the 'most noble works on the modern stage' as it demonstrated that defeats can be 'more fruitful than victories and suffering more luminous than joy'.[16] More surprisingly, however, was Thomas Mann's praise of *Jeremiah* in a letter to Zweig written on 9 September 1917. It is worth quoting in full:

Dear Herr Zweig,

Take my honest and genuinely respectful thanks for your courageous, magnificent work [the German *Dichtung* here suggests a poetic drama – R.G.]. I am still entirely under the spell of it, at present a bit numbed by its Old Testament pathos. I intend to return quite often to it to learn to appreciate its individual beauties. It is certainly the most significant poetic fruit of this war that I have seen to date. There is, after all, no shortage of allusions and relations [:] 'You all wanted it, all, all of you! Your hearts are wavering and more so even than reed. Those who you are now crying "peace", I previously heard raving for war, and those who vilify the king cheered him before.' Yes, yes.

Mann signed with 'repeated cordial thanks'.[17] This comment by Thomas Mann was even more remarkable given that he was working at the time on his *Betrachtungen eines Unpolitischen* (*Reflections of a Non-Political Writer*), which offered a distinctly nationalist stance in its defence of German (high) 'culture' versus mere Western 'civilisation'. Of equal interest, however, is the criticism of Zweig's drama expressed by the Viennese feminist, pacifist, and painter Rosa Mayreder, whose essays on critiquing conventional conceptions of the role of the female are now seen as foundational documents of feminist theory. She noted in her diary on 19 March 1918:

I have read Stefan Zweig's *Jeremiah* with a curious mixture of admiration and indignation. There are magnificent hymnic passages – but the whole is written in a spirit as if two thousand years have passed in vain. Jeremiah begins as a pacifist and ends up as a

Jewish-national chauvinist. The relations to modern Zionism are the only modern features of the drama. It is strange that the Jewish pacifists believe in all naivety that they could unite the ancient conceptions of the Jews as the chosen people with modern internationalism as if the very conception of preferential treatment were not the biggest obstacle for internationalism.[18]

In his political statements during the last phase of the First World War Zweig would go still further by openly advocating 'defeatism'. This plea for an unconditional and immediate end to this war and warfare in general exposed him to massive criticism, even from pacifists like Romain Rolland and the Austrian Nobel Peace Prize winner of 1911, Alfred Hermann Fried, who in 1899 had founded, together with Bertha von Suttner, the pacifist magazine *Lay Down Your Arms*. Paradoxically, Zweig argued even more radically than Thomas Mann ever did, for a non-political stance, but seemingly with an awareness of the illusoriness of such a claim.

Other wartime works

In essence, Zweig's 'war effort' amounted to literary works through which he denounced war. Apart from his play *Jeremiah*, the pieces to consider are two major poems, 'The Cripple' (1915) and 'Polyphem' (1917); his novella *Compulsion* (published after the war in 1920) and his fragmentary story *Wondrak* (unpublished during Zweig's lifetime); and a number of shorter articles, written mostly during the final phase of the war, including his 'Avowal to Defeatism'. Another lengthier political essay stands out in this period, displaying a remarkable maturity in terms of judgement *and* provocative thought, comparable to – as mentioned earlier – his reflections during his Mexican journey (1911), *Why only Belgium, why not also Poland?* (1915).

In the poem 'The Cripple', which makes use, in parts, of the hexametric meter – suggesting surprising allusions to the classic form of the idyll – Zweig, the poet of humanism, comes to the fore. To his bewilderment, the legless and nameless soldier encounters compassion and unexpected care. At the end he even caresses his crutches, a moving gesture of heartfelt emotion, as he experiences genuine brotherhood with people who want to help him. But he is lost for words when he wants to express his gratitude, even though, inwardly, he is filled with 'burning love'. He has nothing to offer but stunned silence and tears in the face of the 'love and light' he, or rather his condition, meets.[19] To a certain extent, the cripple epitomises what has been called Zweig's 'poetics of the defeated', which turns into pure love for the suffering individual.[20]

By contrast, the rhapsodic poem 'Polyphemus' addresses war directly. But it does so with reference to a mythological figure, the one-eyed son of Poseidon and the sea nymph Thoosa, a Cyclops, normally not associated with warfare. As his name suggests he is 'abounding in songs and legends' but unaware of his size and strength. In the ninth book of the *Odyssey*, however, and only there, he is portrayed as a man-eating savage, and it is likely that Zweig derived his characterisation from this source. In the poem, though, Polyphemus is made aware of revenge from the people. They are incensed as well as inspired by the 'breath of the dead' and seek take his one eye out. The poem sees the people walking as brothers 'over the stinking corpse' of the giant 'into the eternal heavens of the world' thus implying the innate sacredness of the earth.[21]

Yet, there is another interpretation possible that rests on the Polyphemus satyr play by Euripides, which Zweig, quite learned in ancient mythology, could easily have known. With Euripides, Polyphemus is a 'pederast', originally suggesting a relationship between an older and a younger man – as condoned in ancient Greece.[22] Attacking Polyphemus in this demonstrative way may therefore also be seen as an act of Zweig finally exorcising his homoerotic tendencies. For it is striking to find that he refers, in his diary of 9 December 1917, to the 'terrible expansion of homosexuality' during the last couple of years, which he noticed in Brussels, Bern, Zurich, and elsewhere. Even though caution in judgement is, as ever, advisable, at this stage Zweig seemed to have subscribed to some 'conspiracy theory' when he suggests and laments that in connection with appointments both academic, social, and military the networks of homosexuals and freemasons seemed to work effectively (Tb, 287).

In articles written between August and December 1918 Zweig insists on a revaluation of *défaitisme* (defeatism) as an essential 'pan-human' right. He argues, however, in favour of 'devaluating ideas' altogether, by which he means ideologies, in favour of elevating human individualism collectively, a neat paradox in line with another fundamental one: defeatism is, after all, an 'idea', too, before it can gain shape in political reality, in this case by ceasing warfare immediately. Another such 'idea' is 'republican consciousness', of which Zweig rightly said that toppling over monarchy does not mean that people have acquired proper 'internal republicanism', meaning political self-responsibility. He regarded this correctly as the result of an educational process.[23]

When in early April 1915 Zweig published in the *Neue Freie Presse* his essay comparing the situation in Belgium and Poland, he showed, once again, political judgement and acumen. His argument reads as follows: why was the whole world concerned with Belgium after the German invasion and not with the Polish territories and the fate of the Jews there, particularly in the Russian-occupied parts? He points out the uncomfortable fact that France had, for far too long, despised Belgian culture and, in particular, cultural life in Flanders. Zweig refers to Baudelaire's contempt for Belgium and his intention to write a book 'against the Belgians'; he reminds his readers of the fact that Maurice Maeterlinck, their most important dramatist, was never admitted to the French Academy and that the boulevard play *Le Mariage de Mademoiselle Beulemans*, which ridicules the Belgians, was one of the greatest hits in Paris theatres. By saying this Zweig did not condone the German invasion of Belgium, but he did accuse France and England of hypocrisy, given that they had for years criticised Belgium's colonial venture in the Congo, deflecting from their own colonial atrocities, whilst ignoring the behaviour of their Eastern ally, Russia, towards the Poles. Zweig demanded that the evident 'Belgian suffering' of spring 1915 must not 'violate the Polish suffering' in the mind of the world – by which he meant in particular the suffering inflicted by Czarist Russia on her Polish provinces.[24]

But it was his novella *Compulsion* with which he attempted to persuade his readers to obtain a pacifist stance. In artistic terms, this is not Zweig's most accomplished novella; it is transparent from the outset that its intention is a didactic and moralistic one. It serves a distinctive message – that of the prerogative of one's conscience.

Ferdinand, the main protagonist, is an artist, having emigrated with his wife from Austria to Switzerland. The 'uncertainty' of compulsory conscription is hovering above him, even though Paula claims that in Switzerland he is free from Austrian jurisdiction. But the outreach of the powerful Austrian Consulate in Zurich makes Ferdinand hide from his 'own fear'.[25] He tries to hide behind his work, his paintings, including an ill-conceived self-portrait whereby his conscience tells him that 'it is a crime to work for your own pleasure now while the world falls into ruin' (WOS, 43). For a short while he contemplates suicide, realising that his wife wants him to be a conscientious objector, but he cannot find the strength in himself to be just that. Communication between him and Paula is strained, mainly because 'words always miss the mark' (WOS, 46), as she points out. Towards the end of the story comes a point when Ferdinand has virtually resigned himself to returning to Austria as a soldier, leaving his wife behind: 'He stood still, musing, hypnotized by the idea of the border' (WOS, 76). But he does not transgress it, returning instead to his deeply caring, committed, and resolute wife. There, in their modest home close to Lake Zurich, he is touched by the fact that in his absence, which she must have thought of as final, she had brought all his paintings 'down from the studio into the living-room so that she could be close to him through his work' (WOS, 81). This sentiment is strongly reminiscent of Friderike's comment to Zweig; as quoted before, it was through his writings that she felt she could be with him all the time (SZ/FZ, 59).

As so often with Zweig's texts, it is also a flash-like realisation (WOS, 80) that makes Ferdinand follow Paula's determination to save him from military service and next-to-certain slaughter. In terms of language, it is only towards the end of the story that the adverb 'uncertainly' loses ground. Until then it is the main mode of any activity on Ferdinand's part. Certainty, however, rests with the female instinct *and* reasoning right from the beginning. Certainty of conviction in an uncertain world is a curious quality, particularly if coupled with a feeling of restlessness and impatience. Furthermore, Zweig was not ready to accept at that time that pacifism was an 'ism' – too, a doctrine – suggesting that ideology was simply inescapable in political connections.

Zweig in the immediate aftermath of the First World War

From 1 May 1919 Stefan Zweig had a new and, as he proudly announced, permanent address: Salzburg, Kapuzinerberg 5. It was more of a small residence fit for someone who referred to himself, if only in jest, as 'Stefan Pascha' (SZ/FZ, 89). At last he was able to take proper possession of what he had acquired during the war, even though the house required renovation and refurbishment, the organisation of which lay mainly in the hands of Friderike. Zweig was in no hurry to experience post-war Austria. During the final phase of the war he spent time with Friderike in Montreux, frequently visiting Rolland in neighbouring Villeneuve and then, until January 1919, once again in Rüschlikon on Lake Zurich, where she stayed in the Villa Seehalde and he in the Hôtel Belvoir, mainly still working on his essay on Dostoevsky and the novella *Compulsion*. From there he observed the end of the Habsburg monarchy and the drastic reduction of the Austro-Hungarian Empire to the small 'Austro-German' republic. In contrast to the majority of German-speaking Austrians, Zweig maintained that joining the German Republic would have fundamentally detrimental consequences for what was left of Austria, that and Vienna would look 'pointlessly large like a hydrocephalus' at the tail end of this conglomerate (Tb, 335, entry of 3 November 1918).

It was only in January 1919 that Zweig informed his ageing mother about his intention to marry Friderike and to move to Salzburg for good. She was 'forewarned' by her elder son, Alfred, of these plans, who felt distinctly less sympathetic towards Friderike than their mother. Friderike's letter to Ida Zweig must have been heart-warming for her, also given the ailing state of her husband Moritz, for her reply to 'Dearest Frau Friederike [sic]' is testimony to her affectionate character. However, before Friderike wrote this letter Zweig gave her a strange lesson displaying, once again, his rather peculiar sense of 'humour': more cutting, if not hurtful, than funny. He told her not to be 'more stupid than usual' when writing to his mother; she should also abstain from mixing her concerns 'with your money mania [*Geldwahn*]', by which he alluded to her concern for her and her children's maintenance following her divorce. Even though the latter point was obviously meant to reassure her, it reveals something uncomfortable about Zweig's attitude towards her. This said, he would go on to do everything in terms of mobilising his connections with the Austrian authorities to secure official permission for Friderike to remarry and to overcome the epic rules and stipulations impeding (Catholic) divorcées like her from entering new marriages. Friderike even took the step of leaving the Catholic Church to facilitate this process, but it was, at first, in vain. It took a further year for the authorities to clear the way for both marrying each other on 20 January 1920 in the Vienna Rathaus, even though, quite bizarrely, the bride was represented at this occasion by Zweig's friend Felix Braun. But this is a different story, to be told later.

Like for so many, 1918–19 represented a threshold experience for Stefan Zweig, and indeed Friderike, with the border between Switzerland and Austria at Feldkirch in the province of Vorarlberg bearing a particularly symbolic significance. For it was at this border-crossing railway station at 4 p.m. on 24 March 1919 that Zweig witnessed – together with Friderike, her two daughters, and their governess, Loni Schnitz, as well as the fellow writer and translator, Erwin Rieger – Emperor Karl I of Austria with his wife Zita, leaving their country for good and entering their exile in Switzerland following the expulsion of the House of Habsburg-Lorraine by the Austrian National Assembly. It was a historic moment, much to the taste of the moment-conscious writer Stefan Zweig, which would feature prominently some twenty years later in his account of things past, *The World of Yesterday*.

The personal threshold experience for both was moving together into the *palais*-like villa on Salzburg's Kapuzinerberg. But even before this happened a discord occurred between the couple of the manor: Zweig wanted to bring his Viennese secretary, Mathilde Mandl, with him. He hoped to set her up on the Kapuzinerberg, too, establishing his personal archive there – Mandl even offered to bring her own bedlinen along – but Friderike put her foot down and refused to accept a lodger of this kind. However, matters relaxed, as indicated by the fact that they signed their letters to each other, at least occasionally, with their pet names 'Stefzi' and 'Mumu'. Whether the latter was taken from Turgenev's novella about a dog with the same name is at least possible.

In terms of literary work amid relocations and renovations, the completion of the Dostoevsky essay, together with the story *Compulsion* and, most notably, his biographical study *Romain Rolland: The Man and his Work*, dominated Zweig's agenda. Like Rilke and others, Zweig was undoubtedly traumatised by the war itself and what its outcome meant – the collapse of ancient bonds and solidarities in what was the Austro-Hungarian Empire.[26] But we need to differentiate between different timelines of this trauma – a more immediate one, especially relevant to the prose written during Zweig's time in Switzerland until he returned to Austria in spring 1919 (*Episode at the Lake Geneva*, *Compulsion*, and the *Wondrak* fragment), and a long-term one that would include his novel *Ungeduld des Herzens* (*Beware of Pity*, 1939), the fragment *Clarissa*, and *Die Welt von Gestern* (*The World of Yesterday*). It is difficult to say whether this trauma was mitigated by the new comparatively comfortable, if not luxurious, living conditions Zweig had secured for himself and Friderike, or whether he tried to compensate for his sense of loss by (over-)indulging in good living in spite of the spartan circumstances of the immediate post-war period, which was marked and marred by deprivation of all sorts, food shortages, and influenza, not to speak of the hardship of traumatised soldiers returning to their families from horrendous front experiences.

Zweig was certain of the envy of others, for, as Golo Mann once pointed out in relation to the living standard of his father in the late 1920s, people in the German-speaking lands tend not to worry about industrialists and film stars living in affluence, but they never condone success and luxury if enjoyed by writers of 'serious' literature. And serious it was what Zweig had to offer – in the case of *Wondrak* so serious a novella that he left it unfinished, at that time in his career a rare occurrence. The story takes his readers to Southern Bohemia in 1899 where they meet Ruzena Sedlak, a shockingly ugly mother of a boy called Karel; he is strikingly healthy whilst she herself has no nose, only two holes. The narrator comments: 'Nature has made us so accustomed to the regularity of her laws that the slightest derivation from their familiar harmony seems repellent and alarming' (WOS, 86). In fact, Ruzena lives apart from the village civilisation in a hunting lodge, fitting for someone who was regarded as the local prey for lusting males. Karel was therefore the fruit of violation; his real father remains unknown. Ruzena has developed into an over-caring mother who is excessively protective of her son. With the arrival of the war, she does everything to hide him in the forest so that he should be spared from conscription: 'a mother on her own against the monstrosity of the world' (WOS, 100). Inevitably, he is eventually found out by the Austrian military police officers, who march mother and son to the village after her literally defending her son back home in the forest with teeth and claws. But this happens towards the end of the war and the Austrian district commissioner realises that this brutal action would generate solidarity between the villagers and Ruzena Sedlak, given that 'long ago the whole Czech people had broken away in their hearts from the Habsburgs, those strange gentlemen in Vienna' (WOS, 101), with whom they felt they had nothing in common anymore and were forced to fight a war which was not theirs. The story breaks off when Karel is sent to the barracks in Budweis (České Budějovice) and into an uncertain future, leaving Ruzena behind in barely concealed despair.

Zweig is at his best when it comes to demonstrating human suffering and hardship in the face of momentous events that appear to be overpowering. But this 'animalistic' female, Ruzena, is endowed by the narrator with more human dignity than the one-dimensional authorities, epitomised by the fact that the title-giving official Wondrak is a mere supporting character in the story and is simply marginalised by events, a non-hero if ever there was one.

To Zweig, heroes of a special kind were individuals like Bertha von Suttner and institutions like the International Red Cross in Geneva. Likewise, he singled out individual writers of the past and present who fell into this category, whom he regarded as misused during the war. There were the 'Three Masters', Balzac, Dickens, and Dostoevsky, whom he saw in this role and to whom he dedicated essays published under this title in 1919, with his portrait of Balzac displaying the kind of rapturing strength that radiates from Rodin's famous sculpture of the writer. The book is prefaced by a short but poignant text, which was one of the first written in his new but historical Salzburg residence. Dedicated to Romain Rolland, it was to explore the 'psychology of the novelist'.[27] And there was his study on the very same writer, whom he credited with the epithet 'greatness'. As Zweig said, the book was written with Rolland's own large-scale 'heroic biographies' project in mind, of which the French writer only completed one – on Beethoven, Michelangelo, and Tolstoy – written in the vein of Thomas Carlyle's and Ralph Waldo Emerson's conception of 'greatness'. Works on Guiseppe Mazzini, Louis Lazare Hoche – the French general in the French revolutionary wars, a strange choice for a pacifist like Rolland – and the 'courageous utopian' Thomas Paine remained unwritten. Instead, Rolland had produced shorter biographies on George Frideric Handel, Hugo Wolf, and Hector Berlioz.

Zweig decided to structure his biography and monograph on Rolland and his work to date (1920) differently to his pre-war studies on Verlaine and Verhaeren, but also in contrast to his essays on Balzac, Dickens, and Dostoevsky. It comes across as surprisingly staggered. The chapters are strikingly short but eminently 'digestible'. It is written in an almost direct contrast to Rilke's study of Rodin (1903) that knows of no chapters or even subheadings. But both approaches share two fundamental points. First, Emerson's comment, 'The hero is he who is immovably centred',[28] which could directly apply to Zweig's vision of Rolland, and second, the very first paragraph of Rilke's *Rodin*, which, in turn, is eminently applicable to Zweig's approach, too:

Rodin was lonely before his fame. And the fame that came to him, has made him probably even more lonely. Fame is, after all, only the epitome of all misunderstandings that gather around a new name.[29]

All biographical approaches by Zweig rest on the significance of the 'demonic' in a writer, meaning something inconceivable, unfathomable, a drive of exceptional and ultimately inexplicable force that unfolds its dynamics in each respective work. In fact, Zweig could only write about a particular personality if he felt that the demonic had been at work in it. In the case of Rolland, Zweig singled out the 'demonic industriousness' as the main driving force, coupled with the French writer's humaneness and concern with the sheer 'musicality' in a character.[30] Zweig saw the latter coming to the fore in Rolland's ten-volume novelistic Franco-German enterprise, his 'Beethoven' novel *Jean-Christophe*. Part of Zweig's 'strategy' was to identify early precursors of this monumental work in Rolland's development. He recognised it in Rolland's 'dream of telling the story of a pure artist who is broken by the reality of worldly affairs', a composing idealist in the company of his own former schoolmates, Paul Claudel, André Suarès, and Charles Péguy.[31]

In none of his later biographies did Zweig return to the structure of his *Romain Rolland*, thus making it particularly distinct within his œuvre. To a certain extent, these short chapters indicate 'thresholds' one needs to cross to get deeper into the extraordinary work of this 1915 recipient of the Nobel Prize for Literature. And this structural device seems to befit the period of thresholds in which Zweig wrote his study. Moreover, with the exception of the book on Verhaeren, it is the only major study Zweig produced on a living author and he did so by alluding to elective affinities between Rolland and himself, especially the 'demonic drive' to work, a concern for the suffering 'defeated' individual, and commitment to what Zweig calls 'our sacred home, Europe'.[32]

Photograph by Friderike, with a note on the back: *Two magnificent specimens, each of them a hero in his respective field*
Heirs of Stefan Zweig

Tracing Demons, or How to Approach Greatness

Between the life and work of any artist falls the shadow of their respective historical time.

Perhaps with this in mind, Jules Michelet, one of the founding fathers of modern historiography, claimed in the preface to the second volume of his unfinished *Histoire du XIXe siècle*, written between 1872 and 1874, that the task of the historian is to 'exhume the unduly forgotten dead for a second life'.[1] For Zweig, who had been familiar with Michelet since his student days, mainly through his work on Taine, biography was the most effective means of accomplishing this macabre task. But by the early 1920s, in the immediate aftermath of the First World War, when Zweig found himself at the beginning of a decade brimming with creativity, history itself seemed to have reached a stage of dilapidation. For good measure Zweig felt compelled to write a pamphlet-like article on the 'tragedy of forgetfulness' (1919), preparing for himself the ground for a multitude of biographical essays, or essayistic biographies. Symptomatically, it was in the final phase of Zweig's life that the problem and meaning of writing history came back to him. His thoughts on the subject he was to present on his 1938–9 lecture tour through the United States – that is to say, to the 'New World'.

One cannot but speculate what Zweig would have made of a comment by the Russian poet Osip Mandelstam, who in 1922 argued that the novel, if understood as a braiding of biographies, had come to an end – for the Europeans had been catapulted out of their biographies. He compared them to balls which collide on the billiard table in accordance with the principle that 'the angle of incidence equals the angle of reflection.'[2] It is telling, though, that Mandelstam regarded

Rolland's epic *Jean-Christophe* as the last word on the great tradition of the biographical novel, originally produced in the shadow of the Napoleon phenomenon. In Balzac's novelistic cosmos, for instance, the one hero or protagonist was then fragmented with the emergence of a multitude of characters, foreshadowing the pre-eminence of the plenty in a growing anonymity of the masses. For Zweig, this was precisely the reason he insisted on elevating the individual in his biographical and novelistic work. With it, he attempted to counteract the massification of culture.

(Tragic) personality and biography

In terms of what 'biography' could mean, Zweig remained discerning. When in 1920/1 his study of Marceline Desbordes-Valmore was finally published, together with some translations of her poems by the then late Gisela Kühn-Etzel, he gave it the subtitle 'Lebensbild einer Dichterin'. It literally means 'life picture of a poetess'. There are implications for the way in which Zweig understood 'life-writing' as it suggests that life can be captured in a verbal image and that the literary image, or picture, can enliven the memory of a person. In his biographical writings Zweig differentiated between *Lebensbild* and *Bildnis*: the latter referring more to the portrait of a person, where *Lebensbild* implies a life-oriented intensification. The latter category Zweig was to apply, too, to his biography of Romain Rolland (1920), whilst he termed his biographies on Joseph Fouché (1929) and Marie Antoinette (1932) *Bildnis*.

Zweig's concern for the individual at that time owed much to his regard for identity, but needs to be viewed in a specific context, in parts defined by what Sigmund Freud termed in 1919 'the uncanny', or rather, 'the unsettling' (*das Unheimliche*), or demonic, with explicit reference to E. T. A. Hoffmann's novella *The Sandman* (1817). Furthermore, there was the powerful verdict on the end of Western, or 'Faustian', civilisation in Oswald Spengler's seminal work *The Decline of the West*. Its first part (*Form and Actuality*) appeared in summer 1918 and its second part

(*Perspectives of World History*) in 1922. As George Steiner pointed out, Spengler's conception of culture and civilisation ought to be seen as a direct response to the German defeat in the First World War, together with a drastically diverse array of works consisting of Ernst Bloch's *The Spirit of Utopia* (1918), Franz Rosenzweig's *The Star of Redemption* (1921), Karl Barth's *The Epistle to the Romans* (1922), Adolf Hitler's *Mein Kampf* (1925), and Martin Heidegger's *Time and Being* (1927).[3] In these works, the individual seemed to disappear. It was up to the novelist, and indeed the biographer, to reclaim some territory for the individual, whereby the divergence in opinion of what constituted a biography was just as drastic. This approach spanned from the aftermath of Julius Langbehn's notorious study *Rembrandt as Educator* (1890), which had reached by only one year after its first release a spectacular thirty-eighth edition, to the works of immensely popular biographers Jacob Wassermann and Emil Ludwig on Christopher Columbus (1929), Kaspar Hauser (1908), Rembrandt (1923), Goethe (1920), and Napoleon (1924), and Friedrich Gundolf's biographies on Goethe (1916), Stefan George (1920), and Heinrich von Kleist (1922) to mention but a few. Biographies on Paracelsus (1927), Caesar (1924), and Shakespeare (in two volumes – 1928) were to follow – the latter as a major addition to Gundolf's earlier groundbreaking study of *Shakespeare and the German Spirit* (1911). A former close disciple of Stefan George and professor of literature at the University of Heidelberg from 1916 until the late 1920s (he died in 1931), Gundolf found himself on a platform that secured him a truly diverse student audience: from Hannah Arendt to Golo Mann; from Claus Schenk Graf von Stauffenberg, who attempted to kill Hitler on 20 July 1944, to Joseph Goebbels, then affiliated with the communist (!) student movement. Gundolf's conception of biography rested on literary works representing forms of life, thus gaining enduring vitality directly from their authors' lives. Emil Ludwig favoured a distinctly psychological approach to his 'objects of greatness', which appealed to his growing readership in the United States of America – to where he, a resolute opponent of National Socialism, emigrated from Switzerland (he obtained Swiss citizenship in 1932) in 1940 having helped in compiling anti-Nazi propaganda.

Not that he had engaged with the works of either of those mentioned, but they were the backdrop against which Zweig regenerated his biographical interests, endowing them with essences of his very own conception of life. It meant that, for the time being, his novelistic fiction took second place.

With Ludwig, Zweig shared a strong lenience towards psychologically motivated biography but also a deep admiration for Walther Rathenau, the German–Jewish industrialist, politician, and writer, the assassination of whom by right-wing radicals in June 1922 sent shockwaves through Germany. Rathenau, at the time of his assassination newly appointed German foreign secretary, could have easily been the subject of a biography by Emil Ludwig – perhaps to a lesser extent by Zweig, given that he preferred to devote his biographical skills almost exclusively to figures of the past, with the notable exception of Rolland. We have already seen how instrumental Rathenau's advice to Zweig was back in 1907 when he suggested that he explore India and the Americas. Since then, the future early icon of the new German Republic had acted as advisor to the kaiser and, much to the envy of France and Britain, effectively organised the raw material supplies in Germany during the First World War. Incidentally, Rathenau refused to come out as a critic of the destruction of parts of Leuven and Reims Cathedral. He saw it as collateral damage of warfare, even though Zweig eventually asked him on behalf of Romain Rolland to distance himself from such military actions. Rathenau even defended the submarine warfare in 1917 but became openly critical of the kaiser, even before the revolution of 1918, for not abdicating sooner. From then on, he advocated peace, constructive negotiations with the Western Allies, and support for the League of Nations. Thus, internationalism had become to him a matter of humane patriotism, a view emphatically shared by Zweig. However, as mentioned before, the radical nationalists in Germany branded Rathenau a 'fulfilment politician', vehemently resenting him for allegedly 'fulfilling' all demands of the Western powers. The hatred generated against Rathenau led to his assassination by right-wing radicals. Before him, key representatives of the political Left like Karl Liebknecht, Rosa Luxemburg, and the

Bavarian prime minister Kurt Eisner were brutally murdered: likewise the more liberal finance minister Matthias Erzberger, denounced by the radical Right as another key 'fulfilment politician'. During the duration of the Weimar Republic from 1919 until 1933, some 300 politically motivated murders were committed in Germany. When Rathenau was assassinated in his car on his way to the Ministry on 24 June 1922 the democratic forces in Germany saw in him the martyr of the Republic; so did Zweig and Rolland. The latter commented in a letter to Zweig from Villeneuve only one day after the assassination:

> These wretched insane characters! Out of raging love for Germany they have killed the country's greatest men – those for whom other peoples envied the Germans! And they did not realize that those deplorable murders would plunge Germany in an even deeper and [more] irreparable defeat than the one that was afflicted to her by the fickle fortune of the arms. (RR/SZ, II, 692)

News of this atrocity affected Zweig profoundly. In his two long replies to Rolland he was full of praise for Rathenau and did not hold back his vitriolic criticism of the situation in Germany: 'I detest politics: What devastates me is the triumph of brutality over the mind [...] This canaille, in its nationalistic idiocy, wants nothing but eradicate independent thought in Germany' (RR/SZ, II, 693). Following these events he could not even bring himself to spend time at the German coast for he feared that the whole country had been penetrated by sympathisers for this assassination. 'I would be disgusted to see all these banners along the coastline; I cannot look at these people at close range if I am supposed to love the idea of the German people and to preserve the image of the greatness of its culture' (RR/SZ, II, 695).

The novellas of life

When mystery takes effect a particular kind of life begins – this wisdom, captured in an untitled poem that prefaced the novelistic cycle *Amok*

(1922), informs both Zweig's biographical essays and fiction throughout his career. It captures the intrinsic connection between 'life' and the 'demonic' that he came to regard as essential for an understanding of the unpredictability of human activity emerging from what he termed 'the underworld of passions'. To a certain extent, Zweig's growing preoccupation with biographical projects, particularly on Hölderlin, Nietzsche, and Kleist, was to serve this purpose – to remind his readers of what German cultural sophistication was (once) 'really' about. He was to publish his take on this trio in 1925 under the title *Der Kampf mit dem Dämon* (*The Struggle with the Daemon*); it was preceded in 1919 by a distinctly European trinity of *Drei Meister* (*Three Masters*), his essays on Balzac, Dickens, and Dostoevsky. But as pointed out already this did not mean that he neglected fiction. The 1920s saw some major novellas written by Zweig and it is worth examining at least a few strands and themes that his biographical essays and novellas shared. On balance, it is fair to say that both genres competed in Zweig's mind and on paper. 'Demons' were present in both cases and exorcising them through writing posed similar problems, with one major difference: according to Zweig, the writers and objects of his biographical essays were themselves driven by their demons and were able not to domesticise but instead 'articise' them, as it were. By contrast, the characters in his fiction had no compensatory outlet for their respective demons or inner forces. They remained exposed to what drove them – mostly into their tragic downfall. In Zweig's mental cosmos, the attribute 'greatness' was reserved for those who were able to live with their demons.

It would be quite wrong to argue that only the new domicile in Salzburg with its favourable living conditions generated this new wave of productivity. Admittedly, the topographically elevated position of his baroque villa – his home in Bath and his final domicile in Petrópolis shared this raised position – somehow reflected his heightened social status and allowed him, by post-First World War standards, to lead a privileged and extremely comfortable life. But he remained as restless as ever. It appears that there was another force at work that 'drove' him: the desire to connect with his pre-war period and to build, at least for himself, bridges across the horrific rupture of the World War. This comes across in Zweig's emphasising that what he was able to present to his publisher, Kippenberg, was a 'closed cycle' of works, some of them originating in the time before 1914.[4] The other 'bridge' between times past and present was Zweig's biography on Rolland, together with a different kind of 'bridge': the first volumes of a new series that he had launched with Insel Verlag, the *Bibliotheca Mundi* (*Library of the World*). This was Zweig's attempt to realise the essence of Goethe's notion of *Weltliteratur* as a way of connecting cultures. The conception of the series and editorial supervision was his. Such was the importance he attributed to this project that he arranged a particular letterhead for use in his correspondence over matters concerning the *Bibliotheca Mundi*.

Matrimonial domesticity in Kapuzinerberg 5?

Naturally, the most personal of 'bridges' between then and now was Zweig's now confirmed marital status. The registry wedding with Friderike finally took place on 28 January 1920, except that she was not present at the occasion but stayed back in their new Salzburg home sorting her husband's letters and books. Instead of 'here comes the bride', it was their friend and confidant, the writer Felix Braun, who represented her together with two male witnesses. This thoroughly male affair, often mockingly commented on, was the result of two things, in addition to problems with the train connection between Salzburg and Vienna: the peculiar regulations for female divorcées like Friderike in the arch-Catholic federal state of Salzburg and the strong sense of sobriety that Zweig had inspired in her. 'You have weaned me off my sentimentality', his now wife wrote to him one day after the weirdest of ceremonies, cheekily asking him: 'How did you spend the wedding night?' (SZ/FZ, 109). The best thing she had to report was the fact that Thomas Mann had sent him, for his autograph collection, the manuscript with corrections of his novella *Die Hungernden* (*The Hungry*). When sorting his letters, Friderike admitted that she felt annoyed by all his *Frauenbriefe* (letters from females). She made the firm point that his newly appointed secretary, Anna Meingast, could not have possibly done this job for she would have had to be under the impression that a 'Don Juan' had employed her. Even though (or perhaps because) Meingast, who lived close by in Linzergasse at the bottom of Kapuzinerberg, remained his loyal helping hand, Friderike's relationship with her was strained.

On the whole, Zweig seemed to have been more absent than present during the first year of marriage in their splendid home, where it was, as said, mostly on Friderike to look after renovation work and other mundane things – such as preventing the Salzburg magistrate from enforcing the quartering of people seeking accommodation, mainly refugees from Austria's by now former Eastern provinces. Zweig, while on a wandering tour through northern Czechoslovakia with his brother Alfred, gave her detailed instruction of how to rearrange the house should there be an inspection: three typewriters should be put side by side so to create the illusion of there being an actual office for three female typists; papers and books should be heaped up strategically so that more living space should look like a study; the larger rooms should be declared as unfit to be heated or partitioned. Eventually, a considerable sum of money was paid to the magistrate for Kapuzinerberg 5 to be spared from any such enforced intrusion. In June and July 1921, Friderike was busy organising the meeting of the English section of the third congress of the Women's International League for Peace and Freedom. The venue was the Mozarteum in Salzburg, and she was able to report back to her 'dear Stefan' that at the official opening praise was heaped on her for this achievement. Madame Rolland gave a paper and Zweig's old friend Pierre Jean Jouve took lodgings in the Zweig 'residence'. Selected few were invited to a garden party in the substantial grounds of Kapuzinerberg 5, all in the absence of the 'lord of the manor'.

Interestingly, there was indeed a permanent lodger in the Zweig villa: Johann Tanner, a local policeman, who was to look after their safety. In 1922, he was succeeded by his colleague, Franz Schirl. That is to say that both Zweigs must have felt security to be an issue. Further support in this direction came when the couple acquired an Alsatian named Rolf, whom Zweig referred to as his 'son' as an equivalent to his two stepdaughters – who naturally also resided in Kapuzinerberg 5. In other words, quite a ménage for someone like Zweig, who was used to a more solitary existence. Confronted with his elderly parents and tensions between them, Zweig must have felt that there was no such thing as lasting domestic bliss. The account of his stay with his parents back in Vienna, which he gave his 'dear Fritzi' in June 1920, was 'deeply sad', as Zweig's father had by then lost all his friends and his mother was suffering from growing deafness; his father died in 1926. Even being with his brother Alfred, who looked after the Zweig textile business, was a mixed blessing. He found him 'ever worried, anxious and on his way of becoming a loner. He never goes to the theatre, is never in company; his entire life passes without genuine pleasure [...] His disinterestedness in all intellectual matters is almost embarrassing' (SZ/FZ, 112). From our perspective, Alfred Zweig remains rather a pale figure mainly due to the loss of his correspondence with his brother Stefan. He was to become more high-profile in autumn 1937. This is evidenced by the few letters that survived, in which he commented on having to deal with rumours about his brother's separation from Friderike; an alleged affair with his secretary, Charlotte Altmann; not to speak of Stefan's unwittingly accrued tax debts in Austria at a time when he had already been living in England.[5] In both letters he comes across as a clear-thinking, very upright, and genuinely concerned brother, who disliked nothing more than insincerity and having to lie to their ailing mother about Stefan's state of private affairs.

But back to the early 1920s. It was, as ever, rare for Friderike to accompany her husband on his various trips and lecture tours, but he reported back to her about his public successes with lectures on Rolland and Dostoevsky from Berlin, Frankfurt, Wiesbaden, Heidelberg, and Zurich. At least the couple made it to Florence together for about three weeks in spring 1921 on what could be called a much-belated honeymoon. Little 'honey' was left, though, around Zweig's fortieth birthday, when Friderike, as mentioned before, had sent her birthday greetings for the slightly wrong date. More importantly, she accused him, in a letter dated 28 November 1921, of trying to push her 'more and more into a corner', distancing himself from her. Whether it meant an effort or not on Zweig's part, Friderike's 'warning shot' seemed to have had the desired effect. He made it back to Salzburg in time for Friderike's birthday, contrary to her worst fears, and in the following year the couple travelled together to Munich, Leipzig, Hamburg, and to the island of Sylt, as well as to Berlin.

'For my heart belongs to the Dead' (Hölderlin)

In one of her letters in autumn 1920, whilst Zweig spent time, again, with his parents back in Vienna following his father's mild stroke, Friderike reported about Sigmund Freud's comment on his studies *Three Masters*. He had admired the essays on Balzac and Dickens but not the one on Dostoevsky, as he was 'dead certain that D. was not an epileptic but a typical hysteric'. Freud even had claimed that all epileptics were demented, a deplorable misjudgement on his part. These studies, together with a review Zweig had published on a 'diary of a half-adolescent girl' edited by a disciple of Freud's (but, as it later transpired, written by himself), prompted Friderike to be unusually blunt about her 'dear Stefferl's' current work: 'I beg you, leave this biographising alone and live for yourself, and listen to yourself. Do no longer write "about" this and that but solely concentrate on your very own writing even if it will take longer to mature' (SZ/FZ, 117–18). But there was one undercurrent in this letter which makes uncomfortable reading as far as Friderike's motivation was concerned as it displays clear signs of her anti-Jewish resentment, even though she was of Jewish descent herself having converted to Catholicism only shortly before her first marriage to Felix von Winternitz. Zweig, or so she argued, should simply not have written about 'such a Jewish book', as she was nervous about what it would do to his reputation in the Kaiviertel (the Law Quarters of Salzburg), where she assumed quite rightly that there would be anti-Semitic sentiments. She ominously added: 'In this matter we [meaning herself – R. G.] have a different taste. Perhaps you will acquire the same before long' (SZ/FZ, 117). Zweig, however, neither stopped 'biographising' nor writing about 'Jewish books'. But in one respect, Friderike had a point with her remark: Zweig was at his best when he combined life-writing and invention. What he told Rolland about his forthcoming volume of novellas, *Amok*, reflected this approach to 'creative writing': 'At long last I can send you my new book. It contains five stories, in parts written before the war and since reworked. They are taken from my private life, no religious creeds like "The Eyes of the Eternal Brother", [...] not about things actually experienced but rooted in my existence' (RR/SZ, I, 709). He felt free to engage with a 'large novel or a drama' and thought of writing shorter books on artists and writers like Frans Masereel and Stendhal, to whom he felt 'related' in terms of the latter's 'passion for psychology and his cosmopolitanism' (RR/SZ, I, 709).

This correspondence with Rolland belongs undoubtedly to the finest of deeply personal exchanges on intellectual questions, and one never tires going through them repeatedly as it bristles with ideas. For example, the letter of 11 October 1922, in which he announced his new volume of stories, testifies to the sharpness of Zweig's observation of his time and of the intellectual climate in Germany. But there are erroneous judgements, too. For instance, Zweig noticed a general mistrust of the people in political parties given the hypocrisy of their main proponents. Instead, he sensed the longing in people for 'anything that could intoxicate them' – a new idealism given that in Germany, or so he believed, the 'moral attraction of Protestantism, Socialism, and Nationalism' had 'died off'. But he clearly underestimated the danger of this 'thirsting' for new ideals and underrated the resilience of nationalism – and other 'isms', for that matter. He associated new idealisms predominantly with the sudden attraction of 'books of wisdom' by Hermann Graf Keyserling and Rudolf Steiner, realising, though, that their partly Buddhistic, partly anthroposophical dimensions had the hallmarks of religious sects. But he also refers to Tagore and Hesse and the phenomenal print runs of their works. He praises the biographies by Gundolf on Goethe and Kleist, as well as the rediscovery of Hölderlin's works, claiming: 'If at this moment a great personality would emerge, who unified in him Nietzsche's gifts, he would find a new faith' (RR/SZ, I, 711).[6]

Zweig himself was tentatively exploring a 'new faith' of this kind, which took him back to his Indian venture of 1908–9. As we have seen, he gave an account of the religiousness amongst ordinary folks, in Benares for example, referring his readers to the Indian legends in the books of Hindu and Buddhist wisdom. He was clearly taken with the guru-like Tagore effect on Europe and in Germany in particular. To a certain extent, this was triggered and supported by the 1921 publication of Tagore's works in eight volumes in German translation, realised by one of the leading publishers for modern literature, Kurt Wolff Verlag in Leipzig. Tagore's tour through Germany in the wake of his sixtieth birthday, which brought him together with Albert Einstein amongst others, was also the reason Zweig reviewed Tagore's volume *Sadhana*, which he called in a letter to Rolland 'sublime' and '*un livre de sagesse*' – 'a book of wisdom'. The form of his review reflected the value he attached to the work in question; it was written as a dialogue between a younger and an older writer conversing about Tagore's fame, whereby the latter rejects the criticism of the former who is sceptical about the Tagore cult in post-war Europe. The older writer argues that no other intellects had considered so deeply the problem of violence, power, and property than those of India, and Tagore in particular. According to Zweig, this had exposed the entire madness of our European bellicose nationalism and therefore this perspective is indispensable.

An unexpected Indian parable

Zweig's own memories of India and essences of such Tagorian wisdom entered his own 'Indian story', 'Die Augen des ewigen Bruders' ("The Eyes of the Eternal Brother"), first published in the then leading literary journal *Die neue Rundschau* in 1921 and in the following year in book form, almost at the same time as Hermann Hesse's Indian novel *Siddhartha*.[7] In a brief comment to Leonhard Adelt, written probably in mid-October 1922, Zweig says that he had to 'discharge some of the things that concerned me', including this novella, for 'within me, scepticism always interferes with the purely productive drive: mere narration does not provide me with a sufficient thrill' – meaning that, given the complexity of the time, he needed discursiveness that is more than just a 'nice plot'. Still, this novella deserves our attention as it introduces Zweig's notion of the demonic, which was to gain a prominence of its own in the collections of novellas and essays to follow: *Amok* (1922) and *The Struggle with the Daemon* (1925), the latter dedicated to Sigmund Freud despite his criticism of Zweig's Dostoevsky essay. We will return to this dedication and its meaning a little later.

Zweig called his novelistic legend a monument of non-violence and thus 'a creed' suggesting that 'all certainty' in the world 'is dead' – in the case of this legend, certainty in matters of law and justice.[8] One can assume, with some justification, that this legend originated in the two quotations from the *Bhagavad Gita* that provided Zweig with the motto for this second of the altogether five specimens of this genre. In all likelihood, it was through Tagore, whom Zweig hosted in Salzburg when the Indian sage arrived there in June 1920, that he learnt about these quotations. It was to be the only of Zweig's legends with an Indian theme; the other four written between 1916 and 1936 focus on Judeo-Christian motifs. In tone and style, the genre of the legend allowed him to indulge in a deliberately antiquated tone of narration. But one traditional feature of legends, the transfiguration of the main character(s) as a sign of the miraculous in operation, is deconstructed in line with the deconstruction of the meaning of 'doing' that the two quotations of the *Bhagavad Gita* pronounce. The quotations in question, modified by Zweig, come from the third and fourth chapters of these pronouncements by Krishna: 'Not by refraining from action does man attain freedom from action. Not by mere renunciation does he attain supreme perfection. For not even for a moment can a man be without action.'[9] And the second one: 'What is work? What is beyond work? Even some seers see this not a right. [...] Know therefore what is work, and also know what wrong work is.'[10] Zweig's modifications consist of using '*Tat*' instead of 'work', a clearly deliberate reminiscence of Goethe's Faust's association with that concept, meaning 'doing', 'deed', or 'action'. Moreover, he adds a final phrase, which is not part of the original: 'The nature of "Tat" is as deep as an abyss.'[11] If anyone wanted to know where he himself stood in relation to his time, or so Zweig claimed in a letter written to Hans Rosenberg on 6 November 1922, he should refer to this story; such was the extent to which Zweig identified himself with this legend. The ambivalence towards 'action' of any sort was clearly one that was Zweig's very own at the time; for it was only one year before his meeting with Tagore in Salzburg that he pronounced in a letter to his wife Friderike that pure idleness and mere leisure were against his nature, quoting words of the artificial creature Homunculus from Goethe's *Faust (II)*: 'Since I am, I have to be active (SZ/FZ, 112).

The story goes as follows: in support of his King Rajputas, the main protagonist of his legend, the noble warrior Virata, leads at night an ambush attack against the king's brother-in-law and arch-rival, killing countless of the 'Counter-King's' men. It later transpires that Virata's brother, Belangur, was amongst those whom he had slaughtered with his flash-of-lightning-like sword. The dead eyes of Belangur stare at him with a look that penetrates Virata instantly and continues to do so in future. When the rightful king wants to honour his noble knight, he refuses to accept a reward for the action that saved the king but cost his brother's life. Virata's interpretation of what had happened is as radical as it can be: 'Anyone who slayed a human being has killed his own brother. [...] He who was party to the sin of killing is already dead himself'.[12] He rejects the king's offer to become his advisor, for he does not want to have any power, but accepts the position of supreme judge of the realm, which he occupies for seven years. During this time, he never passes a death sentence, weighing up every word and possibility. Even when he is confronted with a mass murderer, he resists the temptation to sentence him to death, although the compelling evidence speaks for itself. Instead, he condemns the murderer to life imprisonment in a dungeon. But the convicted criminal, whose eyes penetrate the judge like those of his dead brother, wants to pay with his life for what he has done and accuses the judge of not knowing what he is doing as he had himself never experienced a punishment of this sort, crueller than death. It is only after the judge, in disguise, changes position with the convicted in the dungeon that he realises that 'anyone who passes judgement on others cannot but commit a crime and thus become guilty himself'.[13] Thereafter, Virata abandons his duties as judge of the country, withdrawing from society altogether and eventually even from his family as he realises he cannot escape the eyes of his dead brother. He is regarded by others as 'the star of solitude', admired by some but despised even by his two sons, who are increasingly embarrassed by their father as an embodiment of inaction. Eventually, he returns to his king asking him for a position at court that does not endow him with any power whatsoever. The king entrusts him with the care of the royal dogs. Looking after the dogs is the only activity that will not generate guilt, unless the guard dogs were to harm an intruder. But Virata dies forgotten by all; only his dogs will howl 'two days and two nights' in mourning their dead carer, but then forget about him too.

Arguably, such abandonment of action and rejection of violence is the pinnacle of Zweig's pacifism as translated into literature. It is as much a concise narrative exploration of those crucial pronouncements of Krishna in the *Bhagavad Gita* as a literary transposition of the Schopenhauerian denial of will. Evidently, both interpretations need to be seen as part of the immediate aftermath of the devastating actions and killing overdrive during the World War. Whilst the Indian legend illustrates the moral dilemmas of action, Zweig's other and very different take on 'Indian' motifs epitomises the equally dangerous 'action' of passion. And with that we have reached the world of *Amok*, one of Zweig's most widely read stories – even inspiring some early filmic renderings. Already in June 1923 – that is, half a year after its first publication – the *Amok* volume had reached twelve thousand sold copies, as 'Stefzi' proudly informed his 'dear Fritzi', as they liked to call each other during periods of endearment – not to forget 'Wutzi', the pet name for their Alsatian.

Passions running amok

If read from today's established post-colonial perspective, *Amok* must raise some eyebrows given the racist stereotypes it offers about India, including the characterisations of young Indian women as 'twittering, fragile little creatures' and 'yellow-skinned, dull-minded' ones at that. Incidentally, both are cases where the translator smoothed over the more appalling phraseology in the German original; there the girls are referred to as '*Tierchen*', 'little animals', and the boy is simply a '*Tier*', or 'animal'.[14] But before we climb on a well-saddled post-colonial high horse we need to acknowledge that what is represented here is a fictitious occurrence of the pre-First World War period, presented from the perspective of a frustrated medic who worked in the 'some wretched swamp-ridden station' in the midst of a tropical forest. By unburdening himself to his fellow traveller on board their ship he wants to deconstruct the latter's illusions about the subcontinent:

> oh, I understand, you are fascinated by India, by its temples and palm trees, all the romance of a two-month visit. Yes, the tropics are magical when you're travelling through them by rail, road, or rickshaw [...] Everyone who comes here dreams the same dream. But then a man's strength ebbs away in this invisible hothouse, the fever strikes deep into him – and we all get the fever, however much quinine we take – he becomes listless, indolent, flabby as a jellyfish.[15]

As is evident by now, the story takes place in sub-tropical Dutch India and is told on a sea voyage from Calcutta back to Europe, where and when we meet the protagonist, a German medical doctor who gives an autobiographical account of how he found himself 'running amok' without having committed a crime.

In compositional terms the story is flawless, with the opening reference to a 'strange accident that occurred in Naples harbour during the unloading of a large ocean-going liner' being demystified only in the final paragraph of the story. While the cargo is unloaded, a lead coffin containing the corpse of the second protagonist, an English lady, plunges irretrievably into the sea; her widower, jumping after it, is rescued, however.

It is one of the narrator's particular characteristics that allow us to identify him as Stefan Zweig himself:

> Odd psychological states have a positively disquieting power over me; I find tracking down the reasons for them deeply intriguing, and the mere presence of unusual characters can kindle a passionate desire in me to know more about them, a desire not much less strong than a woman's wish to acquire some possession. (AOS, 18)

But what follows is less a story of acquiring possessions than an account of what it means to be possessed. The medic's journey back to Europe is in fulfilment of a promise he makes to his superior, who implores the medic to give false testimony in his coroner's report about the reason for the woman's death. The medic testifies paralysis of the heart but, in fact, she had bled to death after a botched abortion performed by a Chinese charlatan. Originally, she had come to the medic in his 'swamp-ridden' station, demanding from him that he should perform this termination of her pregnancy, which he refused. Her pregnancy was the result of an extra-marital affair, which she was determined to keep a secret. We learn that her strange personality contributed to the mystery that surrounded her: 'a woman full of pride and hostility [...] reserved in every fibre of her being, glittering with mystery and at the same time carrying the burden of an earlier passion' (AOS, 38).

Given her social standing, clearly belonging to the white colonial elite, this English lady transfixes the doctor to the point of hypnotising, or rather, eroticising him. He hopes for ultimate intimacy with her but is adamant about not complying with her request. After she leaves, he follows her into the urban depths of Calcutta where he encounters her again, but she rejects him to the point of public humiliation. Eventually, after further frantic searching for her as if he were an amok runner, he finds her on her deathbed following the fateful abortion. She now implores him to keep her secret at all costs, which he goes on to do, knowing that it is due to his refusal to treat her that she is now dying. 'Her secret was her legacy', which is transformed into a guilt complex in the medic.

This lady comes across like an equivalent to Keats's '*la belle dame sans merci*' with an 'impenetrable face, hard, controlled, a face of ageless beauty, a face with grey English eyes in which all seemed at peace, and yet behind which one could dream that all was passion' (AOS, 33). And his reaction? 'I trembled with admiration for her demonically imperious will.' Once the word 'demonic' is found in the medic's account there is no stopping him using it: 'I felt the demonic force of her will enter into me, but embittered as I was – I resisted' (AOS, 35). The 'demonic' is as prominent in this story as are 'amok' and 'passion'. It is as if passion itself is running amok after having caused so much psychological and indeed physical damage.

But in this collection of five stories from the 'underworld of passion', some of which, like *Moonbeam Alley*, we have covered already, the one truly *risqué* is *Die Frau und die Landschaft* (*Woman and Landscape*). In order to learn more about the way in which Zweig designed these narrative masterpieces, which reflect his notion of literary construction, we need to familiarise ourselves with some of their actual plots. In *Woman and Landscape*, we find ourselves in an isolated Alpine hotel in the pre-war Tyrol in blistering summer heat, with no rain in sight. To a certain extent the protagonist begins to feel like the medic in *Amok*: 'I will strip myself naked and say – I ... I forgot all shame in that filthy isolation, that accursed country that eats the soul and sucks the marrow from a man's loins' (AOS, 24). The Tyrolian hotel offers comfortable conditions but even they evaporate in the heat. The result is that 'all my senses had a temperature', a fever that epitomised the one the whole world suffered from. The other consequence is sleeplessness and the 'dangerous copulation of thirsting and drunkenness'.[16] The atmosphere depicted in this story reminds one of the fifth part of Eliot's *The Waste Land* ('What the Thunder Said'), written roughly at the same time, in which we hear 'There is not even silence in the mountains / But dry sterile thunder without rain' and a 'hermit-thrush' that 'sings in the pine trees' when its song is mistaken for rain drops: 'Drip drop drip drop drop drop drop / But there is no water.'[17]

The striking feature of *Woman and Landscape* is that its entire depictions of nature are eroticised, if not sexually charged. From this distinctly and unashamedly male perspective, 'nature' is seen like a female expecting a lover. But then a young female, clearly not of age, turns up in the company of her parents, appearing to him like 'Ophelia at a pond'. He senses something 'demonic' in her, but it takes him some time to realise that she is somnambulistic. In her trance-like state she enters his room before him, leading to an intimate encounter which only just stops short of sexual intercourse: 'I kissed and kissed her and felt as if I enjoyed the great, sultry, awaiting world in and through her, as if the warmth that radiated from her cheeks was the exhalation of the fields, as if the quivering land would breathe from her soft and warm breasts.'[18] It is only then that he becomes aware of being together with a non-conscious somnambulistic human being, 'with a demon inside her' – the original says: '*daß ich da eine Unbewußte nahm*', normally suggesting that he had in fact taken possession of her sexually. All that happens during a thunderstorm and just before the release of tension in massive rainfall. Once again, the demonic comes into play, now as a 'lustful fight of heaven with earth, a gigantic bridal night, whose lust I had been able to share emotionally.'

All seems back to 'normal' the next morning when the girl comes down to breakfast with her parents, engaging in serene childlike chatter, except that her sudden focused gaze on the narrator appears to contain some vague memory of what had happened the previous night. But this serious expression on her face soon vanishes and it is as if nothing had ever happened apart from the nightly rain having cleared the air. The point is, however, that the narrator remains alone with his memory of this curious, if not for him fateful, night that told him something about himself and who he 'really' is.

Reference to the demonic does not exculpate the narrators of these novellas; nor does it make soul-searching self-examinations redundant, as confirmed by the narrator of another of the five stories contained in the collection *Amok, Phantastische Nacht* (*Awesome Night,* in the sense of an 'awesome night' but also one that generated 'phantasy'). The atmosphere and setting are known to us already from one of Zweig's earliest prose pieces, *Spring in the Prater*, as it takes place on Derby Day in June 1913 as recorded by an aristocratic reserve officer, the Baron Friedrich Michael von R. When he dies in the first months of the First World War his family gives these papers to the narrator to authenticate their value. Contrary to the family members, the narrator does not regard them as 'fiction' but an account of what really happened on that day and night, namely the 'uncovering of his soul'.

Thanks to a considerable inheritance, the baron is able to live a life of leisure in Vienna's First District collecting precious glasses, antiques of all sorts, and women. In literary terms he is a relative of the 'superfluous man' as known from nineteenth-century Russian stories: spoilt, indolent, a waste of time and space. Even though he claims in his notes not to have had any idea of literary composition, his own way of writing demonstrates his literary creativity. This is to a certain extent due to his realisation that the material of writing, words, are thoroughly 'ambiguous'. It is this very ambiguity that conditions whatever he thinks or does, if anything at all. The account is written four months after the (fictional) occurrences of 7 June. Time is a striking feature in this account and seems to be the only quality that is not ambiguous. We even get the precise moment that something significant happened on that day: sixteen past three in the afternoon – this is when the baron, sitting on a chair near the tribune of the racecourse, hears a particular female laughter behind him. To the baron's mind, even a particular 'second' can be more 'sudden' than another. In this instance it is the flash of inspiration for a peculiar experiment on the baron's part. Judging from this very laughter, he tries to imagine what the woman would look like that matched this laughter. He calls this the 'pre-lust' of his fantasy, only to find that this phantom image of her in his mind does not, as the reader would expect, correspond with the real woman once he sees her properly.[19] In material terms, his bet pays off as his ticket is on the winning horse. He cashes in a large sum, but it comes with a bad conscience. It is then literally on this ticket that the baron will explore the seedy side of the Prater pleasure grounds and encounter the other social half of society. Squandering his win at the horse races he plunges himself into the masses of the ordinary, if not underprivileged, people. Like nature and landscape in the previous story, he sees in the anonymous mass of people a 'giant female body', which triggers in him the passionate desire to copulate with it.[20] Once again, the text and the baron's observations and feelings are sensually and erotically (over-)charged. Allusions to sexuality are everywhere; even when he is throwing his banknotes in all directions, he compares the moment with a frenzy and ejaculation.

Yet, this ecstatic self-abandonment in the masses is void of any proper communication. In fact, he desires to communicate but finds himself in a clear allusion to Coleridge's 'Ancient Mariner', like someone 'who is dying with thirst on the sea'.[21] Eventually, he discovers in himself an interest in the world of his servant and the janitor, realising that there is a secret in everybody's fate. Suddenly, his indifference is gone, and he finds the story of the death of the janitor's little daughter more powerful a tragedy than any by Shakespeare.

Zweig's collection of stories, published in 1922 under the title *Amok*, contains a series of revaluations – of values and emotions, of life's meaning and purpose. As ever, passion runs riot, arguably never more than in one other piece of this collection, *Letter by an Unknown Woman*. The extent of this passion and self-sacrifice is such that we react to it with incredulity, bewilderment, and the feeling that something incredible turned credible. All characters in this story in letter form are without full name except the servant of R., the well-known novelist from *Awesome Night*, who is called Johann. Namelessness and anonymity are the rules of what was a mere game for the writer whose characterisation in the woman's confession-like long letter corresponds with the way in which Zweig clearly wanted to see himself – at least there and then. This applies in particular to the following passage: 'I have never experienced with a man in his tenderness such devotion to the moment, such exposure and glowing of his deepest Being – '. But, this is followed by a sobering conclusion: 'yet only to extinguish itself into an infinite, almost inhuman oblivion.'[22]

It is on the writer R.'s birthday that he receives this letter, or rather a twenty-four-page manuscript 'visibly written in haste by a strange restless female hand'.[23] It tells the story of an extreme passion that had been building up in an adolescent girl for a young writer, the very addressee of this manuscript, who had moved into the house she shared with her mother. In a case-study-like form of self-analysis she describes in minute detail what this building up of her unconditional devotion entailed. When she finally decides to write this text and send it to R., she had also decided to end her life following the death of her eleven-year-old son, the very fruit of their first physical encounter. Time and again, she emphasises that she does not blame R. for anything, not even for the fact that he never recognised her and had evidently forgotten about her. Even when they meet again, years later, by coincidence in a dance club and he engages her for a one-night stand, he takes her for nothing but a high-class prostitute whom he duly pays, to her horror, the next morning. She is to him merely the attractive nameless one, and one erotic adventure more. She describes that she had to give birth in a hospice for fallen women even though thereafter she is to climb the social ladder, supported by her rich suitors but mainly for the benefit of her son's early education and comfort. At every birthday she had sent R. a bouquet of white roses of the sort he had given her after their first intimate encounter, the origins of which, incidentally, he had never investigated. Now, after R. has read this devastating account, he realises that, for the first time, there are no white roses on his birthday. Instead, he is shattered by what he has read, and tries to remember her but without success. His thoughts, however, remain directed towards something invisible, as if it was a remote piece of music.

Why is it so very tempting with Zweig to read his texts autobiographically? Perhaps because nothing is more over the top than the biographical 'truth'. The sheer authenticity and immediacy of these stories have something undeniably compelling simply because they come across as exaggerated and realistic at the same time. They seem like fantasies: at once wild and controlled, completely uncanny and plausible, one-sided and yet strangely balanced in terms of what they disclose about 'the Other'. Once *Amok* was in the public domain,

Zweig was *en route* towards further explorations of the 'demonic' driving forces behind the works by Hölderlin, Kleist, and Nietzsche.

Interlude with Thomas Mann and the 'Ballad about a Dream'

While he embarked on working on these essays on 27 March 1923, Zweig hosted Thomas Mann in his Salzburg villa on the Kapuzinerberg. On this occasion, Mann's first official appearance in Salzburg, he gave readings in the Mozarteum from his epic essay on Goethe and Tolstoy and from the initial version of *Felix Krull*, the memoirs of a confidence man. It is almost impossible not to interpret Zweig's rarely considered but stunningly revelatory 'Ballad about a Dream' (1923) without reference to this visit. It appears from this ballad that Mann's reading must have left a mark on Zweig. The short but significant stay in Salzburg was part of Mann's reading tour, which led him further on to Vienna, Budapest, and Prague as well as to Spain, where he gave readings at the end of April and early May in Barcelona, Madrid, Segovia, and Sevilla.

The seventeen extensive strophes of this *ballade* are only the more remarkable as Zweig had virtually abandoned writing poetry at that time. Its main theme is presented as a duplicated refrain and repeated nine times – to a certain extent like 'nevermore' in Edgar Allan Poe's 'The Raven' – and takes the shape of an exclamation: '*Du bist erkannt! Du bist erkannt!*'[24] It means: 'You have been recognised' but more pejoratively, in the sense of 'you have been found out'.

In today's terminology, what Zweig addresses in his ballad would be called 'imposter syndrome'. Literature on this phenomenon of 'feeling like a fraud' is extensive but examples of self-critical literary accounts are rare; Zweig's poem is one of the few and deserves some attention, particularly in a biographical context that considers the relationship between life and work as its main challenge.[25]

The first strophe concludes by saying: 'And this dream, that found me strange, / Has recognised me more deeply than daylight could.' To a certain extent, this can be read as a personalised adaptation of 'The

Intoxicated Song' of Nietzsche's *Thus Spoke Zarathustra* ('The world is deep, / Deeper than day comprehend'), which presents an insight into 'depth', though *after* a dream has come to an end.[26] What follows is a feeling of exposure to 'a net of a thousand looks', in which the poem's first-person singular narrator feels caught. This happens in a 'dream room' where the persona of the poem suddenly sees a 'fiery writing on the wall' like Belshazzar: 'You are recognised!' This he internalises, fearing that he has been found out. It leads him to harshest self-criticism of the following kind: 'In vain that I have been the guardian of my heart for forty years – / Most secret vice, dark actions / the alien walls now knew about it.' Uncovered is now 'what I had hidden in a dark coffin, behind words with sheets of lies, my innermost being'.[27] He is pestered by these deeply unsettling thoughts throughout the entire dream. When he finally awakes, he first looks at the wall, realising that nothing is written on it and that he remains unrecognised. He puts on his 'colourful clothes of pretence' and continues to work, deceiving people as if nothing had happened.

Is it possible that Thomas Mann's reading from the memoirs of the trickster Felix Krull triggered this response in Zweig, let alone the way in which the great master of prose tackled the comparison between the two literary giants, Goethe and Tolstoy, whilst Zweig himself may have feared that he might be missing the mark in his attempts to approach the demonic in Hölderlin, Kleist, and Nietzsche? Was his conception of writing essays about them inferior to what Mann had on offer? Regardless of these speculations, 'Ballad about a Dream' remains a singular piece of work in Zweig's œuvre in terms of its self-challenging character. A poem being a poem, however, we cannot simply equate its haunted and profoundly disturbed persona with Zweig himself. As much as he portrayed fictitious characters in his novellas, he tells in his ballad the story of a dream and a dreamer. Yet, the level and intensity of an author's identification with a lyrical 'I' tend to be stronger than with their third-person narrator.

Thomas Mann's lecture, *Goethe and Tolstoy*, repeatedly emphasised the notion of *Sachlichkeit*, or objectiveness, which was indeed different from Zweig's emphasis on empathy and emotional involvement with his object of study and narration. But also, *Goethe and Tolstoy* ended with a 'dream', consisting of German culture appearing like a fugue, 'whose voices serve each other and a sublime wholeness in artful freedom [...] preserving traditions and creating something new from them'.[28]

Wrestling with demons and the meaning of a dedication

The next renowned visitor in Zweig's villa on the Kapuzinerberg was Rolland, who stayed for some ten days in summer 1923. Together, they visited Mozart's birthplace and attended concerts given by the International Society for Contemporary Music. Shortly after Rolland left Salzburg, the National Socialists held their party conference in Max Reinhardt's Festspielhaus, of all places, with the young Adolf Hitler as main speaker. The future demon of the German lands, perhaps by then already preparing manoeuvres that led to the (failed) Munich Putsch on 9 November 1923, was already too close for comfort to Zweig's noble domicile.

Otherwise, Zweig spent the incubation period and a great deal of the actual work on what was to become *The Struggle with the Daemon* travelling. When he was to refer to one of those who had struggled with the demon, Heinrich von Kleist, as a 'haunted one' who had not left out any part of Germany 'nor any direction of the wind' in his restlessness, Zweig certainly spoke from his own experience. Despite his new residence towering over one of the most beautiful of European cities, we find Zweig charging around Germany – from Berlin, where he (half-?) jokingly signed a letter to Friderike from 'your until now still faithful Stefzi', to Westerland on the island of Sylt, Weimar, Wiesbaden, Frankfurt, Heidelberg, Nuremberg, and Munich, and in the company of Berta Zuckerkandl back to Paris in spring 1922. Zuckerkandl belonged to the cultural set-up in Vienna-Döbling and was friends with everybody who was anybody in the Viennese modernist scene – from Gustav Mahler to Gustav Klimt, from Hugo von Hofmannsthal to Max Reinhardt and Arthur Schnitzler. She was not only one of the co-founders of the Salzburg Festival but also the sister-in-law of the French president, Georges Clemenceau, thus was as well connected as one possibly could be. Her background was that of the liberal Galician Jewry, with her father, Moritz Szeps, having been an influential newspaper editor and publisher. In Paris she and Zweig took part in the launch of the illustrious *Cercle littéraire* while in Berlin – just a few months earlier he found the city 'insufferable' to the point that he felt he could not give readings there anymore. As he wrote to Friderike, he felt 'nauseated' there by all the busybodies, the hectic toing and froing in all matters of an over-speedy life. 'You should see', he wrote to Friderike three days before his fortieth birthday in 1921, 'how quick the Berliners are even when it comes to making erotic arrangements. This all happens clip-flap without much fuss, directly straight into the matter. Like in a carousel people enjoy the speed of things, a delight and nausea at the same time' (SZ/FZ, 131). To Zweig, Berlin was lacking in mystery; it was the place of the cut and dry anti-demonic, which one also had to know to appreciate the quality of the demonic even more.

Focusing on these 'demonic three' – Hölderlin, Kleist, and Nietzsche – meant taking sides and, to a certain extent, risks. With his major essayistic portraits, together with his suggestions for a *Bibliotheca Mundi*, Zweig was in the business of canonisation. But his 'canon' was distinctly different from the established ones at the time, at least in the context of German literature, as he favoured those who had been sidelined for too long. Interestingly, there are no substantial essays by Zweig on Goethe, Schiller, Gottfried Keller, or Adalbert Stifter but, surprisingly, also none on Georg Büchner or Heinrich Heine. His biographical essays on Hölderlin, Kleist, and Nietzsche, however, stand out, also because they represent his most extensive texts on German authors, whereas the preponderance in this genre is with non-German ones. In fact, it was Friderike who entertained the idea of writing something for children about 'Weimar at Goethe's time' herself when she visited, alone, this iconic place of German culture in November 1922 (SZ/FZ, 141). Symptomatically, she pointed her husband to a female outsider of the Weimar set-up at Goethe's time, Luise von

Göchhausen, the lady-in-waiting to Duchess Anna Amalia: one of Goethe's confidantes and helping hands, yet physically disadvantaged due to her shortness and hunched back. Friderike found it strange that one had never made anything of her in literary terms. True, neither did Zweig take up Friderike's hint, nor was Thomas Mann to make use of her later in his Goethe novel *Lotte in Weimar* (1939).

Even though the dedication of his book *The Struggle with the Daemon* would have been the final touch in Zweig's composition, it is the obvious first thing that his readers take note of when opening the volume. Zweig dedicated the book to Sigmund Freud with the following specification: '*dem eindringenden Geiste, dem anregenden Gestalter diesen Dreiklang bildnerischen Bemühens*' (or, 'to the penetrating mind, the inspiring shaper, this triad of a pictorialising endeavour').[29]

The meaning and implications of this dedication are threefold in themselves, for they suggest the penetrating quality of Freud's thought, refer to him as an inspiration as well as quasi-artist, and reflect a specific quality of these three essays: as seen at the beginning of this chapter already, Zweig preferred the word '*Bildnis*' to 'biography', thus emphasising the visual dimension of his undertaking, but not without granting it a musical dimension in the resounding shape of a triad. The suggestion is that psychology and artistic variety join up to come to grips with the extraordinary complexities of these three personalities in question.

The overarching conception of these biographical essays turned out to be architectural, as what Zweig called the objects of his threefold engagement (*Three Masters*, 1922: Balzac, Dickens, Dostoevsky; *The Struggle with the Daemon*, 1925: Hölderlin, Kleist, Nietzsche; *Three Poets of their Life*, 1928: Casanova, Stendhal, Tolstoy) is sometimes translated as 'master builders of the spirit' or as a 'typology of the spirit' – three times a triad. Central to the conception of this essayistic composition is Zweig's programmatic foreword to the second volume of his trilogy of triadically structured volumes.

Zweig was not the only one who thought in terms of literary triptychs at the time. As it happened, it was in June 1925 when Thomas Mann, too, decided, erroneously as it worked out, that his next project after *The Magic Mountain* should be 'a triptych of novellas, based on the lives of three historical figures: the Old Testament Joseph, the Renaissance humanist Erasmus, and Philip II of Spain'.[30] It was also in this foreword where he generated the notion of the writers in question being 'master builders' of the world, and their respective worlds in particular, which he hoped to show as nothing less than a 'typology of the spirit'.[31] *Joseph*, however, famously was to turn into a novelistic tetralogy, *Philip II* he left to his protagonist, the peculiar historian, Dr Cornelius, in his novella *Disorder and Early Sorrow*, and *Erasmus* turned into one of Stefan Zweig's finest biographical accomplishments. This interest in triadic structures seem to occur when a sense of stability is to be generated. It goes back to the early nineteenth century, when the 1770-born triad Hölderlin, Beethoven, and Hegel pursued this structure as an expression of secularising the notion of the Holy Trinity, enjoying, or so it seemed, the sheer rhythmicality of triadic sequentialisation of thought and expression.[32]

But back to the foreword to Zweig's *The Struggle with the Daemon*. Since it encapsulates his thoughts on the meaning of the demonic and prefigures his approach to writing biography, we will consider it in some detail instead of looking at these essays individually, since they present their readers with different case studies of but one main concern: to show the shaping of individual lives as literary artefacts and writing as a mode of living.

In this foreword Zweig categorically states that he was 'not looking for formulas of intellectualism' when writing these essays but wanted to 'create forms of intellectual and artistic processes'.[33] He reminds his readers of the comparative method of biographising as first introduced by Plutarch. Bringing these essays together happened, or so he argues, in the manner of painting. It meant taking Horace's *ut pictura poesis* (as painting is, so is poetry) principle to another level, namely that of the actual composition of biographies by means of contrast and complementariness.

From his correspondence with Rolland at the time (in particular, a letter of 1 April 1923) we get Zweig's explicit comments on what it was that motivated him to embark on this project. In Hölderlin, Kleist, and Nietzsche he saw 'three demonic characters, the only ones in Germany who did not pact with society, the nation, and their period in history, and therefore were destroyed.' With his book, Zweig wanted to 'proclaim the freedom of the artist, the heroism of suffering' and provide 'a great paraphrase on the demonic'. The psychology behind what Zweig already envisaged as his next volume would be presented as a 'matter of courage, to see and speak the truth'. The point of making such long-term plans was for him to hold something up against the 'fluctuation and agitation in the world of today'. In this respect, and in the way of writing biographies, he called himself Rolland's student and his most recent essayistic study on Gandhi, published in instalments in the newly launched journal *Europe*, a model and measure for his own ambitions. Zweig being Zweig, the sensual, if not sexual, analogy is never too far away. He told Rolland that his way of presenting a personality causes sheer happiness in the reader. 'It must resemble the feeling of a woman when embraced by a man, penetrated and impregnated' (RR/SZ, I, 733–6).

Interestingly, with reference to Thomas Mann, whom Zweig 'respected as a character in terms of his integrity and as a wonderful artist', we read in the same letter about Mann's visit to the Kapuzinerberg that they had 'chatted a lot without completely understanding but also without misunderstanding each other' (RR/SZ, I, 736). Before Rolland, who was still suffering from the aftermath of the Spanish flu, had visited Zweig, he went to London accompanied by his sister, met G. B. Shaw, John Galsworthy, and H. G. Wells, and spent time with the ageing Thomas Hardy in the West Country, commenting on just how detached the English intelligentsia was from what was going on in Europe. We even learn about Rolland's dietary requirements before his visit to Salzburg and know the train he took from Zurich to Salzburg on 30 July 1923, which took a staggering fifteen hours all in all. (Zweig warned him not to come through Bavaria on his own as he feared for the safety of French travellers given the over-heated political climate and nationalist hype there, pointing out to his friend that he would find everywhere posters barring French and Belgian customers from entry into hotels, post offices, and restaurants (RR/SZ, I, 753).)

The question was (and still is), how to be 'heroic' in times of mediocrity, conformism, and collective frenzy? Hence, we find Zweig quoting the opening of Byron's *Don Juan*, 'A hero, I want a hero!' – preferably of Gandhi's quality in Rolland's interpretation and with Hölderlin's, Kleist's, and Nietzsche's 'demonic' substance (RR/SZ, I, 735).

In the programmatic foreword to his trilogy, Zweig defines the demon as the embodiment of an inner fermentation that pushes our 'otherwise quiet Being towards excessiveness, ecstasy, self-expression and self-destruction'. He ascribes a 'volcanic' quality to it, causing a perpetual restlessness in humans. Without the demonic, or so Zweig claims, there can be no great art. But, as Goethe's example shows, there can be a balance between demonic and anti-demonic forces at work. And it is Goethe who serves Zweig as a backdrop for his essayistic 'pictures' of his three demonic protagonists. He suggests that for Goethe it was the circle that provided the appropriate illustration of what he was after: the emblem of rounding off experiences and endeavours, the image of 'returning to oneself with the line of the circle denoting an equal distance between infinity and the centre point, always suggesting growth from within. The demonic, however, is like the parable in geometry: a speedy upward movement followed by a steep decline, in short, a cataclysmic movement.'[34]

What, then, are the striking, or dominant, features of Zweig's 'demonic three'? In Hölderlin, it is the might of the rhythms he perceived as the attribute of freedom in culture and indeed art; Hölderlin is portrayed as the eternal stranger in a world that understood nothing better than to produce alienation for those who refused to comply with expectations and social norms.[35] With Kleist, it is the force of exaggeration, the feeling of being violated by one's own demon, the incessant attempts on producing plans for life only to burn them in the fire of one's own emotions; yet Zweig called him a 'sleepwalker of feeling', exploring the unknown in utter restlessness.[36] And, finally, Nietzsche, the Orphic thinker who felt that he was 'born posthumously'. Zweig saw him in 'perpetual dialogue with his nerves', a man who discovered the value of illness and the will to health that would lead him to 'invent' his own well-being.[37] His demon made him recognise the passion for unpicking deceptions about the truth of, and behind, life.

While Zweig was finishing the second triad of his 'master builders of the world' trilogy he worked on more novellas, most prominently on *Confusion*, prepared his *Collected Poems*, and, as ever, travelled. Travelling relaxed him, as he told Rolland in July 1924. In the same letter he explained that after a change of scene he would return to 'his "Hölderlin" and "Nietzsche"' (RR/SZ, II, 39). To another correspondent of his at this time, a young writer and editor with the endearingly Swabian name Otto Heuschele, he spoke of the stunning 'strength of solitude' (III, 103) that he had detected in these three poets, coupled with their uncompromising 'will to the unconditional' (III, 92). It appears that Zweig regarded all these qualities as components of the demonic, too.

To Zweig, the question of what it is that makes a man a hero remained alive and strangely vital. It included self-contradictions. Whilst, as we have seen, he originally was not prepared to sacrifice everything to artistic work, he now professed, following news of the death of his friend, the composer and pianist Ferruccio Busoni, that his form of heroism was the way in which he gave everything to his art: 'a rare quality in our disillusioned world', he added in a letter to Rolland of 5 August 1924 (RR/SZ, II, 41). The other example was, to him, Lenin, or rather Maxim Gorky's mode of writing about him after his death. Zweig commented on the exemplary 'plasticity of Gorky's depiction' of the revolutionary leader. He mentioned this to Rolland, hoping that his friend would return to his dramatic cycle on the French Revolution and the tragedy of its main protagonists – to a certain extent an equivalent on stage to Zweig's three demonic poets. Incidentally, Rolland's *Robespierre*, the final part of his dramatic cycle on the French Revolution, would be his last work for the stage, published in 1939 in Paris and, interestingly, first performed in Leipzig in 1952. On Bastille Day in 1939 the Comédie-Française took his play *Le Jeu de l'Amour et de la Mort* (*The Game of Love and Death*), part of this cycle, into its repertoire, after its French premiere in 1928 and its first publication (to great acclaim) in Germany in 1925. The play was dedicated to Stefan Zweig.

Zweig (not) in Weimar

One extended unpleasant episode in Zweig's relationship with Germany's cultural heritage sails under the flag of 'Weimar' and mainly belongs in the 1920s. Although meticulously researched in recent years, this episode is rarely mentioned in works on Zweig, but it deserves wider attention for it provides a nutshell of the cultural and therefore always political climate in Germany at that time.[38]

Zweig's interest in Weimar as the hub of German, if not European, classicism is obvious given his works that betray intimate connections with Goethe (as reflected by several references in essays written and published in the 1920s and his novella 'The Elegy of Marienbad' as part of his collection *Decisive Moments in History*) and to an even more intensive extent with Nietzsche, who had died in Weimar in 1900 in the questionable care of his sister, Elisabeth Förster-Nietzsche, not to speak of her ensuing forgeries of her brother's works. Less obvious, yet demonstrative, was Weimar's disinterest in Zweig in the 1920s and early 1930s. He never received an official invitation to give a reading or hold a lecture there. As a private individual Zweig had visited Weimar often, for instance in 1911 and 1913 as well as in 1925 with Romain Rolland. In fact, it was during the latter short stay in Weimar that both visited Nietzsche's sister, who had surprisingly appreciated Zweig's biographical essay on her brother. It appears, though, that both sides avoided any sensitive topics, such as the conservative nationalism that dominated the atmosphere in Weimar then, let alone Elisabeth's rampant anti-Semitism (racist pamphlets by Elisabeth's late husband, Bernhard Förster, entered National Socialist doctrine directly via Hitler, with whom Elisabeth met on several occasions). At least they were able to enjoy the *Jugendstil* ambience in Förster-Nietzsche's Villa Silberblick, designed by Henry van der Velde, a close friend of Émile Verhaeren's. The cultural climate in Weimar was further dominated by the anti-Semitic literary critic Adolf Bartels and Hans Wahl, then director of the otherwise highly reputed Goethe and Schiller Archive and the Goethe National Museum. In short, Zweig had a clear atmospheric foretaste of things to come whenever he visited Weimar in those days.

Furthermore, he would have received news in 1926 when the National Socialists held their party congress in Goethe's town, on which occasion the young Baldur von Schirach founded the Hitler Youth. Incidentally, Schirach's father had overseen the Weimar National Theatre until 1918.

Zweig's main connection to Weimar was with the specialist librarian and literary scholar Alfred Bergmann, who at some stage was scheduled to produce a catalogue of Zweig's autograph collection. Even when Bergmann informed Hans Wahl of the imminent dissolution of Zweig's collection, the Goethe and Schiller Archive did not acquire the Goethe autographs from this collection. One cannot but assume that Weimar felt these autographs, too, were tainted because they had been in Jewish hands.

A collage that speaks for itself
Fremantle/Alamy Stock Photo

Towards European Transnationalism

Forging alliances against the rise of fascism was clearly at the forefront of Zweig's mind in those years. Both the (health-wise) mostly resilient Zweig and the ever-ailing Rolland were constantly on the move in the mid-1920s, at times travelling together. The highly cultivated Czechoslovakian president, Tomáš Masaryk, received them both in turns; Rolland attended the celebrations in Vienna for Richard Strauss's sixtieth birthday as well as music festivals in Cologne and Leipzig. In spring 1924 Zweig was again in Paris, where he met publishers but also Salvador Dalí and renewed his acquaintance with James Joyce.

In late spring 1924, in Boulogne-sur-Mer, Zweig, the reluctant modernist, read Proust, whose 'subtle psychology' impressed him. But he was not overwhelmed by what he saw, as noted in a letter of 5 August 1924:

> All of his characters are, in principle, not terribly interesting because their true human life is all too dominated by the trifles of the 'high society'. I don't think that with Marcel Proust a genuine creator has left us as he was rather a fine and sophisticated psychologist. I can visualize him very well without having known him personally. (RR/SZ, II, 40)

Zweig says '*raffinierter Psychologe*', which can indeed mean 'sophisticated' but also 'sneaky' and 'clever'. The interpretative choice is ours but in one respect, he – as an advocate of the absolute in his 'demonic heroes' – is unambiguous about Proust: rightly, Zweig detected in him 'a spontaneous application of Einstein's theories of relativity' (RR/SZ, II, 40). In any case, the subject matter of relativity concerned him.

After a rare period of – by his standards – prolonged illness in spring 1924, during which he was bed-ridden for one week, Zweig explained to Rolland that he had time for 'unexpected readings and dreams', as only illness and travel 'are the two powers that can rip us out of our continuities and all too daily routines.' It was during this period that he had 'studied new theories about the non-existence of the present and the all-relativity of the world', to him not much more than 'illustrious toying with words and ideas'. This led him to an almost Goethean approach to knowledge: 'My intellectual curiosity refers to things that I can grasp [also in the meaning of sensual comprehension – R. G.] what I see and what I don't want to see I can no longer grasp' (RR/SZ, II, 22). He called this thought a 'rare excursion into the garden of philosophy'.

Zweig confirmed that he had been dealing with such matters and reading biographies about English Romantics, most likely Rudolf Kassner's biographical essays on *English Poets* (1920). This was to 'forget the times we live in', especially 'the political stupidity' that prevailed in Germany – by which he meant the pathetic trial against the right-wing coup plotters of Munich on 9 November 1923, which ended with the acquittal of General Ludendorff and a farcical punishment of Hitler. When Zweig met friends in Paris who were organising collections for the needy in Germany, he was tempted – or so he told Rolland – to tell them:

> Don't deceive yourselves. Germany is still a hotbed of war, and perhaps it would be the only good policy by Europe a cruel one, namely, to appoint a commission that would ensure that Germany could never rearm and protect her from her own political moronism. (RR/SZ, II, 23)

Germans, Zweig feared, did not want to be free, preferring to obey (RR/SZ, II, 23–4). At the same time he knew that it was in this very country where his works had a chance of finding a readership of rarest sophistication, a paradox and dilemma that Zweig shared with his fellow writers, virtually all of whom were to find themselves in exile after 1933.

With Byron, Shelley, and Keats against the political nonsense in a precariously unstable German (and Austrian!) democracy, it is the traditional pattern of behaviour for many a writer, then and later, to assume that 'culture' can save our political souls. As far as Europe was concerned, Rolland pointed out to Zweig that she looked like a once-beautiful old lady – following Rolland's recent visits to Vienna and Prague. He argued that it was high time for Europe to realise that 'on the chessboard of politics' she played at best a subsidiary part by now, whereby he admitted that it was difficult for her to grasp this devalued function in the world given her centuries-old pride (RR/SZ, II, 43). Rolland also did not expect much from the United States in terms of cultural rejuvenation given the country's naked materialism and power-mongering in the Pacific. In this respect, Rolland, like Hermann Hesse and others, had directed his hopes firmly onto Asia, and India in particular, as he made clear in his book on Gandhi, which turned into a world bestseller. Zweig was to follow suit with his works, which made him one of the most widely translated German-language authors in the twentieth century.

To be sure, we are in the year 1924, which was one of Zweig's other 'French years' with three extended stays in Paris, Boulogne-sur-Mer, and Amiens, with his friends Frans Masareel and Léon Bazalgette as fixtures during these visits. France remained his second home in terms of culture and mentality, even though Marcelle as far as one can tell had firmly ceased to feature in his life. At any rate, there are no traces of her, except in the shape of Zweig's continuing interest in the female psyche, a motif that was to stay with him to the very end.

During this period different concerns, interests, and occurrences of all kinds overlap and compete. But this 'reluctant modernist' could come up with thoughts that would turn him into a backwardly oriented prophet. This could happen even in short review articles on minor writers like Erwin Rieger and Paul Wertheimer – the latter, incidentally, a friend of the painter and writer Oskar Kokoschka, whose innovative style of portraiture Zweig had recognised in his account of a landmark exhibition of pictorial art from Vienna, which was on display in Zurich in summer 1918.[1] At the end of this review of August

1921, mainly on Rieger's novel about contemporary Vienna, with the symptomatic title 'Die Zerrissenen' ('The Torn Ones'), Zweig wrote: 'Austria never managed to find a tragedian and hopefully her destiny will never turn out to be so forceful for her to create one.'[2] By then, the bringer of tragedy from, and for, Austria was in the making.

The 'good European'

'Europe' was to Zweig not an abstract concept but the ever-growing result of cultural endeavours, often against the grain of the nationalistically narrow-minded politics of the day. After 1918 Zweig increasingly looked for personalities that generated, and engaged in, cross-national cultural activities. 'Europe' therefore, according to Zweig, depended on the ethos of values and their personifications. One such embodiment of the 'homeland Europe' Zweig identified in the Danish literary historian and *homme de lettres* Georg Brandes, as testified in his homage when Brandes turned eighty in spring 1922. In it, Zweig argued that Europe had again been reduced from 'our highest spiritual concepts to a merely geographical one' by the senseless antagonisms between her peoples. He spoke of the 'brotherhood of the great minds', which Brandes had investigated in his works on the *Main Currents in Nineteenth Century Literature* with detailed references to trends in Russia, Scandinavia, Italy, Germany, Belgium, and England, thus counteracting the political madness that had raged in Germany, England, and France at the time. He saw in Brandes, who for the first time recognised the 'genius of Nietzsche', the ideal representative of the latter's conception of the 'good European.'[3] The idea of the 'collective individual', which Zweig was to develop further in his speech in Florence on 5 May 1932, gained shape here for the first time, although in reverse weighting: Brandes, the superior scholar of comparing literatures, who was able to distil specific themes of commonality *and* difference, represented through his scholarship the ideal of a European cultural collective.

Whether Zweig himself was consciously trying to live the life of a 'good European' belongs to the realm of speculation. In his pursuit of identifying 'good Europeans' as counterweights to the destructiveness of nationalist frenzy – even during the so-called 'Golden Twenties' – he would not limit himself to great individuals (of the past). In his tireless networking and support for younger writers he, like Hermann Hesse, precisely served this very ambition. Even when his own career, thanks to by then already countless translations of his works, was nothing short of glittering on an increasingly international parquet, Zweig would encourage, if not mentor, talented but hitherto unknown writers. Among them were Erich Ebermayer, Walter Bauer, and, later, Richard Friedenthal. But it was, as mentioned before, the twenty-four-year-old Swabian Otto Heuschele whose *Letters from Solitude* he graced with a substantial afterword about the rapidly disappearing art of writing proper letters. His brief characterisation of Heuschele is telling for what Zweig associated with the future of any writer: 'He lives in a small German town [that is, Waiblingen, near Stuttgart – R. G.], but his heart is leaning at the heart of the whole world where it is beating the loudest' (III, 127). But this heartbeat of the world with its cosmopolitan rhythms must be transferred into the quietness of reflection as provided by the form of the letter, or so Zweig argued. For Zweig, nothing was unworthy of his attention that contributed somehow to transnationalism, even though he ultimately shied away from unreserved support for Count von Coudenhove-Kalergi's conception of Pan-Europa and its actual movement. But, in principle, he found the Pan-Europa idea 'necessary and immensely sympathetic as long as it would one day not be directed against Russia and Asia', as he put it in a letter to Rolland of 25 October (RR/SZ, II, 187). He was then referring to the third Pan-Europa congress in Vienna (1926), which was followed by a string of events all over Europe to promote the spirit of transnational cohesion. Surprisingly, Zweig found these kinds of activities rather futile and felt that only a small circle of dedicated Europeans could make a difference. By then he regarded cosmopolitanism as 'morally without any value', for it folded like a pocketknife whenever there was a real war, as he explained in a letter to Siegmund Warburg on the day of the Vienna congress (25

October 1926). Remarking on Tagore's exhaustion following his recent European tour, Zweig even decried 'the nouvelle manie' of European writers like Thomas Mann and Paul Valéry to travel as missionaries of the European spirit, calling it even a *'maladie contagieuse'*, an infectious disease, which made writers of this eminence 'compete with film stars' (RR/SZ, II, 187). This, coming from Zweig, was a bit rich given his at times frantic travelling and lecturing literally all over the place.

Zweig's 'good Europeanness' consisted indeed of travelling for the sake of working and, in so doing, joining up different hemispheres – for instance in November 1925 when he travelled to Marseille, where he worked on his free adaptation of Ben Jonson's *Volpone*, or *The Fox* (1605/6). In February 1926 Zweig would celebrate Romain Rolland's sixtieth birthday with lectures in several German cities along the lines of what he had done for Émile Verhaeren before the First World War. In early spring of the same year, he was to revisit the south of France, this time accompanied by Friderike, as always somehow incorporating Paris and places in Switzerland 'on the way'.

Volpone in Marseille; the Elizabethan playwright in Zweig's 1920s Europe; the Venetian Renaissance setup with lustful evil characters obsessed with material values, preferably gold, transposed into the 'Golden Twenties', the glitter and affluence of which Zweig mistrusted; social comedy on the importance of being ridiculously serious and seriously ridiculous; and all this topped by the subject of the travesty of inheritance – small wonder that Zweig's comedy was one of his greatest theatre successes. It provided him with additional means to augment his by then already considerable autograph collection. Moreover, it turned the stage into a European space parading all its rotten values.

What Europeanness meant to him becomes abundantly clear from a letter he wrote to Richard Specht, who was preparing a biographical essay on Zweig to be included in the first collected edition of his works in twelve volumes with Wremja publishers in Leningrad; it appeared between 1927 and 1932 with a foreword by Maxim Gorky, who was also the likely initiator of this edition.[4] Zweig was sure by now that he wanted to be noticed by a wider public.

First of all, he suggests to his young friend that he should portray him as an 'initiator', by which he means a pioneer in terms of activities and attitudes, such as his *Jeremiah* being 'the first artistic work in the war against the war'; furthermore, he mentions the joint reading he gave with the French writer Pierre Jean Jouve in Zurich in 1917 and his widely translated first-time monographs on Verhaeren and Rolland, as well as the first major study on Dostoevsky and on the Czech poet Otokar Březina in German. Through works like these he had, 'to a certain extent, overcome the Viennese in him' and attained European dimensions. And there is an interesting stylistic argument with which he supports his transnational ambition. With the book on Rolland, he had known in the first place that it would be translated. With that in mind he claimed to have paid particular attention to the clarity of his language and way of arguing 'because I asked myself with every sentence whether it would be comprehensible and valid beyond German.' He then adds as a *post scriptum*, underlining the significance of the prescriptive guidelines he has given to Specht, 'To me, it is naturally important that your essay brings across how I was aiming towards Europeanness originating in my Viennese background, something I have really achieved in my books and through their translation into all languages' (III, 174–6). Even though the latter point was a slight exaggeration at this stage, the claim itself was certainly not unfounded.

News of the death of another genuine European, the poet Rainer Maria Rilke, came as a profound shock to Zweig at the end of 1926. In his commemorative address, delivered on 20 February 1927 in the Residenztheater in Munich, Zweig was to celebrate Rilke as the 'last pure poet', who had lived a life in creative solitude without the posing and the priesthood-like attitude of the circle around Stefan George. Preceding his memorial speech, he described Rilke in a letter dated 4 January 1927 to the writer and literary critic, Detmar Heinrich Sarnetzki, as the rarest of breeds in our time: a 'lyrical human, one of the finest blossoms of our culture that is unlikely to grow again on the parcelled fields of technology' (III, 179).

'Europe' remained the main focal point in his biographical studies for years to come, including the final part of his trilogy of literary masters with Casanova, Stendhal, and Tolstoy (*Three Poets of their Life*). The purpose of these studies, or so he explained to his friend Victor Fleischer, was to examine 'forms and limitations of autobiography' (III, 197). As collective titles he considered *Stages of Self-Representation*, or *Three Creators of Selfhood*. This preoccupation with the Self was presented by Zweig as a hallmark of European literary culture – with its obvious downside of excessive self-centredness. His European concern culminated in the mid-1930s when he, by then half-exultant, embarked on his biographies on Erasmus of Rotterdam and his double portrait of Calvin and Castellio. As there is no such thing as a 'last word on Europe', these were not his last ones either – as we shall see when we later consider his time in England as from the mid-1930s.

The 'Eurosceptic'?

Ambivalence and contradictions are the hallmarks of a critical mind. By May 1927 Zweig for once seemed to have grown tired of Europe. He wanted to see India again, Russia, and other countries – the further away the better, as he put it in a letter to Rolland of 6 May (RR/SZ, II, 226). The League of Nations had invited him to a lavishly funded conference in Paris, but he declined. Instead, he found echoes of Rolland's maxim resonating in himself: one needs to guard one's own solitude. Unbeknown to both, Rilke had once argued along similar lines but with reference to lovers. According to him, they should appoint each other as custodians of their respective solitude.

With Rolland he attended the Beethoven festivities in Vienna at the occasion of the centenary of his death in 1927. Yet, they left disappointed, mainly because musicologists surrounding the doyen of this guild, Guido Adler, had monopolised and thus 'spoilt' the occasion with the tedious dryness of their lectures: 'Why is it that these professors always want to jostle into the most beautiful things in the world with their scholarly boredom', Zweig asked. A different matter was to listen to Wilhelm Furtwängler conducting the *Eroica* in Salzburg. Zweig speaks of this 'incomparable genius of precision, clarity and strength.' What impressed him was the conductor's 'richness of nuances, coupled with such rhythmic intensity.' To Zweig's ever-sharp and knowing ears, he even surpassed as a conductor the late Arthur Nikisch and Gustav Mahler (RR/SZ, II, 226, 204, 235).

There are a few indicators that help to assess what Rolland called the 'psycho-physiology' of Zweig at this time. The 'intensity' he noticed in Furtwängler's conducting was something that he wanted to appropriate for his own work. He felt he needed to resist distractions that would only lead to proliferation. Furthermore, he grew suspicious of his own overwhelming success. His *Volpone* was exceedingly well received; audiences clearly got the message in the sense that this bitter comedy was the anti-glitter of the season, a critical response to the materialism of the 1920s that was on its way to the Great Crash of 1929.

Rebels began to interest Zweig, such as the German revolutionary and friend of Georg Forster, Adam Lux (1765–93), supporter of the French Revolution and its 'dependency' in Mainz, whose delegate he was in during the short-lived republican Rhenish–German National Convent (1793). Together with Forster, the Convent sent Lux, who had written a doctoral thesis on *De enthusiasmo,* to Paris asking for official sanctioning of the Mainz Republic becoming part of the French Republic. In Paris, he involved himself in the dispute over Charlotte Corday and her execution following her killing of the radical Jacobite Jean-Paul Marat, defending her in a pamphlet with the consequence that he ended up under the guillotine himself. Somewhat in competition with Rolland, whose works on the French Revolution he admired, Zweig researched Lux with the aim of writing a play about him. After conducting further research to that end in Mainz in late November 1926 he wrote to Rolland from there, mentioning the 'thin dossier' on Lux but, most importantly, his lecture about his close French friend, which Zweig had given the day before in 'a beautiful old hall where Mozart performed 200 years ago for the Archbishop', except that he, Zweig, had had a 'larger audience' than this genius of geniuses. But it was in the same letter that Zweig admitted that he had enjoyed 'too much success as of late', which made him wonder how to deal with such permanent success. He even wished to experience setbacks to sober himself up. Working on someone who had written on 'enthusiasm' was therefore clearly the wrong remedy. Perhaps it was consequential, then, that his drama on Adam Lux remained a fragment.[5] 'I need more lively currents to intensify what I intend to say at a later stage', Zweig remarked somewhat mystifyingly (RR/SZ, II, 250). What he meant were influences from outside Europe and outside of literature, of which he had – temporarily – become as weary as of 'Europe'. Hence, he admired Rolland for his friendships with the Bengali scientist and, since 1920, Fellow of the Royal Society, Jagadish Chandra Bose, who studied analogies between plants and animals, professing the 'unity of all life', and Albert Schweitzer, the anti-colonial sage of Lambarene and extraordinary medic, theologian, and expert on Bach's organ music, whom Rolland had known from his schooldays.

This said, Zweig's focus remained firmly European after all, and in mid-March 1929 he delivered a lecture on the 'European idea' in Brussels. Moreover, by the time he abandoned his work on Adam Lux, mainly due to the shortage of source material available to him, another 'rebel' was in the making, again in the contexts of French (post-)revolutionary history and of a new biographical work he had embarked upon – chiefly to his own surprise, the chameleon of power and inventor of the secret police, Joseph Fouché. When he came back to the subject of Lux, albeit sporadically in summer 1928, he explained to Rolland in a letter of 24 July that this subject matter had matured in him since the Russian Revolution. It would take the shape of a 'dramatised biography [...] with no females in it, no word about love, only disappointment about the reality and the contrast between revolutionary ideal and realism' (RR/SZ, II, 290). But a different subject matter took the place of Lux. Zweig gave a first indication of its nature when he discussed his and Rolland's approach to Tolstoy. Almost as an (undated) aside Zweig noted, 'I admire a human who does not attain perfection and is suffering from this failure'.

We find the main character of his new play quite in line with this thought. He called it, in an extrapolation of St Matthew's reference to the rich and the poor, *Das Lamm des Armen* (*The Lamb of the Poor*).

In it, we meet Fourès, a lieutenant in Napoleon's Egyptian military expedition, a decidedly honourable man, who resists being corrupted by power but is eventually forced to succumb to it. *The Lamb of the Poor* turned out to be the last work Zweig wrote for the stage. It is a tragic comedy that centres on Bonaparte in Cairo, who falls in love with Bellilotte, the wife of Fourès. She had followed her husband to Egypt against strict orders from Bonaparte. But now that she is in Cairo, the 'citizen general' sends his unassuming lieutenant back to Paris as a courier on a 'special mission' so to have a free hand for Bellilotte. In Paris, Fourès's brother is supposed to keep him there as long as possible. (Strangely, Zweig dedicated his play to his brother Alfred!) But the English get hold of Fourès's ship and release him from his alleged duties, meaning that he is free to return to Cairo where he is confronted with Bonaparte's *fait à compli*. Soon after, the 'most powerful Frenchman' on the planet returns to Paris, declaring himself 'first consul'. Bellilotte explains herself by pointing out that she, a vulnerable female on her own, without protection, was unable not to 'serve' Napoleon. By then, she is officially separated from her husband, who is offered promotion and a military command elsewhere in compensation for the loss of his wife. But Fourès rejects this trade-off and, in the view of Bonaparte's assuming of superior power over France, declares that he would rather see the English take over Egypt than Napoleon France and his wife. He is first accused of treason but is then sent back to Paris where he tries to mobilise resistance amongst the ordinary people against Napoleon. There, the authorities demand from him that he should renounce any further activities against the first consul in the name of the '*raison d'état*' considering that Napoleon now has to focus on preparing his military campaign in Italy. Once again, Fourès refuses to comply. It is only when Bellilotte, on instigation by Fouché, talks to him that he is persuaded to give in. It is the 'tragedy of resigning' to the inevitable that interested Zweig, the tragedy of the ordinary fellow who is confronted with helplessness. He is the 'lamb', who has been robbed of everything but has retained his dignity.

The rebellion against Napoleon is aborted; for Fourès is neither a Kleistian Michael Kohlhaas, nor a Haitian Toussaint Louverture, let alone a Jean-Jacques Dessalines, who would risk absolutely everything for the sake of a rebellion.[6] Fourès stands for the 'rebellion of dignity', non-violent opposition against authority, and the exposure of the unworthiness of dictatorial power. In that sense, *The Lamb of the Poor* accurately reflected and criticised the move towards unlimited authoritarianism. In overtly political terms, Zweig declared in a letter to his publisher, Kippenberg, on 7 July 1931 that 'Either customs barriers within Europe will be abolished in the immediate future, or Europe is finished' (III, 294).

As far as the reception of *The Lamb of the Poor* was concerned, Zweig was far from hoping for what he had previously termed a desired 'setback' in respect of his successes. On the contrary, once it was out, he wanted to see it succeed. And, yet again, it did – even though the Vienna Burgtheater only staged seventeen performances, which was good but clearly not good enough for Zweig, who wrote to the producer Erhard Buschbeck on 14 June 1930 in strongly ironic terms: 'As I can see, this week, too, you are making your performing schedule only a strictly vegetarian basis, excluding lamb's meat. Has the lamb finally been slaughtered?' (III, 273).

After its premiere in Hanover on 15 March 1930, which Zweig attended, he travelled to Berlin to visit Albert Einstein. This matched his intention to familiarise himself with 'modern progresses in the sciences', even though he deplored the fact that his 'mathematical and biological foundations' were insufficient. At the end of the 1920s, following yet another lecture tour through Germany, he reported back to Rolland in a letter of 21 November 1927 that he was astounded by the economic affluence there: theatres, cinemas, lecture and dancing halls 'were bursting' with people; and they are buying 'left, right and centre – books, paintings, buildings'. This did not look like a defeated nation, Zweig suggested, but like one full of strengths. But he also noticed the shortcomings when remarking on the Germans' appetite for work: 'They work incessantly', he said, which 'ruins their body and soul'. The inequality in wealth distribution also concerned him. The rich, or so he told Rolland, had quadrupled their wealth whilst millions of people were trapped in badly paid jobs. By now, he said, 'the German industrialists have more power than in the days of Wilhelm II.' But what will happen, he asked, when one day this 'incredible German strength will become apparent to others'? And, not only because he was writing to Rolland, he hoped for a true 'alliance between Germany and France', adding: 'I shiver with anxiety when I think of a [new] European conflict' (RR/SZ, II, 259). Ten years hence and Europe would be at the brink of the next catastrophe.

When the Romanian publicist, Eugen Relgis, asked Zweig in October 1930 whether 'he has already noticed something like a "European spirit"', he stated: 'Not really but rather certain common European interests. The large industrial companies have by now agreed matters in practical terms [of supplies and production – R. G.] whilst artists and intellectuals limited themselves to talk about European unity.' He recommended being wary of those who pronounced emphatic pacifist views but were the 'loudest warmongers' between 1914 and 1918 (III, 283). Interestingly, Zweig had written to the very same addressee one year earlier on 8 November 1929 about his doubts regarding the concept of 'humanitarianism', which appeared to him too feeble to cut any ice with nationalists in Europe (III, 257). To a certain extent, Zweig would revisit the problem of 'humanitarianism' when he embarked on his biography on Erasmus of Rotterdam, his 'triumph and tragedy' as he was, tellingly, to call it.

The Russian perspective

Like with Thomas Mann, whose novelistic protagonist Tonio Kröger spoke of the 'sacred Russian literature', Zweig concerned himself with two of its major exponents, Dostoevsky and Tolstoy; moreover, he was even friends with the figurehead of the 'new' Russian literature under Soviet auspices, Maxim Gorky. Not only was it in Soviet Russia where the first edition of Zweig's *Collected Works* appeared, but he also was invited to deliver one of the guest speeches on Tolstoy at the grand festivities to celebrate the centenary of the writer's birth in September 1928 in Moscow. Equally remarkable was that he only learned about this honour after his arrival. He improvised his speech in the great opera house in front of some four thousand people. The following day he took part in the opening of the Tolstoy House and was then taken to the Tolstoy estate in Yasnaya Polyana, where he met members of the Tolstoy family, including his daughter Sascha, who oversaw the country school founded by her father. There and elsewhere on his Russian journey Zweig was in the company of the Ukrainian-born, highly cultured Anatoly Lunacharsky, the then still people's commissioner for education, originally appointed by Lenin. He was a prolific writer along the lines of Marxist aesthetics with major essays on Pushkin, Shaw, and Proust to his credit. His play *The Liberated Don Quixote* had been staged by the Volksbühne in Berlin in 1925. Zweig would have heard the official version of Soviet-style cultural policy from him, probably counterbalanced by what the writer Boris Pilnyak would have told him about the real situation in the Soviet Union. A great deal of what Zweig reported back to Rolland, who was himself expertly versed on Russian matters, seemed to have been based on information provided by Pilnyak, whose prose *The Naked Year* (1922) had given an expressive account of the chaos surrounding the post-revolution civil war in Russia of 1919. Barely one year after Zweig met Pilnyak and following the publication of his novella *Mahagoni* with a Berlin–Russian emigré publisher, he was subject to an infamous hate campaign, which led ten years later to his execution. By then Lunacharsky, too, was disempowered by Stalin and probably liquidated on his way to Spain, to where he was sent as the new Soviet ambassador.

Zweig went on a one-day excursion to Leningrad, retracing Dostoevsky's steps, and found to his satisfaction that his essay on Tolstoy, printed separately in book form, was being sold everywhere. Encounters with Gorky rounded off what he saw as an altogether fascinating excursion. Zweig felt that it needed to be repeated and extended if ever he wanted to engage himself more fully in promoting further links with Soviet Russia's cultural scene. His two letters to Friderike, written from Moscow's Grand Hôtel at Revolution Square, sounded breathless, bursting with short accounts of his activities. But Zweig's most important impressions found entry into two letters to Rolland written in Salzburg soon after his return from Russia, dated 21 September and 3 October 1928 (RR/SZ, II, 296–301, 303–7). He argued that the present Soviet government (in 1928) could not be blamed for the severe economic difficulties Russia found herself in but identified it as a fateful czarist legacy. But he considered the abolition of any freedom of speech a crime for which the Soviet government must take the blame. Likewise, Lunacharsky's (higher) education policy, which privileged the 'sons of peasants and workers' in terms of access to universities to the disadvantage of the children of intellectuals and civil servants, had led 'to suicides of school leavers'. Zweig discussed the implications of the devaluation of the ruble, the ill-conceived engagement in warfare with China over its territory and with the British over the oil fields of Baku; he understood the vital necessity of German industrial investment in Russia, to the dismay of the French and British governments, and repeatedly pointed, if not marvelled, at the 'incomparable ability of the ordinary Russian people to bear economic hardship patiently'.

Zweig's comments on the type of German investment in Russia demonstrated that he was the son of a factory owner after all, and not only his brother Alfred; he clearly saw that the American loans for Germany, provided as part of the Dawes Plan (1924), that were intended to make it easier for Germany to repay war reparations as stipulated by the Versailles Treaty, were in parts passed on to Russia by German industry. Under this scheme the United States gave loans of US$25 billion to Germany to enable the rebuilding of her industrial capacity, so to generate higher tax revenues that were needed to meet reparations – which were, as from 1924, reduced to $50 million per year. (When these short-term loans were called back literally overnight following the Wall Street Crash one year later, further German investments in the Soviet economy were stopped – something that of course could not have been foreseen in autumn 1928!)

This said, Zweig feared the formation of a 'social nationalism' in Russia, as many Russians felt 'betrayed' by the Western powers that seemed to have favoured the czarist regime, albeit in a modified form. Zweig clearly wanted to correct the many 'lies that have become common currency' in the way in which the media in the West report about Russia. Zweig had hardly spent a fortnight in Russia and, with characteristic enthusiasm, wanted to help organise 'congresses and cultural events' with Russian participation in order to produce something 'connecting' between these two spheres within the European continent. For too long, Zweig said, 'mutual understanding has become the business merely of businesspeople, an unworthy haggling, to which we intellectuals have unconsciously contributed some table music' (RR/SZ, II, 307).

On balance, Zweig was clearly impressed by the strenuous attempts of the Soviets to overcome the czarist Russian legacy of an unspeakably drastic social division between the over-affluent few and the impoverished masses. But these efforts did not blind him, like so many fellow writers from Western Europe who were on 'official visits' to the Soviet Union, to the brutal dictatorship of the party officials, let alone Stalin's increasingly iron grip, thinly disguised as 'policy making in the interest of the proletariat'. But, if push came to shove, Russia, for Zweig, remained the country of Tolstoy and Dostoevsky. Still in 1931, when he was asked to summarise what it was that fascinated him about Dostoevsky, he noted the following on a paper only found recently (2021; the addressee is not known):

> Time and again, I read Dostoevsky and always with the same admiration. Because with his psychology he was ahead of his time; and because of his political divinations he had an anticipatory feel for the future [and] he is timelier than ever; his characters are so durable as any of a great writer can be, like those of Shakespeare and Balzac; those who wanted to imitate him were never able to reach the ultimate forming art of his creative power, for his emotional intensity remains unattainable.
>
> The fact that beside him stands like a giant the other Russian colossus, Tolstoy, should not blur our vision for his greatness. The one does not cancel the other. They are like two enormous mountain areas, each of a different formation and geological layering. From the height of the one, one recognises the greatness of the

other. They complement each other like Michelangelo and Leonardo da Vinci, Goethe and Schiller, Shelley and Keats, and their simultaneity in the very same hour and nation has created one of the great moments in the history of thought.[7]

Across the nations such complementariness was possible, too, as Zweig himself and Rolland demonstrated, even though this most intensive of intellectual relationships that Zweig enjoyed was to be put to the test when Rolland, between 1928 and 1931, became too enamoured with the Soviet experiment – at least for the taste of his friend.

Friderike Zweig (1882–1971)
Franz Xaver Setzer

The Torch of Eros, or The Confusion of a Reluctant Modernist

By August 1927 Zweig felt drastically overworked and rightly thought that it was time for a break. While on the domestic front gas heating was installed in his Salzburg villa under Friderike's, as ever, competent supervision, supported by a newly appointed caretaker, Zweig had taken refuge from all the domestic noise and dust in Zuoz in the Lower Engadin – mainly to wean himself off excessive amounts of smoking and coffee. He proudly reported to his 'Fritzi' that he had been doing gymnastics at half past seven in the morning in the freedom of nature, only in 'panties' whilst other guests were still wrapped in their woollen blankets. After a warm then cold shower he would be dried off by 'a pretty assistant'. Unfortunately, in his report about life in the Kurhotel in Zuoz in a letter of 5 August, Zweig could not help but say that all was 'very decently posh, *almost no Jews*, only Swiss and Germans' (SZ/FZ, 191, my emphasis). But only three years later Friderike had reason to report to Rolland that 'Stefan suffers from exhaustion', adding alarmingly, 'He tries to do too many things, smokes excessively, which exhausts him even more and often he does not find the strength to think things through to the very end' (RR/SZ, II, 391).

As of late, Friderike, whom he called at times 'dear child' or even 'Bubili', had been busy compiling with her eldest daughter Alix a comprehensive bibliography of all of Zweig's writings. (By contrast, Suse, the younger child, only wrote monosyllabic greetings to her stepfather, much to his annoyance. She was eventually sent to an English Quaker boarding school in Glad on Lake Geneva. But both daughters remained distant, if not stand-offish, towards Zweig.) Friderike even suggested that a biography should be written about her husband and recommended that their literary friend Erwin Rieger do so. This project was indeed realised and appeared as the first biography on Zweig in 1928.[1] But such noble activity did not spare her from criticism by her 'dearest Stefzi' whenever anything irritated him. And easily irritable he was.

But more was at stake at the time. Periodically between 1925 and 1931, Zweig was in search of the 'great novel', somewhat reminiscent of Franz Schubert's desire to compose 'the great symphony'. By now, Zweig was the master of the smaller-scale novella, but it seems that in any writer who perfects the art of the short story burns the desire to expand and compass a fictitious world more fully, or rather to create a novelistic world of one's own. Zweig's tendency to overwrite at times, particularly in his longer novellas, but rarely in his essays or biographies, was due to his overflowing imagination. His pleonastic style in places reflected his indulgence in verbal imagery and tendency to bask in metaphor. It was his way of demonstrating the sheer delight in sensualising his language.

There is something undeniably physical about the way in which he wrote. To him this seemed to have been the precondition for the literally 'touching' quality of his prose, most prominently in his extended novella *Verwirrung der Gefühle* (*Confusion*, 1927), the title piece of his second major collection, or cycle, of fiction. Arguably, it was a substitute for the 'great novel' he had in mind. When it seemed to come about in the beginning of 1931, interestingly at the French Riviera, where he spent time with his now friend Joseph Roth, it turned into *Rausch der Verwandlung* – meaning 'intoxication', or rapture, 'of transformation' – but known in English under the rather bland title *The Post Office Girl*. It remained a fragmentary novel about a young woman suddenly taken out of her original social context with unexpected consequences, as the main protagonist, Christine, commits a crime to help her impoverished lover, Ferdinand. The fragment was published posthumously in 1982 and, together with Zweig's only completed novel, *Beware of Pity* (1939), inspired Wes Anderson's 2014 filmic comedy-drama *The Grand Budapest Hotel*.[2] But more of that later. For the moment we remain in the late 1920s, with *Confusion*[3] and the original five 'historical miniatures' that changed the world, *Decisive Moments in History*, which both appeared in 1927.[4] It would not be overstating the point if one referred to these novelistic essays on crucial historical occurrences as the eros of the moment, stretched over one day in the story *Twenty-Four Hours in the Life of a Woman*.

And there is more: for instance, the much-underrated fragmentary novella *Widerstand der Wirklichkeit* (*Journey into the Past*), on which Zweig worked sporadically between spring 1924 and the early 1930s, and also the four shorter prose pieces of the *Small Chronicle* (1929), consisting of 'The Unseen Collection' (1925), 'Leporella' (1928), 'Buchmendel' (1929), and 'Episode at the Lake Geneva' (1919), which we have already considered. Amongst Zweig's book reviews of the time, one stands out: his 'Notes on Joyce's *Ulysses*', published in October 1928 in *Die Neue Rundschau*. It is this review that justifies us in referring to Zweig as 'the reluctant modernist', for reasons that will become clear when we examine this text more closely.

The unlikely Joycean

When Zweig met Joyce again in Zurich on 10 October 1918, both were remarkably unafraid of infecting each other with the raging flu epidemic, given half of the city was 'down with the disease and up to a dozen deaths every day'. Zweig noted in his diary:

> Spent the afternoon with James Joyce, the Irish poet, gaunt-looking, stuffy, sharp, clever, but very 'quaint'. He has lived for 14 years in Trieste and loves this city because it did not claim any taxes from him: his poetic work he has begun considerably later, that is he has worked on his novel for 10 years. Now, an Irish Odyssey will appear in a periodical without his having completed it – strange circumstances also given the fact that no printer in England was willing to take his work. He appears an odd man out and like all such ego-fools he is only concerned about himself: in 14 years of living in

Trieste he did not even go to Fiume, Agram, or Vienna; here, too, he lives completely in a cave. (Tb, 328)

Ten years later, and six years after the publication of *Ulysses* in its first German translation, Zweig read and wrote about what Joyce, clearly another 'good European' from Zweig's point of view, had announced to him during that Zurich meeting. Before he sat down to accomplish this challenging task, Zweig mentioned to Rolland in a letter of 25 October 1926 his most recent reading:

> Nothing much of significance. But for entertainment I only read Jack London and Joseph Conrad. There are times when I am tired of psychology and I want to read like a child reads fairy tales, proper plots, miraculous adventures; at times like these one page of Proust, and even Dostoevsky unnerves me.

In matters of psychology, 'I practice it myself by reading about lively lives, that is biographies.' He then alluded to a biography of 'a Renaissance musician and murderer', that would interest him but whose name he had forgotten (RR/SZ, II, 187). The musician in question was, incidentally, Gesualdo. On balance, though, all this did not really prepare Zweig for any appreciation of *Ulysses*.

Like with his best reviews, with this one on *Ulysses*, too, Zweig sought contact with the reader.[5] As seen before, he did so occasionally through presenting his thoughts in the form of dialogue. With this review of *Ulysses*, however, he tried to generate interest by way of structuring his text with the use of cunning keywords: 'manual for reading', 'genre', 'origin', 'face', 'art', and 'summary'. One could title this review 'From bewilderment to admiration', as Zweig initially obtained the perspective of the bemused reader, who cannot make head or tail of what he is reading. In a rare spurt of irony, the 'manual' recommends obtaining a 'solid position', given the weight of the volume together with all the patience and sense of justice one can muster, before embarking on reading this novel in a decidedly comfortable chair. This is followed by the question as to whether *Ulysses* is a novel

THE TORCH OF EROS, OR THE CONFUSION OF A RELUCTANT MODERNIST   181

at all. It is made to sound like a rhetorical question given that he saw in it a 'witches sabbath of the mind, a gigantic capriccio, a phenomenal cerebral *Walpurgisnacht*.' What follows is a cascade of qualities, of which the 'filmic' is the first and foremost. Scenes speed past the reader's eye with 'ingenious details' – a hitherto unseen parallelism of layered thoughts and emotions, an 'orgy of psychology' with sudden application of slow motion. On offer is a 'tarantella' of impressions, subtleties, and banalities, 'theology and pornography'. Zweig calls it mind-spinning prose, placing the reader for hours on what feels like a roundabout. But at this point we get an indication of the reviewer Zweig beginning to admire what is before him:

> there is the consciously modernistic verbal music by James Joyce, which lends itself here to one of the cleverest language orgies in any known tongue. There is something heroic in this book and, at once, something that parodies art lyrically [...] something unique, unrepeatable, and new.

Under 'origin' we find Zweig's assumption that there must have been something violently evil that had happened to Joyce back in the Dublin of his youth, starting with the 'gloriously taboo-free autobiography of Stefan [a self-identificatory spelling of the first name on Zweig's part!] Dedalus' in *Portrait of an Artist as a Young Man*, followed now by this 'cruelly analytical Oresteia of the soul'. Zweig perceived in *Ulysses* boundless cynicism, resentment, and a vibrating temperament.

The 'physiognomy' of this novelistic composition offers an 'interpretation' in line with Zweig's ever-biographising interest. When remembering Joyce's facial expressions between reading sessions of *Ulysses*, he detected in it strong features of a 'pale suffering fanatic with a quiet voice, a tragic eye behind over-cut spectacles', who regarded 'his hatred and blasphemy as something sacred', a man 'who had suffered as a teacher in the Berlitz School, a treadmill for the mind' and whose twenty-five years of exile and austerity 'had made his art so sharp and cutting.' Zweig identifies greatness in this face, but the real greatness is in his hatred, 'only redeemed by irony'.

From then on, in the paragraphs called 'art' and 'summary', Zweig displays a firework of appreciative comments that try to match the 'firework' of Joyce's colourful language, or should one say 'languages', as Zweig points out what he calls Joyce's 'orchestra' of vowels and consonants with all imaginable registers of language – from gutter jargon to dialects and scientific vocabulary, nothing short of 'verbal acrobatics'. Zweig was struck by this manifestation of what he saw as a 'pan-European Esperanto', the language of *Ulysses* as the *lingua franca* of Europe – Joyce could not have hoped for more extraordinary a review and resumé: 'In the history of English prose a new chapter begins with James Joyce, of which he is at once the beginning and end.' *Ulysses*, or so Zweig concluded, is incomparable. Comparisons with Homer were 'as lopsided as the Leaning Tower of Pisa'. In terms of Zweig's 'fantasy of visions' and exaltation he saw Joyce in proximity of Dostoevsky, only to arrive at the conclusion that *Ulysses* is like an 'erratic bloc', a meteoric solitaire in the landscape of literature, which commands 'respect', a word repeated three times at the end of his review, which by itself is a unique piece in contemporary responses to *Ulysses* and in Zweig's rich palette of reviews. His own fiction, however, shows that he was able to admire Joyce but without showing any traces of being influenced by him.

(The eros of) *Confusion*

For genuine authors, creating a text is a lasting encounter between the author's self and the Other in him or her. Hence it must at least be part of their biography, like any other turn in their lives. Zweig in the mid to late 1920s proves the point, for instance through his story *Vierundzwanzig Stunden aus dem Leben einer Frau* (*Twenty-Four Hours in the Life of a Woman*).

Given Zweig's connoisseurship of French literature, there is a likelihood that he knew Constance de Salm's novel *Vingt-quatre heures d'une femme sensible* (*Twenty-Four Hours in the Life of a Sensitive Woman*, 1824) at the time when he devised his novella *Twenty-Four Hours in the Life of a Woman* (1927), a century after de Salm's sensually provocative narration.[6] It seems too obvious for words that this very title, save Zweig's omission of the word *'sensible'* (*'empfindsam'*, or 'sensitive'), should have influenced Zweig's conception, for which there is, however, no conclusive evidence. At any rate, the intriguing difference between the two pieces of fiction is that de Salm's is epistolary in design whilst Zweig offers a coherent narrative in the shape of his protagonist's reminiscence. Whilst de Salm's *Vingt-quatre heures* proposes to examine how many letters on the intoxicating and confusing effect of love and jealousy a 'sensitive female' can write in the course of one day,[7] Zweig's novella offers the experience of a particular moment that seems to extend over one day, containing a recalled moment of the past. It is the story of an Englishwoman, Mrs C., on vacation on the French Riviera, who suddenly feels compelled to unburden herself on the narrator by telling him a story that had taken place twenty-four years ago. The suddenness of this urge is triggered by an incident in the hotel where Mrs C. and the narrator find themselves: the wife of a guest and mother of two daughters elopes with a young man whom she had only met the day before. This situation, which is much talked about among the guests, reminds Mrs C. of her own former affair with a hopeless gambler, who eventually committed suicide.[8] His main asset was his exquisite pair of hands. They took centre stage on the roulette table and were the very first thing that Mrs C. noticed about him, as they seemed to act independently from the male to whom they belonged. Evidently, there are echoes of Dostoevsky's story *The Gambler* but with a changed perspective: it is through Mrs C. that we observe the unfolding drama of her trying to help this hopeless case of a roulette addict. But first we learn about her long-standing inability to talk about what happened between them there and then. Mrs C., like de Salm's despairing heroine, is baring her soul before the narrator – or in the case of *Vingt-quatre heures*, to her best friend. But it seems that Zweig, who knew well how to keep secrets about his life, appears himself in the shape of the novella's narrator and Mrs C.'s psychotherapist, as it were, and in the fictitious incarnation of the gambler. In his novella Zweig shows how two obsessions collide: the addictive passion for loving and for gambling. Indirectly he alludes – through describing these passions, which are the real 'protagonists' of his novella – to his obsession with writing. In terms of their intensity, they match the sheer vigour of de Salm's depiction of jealousy in her nameless female protagonist. Both de Salm and Zweig abandon the idea of controlling passions in a Cartesian way; instead, they focus on analysing their nature and effect.

Mrs C.'s secrets make up one of the three novellas that constitute Zweig's 1927 collection *Confusion*. With this collection, Zweig was to score yet another major success as far as its reception and, indeed, sales were concerned. However, in terms of subject matter, male homosexuality, the title story *Confusion* was undoubtedly the most daring, and was received as such.[9] Prior to the first edition with Insel Verlag in 1927, its director Anton Kippenberg asked Zweig for modifications of some more delicate passages, acknowledging however that Zweig had treated this 'most precarious of topics' with admirable subtlety.[10] This view was shared by Romain Rolland and Franz Werfel, but most notably by Freud, who regarded *Confusion* and *Twenty-Four Hours in the Life of a Woman* as 'masterpieces'.[11]

What was it that made *Confusion* so extraordinary a novella? It was indeed not homoeroticism itself that offered an 'unheard-of' subject matter, to use Goethe's over-used definition of a novella once again, but the subtlety of its treatment. Zweig transposes the platonic love as known from the Socratic dialogues into a pre-war academic set-up, but shows the stages of an established professor falling in love with his student and assistant. But the starting point is the latter, now himself a highly regarded philologist, whose colleagues and students have honoured him on the occasion of his sixtieth birthday with a Festschrift consisting of a bibliography of all his works, remembering this well-guarded secret of his life. When he sees the reams and reams of titles of his publications that he finds compiled in the Festschrift, he feels alienated from them. He cannot identify with his life's work, and deep down there is a psychological reason for it.

Part and parcel of this recollection of his student days is his falling in love with his professor's young wife, a sporty, attractive, but somewhat androgynous female. Once again, as so often with Zweig, the reader's temptation to interpret this story as an autobiographical revelation on Zweig's part is almost as strong as the sexual temptations displayed in the narrative. Giving in to such temptation would simply mean to credit the author's imagination with one-dimensional simplicity. Zweig's authorship, as should be clear by now, was of a different kind and calibre. In any case, there is considerably more to this story, as we are not for nothing entering the academic world. First, there is the reflection of the sexagenarian philologist about the pitfalls of his work; this precedes the recollecting of his student days and his troubled, or indeed 'confusing' life in the house of his revered scholar, who had offered him lodgings in payment for work as his research assistant. Whilst the young student lodger falls in love with the lady of the house, the professor does so with the student. But he also exploits his capacity for work and exposes him to drastic mood swings, with the result that the young assistant does not know where he stands and what to make of the situation. Since the professor seems to hope for a cross-gender *ménage à trois* he is much less upset about his wife's feelings for his assistant than the student is himself. Eventually, the professor reveals himself to his assistant and tells him about the traumas of his passion, the humiliations he suffered, and his desperate attempts to overcome his resistance against women. He speaks of the sordid milieus he found himself in, always living in fear that he might be discovered, and his ill-fated attempt to overcome 'all these crooked, intimidated, perverse, fantastic forms in which the sexual instinct, wandering from the usual way, seeks and knows itself in the meaner areas of big cities.'[12] And now he encounters this unexpected 'messenger of male youth' but he 'came too late, at the last sunset hour'. It is their final encounter before the young student leaves what had become an untenable situation. In his study, the professor kisses him:

> It was a kiss such as I have never received from a woman, a kiss as wild and desperate as a deathly cry. The trembling of his body passed into me. I shuddered, in the strange grip of a terrible sensation – responding with my soul, yet deeply alarmed by the defensive reaction of my body when touched by a man – I responded with an

eerie confusion of feeling which stretched those few seconds out into a dizzying length of time.[13]

Zweig's publisher will have had passages like this one in mind when he praised his author's subtlety in rendering this 'most delicate of subject matters'. And subtle it is, only matched by the way in which the professor, a philologist of English, describes his approach to the study of literature as a key to the culture of a country:

> So now do you see why I don't begin my course of lectures in chronological order, with King Arthur and Chaucer, but with the Elizabethans, in defiance of all rules? And do you see that what I most want for you is to be familiar with them, get a sense of that liveliest of periods? One can't have literary comprehension without real experience, mere grammatical knowledge of the words is useless without recognition of their values, and when you young people want to understand a country and its language you should start by seeing it at its most beautiful, in the strength of its youth, at its most passionate. You should begin by hearing the language in the mouths of the poets who create and perfect it, you must have felt poetry warm and alive in your hearts before we start anatomizing it.[14]

Analogously, physicality and emotions must be experienced before they can be analysed. What is advocated here can be termed 'emotive philology', or the poetics of emotion, something with which Zweig was intimately familiar himself.

The third story of this collection of three, *Untergang des Herzens* (*Downfall of the Heart*), is usually given a short shrift as the least accomplished in narrative terms. Freud's verdict stuck that the suffering of the main character, a self-made affluent Jewish merchant named Salomonsohn, was not sufficiently plausible. The story is about an aged father with an ailing heart who suffers from estrangement from his wife and daughter. They profit from, and bask in, his hard-earned wealth but regard him as socially inadequate. When they holiday at Lake Garda, his daughter has a brief affair with one of the smart young gentlemen, which upsets her father to an almost irrational extent, as he sees her morally on a downward spiral. He fears that she will cheapen herself for the sake of fleeting carnal pleasures that are incompatible with his moral principles. Finally, he becomes a recluse, giving away his money to people in need and refusing to have to do anything with his family anymore. Only in utter solitude does he find peace with himself.

Salomonsohn represents an extreme case of someone who comes to radically guard his solitude, even at the price of ostracising himself and turning anachronistic. With his principles, he steps out of time and allows himself 'to sink his heart' further and further. He will die of a 'sunken heart', as it were, but also because of his inability to find the words for what he feels. Notwithstanding Freud's criticism, one can credit this story for its ability to show a man trapped by his deficient communicative faculties. Salomonsohn, too, suffers from 'confusion of his feelings' and their swirling stream in him. The reader's heart goes out for the protagonist's 'sunken heart', so to speak; for it is this very heart that appears to be the main protagonist of this novella. For fear of shame about what his daughter had done – in his eyes she had cheapened herself beyond belief – 'his heart, his dark heart, made no sound and quietly soaked up that strange torrent. Soaked it up like a sponge, became heavier and heavier with it, his heart was already swelling with it, brimming over, it was spilling into the narrow frame of his heart.'[15] At the same time, this story also shows how moral conviction, if as inflexible and dogmatic as in this case, can become an illness.

Small wonder that Zweig would then turn his creative attention to another 'trio', this time representatives of what he termed *Heilung durch den Geist* (*Healing through the Mind*), essentially novelistic essays with the idea in mind to depict psychoanalysis in the context of the history of ideas, interestingly dedicated to Albert Einstein, whom he had met at various occasions around 1930. These essays were on Franz Anton Mesmer, the American Mary Baker Eddy, whose foundation document of Christian Science, *Science and Health with Key to the Scriptures* (1875), Zweig treated with critical sympathy, and Sigmund Freud. Freud's appreciation of Zweig's approach was somewhat tainted by the fact that he found himself in the company of Mesmer and Baker Eddy, but he credited Zweig in a letter of 7 February 1931 that Zweig had clearly learnt a lot about psychoanalysis. Somewhat provocatively, he expressed his assumption that Zweig had 'not known much about psychoanalysis before he had started to write this book.'

In this context it is worth considering another novella on which Zweig was working at the time, *Widerstand der Wirklichkeit* (*Journey into the Past*, 1929), but that he did not attribute to any of his collections, instead leaving it unpublished. As it happened it was to be Zweig's penultimate novella, only to be followed his final masterpiece in this genre, *Chess* (1942). The novelist, biographer, and critic Paul Bailey sensed 'a distinctly Chekhovian air' in *Journey into the Past*.[16] This is fitting given that Zweig was particularly concerned with 'Russian affairs' in politics and culture during the time of writing this novella, even though there is no actual Russian motif in what the original German title intriguingly calls *Resistance of Reality*. In fact, this is one of the few rather abstract titles of any of Zweig's novelistic works, and it can also be read as his very 'resistance' against plain realism in literature. After all, he never grew tired of emphasising the imaginative quality in writing, which, as we have seen, also informed his essays and underlying conception of what makes a biography 'lively'.

At first sight, the setting – this time in Frankfurt – is comparable to the one we encountered in *Confusion*. A young man, in this case a recently graduated chemistry student called Ludwig – the other characters are unnamed – comes into the elegant house of the company director in whose laboratories he is working. He is employed as the director's private secretary and is entrusted with knowledge of all the secret documents of the laboratories. Soon, he develops tender feelings for the director's wife, which are duly reciprocated, but, to everyone's surprise – suddenness is here, too, the name of Zweig's narrative game – he is sent to Mexico to build up a subsidiary industrial plant. The idea is for him to return after two years, but the outbreak of the First World War makes this impossible. The narrator comes up with a term that was to acquire proverbial quality after the Second World War, normally attributed to Churchill in his speech in Foulton, Missouri on 5 March 1946. But Zweig, the unfailing anticipator, or rather, the narrator of *Journey into the Past*, was there first: 'An iron curtain had come down between the two continents, cutting them off from each other for an incalculable length of time' (JiP, 68). It is then, after nine years, that he returns, only to find that the company director has died in the meantime, but that his widow is still devoted to the now not-so-young chemical industrialist. Their re-encounter is intercepted by long stretches of memories, which provide both comfort and annoyance. Because he feels that he 'cannot say anything right to her', the prodigal lover asks himself: 'What makes me keep comparing the past with the present? [...] The past always comes between us, the time that has gone by' (JiP, 104).

The main question that this novella raises is what recollections, memories, do to us. For Zweig, this was to become an increasingly pressing concern given that he was, in principle, an advocate of the present moment, even though 'memory' grew ever stronger in him the more he saw his former world disintegrate and disappear. The narrator's statements on memory are strikingly profound and decidedly poetical, for instance in passages like this one:

> It is not in human nature to live entirely on memories, and just as the plants and every living structure need nourishment from the soil and new light from the sky, if their colours are not to fade and their petals to drop, even such apparently unearthly things as dreams need a certain amount of nourishment from the senses, some tender pictorial aid, or their blood will run thin and their radiance be dimmed. (JiP, 70)

But there is more to these reflections than mere abstract thought. It is testimony to Zweig's art of narration in that he combines a visual impression with a flash of recollection, in this case of two verses by Verlaine which Ludwig once quoted to her during one of their pre-War intimate encounters. First, the visual image perceived by the reunited couple when they find themselves in the old quarters of Heidelberg at night: 'whenever a lamp by the roadside cast its light on them at an angle, the shadows ahead merged as if embracing, stretching, longing for one another, two bodies in one form, parting again only to embrace once more, while they themselves walked on, tired and apart from each other' (JiP, 105). It is at this moment when Ludwig remembers the verses: '*Dans le vieux parc solitaire et glacé / Deux spectres cherchent le passé*' (JiP, 106). ('In the old park, in ice and snow caught fast / Two spectres walk, still searching for the past.') These 'two' can be shadows and/or ghosts.

When Zweig was writing this novella, the past was indeed still the vague destination of a 'journey' that attempted to resist 'reality', although in vain. But worse was to come: the past was about to haunt this ever-restless writer who sought nothing more than tranquillity, albeit for mere moments.

The sceptic
Heirs of Stefan Zweig

Political Ridge Walks

By 1929 Zweig admitted: 'Involuntarily, I become increasingly radical.' Reason being, he was seriously disenchanted with capitalism, which – according to him – was about to 'suffocate Europe' (RR/SZ, II, 323). This he wrote in March, months before the Wall Street Crash. By contrast, and at least some shortcomings considered, the new Russia seemed to offer an ideal alternative to the West's moral bankruptcy. The 'discrepancy between need and affluence' was never greater than now, Zweig claimed in a letter to Rolland on 18 February 1930 (RR/SZ, II, 353). In the autumn of the same year, he added: 'Europe wants to commit suicide as it failed to do so in 1914 for good' (RR/SZ, II, 393).

There is something at once remarkably astute and staggeringly naïve in the way in which Zweig assessed the political situation around 1930; he was often stunningly insightful and never short of realistic foresight, but at times conditioned by wishful thinking. Yet again, Zweig's correspondence with Rolland provides crucial pointers, with both, more than once, controversially arguing over finer political details, particularly in respect of developments in Soviet Russia. What is striking is the mutual intellectual intensity with which this happens. At the time, it was mostly Rolland who felt in a slightly superior position in matters of political judgement, claiming to be better furnished with insider information, particularly about Russia. Rolland was also to express his misgivings about Zweig's, at times, more lenient attitude towards Italian and South American fascism. But both shared a vehement disgust at the German and Austrian variant of fascism. Furthermore, Zweig expressed deep disappointment in the League of Nations and even drafted a manifesto against this institution, which he denounced as a mere 'chatterbox' indulging in diplomatic intrigue. Sadly, it is the very word with which Hermann Göring was soon to defame the German Reichstag and with it the idea of democracy. Zweig called the League an office housing a bunch of 'well-paid sleepy officials without any proper European conviction unwilling to do anything against the rise of Fascism' (RR/SZ, II, 419). Rolland confirmed that all of his friends had also given up hope in the League for the same reasons, expressing doubts as to whether a manifesto of this kind could have any effect whatsoever. By October 1931, Zweig clearly predicted the arrival of a 'fascist Austria and Hitler Germany' (RR/SZ, II, 433). In spring 1931, he read the first volume of Otto Bauer's study *Capitalism and Socialism*, which dealt with ill-fated over-rationalisation owing to the propagated supremacy of the 'spirit of engineering' that would hand humanity over to machines. Forever looking out for potent symbols, Zweig left no stone unturned before he obtained permission to see with his own eyes the massive gold reserves in the cellars of the Bank of France, which appeared to him a bit like the 'Rhinegold' in Richard Wagner's decidedly anti-capitalist operatic tetralogy *The Ring of the Nibelung*. But, in February 1932, he also compared it with:

> Verdun, 28 metres underground, an entire subterranean city, unconquerable, full of provisions for eight weeks with its own water and electricity supplies – above, one could have shootouts in the streets, set the city on fire, throw bombs to satisfy the murderous desires of generals: but down there it will be quiet, gold and shares are properly safeguarded behind steel doors and concrete. (RR/SZ, II, 443)

He was 'grateful to have seen the two poles of our world: the red flag over the Kremlin and the cellars of the Bank of France' (RR/SZ, II, 444). The exact position of the swastika in this world still had to be determined, even though the Italian fascist emblem, the perched eagle clutching *fasces*, or so-called lictor bundles, had its firm place since Mussolini's march on Rome in October 1922.

Zweig's relationship with Mussolini, if one can call it such, is an intriguing one. Like Rilke and others, Zweig saw in the Italian 'duce' a milder version of a dictator – at least until 1938, when Mussolini introduced racial laws against the Italian Jewry and did not do anything to obstruct the annexation of Austria by Hitler's Germany, let alone the subjugation of Czechoslovakia in the Munich Agreement of the same year. Zweig visited Mussolini's Italy in 1930 with Friderike, where he saw Gorky again, who was on convalescence in Sorrento, and spent time in Verona, Milan, Florence, Naples, and Rome. He wanted to see for himself what life in fascist Italy was like and returned in May 1932, lecturing, as mentioned before, on the European idea in Florence and Milan. But there was another reason for Zweig to even get in contact with Mussolini directly. The wife of the anti-fascist Giuseppe Germani, a supporter of the leading Italian socialist Giacomo Matteotti – himself murdered by Mussolini's people – who found himself in captivity without a trial, turned to Stefan Zweig in early 1932 to support her husband. And that he did, namely by writing a personal letter to Mussolini asking for Germani's release. He told Rolland that taking this step was not easy for him, but already on 17 January 1933 he reported to his friend that Mussolini had pardoned Germani. Zweig made a characteristically enthusiastic comment:

> I think I have scored the greatest success of my life, even more than winning the Nobel prize, for I have saved Doctor Germani [...] Despite of everything, I have to admire the energy of this man [i.e. Mussolini – R. G.], who is ruling the world [sic!] but responds so quickly to a simple letter sent recorded delivery. I lay down my arms! I am sure nothing has impressed him more than my sincerity.

And he added that he had not written a single submissive word, which could have compromised him and caused him embarrassment. Interestingly, Zweig had not considered the option of publishing it as an open letter in the first place, but noted that, by design, 'My letter can be published in any newspaper' (RR/SZ, II, 487). In addition to this personal intervention, Zweig wrote another letter to Mussolini thanking him for pardoning Germani, which sounded considerably more 'submissive', and which only came to the surface quite recently. Written on the day when he reported the release of Germani back to Rolland he felt the need to thank '*il Duce*' with the following words: 'Your Excellency, I was deeply moved and immensely grateful when I learnt today about your magnanimity. I feel truly touched by your benevolence.' He referred to Mussolini as a leader of a state, who tried to manoeuvre his 'country through a rough sea into which world history has turned itself.'[1] In May 1932, after his return from Florence and Milan, where it was surprisingly possible for him to speak before a thousand people in the Palazzo Vecchio on his conception of Europe, he summarised his impressions to Rolland as follows: 'One cannot deny that Mussolini with his great intelligence has done a lot of good: the public finances are in better shape than elsewhere, large-scale engineering projects are happening and the optimism hammered into people's minds generates some excellent economic drive.' At the same time, he believed that Mussolini feared nothing more than free speech. He noted that censorship was rife and with it the complete suppression of the press and silencing of any opposition.

This makes uneasy reading, also since Rolland pointed out to him that Mussolini would act in this way purely for tactical reasons. The uneasiness about Zweig's attitude here is not helped when we read Zweig's comment on the presidential elections in Germany in March 1932. He argued that he would have preferred Hitler to win against the geriatric Hindenburg; at least one knew what Hitler stood for, as he explained to Rolland (RR/SZ, II, 451). But he saw the predicament for the German socialists, who felt they had to support the old imperial general, whom they despised, to stop Hitler. Matters are not helped when he 'explained' to Rolland over Easter 1932 the outcome of the German presidential elections: 'I hope', he wrote to his more sceptical friend in Villeneuve, 'that you were not deceived by the newspapers, which call the election of Hindenburg a victory. Truth be told, it is an increasable victory for Hitler. A single man, who emerged from nothingness, managed to score 12 million votes, without support, and forces the Socialists to commit hara-kiri' (RR/SZ, II, 455). Here, Zweig fell for Hitler's own propaganda that presented him in precisely that light: having come from nowhere, relying on nothing but the support of 'the people'. That major industrialists, influential bankers, as well as the eldest son of the abdicated German emperor, Prince Wilhelm, openly supported Hitler was a well-known fact. In the next paragraph of his letter, without any transition, he switched to Pearl S. Buck and her novel *The Good Earth* for lighter relief. But he reported that he had also read a new book about Gandhi by Charles F. Andrews, an Anglican priest and missionary, and friend and supporter of Tagore and Gandhi, who identified himself entirely with the Indian struggle for independence.[2] Perhaps most importantly for Zweig though, he began to 'dream of a book on Erasmus of Rotterdam', which was to become reality only two years later (RR/SZ, II, 457–9).

'I have noticed a certain volatility in your thinking', Rolland remarked at the end of May 1932, and he was not mistaken given Zweig's increasingly ambivalent attitude towards Soviet Russia. By 1932, there was reason enough for such ambivalence, and Rolland would have been well advised, too, to grow more critical of developments in Stalin's realm. For it was on 23 April 1932 that his state Communist Party passed a widely publicised decree that amounted to *Gleichschaltung*, or enforced conformity, between state and literature, demanding from writers total loyalty towards the Stalinist regime. Two years later, and 'socialist realism' as well as partiality of writers had become absolute doctrines, a fact that was not enough to shake either Rolland's, nor André Gide's, H. G. Wells's, or George Bernard Shaw's admiration for the Soviet Union.

However, the more politicised the atmosphere became, the less inclined Zweig was to 'engage' with it. What Zweig had said to Rolland shortly after Walther Rathenau's assassination in June 1922 still rang true to him: 'Politics disgust me.' And yet, Zweig's letters of the time betray an acute interest in anything that occurred on the political stage. The dimensions of his perspective remained global but its focus around 1930 was distinctly Austrian and German. Some of his poignant analyses were truly astounding, demonstrated in his responses to the following four out of six survey questions on the human (political) condition in autumn 1930:

1. *Why is the young generation of today so war-minded?* 'Because of a false inferiority complex when confronted with the forty- and fifty-year-olds, who had experienced the front line. Towards them, they would feel ashamed if they expressed pacifistic sentiments and pretend to be militarists as a sign of their "manliness".'
2. *Are books about the war helpful for generating pacifist beliefs?* 'Unfortunately not. The kind of "romanticism" and excitement the young are looking for they find in those books, regardless of their pacifist orientation. Besides, these books were written by authors who returned from the war and, in so doing, generate hope in the young that it is possible to remain unscathed whilst in combat.' To that, Zweig added a comment that betrays the true writer: 'If only the dead could speak, only their voice would make a real impact' – the implication being: true writers can do just that and turn the dead into witnesses of the horrors of war.
3. *How do I view the present condition of Europe between Revolution and Fascism?* 'What people can least cope with is uncertainty, and this very uncertainty weighs heavy on our world today. Nobody knows what might happen in the next moment, all values are swaying, nothing is stable. But the people desire certainties and thus move unconsciously towards such tendencies or regimes that promise genuine order. For most people, the question whether revolution or fascism will provide it is irrelevant; they all want an end with horror rather than a horror without an end, and no sooner will there be peace until the unification of the states in Europe will provide for some 250 million people a steadier development.'
4. *Do you detect already a European spirit?* To this Zweig replied, somewhat surprisingly: 'Not really. The large industrial companies have managed to unify whilst the artists and intellectuals limit themselves to talking about European unity.' He argued that too many intellectuals attacked other countries over their nationalistic tendencies but not their own. But 'genuine and honest pacifism must first be directed against

bellicose and nationalistic tendencies in one's own country' (III, 282–3).

Furthermore, Zweig insisted on the never-resting quiet voice of the intellect that keeps questioning, and challenging, the impulsiveness of the human (subconscious) drives. When asked about his own work at the time, he referred to his pen portraits (of Mesmer, Baker-Eddy, and Freud), which he presented as moral still images – against the madness of his time.

Regardless of his emphasis on 'steadiness' as a wishful situation, Zweig himself remained under the spell of 'suddenness' even when he decided to keep a diary again. It happened 'suddenly', the first word he wrote down in his entry of 22 October 1931. It was triggered by what he termed a '*Vorempfinden*', or 'pre-sensation', for war-like times, by which he meant 'inner social upheavals' and, in Austria, possibly a fascist 'revolt'. But it was news of Arthur Schnitzler's death that made him aware of the necessity to reflect, again daily, of what was happening around him. The 'disgust of Austrian politics' coupled with his alienation from the reality of national citizenship, which he called an 'artificially galvanised mummy' became, once again, paramount in his thinking (Tb, 343). In addition, only-too-blatant signs of anti-Semitism in Austria appalled him. The most recent one at this time occurred at Schnitzler's funeral when Zweig noticed that no state official was present and 'the University of Vienna was silent' (Tb, 344). He repeated this point in a letter to Felix Salten in early November when he mentioned the consistent snubbing of Freud in Vienna, as well as the fact that both the vice-chancellor of the University and the minister for culture and science abstained when Albert Einstein gave a lecture in Vienna. But observations like these could tempt Zweig to come to rather rash judgements:

> I have nothing against National Socialists who are honest enough to announce on placards 'Jews not permitted'; at least with those we know what they are after. But I hate the cowardice of the Austrian authorities, which pretend that there are no differences and in

closed rooms greet you with phrases like 'My devotion!', yet otherwise display their concern in public that one could mistake them for philo-Semites if they had said anything [laudatory] at Schnitzler's funeral. (III, 303)

Occasionally, Zweig's political judgement was in danger of slipping around that time, for instance when, as seen, he felt that Hitler was the better choice than Hindenburg to become president of the Weimar Republic, or when he regarded the election victory of the National Socialists in 1930 as an understandable rebellion of the youth. For that he was heavily criticised by Klaus Mann, otherwise one of his loyal young admirers; relations turned sour after 1933/4 for a while, when Klaus Mann's exile periodical, *Die Sammlung* (*The Gathering*), to which Zweig had contributed an article for its first issue, turned out to be openly political – that is, anti-Nazi – without prior consultation with contributors. The title of the magazine will have appealed to the passionate 'collector' Zweig ('*sammeln*' in German means both to gather and to collect) as much as the names of its patrons (André Gide, Aldous Huxley, and Heinrich Mann) but, in particular, its promised non-political stance, which seemed to guarantee its wider European cultural mission. Zweig was not alone in protesting against the politicised nature of this newly launched magazine. Thomas Mann, René Schickele, and Alfred Döblin distanced themselves, too, from their affiliation with *Die Sammlung* in messages to the authorities; they did not want to risk their books being banned from sale in Germany nor their publisher, S. Fischer Verlag, coming under pressure. Stefan Zweig, too, had written a confidential letter to his publisher, Kippenberg of Insel Verlag, to that effect but, in Kippenberg's temporary absence, the Insel editor gave the letter to the magazine of the German Booksellers Association for publication without prior consultation with Zweig. He, therefore, felt betrayed by his long-standing publisher and exposed as an opportunist. The rift with Insel Verlag was inevitable, as Zweig explained in a letter to his US publisher Ben Huebsch of 6 November 1933 (IV, 63–4).

But back to 1930. Klaus Mann had published an open letter to

Zweig under the title 'Youth and Radicalism', republished later in his essay collection *Auf der Suche nach einem Weg* (*In Search for a Path*). He attributed such significance to his letter that he also included it in the German version of his autobiographical acount *Der Wendepunkt* (*Turning Point*). It deserves to be presented in full, as Klaus Mann did not beat about the bush:

> There is also something like 'understanding everything', a willingness towards the youth that goes too far. Not everything about youth does point into the future. I say this as I am young myself. A large section of my peers – and younger ones still – has engaged itself with a vigour that should be reserved for forward movements in going backwards. We must not condone that under any circumstances. Under no circumstances!
>
> But you are doing just that when you refer to the terrifying results of the recent German general election as a 'perhaps unwise but, in principle, a natural and by all means welcome revolt of the young against high politics'. Your normally delightful sympathy for anything youthful allows you, I fear, to overlook what this revolt consists of. What is it the National Socialists want? (For it is them that matter in this moment and not at all the Communists!) In which direction does their radicalisation turn? This is what matters. Radicalism by itself is nothing positive, especially not if it manifests itself not exactly rapturously but rowdy-like and without imagination as with our knights of the swastika. ... It is thus a matter of fact that I reveal my very own generation to you, Stefan Zweig, or at least that section of it for whom you have found excuses. Between them and us no connection is possible. At any rate, those would be the first who would refuse such a connection with rubber truncheons. With the help of psychology, one can understand everything – even rubber truncheons. *But I do not want to understand them, I reject them.* I force myself to claim, even though this is against my honour as a writer, that the phenomenon of hysterical neonationalism is of no interest to me whatsoever. I regard it as nothing but dangerous. This is *my* very own radicalism.

People born in 1902 were able to say: '*La guerre – ce sont nos parents.*' But what if those born in 1910 had to say: '*La guerre – ce sont nos frères...?*' Then that would be the time when we had to feel ashamed to our inner core to have belonged to a generation whose drive to be active, thus its radicalism, had turned in such a gruesome way into something negative.[3]

Zweig did indeed always argue from a psychological point of view. But it was true that he suggested towards the end of the Weimar Republic, again in a letter to Rolland in March 1932, that, within the democratic framework of the Weimar Republic, he found it better to have 'Hitler's lunacy rather than lies!' (RR/SZ, II, 452). There is little doubt that around 1932 Hitler at once fascinated and appalled Zweig; sometimes his political judgement could be far off the mark, for instance when he surprisingly stated in a letter to his friend Victor Fleischer of 21 November 1931 that 'the worst for Germany is probably over' (III, 310). At the same time, he feared that a Germany under Hitler would be welcomed by France but would single out Poland as its first victim. As for Austria and the Balkans, he deemed their 'situation catastrophic' in April of 1932 (RR/SZ, II, 456). The 'dream' he held against these auspices was his project on Erasmus of Rotterdam. But he was still busy with his biography on Marie Antoinette.

The impression one gets from Zweig's comments on politics at that time is that he was dramatically wavering between being political and trying to be non-political. He felt mentally unsettled and yet anchored in his work, although not 'serene' enough, as he mentioned in passing to Rolland, to engage in producing a libretto for Richard Strauss, who wanted some kind of *opera buffa*-like scenario from him. When he visited Strauss in his home in Garmisch-Partenkirchen on 20 November 1931, he reflected on what this composer represented for him in one of his longest diary entries during this time. To Zweig, Strauss came across as the epitome of a non-political artist and he puzzled him for one reason in particular: in Strauss he encountered the personified contradiction of his belief in the 'demonic' drive to which, according to Zweig, every real artist was subjected. But the composer puzzled him, for in Strauss he encountered the non-demonic, non-driven artist, who simply invested his musical intelligence into his compositions, coupled with dutiful perseverance. Zweig's letter to Strauss that preceded his visit contained but one indirect 'political' hint: that a work of art should be genuinely 'European' and have 'universal effect' (III, 305). It was to be found in Ben Jonson's *The Silent Woman*. Zweig began work on a libretto version in October 1932.

It seems strange to hear about a writer and prominent figure on the lecturing circuit of the time suffering acutely from what he termed, in a letter to Felix Salten of November 1931, 'publicity complexes': his virtual inability to be seen as a political activist or be celebrated in public (III, 302). Whenever it happened – and nowhere more exuberantly than in the late 1930s in Brazil – he found it too burdensome for words. In exile, he was to admire Thomas Mann for being able to perform in public on behalf of democracy, but Zweig himself preferred not to have to expose himself. Would it be a case of over-psychologising if one assumed that his very different kind of 'self-exposure' before 1914 had spoilt Zweig's appetite for presenting himself, no matter how different the circumstances now were?

However, the real test for Zweig's political stance(s) was to come after 1934 following the dramatic changes in Austria, pre-shadowed by his (former) countryman Hitler coming into power on 30 January 1933. Hitler, who was granted German citizenship by the municipal authorities in Braunschweig only in 1932, following seven failed attempts, had renounced his Austrian citizenship seven years earlier and lived the life of a stateless individual. In one respect, Zweig held possession of Hitler, namely in the shape of an autograph on the outline for a speech Hitler made in Berlin in 1928, which was part of his extensive collection of autographs – in the early 1930s one of the largest private collections worldwide, with over 650 items or so.[4] To a certain extent even this collection was a private 'political' statement, at least in terms of *Kulturpolitik*, as it focused on testimonies of creative processes in European culture.

Last days in Salzburg
Heirs of Stefan Zweig

Life Amidst Crises: Stefan Zweig at and around Fifty

When a man has reached his fifty-second year without being, materially, the worse for wear – when he has fair health, a fair fortune, a tidy conscience and a complete exemption from embarrassing relatives – I suppose he is bound, in delicacy, to write himself happy. But I confess I shirk this obligation. I have not been miserable; I won't go so far as to say that – or at least as to write it. But happiness – positive happiness – would have been something different.[1]

Thus wrote Henry James's 'man of fifty' in his diary under the date of 5 April 1874 – not quite a leaf out of Goethe's novel *Wilhelm Meisters Lehrjahre*, with a chapter of the same title, nor of Stefan Zweig's notes when he turned fifty on 28 November 1931, but an apt reflection of a moment of transition, or rather a threshold from satisfaction to the realisation that 'real' happiness would be something else, next to impossible to define.

By 1931 it appears that Stefan Zweig was in crisis mode, for personal and political reasons, and this was not to change for the final ten years of his life. 'Happy' he was, considering his growing fame as a writer; considerably less happy given his private circumstances. Yet, there was for the time being no younger lady in sight as in Goethe's novel – Friderike remained in charge for the time being – nor was his brief time in Florence, where he had spoken about the European idea, long enough to indulge in reminiscences about previous times gazing at the unmatched beauty of this urban treasure on the banks of the 'yellow river' Arno and its 'violet hills', like Henry James's protagonist. However, he confessed to Friderike that the women in Florence were 'desperately beautiful'. One can only speculate what she made of remarks like this one.

'Objective' concerns regarding the state of the world and atmospheric problems back home in Salzburg – Friderike called their villa by now a 'far too wide overcoat for a freezing soul' (SZ/FZ, 247–8) – coincided in Zweig's perception. He wrote in his diary about his anticipation of domestic 'critical and war-like' times, not to mention the disrespectful behaviour of his two stepdaughters, Alexia and, to a slightly lesser extent, Suse, towards him. By now twenty-four and twenty-one years of age, both had become a source of profound irritation for him, creating an 'atmosphere of stupidity and callous impertinence'. Zweig, personally, and his creativity felt increasingly 'suffocated' by it (Tb, 346). What had triggered the latest spurt of annoyance in Zweig was a sorry episode on New Year's Eve in 1930, which he regarded as a bad omen for his fiftieth year. Zweig was about to show his guests, amongst them the actor Emil Jannings, the precious items in his villa when he suddenly heard gramophone music from the quarter of the house where Alexia and Suse lived, celebrating the New Year with their friends. Zweig had explicitly forbidden them to play the gramophone that night, but they drew their mother to their side and went ahead regardless. Zweig took this as a severe breach of trust between him and Friderike.

Undoubtedly, Zweig was hyper-sensitive, if not excessively touchy when it came to preserving his own sphere. Clashes with Friderike increased in frequency and intensity, during which she did not mince her words either. When reading his essay on Freud, for instance, she commented: 'For the first time I sense that you have once studied philosophy with success (as I often doubt that).' In the same letter, of October 1930, she criticised his personal value judgements and his preference for superlatives, which she regarded – with some justification – as ill-conceived, if not damaging (SZ/FZ, 238). At that time Friderike developed a special interest in the all too deceiving 'scientific objectivity', which she intended to apply to a biographical essay on Louis Pasteur.

Entanglements with Marie Antoinette

Every so often Friderike bemoaned Zweig's willingness to accept more public engagements and to provide more support for people than he could muster – a strange enough phenomenon for a writer who, as we have learnt, was rather reticent when it came to public appearances. Friderike could indeed claim to know him better than anyone else, and in a letter of 5 August 1930 she challenged him on this contradiction, pointing out his anxiousness towards other people and his (false) promises to support them. Moreover, she found his oversensitivity increasingly annoying and 'unmanly', complaining that this sensitivity would not translate itself into affection for her or consideration of her feelings. In short, she accused him of selfishness – in flat contradiction to his otherwise utterly selfless attitude towards people in need. But Friderike was perfectly able to see through even this side of his character when she concluded her letter with the following remark: 'Once before, during the last months in Switzerland, I had to shake you out of your inner discrepancies (on the one hand a revolutionary, on the other hand a capitalist's son). Now, I try to disentangle the discrepancy between a saint and a nervous wreck.' And she added, signing with her endearing pet name, 'Be greeted and kissed and excuse my frankness. Don't reply. I know already all pros and cons. Most heartfelt Mumu' (SZ/FZ, 231). Zweig did indeed not reply to this frank but not entirely unfair assessment of his 'discrepancy'-ridden persona. Still, in the same month she remarked that the only thing she could be sure of with him was that, as ever pleasing himself, he did whatever he wanted. He was an artist after all, and his current main preoccupation was his literary biography on Marie Antoinette. What interested him in this tragic figure Zweig explained in the introduction to his biography:

> The life of Marie Antoinette is perhaps the most single example in history of the way destiny will at times pluck a mediocre human being from obscurity and, with commanding hand, force the man or the woman in question to overstep the bounds of mediocrity. [...] Had it not been for the outbreak of the Revolution, this

insignificant Habsburg princess, who had married a king of France, would have continued, in her cheerful and untroubled play-world, to live her life after the fashion of hundreds of millions of women of all epochs. She would have danced, chattered, loved, laughed, made up her face, paid visits, bestowed alms; she would have borne children, and would at long last have died in her bed, without ever having lived in any true sense of the term.[2]

Zweig ascribed to history 'diabolical cunning' by 'making a spoilt darling of Marie Antoinette' only to stand trial and end up on the guillotine. First, or so one could say, the 'demonic' in her was diluted, but eventually thickened to an extraordinary extent. The very 'discrepancies' of which Friderike had spoken about in relation to Zweig, he saw materialise under his hands when writing on Marie Antoinette, except in an even more drastic form. If ever the saying 'the plot thickens' rang true, it did so in the way in which Zweig portrayed this character that learnt to wrestle with her own mediocrity and, eventually, surpass herself. The final six chapters create the impression of condensation of time and, at once, expansion of emotion. It is this ability of Zweig's that makes his biographies so appealing. The interplay of the acceleration of time and of slowing it down when it comes to capturing individual moments creates a tension that keeps regenerating interest in the plot. Zweig was to excel in this mode of biographical writing in his *Mary Stuart*. The extent to which Zweig found himself 'involved', if not intertwined, with Marie Antoinette's fate became clear when his friend, Carl Zuckmayer, told his wife, after she asked him what he and Zweig had discussed so intently, 'the latest gossip in the French Revolution as he is working on his Marie Antoinette.'[3]

To a certain extent, many of the characters in Zweig's fiction competed in vain with those historical ones to whom he dedicated a biography, or even only a biographical sketch. Whenever he was in doubt about who should take precedent over the other, his fictitious personae, like now the 'post-office girl', had to take a back seat. At any rate, one of the most fascinating aspects of reading Zweig lies in discovering the interrelationship between his fictitious and historical characters, with he himself hovering between them.

As we have seen, Zweig's evolving sense of himself required the extreme experience of a world catastrophe – the First World War. It turned out to a be a drastic catalyst of energies within himself, which expressed itself in pacifist beliefs. Thereafter, the international rise of fascism and National Socialism – or more accurately, Hitlerism, with its rampant anti-Semitism – contributed decisively to his growing awareness of his own Judaism. Consequently, whatever offered itself to him in terms of literary and biographical material, as from the early 1930s, Zweig treated in relation to his time and its traumas. It took him until May 1936 to recognise and express this fact in a letter to Joseph Roth, by now his deeply troubled and burdensome friend, whose demands on Zweig must have driven him more than once to the point of exasperation. Zweig wrote: 'By now I cannot but write things that relate to [our] time and from which something strengthening emerges regardless of the tragical dimensions.'[4] But a precious menorah was not part of his villa's inventory, although it was the subject matter of the last and most substantial of his *Jewish Legends*, more of which later.

The photographs of this time show an always distinguished-looking gentleman, taking his coffee in the garden, sometimes writing *en plein air*, but also sporting his lederhosen with an open-collar shirt and a folkloristic *janker*, to the surprise and quiet amusement or even irritation of his guests.[5] The writer and dramatist Carl Zuckmayer, a good friend during Zweig's last years in Salzburg, was particularly amused when visualising him turning up for a meeting in Berlin in his folkloristic outfit. Quite possibly, Zweig frequented the Gollhofer textile shop – then in Salzburg's Getreidegasse opposite Mozart's birthplace – owned by the very family that would eventually buy his villa on the Kapuzinerberg in 1937.

Symbolically, Friderike had presented Stefan with an iron-wrought garden gate for the lower entrance to their premises, to exclude the outside world from what was supposed to be their retreat and sanctuary. By the late 1920s and early 1930s they were inundated with visitors, but Zweig received many of them in the coffee houses of Salzburg, preferably the Café Bazar right on the banks of the Salzach river. Few visitors were admitted to his villa; even Joseph Roth stayed in the Hotel Stein at the foot of the Kapuzinerberg. Zuckmayer, who lived in Henndorf near Salzburg, surmised that Zweig was living 'up there' amid his autographs and reliquaries, not to forget the company of Beethoven's desk.

During the Salzburg festival season in summer Zweig famously left Salzburg either for the remote North Sea coast or a grand hotel at Thumersbach near Zell am See, to where his secretary had to travel from Salzburg with a typewriter for taking dictations.[6] In summer 1930 Zweig had chosen Hamburg, the 'strangest of all places for summer' as he put it, to continue writing his study on Freud.[7] But in 1933 Zweig broke with this tradition, attended some of the productions, and received guests on the Kapuzinerberg, including the conductor Bruno Walter and the composer Richard Strauss. Photographs and film snippets show a surprisingly relaxed Zweig, reminiscent of the photo taken on New Year's Eve 1932, which he celebrated with Zuckmayer in a public restaurant in Salzburg. The serene pictures of summer 1933 do not disclose what had happened behind the curtains though.

It was, after all, the first Salzburg Festival after Hitler came to power. The festival, later called by Zweig the 'artistic shrine of Europe', heavily relied on visitors from Germany. But following the introduction of a 'law concerning travel to the Republic of Austria', decreed by Hitler in a retaliating response to Austria's decision to declare the NSDAP illegal, Germans wishing to travel to Austria had to pay one thousand Reichsmark. Small wonder that the number of German visitors dropped drastically from 15,681 in 1932 to a mere 874 in 1933, resulting in a near collapse of the festival's budget.[8] Likewise, 'the press boycott imposed by the Third Reich as a further measure against Austria was a serious blow.' Not one of the German music and theatre critics registered for the 1933 festival came.[9] But the Dollfuss government underwrote the losses and extended large subsidies for the festival, as it was now regarded as a symbol of Austrian independence from Nazi Germany. It was Austria's new secretary for education and culture and soon-to-be prime minister (after Dollfuss's assassination one year later), Kurt Schuschnigg, who branded Salzburg and its festival a cultural bastion against National Socialism, notwithstanding his own Austrofascist policies. The state of ideological affairs there and then in Austria could have been labelled political schizophrenia on the political Right, a phenomenon that, to understand, requires some attention in the following chapter to the paradoxical complexities in Austria that drove Zweig and many others to despair and out of the country.

It became clear from the outset that the National Socialists, and Hitler in particular, wanted Wagner's Bayreuth to be the hub of the festival life and not Salzburg, which was intimately connected with the allegedly 'Jewish' legacy of Hugo von Hofmannsthal, Max Reinhardt, and between 1934 and 1937 the staunch anti-fascist conductor Arturo Toscanini. The latter, together with Bruno Walter and Thomas Mann, found himself on the terrace of Zweig's villa. Zweig attended opera rehearsals with his friend, the actor and long-standing assistant of Max Reinhardt, Richard Metzel, who was forced to emigrate immediately after the *Anschluss*.

A fortunate and a troubled friendship

At times of personal crisis Zweig felt, for good reason, that he could rely on loyal friends. He was a master of forming friendships, even though he sometimes struggled to differentiate between who was a friend or a mere acquaintance.[10] Age gaps and rather drastic differences in terms of temperament, style of writing, and outlook on life were no hindrance to him for forming these friendships; one such example was the poet and novelist Alexander Lernet-Holenia, sixteen years Zweig's junior.[11]

As a young poet, Lernet-Holenia had also been Rilke's protegé and Zweig was, in fact, a genuine admirer of his mythologically informed poetry and eventually his prose – most notably his proto-surrealist novella *Der Baron Bagge* (1936).[12] In a letter to Lernet-Holenia, written from Zweig's by then favourite Hotel Regina in Vienna to his friend's villa in St Wolfgang, Zweig called it a 'masterpiece' – and clearly meant it – thanks to the 'positively magical' way in which 'dream and reality glide seamlessly into one another, creating a realm of visionary luminescence, a visual plenitude whose colour derives from fever and coursing blood: you wrote this novella in a state of heightened inspiration such as I have seen otherwise only in your poems'. To Zweig the latter were only second to those by Hans Carossa amongst the German poetry after Rilke. This is followed by the highest praise Zweig was capable of: 'The one work with which I can compare your masterful prose is Hofmannsthal's *Andreas*', which Zweig regarded as the pinnacle of modern prose written in German.[13] Small wonder that Zweig had suggested to Richard Strauss that Lernet-Holenia be his 'successor' as librettist – unexpectedly, though, to the latter's dismay. But there was more to this friendship with Lernet-Holenia than Zweig's praise for *Der Baron Bagge*.

In the second half of the 1920s, in particular, Zweig enjoyed Lernet-Holenia's company. With his dramatic works such as *Demetrius* (1925), *Österreichische Komödie* (1926), and *Saul Alkestis* (1927) this young writer with his elegant and 'aristocratic' appearance, awarded with the prestigious Kleist Prize, was a frequent guest in Zweig's Salzburg villa. Lernet-Holenia clearly brought much-needed lightness of being into Zweig's domestic set-up. In literary terms, more was to come in 1928 – from Zweig's point of view, something experimental at two levels: the co-authoring of a social comedy and co-authorship under but one pseudonym, Clemens Neydisser. The title of their comedy, *Quiproquo*, was taken from *Der Rosenkavalier*, specifically Baron Ochs's comment when looking in the third act from the Marschallin to Octavian and back trying to work out their relationship: 'I do not know what to make of all this quid-pro-quo'.[14] Zweig's and Lernet-Holenia's comedy of mistaken identity can be read as a parody of *Der Rosenkavalier* – one likely reason why Strauss rejected Lernet-Holenia as his future librettist after Nazi policies made it impossible for the composer to continue working with (Jewish) Zweig after the difficulties with his opera *The Silent Woman*.

This erotically charged comedy, *Quiproquo*, with fraught relationships between three ladies and three gentlemen, indeed contained experiments with identity on stage and of authorship. Neydisser was soon identified as a name connected with Lernet-Holenia (on his maternal side) but Zweig's part in it remained hidden. That very fact Zweig seemed to have liked; for although he did not mention Lernet-Holenia in *The World of Yesterday* he speculated that he should have published (all of?) his works under pseudonym – for the sake of getting more excitement and thrill out of life by doubling oneself up through a pen name.[15] The last surviving sign of their friendship was Lernet-Holenia's letter to Zweig of 8 October 1937. It is not known whether Zweig responded given that Lernet-Holenia was in the habit of destroying most of the letters he received, including his manuscripts once they were published. (Rilke's letters to him only survived because a relative of his, convinced of their value, decided to secretly copy them.) In this letter Lernet-Holenia expressed the hope that they would see each other again, adding: 'This hope is more fervent and heartfelt than ever!'[16] Connections broke off after the annexation of Austria. It seemed that Lernet-Holenia remained completely oblivious, or blue-eyed, to the reasons of the termination of this contact. In a letter written after the Second World War, Lernet-Holenia attributed Zweig's suicide to his depressive tendencies: 'The strange pessimistic disintegration that brought Zweig's end began to show itself soon after I met him, around 1926. In long conversations I tried to cheer him up. But he was so downcast that hardly anything I could say reached him.'[17] But, as Arturo Larcati has pointed out, Lernet-Holenia spoke 'not a word about the anti-Semitic attacks on Zweig or his persecution by the Nazis – any more than the reasons for Zweig's exile'.[18] In this respect Lernet-Holenia's reaction there and then was identical with Richard Strauss's.

One of the most productive but also testing friendships Zweig had entered was the one with Joseph Roth.[19] Its lasting testimony is the correspondence between them stretching from September 1927 to December 1938 – that is, shortly before Roth's death. Many of Zweig's letters to Roth are lost, a fate that those of Roth's other correspondents share – not surprisingly, given Roth's chaotic lifestyle. But this imbalance, which forces the reader to second-guess Zweig's responses, is a fair reflection of what emerges from these letters: a writer (Roth) in increasingly desperate need to find an anchor in life. To a certain extent both were kindred spirits, although at opposite ends of their Jewish origins: Viennese affluence on Zweig's part against Galician poorness on Roth's side. Whilst Roth's Jewish orthodoxy turned Catholic with strongest monarchical leniency, Zweig kept both at arm's length. Roth approached Zweig seemingly subservient and yet entirely aware of his own worth, whilst Zweig, no sooner had he realised Roth's problems (a deeply troubled marriage, feelings of guilt in view of his wife's mental illness, excessive alcoholism), adopted the role of the good Samaritan. Even when he realised that Roth was a lost cause Zweig never gave up on him, supporting him morally, financially, and with good advice; the latter Roth often acknowledged with irritation and indignation.

But most and foremost both were writer-friends, and even in later years Zweig would look to Roth for advice in matters of writing style: 'In stylistic terms I am not quite certain', he wrote to Roth around 20 May 1936, when he was about to finish his Jewish legend *Der begrabene Leuchter* (*The Buried Candelabrum*), adding: 'For that I need your scrutiny' (JR/SZ, 316).

We have already considered Zweig's early confessionary letter to Roth of 17 January 1929, in which he stated that 'the real life' for him was a 'double life'. At times, one gains the impression that Zweig felt his own crises mitigated when compared with Roth's traumas. But he seemed to have been grateful for Roth's often-detailed stylistic criticisms, for instance when Zweig sent him the proofs of his essay on Franz Anton Mesmer in September 1930. A less assured recipient than Zweig would have been profoundly disturbed by the extent of Roth's criticism of his writing style, addressed, almost mockingly, to 'my dear, dear, revered professional!' Roth's point was not invalid when he argued that, sometimes, Zweig's 'beautiful wealth of associations threatens to tyrannise [him ...]' (JR/SZ, 47).

In matters of political judgement, they agreed by 1930 that Europe was 'a corpse gradually committing suicide' (JR/SZ, 53). Roth, however, remained a staunch monarchist, whilst Zweig had grown entirely disillusioned by politics altogether. Roth was even more uncompromising in denouncing any traces of fascism, whilst Zweig, like many other Austrians, including Dollfuss and Schuschnigg, saw in Mussolini (until 1938) the guarantor of Austria's independence. Whenever Zweig urged Roth to abandon heavy drinking and not to indulge in the consumption of alcohol, his friend tried to explain to him what this addiction really meant: 'Believe you me, never has an alcoholic taken less delight in consuming alcohol than I.' His comparisons are striking: 'Do you think that an epileptic likes his fits? Does a madman enjoy his riotous attacks?' (JR/SZ, 141.) At the end, Roth begged his friend to visit him, and one feels the pain in Roth when Zweig announced his departure to South America. News of this kind made Roth feel deserted and abandoned and left him in limbo. Nothing is more telling than a photograph taken of both in Ostend in 1936, in fact their last meeting in person. It shows Zweig smiling benignly at Roth over his shoulder whilst Roth seems brooding into the camera, a sceptic and a lost one, even during the reunion with his friend. Roth believed in the existence of what he termed in a letter to Zweig on 2 August 1937 the 'umbilical cord of friendship' through which he received his most important nourishment (JR/SZ, 339). And yet, this friendship ended on a discord, with Roth embittered by Zweig's attitude towards Friderike, with whom he sided in his marriage conflict, and what he called Zweig's 'defeatism'. His last letter to Zweig sounds agitated and has to do with Friderike's and her daughter Suse's situation in Paris. Both were taken by surprise there when the *Anschluss* was enforced on 12 March 1938. They were unable to return to Austria, and whilst back in Salzburg her second daughter, Alix, tried to salvage her mother's belongings but in vain. The Gestapo confiscated them. It appears, as Oliver Matuschek assumes, that Zweig may have asked Roth to support his estranged wife in her attempts to get her possessions out of Salzburg; precisely the kind of thing, namely personal possessions, Roth was disinterested in. Roth's last letter to Zweig reads as follows: 'Dear Friend, Of course I will talk to your wife. I have never had the ability – even long before this catastrophe [i.e.

the *Anschluss* – R. G.] – to understand furniture and the like. I shit on furniture. I hate houses. I will tell your wife that.' He then moves on to criticise Zweig directly: 'I can't see why you, dear friend, say that our situation is "hopeless". If ever then now: We have the obligation to show absolutely no sign of pessimism. [...] You are a defeatist' (JR/SZ, 373–4).

It is unclear whether Roth was familiar with Zweig's essay on defeatism of 1918 and alluding to it then, but in one respect he was the opposite. When it came to writing Zweig remained committed to finding the best possible parable or paradigm to express his growing mistrust in a world perverted by ideologies, ready to betray the principles of humanism. With his biography on Erasmus, he exemplified the paradox that one has to set oneself apart from the others in order to have a cultivating effect upon them. Was this a curious case of left-wing elitism or conservative progressiveness? At any rate, it reflected a scenario in which the far Right and communists in Germany joined forces in a general strike, which saw Goebbels and Thälmann marching side-by-side through Berlin to bring down the Weimar Republic. In terms of politics in the early 1930s, the left hand did indeed know what the right hand was doing, and vice versa.

During this time of perpetual economic and political crisis, Zweig's exchange with Rolland was, once again, the most edifying experience for him, regardless of their growing differences over the meaning of Soviet communism. Rolland was working on what he called 'Adieu au passé' ('Farewell to the Past'), having completed his study on *Goethe et Beethoven*; the latter could easily have been written by Zweig himself. In Berlin, Zweig talked on the wireless about 'history on stage', to which he had recently contributed with his 'Napoleonic' play *The Lamb of the Poor* – performed to much acclaim in 1930 in Vienna, Breslau, Hanover, Lübeck, and Prague. Rolland made his mark with the preparation of the Amsterdam congress 'against imperialistic warfare', which took place at the end of August 1932. It was intended as an international manifestation of pacifism, but it failed in the sense that it did not connect with efforts to support democratic ideals nor a call for a radical demilitarisation of *all* European states. The political establishment did not participate in the Amsterdam conference. Zweig, quoting Heinrich von Kleist, spoke of the 'fragility of the world' by which he meant the loss of faith in a legal system that failed to stand up against political radicalism.

Fragility of this kind found its personal equivalent in the fragility of Zweig's domestic environment. The atmosphere at home continued to be poisoned for him by Friderike's two daughters, whose 'stupidity and presumptuousness' drove him to despair. He confessed to Friderike: 'I am suffocating and with me all my [creative] activity' (SZ/FZ, 246). His response was an ever-frantic changing of places and hovering between the past and present. A Rolland-like 'farewell from the past' was never an option for Zweig. In Friderike's absence he enjoyed the company of Marie Antoinette as dauphine. 'Next week Ludwig XV will be killed, and she becomes Queen', he wrote to his wife on 12 September 1931 (SZ/FZ, 246). Once again, the past had caught up with his daily life as biographising superseded fiction.

With Lotte Zweig, née Altmann (1908–42) in Rio de Janeiro, November 1940
Heirs of Stefan Zweig

The Uprooting of an Austrian, or Fascist Trauma and Early Exile

Exile is the result of persecution of whatever degrading shape and humiliating form it takes; it can be preceded by a feeling of uprootedness, a lost sense of belonging, and fundamental estrangement from one's culture of origin. Each of those factors applied to Zweig by the beginning of 1934. But something else must happen for these sensations to lead to an actual decision to emigrate, let alone official measures to take effect that enforce emigration for political reasons. In legal terms one therefore differentiates between voluntary and decreed exile.

In Zweig's case we have learnt that his disenchantment with Austria, and Salzburg in particular, had already gained momentum during the late 1920s. It was to become acute in the second half of 1933, when his London flat in 11 Portland Place already looked like more than a merely temporary 'escape' from both domestic turmoil on the Kapuzinerberg and from Austria's (and indeed Europe's) economically and ideologically induced political crises. Events in early 1934 made it plain to Zweig that permanent residency in Salzburg or elsewhere in Austria was for him no longer an option.

Just how much the subject of exile was on his mind becomes clear when we read the first pages of the fourth chapter of Zweig's *Fouché* biography, which covered the three years before Napoleon's *coup d'état* in 1799 – the event that brought Fouché back to power. The chapter begins with a prompting surprise in the shape of a question: 'Has ever anybody produced a hymn to exile, this fatefully creative power that raises the human in his fall in the tough compulsion of loneliness only to gather the shaken strengths of the soul in a different way?'[1] In fact what the reader gets is Zweig's hymn to exile in prose, as he refers to 'exiles' of all sorts: to those of silence and contemplation, from Moses to Christ, Muhammad to the Buddha; to Milton's blindness and Beethoven's deafness; to the imprisonment of Dostoevsky and Cervantes; and to Luther's seclusion on the Wartburg, Dante's exile, and Nietzsche's too in the heights of the Engadin. One could add Ovid's exile in Tomis (today's Constanta) and the seclusion of Montaigne in his library tower. Perhaps even Zweig's very own stay in Switzerland during the final phase of the First World War would qualify, given the diversity of exiles he mentions.

Austrofascism's political schizophrenia

By February 1934 the meaning of 'exile' for Zweig gained in profile and urgency. It was the beginning of Zweig's *annus extremis*, a year conditioned by extreme emotions and occurrences. From 10 until 13 February in Vienna, Zweig found himself in an atmosphere of civil war with brutal repression of the Social Democratic Party's Republican Protection League by the state authorities and the military. Austrians were at war with Austrians, causing deep rifts within an already problem-ridden society. Zweig was appalled by what he experienced in the capital of a seemingly defunct state but did not comment on it in public. Regardless, as a Jew and friend of Romain Rolland as well as Maxim Gorky, a writer who had visited the Soviet Union back in 1928 and entertained friendly relations with Austrian Social Democrats, whose party was banned in February 1934, Zweig aroused suspicion amongst the arch-conservative authorities.

Back in Salzburg, the first thing Zweig did was to write a report about what he had witnessed in Vienna for Rolland's benefit. His letter dated 14 February 1934 is a document of utter desolation in view of fascist supremacy in Austria under Dollfuss and his military right hand, the leader of the Home Guard (the former Prince) Ernst R. Starhemberg, who exercised utmost brutality in quelling the resistance of the workers. Whilst in Paris the workers successfully mounted a general strike against the rise of fascism in France, such attempts crumbled in

Austria (mainly in Vienna and Linz) before they even started. Cultural sophistication and cruelty clashed on one and the same day, as Zweig pointed out. He had attended a matinée performance of one of Beethoven's piano concertos with the pianist Wilhelm Backhaus. Only hours later, 'innocent people were slaughtered' (RR/SZ, II, 558). But just four days after he had written this letter to Rolland, Zweig was to experience a traumatising moment literally at his doorstep. On the morning of 18 February four police officers searched his villa on the Kapuzinerberg for weapons in support of the Republican Protection League. This intrusion and violation of his private sphere and personal freedom upset Zweig, the declared pacifist, to such an extent that he decided to leave Salzburg, via Zurich and Paris, at once for his new haven on the British Isles: 11 Portland Place, London W1. He was determined to relocate his permanent residency to London and asked his brother Alfred to deregister him with the Salzburg municipal authorities, and his lawyer, Dr Karl Stiassny, to terminate his taxation obligations with effect from 28 February.

Unfounded rumours began to circulate in Vienna that Zweig had spent time in Paris to spread lies about Austria and the present situation, exaggerating atrocities committed by the state against its opponents. Another prominent Austrian left the country under similar circumstances and auspices, the artist Oskar Kokoschka. He decided to go to Prague with his sister following the death of his mother in spring 1934, but he, too, ended up in London at the end of 1938.[2] Even in later life, Kokoschka blamed the Austrian civil war for her premature death; he argued that his patriotic mother could not bear to see her country's ripping itself apart.

From the point of view of the German National Socialists, or rather, Hitlerists, Engelbert Dollfuss's Austrofascism did not go far enough. Their Austrian equivalents' demand to be part of the government was rejected by Dollfuss, even though Mussolini had urged him to accept them. But the bizarre fact was that Dollfuss continued to regard the Social Democrats as the real enemy of the state and his arch-Catholic regime, but, perversely, not the National Socialists, even though he banned the Austrian branch of Hitler's party on Austrian soil. As an ideology, Austrofascism was nothing short of political schizophrenia. It included a 'mission statement', published in 1933 by the Austrian Home Service, directed against the most fateful Austrian export item to Germany – Hitler. According to this mission, Austria was to be 'at the centre of a unified western world sheltered by the peace of Christ. [...] Austria will never allow itself to be taken out of spiritual attachment to the whole German world: nothing and no one will achieve this, not even the one-time Austrian citizen Adolf Hitler in his battle against his former fatherland.'[3] Instead of providing a democratic alternative to Hitlerism, the emphatically Catholic Austrofascists indulged in dictatorial governance and illusions about Austria's actual influence on the European stage. Worse still, although 'anti-Semitism never became government policy during the period of Austrofascism', it remained a fixture in public discourses. For instance, in periodicals of the Austrofascist paramilitary units, the so-called 'Heimwehr', 'the Jewish question' moved more and more into the foreground. The 'Jewish' mentality, or so they argued, manifested itself in 'materialism, Marxism, Liberalism and the like'.[4] In other words, the Austrofascists continued the anti-Semitic rhetoric that was rife in the Austro-Hungarian monarchy and was officially sanctioned by people like the then mayor of Vienna, Karl Lueger. (Only in recent years was the Viennese monument for this rampant anti-Semite sprayed with the word 'Disgrace'. Since then an open competition has been won by the artist Klemens Wihlidal, resulting in an ingenious decision by the municipal's culture committee to tilt the Lueger statue by 3.5 degrees to the right. What will then be seen is a monument in a permanently precarious imbalance, which is perhaps more visually suggestive than simply toppling it over.)

All this said, it was Dollfuss who, in January 1934, secured a guarantee for the continuation of an independent Austria through the League of Nations from England, France, and Italy. This turned into an official declaration by the League of Nations on 17 February 1934. It was the card that Kurt Schuschnigg, Dollfuss's successor as prime minister after his assassination, continued to play until the fulfilment of the *Anschluss* in March 1938. Small wonder that the aftermath of Dollfuss's chancellorship ranged from his being labelled a misguided dictator to the first opponent against Hitler.[5] Incidentally, Joseph Roth had not given up the idea of reinstating the monarchy in Austria to stop Hitler. Even a fortnight before the *Anschluss*, Roth on his last visit to Vienna hoped to be received by Schuschnigg, whom he wanted to persuade to resign and hand over to Otto von Habsburg. As it happened, he only met the undersecretary of national security, Michael Skubl, who advised him to leave Austria urgently (JR/SZ, 535).

Zweig in turmoil

For Zweig, though, personal drama was to follow. Tensions with Friderike mounted to a clearly unbearable extent, partly due to their different assessment of the political situation in Austria and Zweig's decision to distance himself from Salzburg – including their Kapuzinerberg domicile and thus his wife – for good. On 24 March 1934 Friderike arrived in London with the intention to make the small apartment in Portland Place more comfortable and to dissuade Zweig from his plans. Some emotional relief from the ongoing controversies with his wife is documented on a photograph taken in the park of Hampton Court in spring 1934. It shows Zweig with the Viennese ballerina Margarete Wallmann, whom he adored. She granted him the role of her best man when she got married.

It was with characteristic concern for mediating between cultures that Zweig, even in his tense semi-domestic situation in 11 Portland Place, thought of suggesting that an English play that had impressed him be performed in Vienna. The case in mind was John Drinkwater's *Abraham Lincoln* (1918).[6] In fact, it was realised in Vienna's Burgtheater in November of that year as part of the 'Voices of the People' festival series. As it happened this play on Lincoln was performed at the end of the very year when Dollfuss had been assassinated by Austrian National Socialists. This was in the tradition of stage works by British authors being first performed in Vienna, most prominently the premiere of George Bernard Shaw's *Pygmalion* in 1913, then in 1914 in London.

However, Zweig's more immediate concern was that he needed a new secretary to cope with the sheer amount of work, not least on his heavily researched biography on Mary Stuart. Ironically, it was Friderike, or so she later claimed, who had managed the search for a suitable secretarial candidate and chose a certain Elisabeth Charlotte ('Lotte') Altmann, born in Katowice on 5 May 1908. But it was probably through the London correspondent of the *Neue Freie Presse*, Peter Smolka, known to the Zweigs and Altmanns, who established this contact.[7] Be it as it may, Lotte Altmann's maternal great-grandfather was Samson Raphael Hirsch, the founder of the Israelite religious society in Frankfurt am Main. Together with her brother, Manfred Altmann, and his wife, Hannah Altmann, both medical doctors, Lotte emigrated to London in June 1933. It appears that it only took a very short time for Stefan Zweig to 'appreciate' Lotte's personality and secretarial skills, based on a sound education. To Roth he wrote in May 1934: 'A young woman is good to me here, me, a fifty-three-year-old.' In the same paragraph he conceded, though: 'My pessimism in respect of politics is without bounds' (JR/SZ, 164).

The affection between the twenty-six-year-old Lotte and the famous author continued to grow deeper, also during a first period of absence in summer of that year when Zweig and Friderike went back to Switzerland (Zurich and Klosters), whilst in Vienna *Triumph und Tragik des Erasmus von Rotterdam* (*Triumph and Tragedy of Erasmus of Rotterdam*), appeared in a special edition by Zweig's new publisher, Herbert Reichner. A meeting with Richard Strauss followed and, briefly back in Salzburg, he gave what turned out to be his final reception in his Kapuzinerberg residence in honour of two conductors, Bruno Walter and Arturo Toscanini. After some time in Vienna and Baden, near Zurich, Zweig would go back to London on 9 September for further work on *Mary Stuart* and a reunion with his secretary – soon turned lover.

But first, the ever-restless Zweig arrived in late autumn 1934 back in Zurich, where he joined Friderike for a continuation of his journey to the Côte d'Azur – but via Paris. Trying to trace Zweig's steps in terms of movement and work, if only for a few months, can cause breathlessness in the biographer. By 1934 the speed in Zweig's life had reached a new level, and the more he felt that his space for manoeuvring was restricted, the more frantic his movements seemed to have become. As ever, Zweig needed external or internal pressure to produce. Relaxation was to him more of a health hazard than a cure. Excessive travelling helped him in building up such pressure, which was by then, more than ever, combined with emotional turmoil.

To Nice, then. The Zweigs had booked themselves into the Hôtel Westminster on the Promenade des Anglais; an English touch was by then clearly indispensable for him. Shortly after their arrival, Friderike's daughter Suse, most likely to Zweig's displeasure, joined them too. But he claimed that he needed the presence of 'Fräulein Altmann' to make progress with his biography on Mary Stuart, and Friderike accepted this demand – suspecting something without knowing or having any proof. Matters of publishing business were conducted jointly, at least on one occasion when two American literary agents (Reece & Bing) visited Zweig. 'You can join if you so wish', he wrote to Friderike following some annoyance on his part that she had not turned up in time for lunch (SZ/FZ, 279). She was to make sure that Lotte should be present to take minutes of the meeting.[8] Did they also go together to the dreamlike village Èze, with its incomparable views onto the Riviera? Did Friderike frequent the Avenue Jean Médecin, one of the finest shopping streets along the Côte d'Azur? She did once for sure and came back earlier than expected to their suite in the Hôtel Westminster, only to find her Stefan and his Lotte in amorous embraces.

Joseph Roth stayed in the neighbourhood with his (still-)partner, the volatile Manga Bell, as did Heinrich Mann with his girlfriend, Nelly Kröger. To avoid any more embarrassment and tension Lotte retreated into the higher regions of the border area between the French Alpes-Maritimes and the Italian Piedmont to a village 2,000 metres above sea level, Sestriere. Staying there was good for her asthma and a conducive place for reflecting on her relationship with the revered author. The result was a declaration of love to him. Zweig received the letter on 10 January in Villefranche-sur-Mer before leaving for America to give lectures on invitation by the Jewish Telegraphic Agency. Curiously, he handed it unopened to his wife and Friderike produced a (deliberately?) incomplete transcript of it. The letter would have confirmed to Friderike what she had seen and sensed before: deep feelings for Stefan on the part of Lotte and her longing to be together with him. Perhaps she read with surprise that Lotte spoke of her in decidedly amicable terms, kind and respectful feelings that remained unchanged until the end of Lotte's life (SZ/FZ, 280).

On his return from New York Zweig only fleetingly visited London (and Lotte), moving on to Vienna where he stayed for eleven weeks in the Hotel Regina at the then Dollfussplatz (today's Rooseveltplatz). He had come to look after his ailing mother and check on the production of his *Mary Stuart* biography with his newly acquired Jewish publisher Reichner. Joseph Roth had not a good word to say about Reichner and branded him a Jewish anti-Semite ready to appease the Nazis on purely commercial grounds. This verdict he extended to a whole range of other publishers, too. To be fair, at this point in time Reichner simply tried to ensure the distribution of Zweig's works in Germany as Fischer did with Thomas Mann's. It was only in March 1936 when Zweig's books were officially banned by the Nazi authorities.

Zweig's other main concern by mid-1935 was the sale of his house in Salzburg, which Friderike continued to resist, knowing that this would mean a decisive step towards their formal separation. It was something that she still felt too painful to contemplate.

But no sooner had Zweig completed and published his biographies *Erasmus* and *Mary Stuart* that he embarked on his next project: a dual biography, or rather confrontation, between the French humanist Sebastian Castellio and the Swiss reformer Jean Calvin. Even more than Erasmus, Castellio turned out to be a role model for Zweig. In practical terms it meant that, now again back in Zurich, where he researched both historical figures, he needed support from Lotte and called her back from London to join him in the Hotel Bellerive au Lac.

With Castellio against tyranny, or *The Right to Heresy*

It was a risky venture on Zweig's and his new befriended Viennese publisher's part. *Castellio gegen Calvin oder Ein Gewissen gegen die Gewalt* (*Castellio against Calvin or A Conscience against Violence*) was Zweig's second book with Herbert Reichner as first publisher. Since March 1936 Zweig's books could no longer be sold in Hitler's Germany, in line with a secret list of banned authors. But it was possible for customers to order his books directly from Vienna – at least for the time being. This accounts for the fact that the first print run of five thousand copies was sold by June 1936, only weeks after its first publication. In the same year, already, an English translation appeared under the poignant title *The Right to Heresy*.[9]

For Zweig, the risk was twofold. His continued affiliation with the 'non-political' Jewish publisher Reichner was criticised by fellow emigrés given the publisher's ongoing contacts with Germany, which were regarded with suspicion; Reichner's political stance seemed unclear, and not only to Joseph Roth. In terms of content, the problem was that a principally theological conflict in the period of the Swiss Reformation could have been viewed as mere escapism. But this was evidently not the case and Reichner had published, in 1935, the first novel of a young literary progressive, Elias Canetti, called *Die Blendung* (*The Blinding*). In fact, Zweig's reputation among exiles improved after the publication of this study on the force of conscience. Its relevance for assessing the situation in Europe in 1936 was positively recognised by critics, and the message Zweig tried to bring across in his distinctly 'political' introduction was, by and large, well taken.

Zweig presented his readers with the confrontation between a Cromwellian 'Protestant dictator' (Calvin) and a humanist (Castellio). It is interesting how Zweig uses 1930s terminology to describe Calvin's actions, in that he speaks of Calvin's '*Machtergreifung*' (seizure of power) and his attempt to subject an entire people to a particular ideology through '*Gleichschaltung*' (enforced conformity). His Calvin is a sixteenth-century Robespierre, incapable of finding enjoyment in earthly matters. Zweig regarded Calvin's asceticism as the 'foundation of his despotism'.[10] Like in several of his other biographical works Zweig emphasises, even more with Calvin and Castellio, their features as mirroring their respective characters. Critics have called this mode of characterisation 'psychologising physiognomy'.[11] In fact, Zweig's method can be seen as an homage to Johann Caspar Lavater's conception of physiognomy, but also as a critique of practices rooted in the racial discrimination of the time. But it can also mean that Zweig had – to a certain extent – succumbed to this practice himself.

The Castellio material was to Zweig as important as the Jean Calas case to Voltaire, which prompted him to write his treatise on tolerance, and the Dreyfus affair to Zola, resulting in his rousing reflection 'J'accuse', to which Zweig also alludes in his introduction to Castellio. But it is the Castellio motto of 1562, taken from his treatise *De arte dubitandi* (*On the Art of Doubting*), that sets the tone for the entire study: 'Posterity will not be able to fathom that we had to live once again in such dense darkness after it had been bright before.'[12]

As it happened, Thomas Mann argued quite similarly around that time, possibly influenced by his reading of Zweig's study. In his diary, Mann recorded on four days in May 1936 his engagement with this book, summarising his impression in a letter to Zweig: 'In recent times I have rarely read a book like your Castellio so completely captivated by the subject matter and your shaping of it! It is a sensation, deeply stirring, all disgust and all sympathy of the day concentrated on but one historical object that tells us: It is always the same. This is both bleak but also comforting.'[13] What Thomas Mann really thought about Zweig – his *Castellio against Calvin* and, in general, his way of writing – he confided to his diary; it makes distinctly less pleasant reading. He found the subject indeed 'interesting', if not gripping. But Zweig's 'shaping' of it, his '*Gestaltung*' was from Mann's point of view, deplorable. He refers to it as 'ordinary', 'bland', and 'submissive' – meaning not sufficiently adequate for the subject matter.[14] These comments were almost identical to the ones Mann made after reading Zweig's *Erasmus*, whilst others credited Zweig for having unequivocally taken Castellio's side and with it that of 'conscience'. With *Erasmus* he wanted to show the dilemma of a person who refused to side with any 'party', as he had explained to Thomas Mann in a letter dated 3 November 1933.[15]

At the time, Thomas Mann rejected Zweig's approach to Erasmus because he had himself intended to write about him. For a moment – on 2 April 1934 – he even compared himself to Erasmus in relation to a new form of 'Lutherdom', meaning the National Socialist 'revolution'. Mann criticised Zweig's comparison of 1933 with the Reformation period because it would give National Socialism too much credit. But he reacted with outright anger when reading Zweig's *Mary Stuart*, calling it a 'subordinate and trivial book in view of all the blood, passion, and history, sloppily written with continuously vulgar parentheses. This kind of authorship that messes up good subject matters, is a pestilence.'[16] Thomas Mann's second son, the historian Golo Mann, was to inherit his father's verdict of Zweig and the way in which he wrote biographies. Whether envy of Zweig's undiminished success was one the reasons for Thomas Mann's comments remains anybody's guess.

However, had Zweig known the extent of the revered Thomas Mann's deprecation of his works, he would have been devastated, as was Friderike when she saw the short and cool comment by Thomas Mann on her former husband's suicide. But more of that under the final chapter, 'Notes on Zweig's Legacy'.

But none of Mann's partly sarcastic, partly facetious comments can diminish Zweig's achievement and resonance. For the so-called 'inner emigration' in Nazi Germany and the resistance against Hitler, Zweig's *Castellio against Calvin* could have served as a vade mecum, given its advocacy of conscience over obedience. As far as Thomas Mann's comment on present-day concerns in relation to historical subject matters was concerned, his very own *Joseph and His Brothers* tetralogy, in particular the final part, *Joseph the Provider*, illustrates the case. It offered an explicit homage to President Roosevelt's New Deal. Likewise, in *Doctor Faustus* the reader is provided with a running commentary on contemporary history by the narrator, Serenus Zeitblom. Zweig's comment in his work on Castellio captures this point poignantly:

A truly human person cannot remain without inner agitation when he observes inhuman action. The hand of an honest writer cannot calmly draw cool verbal fundamentals when his soul is quivering in view of the madness of his time, his voice cannot sound measured when his nerves are on fire with fair outrage.[17]

In Castellio's case this point was reached when he learnt of Calvin's condemnation of the Spanish freethinker Michael Servetus. In Zweig's book, Servetus's tragedy unfolds in the two central fifth and sixth chapters, when the Spanish 'heretic' ended up on a pyre in Calvin's Geneva. Servetus's 'crime' was to have questioned the meaning of the 'Holy Trinity' as he regarded it as incompatible with the unity of the divine Being and Spirit. This act of brutal tyranny prompted Castellio to write a public accusation against Calvin, which, in turn, led to a massive campaign of vilification against Castellio instigated by Calvin. But Castellio, who turned into an emigrant, did not end up on a pyre but died of exhaustion before he could have been forced to stand trial. His restlessness saved him from being condemned to death by a Calvinist jury, in real terms an ideologically corrupted court of justice. *Castellio against Calvin* was indeed Zweig's most pronounced and provocative statement on his time; anti-Fouché and determinedly humanist, he was ready to put his conscience on the scales of time.

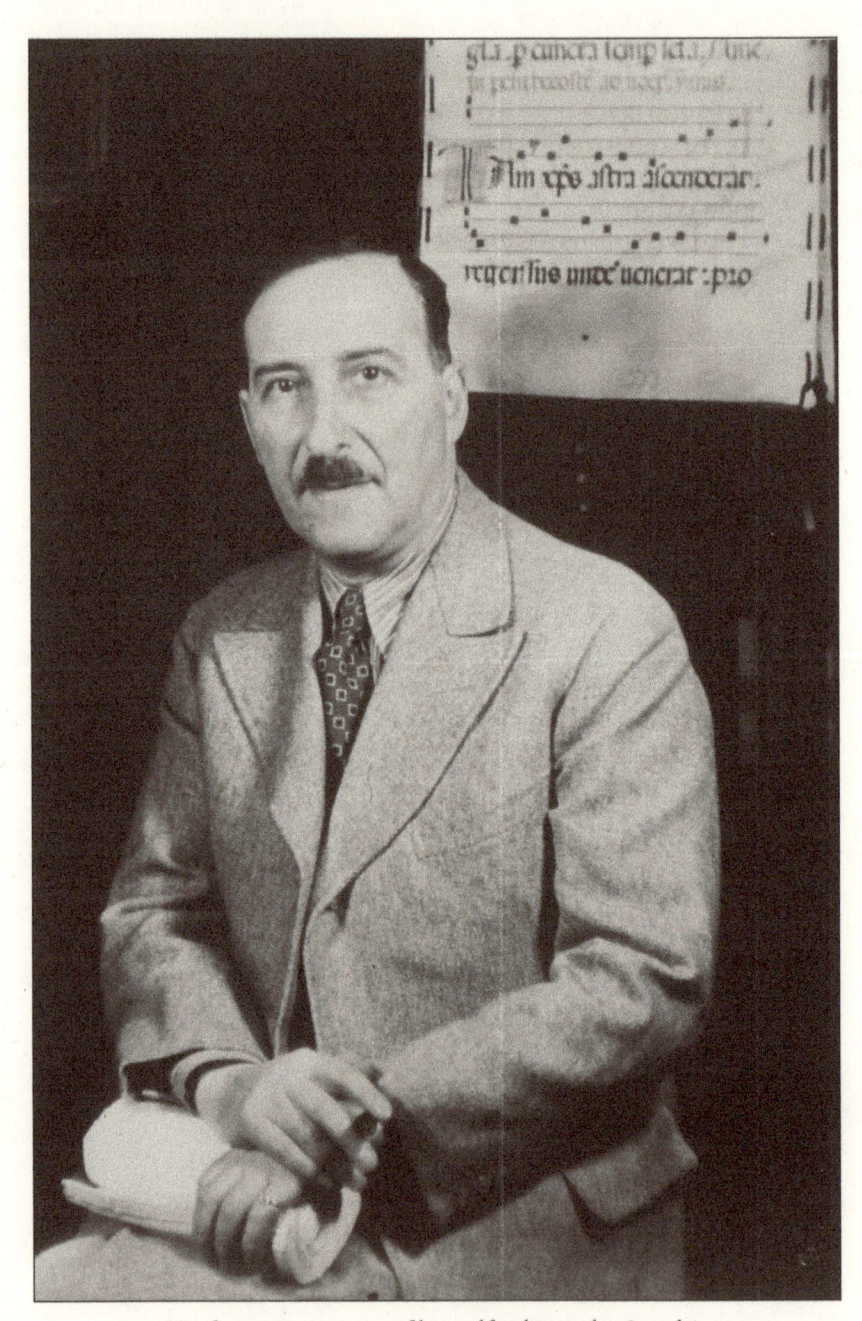

His favourite portrait of himself, taken in his London
flat in Hallam Street on 6 April 1939
RMN-Grand Palais/Gisèle Freund, reproduction de/Dist. Photo SCALA, Firenze

How to Become an Alien and Experiencing England

Zweig's own 'tale of two cities' comes in the shape of a brief '*Tagebuchblatt*', a leaf from his diary, depicting one of several journeys from Paris to London, in this case dated 27 September 1935 (Tb, 383–90). It captures the moment of departure from Paris in the early hours of the morning, thoughts on travelling as repeated *rites de passage*, the annoyance of border controls, and finally his arrival in London. There was the 'chaos' of Paris, which – paradoxically – came across to Zweig as a particular kind of 'order'. Zweig succumbed to the fascination of a city awakening, as would a 'locomotive set itself in motion', generating a specific rhythmicality. The tribute to the times consists of a mad rush for the recent news with the question: 'Has war broken out in, and over, Abyssinia already?' This is followed by the relief of sitting in a train carriage. Its rolling forward had a calming effect on the passenger, Zweig, and he concluded, again paradoxically: 'Travelling is like resting in the restlessness of the world.' He then reflected on the fact that as a human being of the twentieth century one is – as a state citizen – property of the state, which becomes obvious when crossing a border. The assumed authority of the border and its controlling mechanisms upset Zweig the traveller. Comparing it with the time before the First World War, he regarded border controls as a tall order and infringement of his personal freedom. This waiting forever at borders riled him and aroused in him feelings of revolt and anger. He felt that whilst the French seemed more relaxed when checking passports of those leaving the country, the English border guards made a meal of it. He regarded such controls as epitomes of a country's mistrust of foreigners. Remarkably, he predicted a time when these border controls would take longer than the actual journey.

Once the tall order of border control intervention was behind him he finally arrived in London, first in 'unspeakably ugly, grey and sooty suburbs with occasional glimpses of green vegetation.' No sooner had he reached the centre of London, he felt trapped by the imperatives of commerce. But London appeared to him (in 1935) not merely as a hub of commercialism but as a 'polyp whose thousand tentacles stretch over five continents to suck from them their strength, wealth, and energy'. He stood in the middle of Piccadilly, with all its sensual attractions, illuminated advertising, and cinemas that generate stultification of the many at the expense of the few who are still willing and able to reflect what is really happening in the world. Zweig felt that Europe, and London with it, was by then void of any 'great idea' and had sunk into the pitfalls of mere consumerism, which could not but lead to a corruption of the mind. It was in London where Zweig experienced the simultaneity of occurrences most acutely. But what bound Paris and London together in that moment was the question that had dominated the papers. Once again he asked himself: 'Has war broken out in, and over, Abyssinia already?' In other words, Zweig observed the impact of the mass media in urban settings; they constantly make us wait for the next news or disaster. But, or so Zweig argued, instead of waiting for what the media have to tell us, deliberate misinformation very much included, we should use the 'weapons of reason' to create a better world for ourselves.

As evidenced by this 'leaf from a diary', Zweig had by now become a migrant and exile himself, uprooted like Castellio, Calvin's resourceful adversary. Zweig had become, first by choice, basically since 1933, a migrant; then, by circumstantial forces, a stateless individual, due to the *Anschluss* of his former 'home country' in 1938. It meant that his Austrian citizenship had ceased to exist, with restrictions of movement as a consequence. Having become alienated from his country of origin he was now an alien in England. His by now beloved secretary Lotte Altmann, who by spring 1933 was banned from continuing her studies in Frankfurt on racial grounds, followed, emigrating to London with her brother – the surgeon Manfred Altmann – and his family, using her German passport.

Arguably, this experience of diaspora brought Zweig once again closer to the Jewish heritage in him. It was therefore only consequential that one major 'fruit' of his time in England was to be the previously discussed Jewish legend *The Buried Candelabrum*. But his ambivalence towards Judaism remained. By the same token, his growing ambivalence towards England did not prevent him from continuing to entertain Anglophilic sentiments, albeit reluctantly.

On the one hand Zweig considered, in August 1935, a manifesto on the preservation of the dignity of Jewish people, which he had intended to discuss with Chaim Weizmann, the then president of the Zionist World Movement, in Zurich; he even had planned to edit a Jewish Monthly. Both plans came to nothing. On the other hand, he would refer to himself and, somewhat presumptuously, to Lotte Altmann on one of his first postcards to her as 'we blasphemous non-believers'. And, at the time when he developed thoughts for the Jewish manifesto, he lamented the quality of guests in the Bohemian spa town Marienbad, again in a letter to his *'liebes Fräulein Altmann'*: 'Only the forests are dreamlike-beautiful, not the people; it is as if Tel-Aviv had relocated itself into the Bohemian woods.'[1] Did he ever consider whether remarks like these could have offended his Katowice-born Jewish secretary Lotte?

One of the first letters he wrote from his new abode at 11 Portland Place, in autumn 1933, was to Thomas Mann. Work had brought him here, he said, meaning his *Erasmus* and the desire to find emotional relief 'from the political tensions in Austria', something he felt was 'utterly necessary.' He admitted being exhausted by the 'daily demands' on him to make the right decisions in matters that were constantly forced upon him.[2] He confessed to Mann that it was 'liberating' to have written to his highly esteemed writer colleague whom he greeted 'with love and devotion'. Laconically, Thomas Mann registered receipt by noting, in his diary, letters, 'one of them by Stefan Zweig, who is recuperating in London from continental Fascism.'[3]

Originally, Zweig believed that his 'visit to England would not take long' but at least he now knew where he would wish to live when the situation in Austria became even more unbearable. Here in England, he informed Mann, 'the sense for what really matters is still alive – books are being bought, theatre and concerts are attended, the people love their home, their landscape, their animals and even though they appear rather cool and reserved, they are friendly minded towards the other; nobody is interested in the neighbour' and that their private lives seemed to absorb them all.[4] Initially, work was his main reason for being in Britain, to be precise research for his biography on Mary Stuart, which included trips to Scotland with Lotte who, from 1934, soon become an indispensable collaborator and confidante, to say no more about matters of their hearts.

Zweig on the 'Spirit of England'

For the ardent Francophile Stefan Zweig, London was not an obvious choice.[5] He was not a complete stranger to the city, but this was his first visit to the world-metropolis-on-Thames for more than twenty-five years. As seen already, his pre-war impressions found their entry into two travel essays, 'Hyde Park' (1906) and 'Oxford' (1907). London he had termed a 'cyclopean city' with the arms of a polyps, whilst Oxford had appeared to him, as mentioned before, like the one half of Britain's brain with Cambridge being the other. Apart from his essay on Dickens he had another piece on England, which appeared in the *Neue Freie Presse* of 25 January 1924, called 'The Genius of England', or perhaps best translated as 'the spirit' of England.[6]

On the day this piece was published Zweig arrived in Paris for a stay in the Hôtel Beaujolais, whilst in his Salzburg villa central heating and a more comfortable bathroom was installed. The occasion for this publication was a particular one – a contribution to a special edition of the *Neue Freie Presse* on 'England and Austria'. It contained well-wishes for Austria from the new Baldwin government, including the treasurer, Neville Chamberlain, and the chair of the Privy Council, Lord Parmoor, as well as, interestingly, the Irish President Cosgrave, the writer John Galsworthy, and others, with Stefan Zweig as one of the 'most prominent of Austrians'. The leader, 'England and Austria', went out of its way to praise 'the heroic struggle' of the new Republic of Ireland for its sheer 'existence and freedom in the context of the British people'. It commended the 'lightness of dealing' with things as the essence of the 'English spirit'.

Zweig's approach in his contribution was fit for the purpose: no critical, let alone deprecating word about England at this occasion. However, when he declared that the 'actual work of the English spirit was being the greatest architect of mankind' and that English nationalism, in principle Zweig's archenemy, 'transcended itself into worldliness', exaggerated praise turned into folly. Now even the state and the principle of statehood, which Zweig had declared untrustworthy because of the 'Great' War barely three years ago, he was able to regard as something art-like. The elites of the country, or so he argued, would learn the 'secrets of an artistic way of running the state' like a musician would internalise 'the basso general and counterpoint'. State rituals in England had something religious about them. Moreover, he pronounced England's political culture as the main stabilising factor in the world of 1924. He spoke of England's 'European mission' to exercise constraint over the young in their aspirations, already in overheated states in post-war Europe, and referred to the 'genius of England' as an indispensable part of the European spirit.

This act of idealisation was based on pre-war memories of England and the will to project his political ideals onto a historical and political entity that had seemingly emerged strengthened from the First World War. Furthermore, Zweig applied a phrase by Goethe onto the 'English spirit': exercising 'leniency but with a great will' against the backdrop of an 'immeasurable danger' from which only 'unified forces' could save the Europeans. Zweig saw 'forces' of this kind bundled together in England's resolve to salvage civilisation from the wreckage of nationalistic antagonisms.[7]

Mixed feelings about England

Small wonder that the reality in England in 1933 and later did not quite match Zweig's high-minded conception of the country. To be sure, the intricacies of British politics and society never became his domain. Despite the success of his historical biographies with the English book market, he remained an outsider to the English literary establishment.

But first things first. As we have seen already, Zweig returned to Austria (Vienna and Salzburg) before Christmas 1933, only to return to London after the searching of his house in Salzburg in February 1934. On 27 February he informed Rolland that he intended to stay in London, 'regardless of what is going to happen in Austria' (RR/SZ, II, 561). Zweig, in his voluntary exile, first waxed lyrical when it came to his feelings for London, and the British Museum in particular. In a letter to Anton Kippenberg of Insel Verlag, who had been his publisher for the last thirty years or so, Zweig wrote on 31 March 1934 about London: 'The city is wonderful, one can live the way one wants to and is miles away from politics [...] For years I have not felt better at any other place.' The reading room of the British Museum turned into his second home in London; in the same letter he called it 'the most beautiful library in the world where one cannot sense the political idiocy; instead, there one can concentrate properly.'[8] Soon, though, he was to express his annoyance at what he, and others, perceived to be political indolence on the part of the British government versus Hitlerism and fascism in Europe, with open support for both amongst the British elites. It was an embarrassing price to pay for the non-political atmosphere he cherished as a favourable condition for his work. His productivity, however, was undiminished. Apart from *Erasmus* (1934), *Mary Stuart* (1935), and *Castellio Against Calvin* (1936), Zweig, who was still an Austrian citizen and able to travel back and forth to Austria and elsewhere (bar Germany) wrote and published during his voluntary exile *The Buried Candelabrum* (1937), *Magellan* (1938), and the novel *Ungeduld des Herzens* (*Impatience of the Heart*, or *Beware of Pity*, 1939). As Richard Dove points out, the real traumatic calamity began for Zweig when he found himself stateless after the *Anschluss*. He expressed his calamity to Rolland in no uncertain terms, declaring: 'I would not dream of applying for British citizenship [...] as the bureaucracy that goes with it disgusts me. I do not like to live in London [anymore]. I feel lost here. I do not want to become English if this is possible. My dream is to go to South America perhaps' (RR/SZ, II, 677–80). He soon realised that 'in today's world being without a passport is like being a fish without gills.'[9] But his attitude towards London changed significantly once he could associate it with Lotte's presence there. *L*ondon and *L*otte turned in him into an alliteration of the heart. In a letter written to her from Klosters on 14 August 1934, Zweig summarised the development of his feelings for the city thus:

> Here, in Klosters, it is quiet and light, a wonderful breeze from the mountains, but I strangely I am longing, here of all places, for being in London. I do not really understand how things developed in me in relation to this city. At first it left me indifferent as I viewed it simply from the point of view of my work; after all, London is not really an inviting or welcoming city but rather closed up, a city with lowered blinds. But the more I got used to it, the more I discovered; I learnt to love the colours and the cityscape, its special atmosphere, even its anomalies and peculiarities. [...] By now, I would love to live in London for good.[10]

Chances are that Lotte got the hint, even at this early stage in their relationship and despite the formalness of Zweig's approach to her, at least in his letters. Until the end of 1938 she remained his '*liebes Fräulein Altmann*', or 'Miss Lotte'.

However, for Zweig, autumn 1934 in London was marked by a strange visitor, who could not have been more different from him, and who had even more mixed feelings about England, and London in particular: Bertolt Brecht. The story of their predictably fraught meeting has often been told but one of its aspects is simply too good not to be mentioned. The composer, and Brecht's musical mastermind, Hanns Eisler brought them together, allegedly on Brecht's request but perhaps right from the start with malicious intent. This is what happened, in Eisler's account:

> I asked: 'What shall I play?' and Brecht said: 'Play Mr Zweig "Song of the Invigorating Effect of Money".' So I played it for him. I just

> knew things would turn out badly. To play for a man famous for his wealth (inherited wealth) – the man who financed the Insel publishing house, financed his whole career – that song! When you hear the text of it ... Zweig listened to it with a stony face [...] He said it would all be very interesting, quite simply 'interesting'.[11]

Zweig's subtle but poignant 'revenge' for this insult was that he invited Brecht, and him alone, for lunch at some Lyon's Corner House in Oxford Street, 'one of these awful mediocre London restaurants' – a 'treat' for which he paid a mere two shillings and sixpence, as Brecht later confirmed to Eisler. Neither to Brecht nor to Eisler did the question occur why Zweig was so popular a writer and what his literary recipe was to sustain this amazing resonance even under the harsh conditions of exile.

At the time and for the remainder of his life in exile, Zweig's main concern was to preserve his German language – to the point that at some stage he stopped reading English books, pronouncing: 'I do not want to move into another language; we are doomed to have to continue to write in a language that ignores us.' Adopting British nationality meant to him pretending to be someone who one was not.[12] But practical concerns got the better of him – perhaps also due to concern for Lotte following his protracted and stressful divorce from Friderike on 22 November 1938 – and having completed the necessary five-year residence in Britain in December of that year, Zweig did apply for British citizenship, which was granted to him in January 1940. Tellingly, he concealed in his memoirs *The World of Yesterday*, the working title of which was 'My Three Lives', with first notes written at the end of 1939.

His account in *The World of Yesterday* of his years in England and the way he wrote about them in his letters suggest a life in anything but 'splendid' isolation. In fact, he had friends in London, like the actor and playwright John Drinkwater, the novelist Hugh Walpole, the publisher Desmond Flower, the literary scholar William Rose, and his fellow exiles Max Herrmann-Neisse and Robert Neumann, with whom he dined regularly.[13] He gave a few public lectures on 'The Meaning and Beauty of Autographs' at the Sunday Times Book

> [1937] WRO 5/ZWE
>
> My dear Rose, it would of cause be a pleasure for me to give a lecture on Rilke, but first it would be immodest to speak a whole hour in my bad English and then, I feel not enough authority in me to give a good lecture in English. What I would like to propose could be, that I deliver on the first evening a little speech of about 10 minutes, saying, you will hear much about the poetic work of Rainer R. R. by excellent speakers. Perhaps you want also to have a picture of the man, who wrote those poems and as I am one of the few here in England, who have known him for years, I will venture to tell you a little about being the man — and then speak about ten minutes. And of cause Sidgwick & Jackson could include it in her little book.
>
> Truly yours
>
> Stefan Zweig

Letter to William Rose about giving a lecture on Rilke in London
William Rose Archive, WRO 5/ZWE. Senate House Library/University of London

Exhibition in November 1934, was interviewed by the BBC on television, and lectured on Rilke to students at King's College London and on musical culture at the Austrian Embassy when, in September 1937, the Vienna Philharmonic gave concerts in London under the baton of his friend, Arturo Toscanini.[14] But in all instances, Zweig's main concern was his proficiency in English. He feared that his English could be 'too compromising' for the organisers of such events, as he confessed to his young friend Desmond Flower.[15]

To a certain extent, Zweig settled in London to feel unsettled. He claimed to be isolated only to make the most of his contacts abroad. This might account for his extensive, if not, once again, excessive travels. At least between 1935 and 1937 Zweig used London as a hub for his work and a glacis for his elaborate travels. 1935 found him in the United States in the company of Toscanini and Schalom Asch. In the summer he spent time in Pontresina (Switzerland), Salzburg, Vienna, and Marienbad; later that year he was in Villeneuve visiting Rolland and then in Paris, only to be back in Vienna for Christmas and New Year. In 1936 it was Nice, Boulogne-sur-Mer, and Ostend, meeting Joseph Roth and his partner, the writer Irmgard Keun, his chess partner, Emil Fuchs, and the journalist Egon Erwin Kisch. From June to October he gave readings in Brazil and addressed the PEN Congress in Buenos Aires. Then, after an interlude in London and his new flat in 49 Hallam Street, he travelled to Paris, places in Switzerland, and, for the penultimate time, to Salzburg. In 1937, Zweig engaged in what was to be his final Italian journey to Milan, Naples, and Rome. Then, following the clearing of his Kapuzinerberg villa in May and thus his final stay in Salzburg, he went to Prague to visit Max Brod. The next thing he would hear from Salzburg was the burning of his books on the Domplatz on 30 April 1938. His last journey as an Austrian citizen took him, with Lotte in January 1938, to Portugal, followed by stays in Marseille and Paris. Thereafter, only special permits allowed him to travel again to New York in December 1938, followed by his second US lecture tour to several cities, including one excursion to Canada (Toronto), again accompanied by Lotte, whom he would marry on the 6 September 1939. Lotte managed to travel to Katowice for what would be her last visit to her hometown in early November whilst the Salzburg courts and two lawyers were dealing with the divorce proceedings of Stefan and Friderike Zweig. Zweig, back in London by himself, felt lost, as comes across in a postcard he wrote in English to Lotte in Katowice:

Dear Miss Lotte, [...] I am very lazy, nothing goes ahead, – from nowhere comes any good news, especially not from Salzburg, where there seems to be some official opposition and altogether I feel very tired of London and would prefer my voyage [lecture tour through the US – R. G.] could start a month earlier.[16]

Salzburg in Bath

Three months before the incorporation of Austria into Hitler's Reich Zweig had visited Vienna for a last time, mainly, as he explained to Rolland, to see his ailing mother and to bid farewell to his native city. From March 1938 he was officially an exile and from then on, he could not help but try to find 'Austria' – and, regardless of what he had to experience there, Salzburg in particular – elsewhere. News about the death of his mother reached him on 23 August.

By 1939 a move to Bath, or least away from London, had become a necessity. Following the *Anschluss* and the German occupation of Czechoslovakia in an open and cynical breach of the Munich Agreement, London, like Paris, was crowded with refugees. Zweig felt challenged beyond his limit, and 'spent much of his time writing letters concerning visas, permits, affidavits and visiting the Jewish Refugees Committee in Bloomsbury.'[17] It was more than he could bear, as he confessed to Rolland: 'For months I have been unable to work [...] I am the victim of an avalanche of refugees. Since November, this stream has increased to a worrying extent and the entire tide rolls towards London. Yes, one gives good advice and money, but the brain and heart can no longer bear these sorrowful stories' (RR/SZ, II, 704–5). One might raise eyebrows given the vocabulary Zweig, the humanist that he was, uses to describe this 'refugee crisis', which sounds closer to the description of a natural catastrophe, a human 'tsunami' which threatened to bury him but of which he was a part himself.[18] However, he felt that he had to protect himself, his work, and his togetherness with Lotte. But what was tested most in him was not so much his patience and endurance but his pacifist principles, in view of what had unfolded before his eyes in Europe. Fellow writer Franz Werfel observed, when he met Zweig in London in summer 1938, that 'Zweig would go pale and turn away, when others in his company called for war.'[19] The very foundations of Zweig's beliefs were shaken to the core and in danger of cracking. For what else but collective military intervention against Hitler could fulfil Zweig's wish for a more active role of Britain, given that all tentative measures taken in the name of 'appeasement' had failed dramatically? At some stage he must have asked himself whether his pacifist principles were also as dogmatic as the kind of ideologies that Castellio had stood up against. It was a fateful circle by which Zweig felt trapped.

Bath seemed to offer some 'cosmetic' escape from London on the British Isles, which he saw as being increasingly endangered, too. The undulating landscape of Somerset, with Bath as its urban idyll of Roman origin, seemed to provide for Zweig an optical equivalent to the *Salzburgerland*, save the 'real' mountains there. Just before the outbreak of the Second World War Zweig and Lotte moved to Bath, where, in August 1939, he bought a house named Rosemount on Lyncombe Hill. It was, as it were, Zweig's wedding present for Lotte, and where he hoped to devote himself entirely to his major biographical project on Honoré de Balzac. He even called one of the rooms the Balzac room, where he assembled the substantial amount of material he had collected on France's novelistic giant.

For that reason, it was fitting that the only journey Zweig made from Rosemount was to Paris in April 1940, to lecture on 'The Vienna of Yesterday' – literally in the last minute before Hitler's Germany attacked France on 10 May. For the last time, Zweig met with his Francophone friends: Frans Masereel, Paul Valéry, Alzir Hella, Georges Duhamel, Jules Romains, and Roger Martin du Gard. The lecture was a dry run of his major work, *The World of Yesterday*. Together with his novel *Beware of Pity* it provided a final testimony of what Zweig wished to see remembered *because* it was irretrievably lost.

Waiting, waiting, waiting and soon despairing and the farewell to Freud

With the outbreak of the Second World War Zweig, now an 'enemy alien', became a diarist again, at least for a short while. Once again, he said, he wanted to provide himself with a 'picture of the time' only to give up his attempt after 17 October 1939. Following the German invasion of Denmark, Norway, Belgium, the Netherlands, and France he started recording events again in diary form on 22 May 1940, and continued to do so until 19 June 1940 when his suitcases were packed for his final departure from England to Brazil via New York. The diary contains snippets of impressions of what it was like to live through the so-called 'phoney war', a period, in Zweig's words, of 'waiting, waiting, waiting and soon despairing' (Tb, 473). From his point of view this 'phoniness' was nothing but political suicide.[20] The entries amount to a record of Zweig's despair at the increasingly hopeless-looking situation, with the likelihood of a German invasion of the British Isles growing by the week and what looked like to him the complete inactivity of both the British and French governments – an object of controversy amongst historians to the very day.[21] Even though he spoke with admiration of the English calm, endurance, and resolve to resist Hitler, he remained critical of the British government acting only tentatively and all too late. Zweig noticed with dismay that people were asked to keep a distance from any German or Austrian in their vicinity. He felt humiliated by such treatment, realising that as a German-speaking Jew he was doubly exposed as he sensed resentment, if not hatred, of Jews among ordinary people in England, too. His resumé reads: 'I should not stay in this country after the war. I am tired of all ideas of future' (Tb, 425).

Significantly, the first part of his war diaries is in English whilst the second part of his notes he reversed into German. Zweig's English diary illustrates his concern that he could not effectively communicate in English; and yet the irresistible flow of his prose, his agitation and despair, come through quite clearly despite his Germanic syntax and stylistic glitches:

> I regret only to have no opportunity to write as I am unable to do it in English and have nobody here to rectify my mistakes and to give more colour to what I want to say; that's what me oppresses most, that I am so imprisoned in a language, which I cannot use – how different was it in those times in Austria and Switzerland; where I could speak in my own language and even encourage others. (Tb, 418)

Moments of reprieve were rare. One of them was on 5 September 1939 when he and Lotte spent a fine day in Bath, which felt as remote as possible from any thought of 'war in the world'. It was, incidentally, one of the few occasions when he refers, albeit very indirectly, to Lotte in his diaries – but only through one pronoun, 'we': 'Lunch in the Spa – what a marvellous view and in the afternoon we make a walk from Clareston to the hight [sic!] – how wonderful nature can make forget the silliness of mankind' (Tb, 421). It is odd to find that Zweig, in these diaries, does not with one word consider Lotte's feelings; her perspective on the move from London to Bath, not to speak of the war itself, seem irrelevant to him. This is just as surprising as the ignoring of her and Friderike in *The World of Yesterday*, given that as a narrator and biographer Zweig was an absolute master at understanding the female psyche.

Zweig's last public appearance in London was on 26 September in the London Crematorium in Golder's Green, when Sigmund Freud was buried. In his diary he noted the conspicuous absence of English literati, let alone government officials, from the ceremony. It must have reminded Zweig of the absence of any government officials in Vienna at Arthur Schnitzler's funeral. Zweig spoke in German after Ernest Jones, one of Freud's closest collaborators. It was as if all of Zweig's by then next-to-dormant rhetorical skills and verbal artistry was enlivened by this task. On barely four printed pages Zweig put together an *hommage* of Freud as a 'discoverer' and explorer of the soul, and a manifestation of what it means to believe in the independence of mind in a heroically free spirit who worked against all odds. When Zweig deliberately used the expression '*Finder und Führer*' to describe Freud's character, a discoverer and leader, he told his fellow mourners that even the word '*Führer*' could not solely be claimed by the destroyers of culture and civilisation. By implication he argued that it still made sense to identify real leaders like Freud, whose example he characterised as follows: he was 'on the one hand cautious, carefully examining, reflecting sevenfold and doubting himself'. But once he was certain of a particular insight, he would defend it against the entire world if necessary. Freud's courage consisted of 'defending findings that others did not want and did not dare to find, let alone spell out or stand by'.[22]

Just how much Zweig was moved by this occasion is reflected by a diary entry, the English of which is even more shaky than usual: 'How kind Mrs. Freud says me, that the dear master loved me so much and expected always the day, when I came to visit him, all the relatives show themselves extremely kind and grateful to me' (Tb, 430).

Freud, during the last one-and-a-half years of his life following his emigration to London, must have indeed appreciated Zweig's frequent notes from Hallam Street and then Bath. Zweig visited him shortly after his arrival in London with the young Salvador Dalí, a great admirer of the founder of modern psychology. Zweig's and Freud's exchanges remained indeed relatively intensive right to the end of Freud's life.[23] In his last letter to Freud, dated 14 September 1939, Zweig informed him of the fact that, as an 'enemy alien', he could only move within a radius of five miles from the marketplace in Bath, adding:

> Here, I vegetate, silly and useless, not yet able to work properly and remote from all friends. I could laugh at this folly considering that I could be more useful than even civil servants in the Ministry of Propaganda [he refers to the Ministry of Information in the later Senate House, University of London – R. G.] – but this situation even spoils my joy in visiting you, which makes me sad ... [and yet] we need to remain steadfast – it would be pointless to die now without having seen the hell ride of these criminals beforehand.[24]

Visitors in Bath he had indeed only very few, among them the young writer Richard Friedenthal, who was to become his secretary and first biographer, and editor of his works, and the French art critic Louis

Gillet. Friedenthal stayed from January until February 1940, when his internment set in. He was to write a fine novel about this experience, which he called *Die Welt in der Nußschale* (*The World in the Nutshell*, 1956).[25] Idleness was a luxury Zweig felt he could not afford. Friedenthal had hardly arrived in Bath when the long black-out evenings began, and Zweig suggested to his visitor and soon confidant to use this time for a translation of Irwin Edman's book *A Candle in the Dark*. He had met Edman, who held the chair for philosophy at Columbia University, in early 1939. He praised the book in one of his last letters to Rolland on 13 February 1940, calling it 'clear and courageous' in contrast to the lukewarm political views he had encountered among English writers and journalists (RR/SZ, II, 718–19). In his foreword to the translation Zweig wrote that the authors had 'no intention to sublimate their personal disturbance over the catastrophe of our European civilisation but to ask – with Edman – how to safeguard ourselves intellectually in the chaos of our time.'[26]

In political terms, the other reference Zweig makes in passing in his letter to Freud is more intriguing and corresponds with an opaque reference to his visit to this very Ministry of Information, which was indeed modelled on Goebbels's ministry for propaganda, and a meeting he joined there with 'two gentlemen' on 27 May 1940. It is possible that one of the participants was Sir Arthur Beverly Baxter, the Canadian–British journalist: right hand of the newspaper tycoon Lord Beaverbrook, editor-in-chief of the *Daily Express*, member of parliament for the Tory Party, and fervent supporter of Chamberlain's appeasement policy. It was for Baxter that Zweig had written a memorandum on the political and strategic significance of Trieste on 4 January 1940. This text, unearthed only in 2019,[27] betrays Zweig as a sharp political analyst with a clear sense of strategic necessity – somewhat surprising given his pacifist beliefs but, perhaps, a document that evidences at least a slight shift in his stance on timely military intervention. Zweig must have had information about German intentions to annex Trieste for strategic reasons (which in fact happened in September 1943 when, after the Badoglio government agreed peace terms with the Allies and the Italian army was dissolved, the Wehrmacht established a 'operational zone' under the name 'Adriatic coastland' with Trieste as its centre) and rightly identified Trieste as the 'corpse in the cellar of German–Italian relations', recommending that Britain alert the Mussolini government of Germany's plan. His idea was to drive a wedge between the two dictators, which would, or so he believed, shorten the war – by then declared but not acted upon, with the tragic exception of Poland.

Although Zweig's memorandum did not bear fruit it showed, nonetheless, that he was not completely isolated. But especially the second part of his war diaries of 1940 shows just how sceptical he had become in terms of his own prospects. He expressed 'tiredness' when he came to contemplate yet another self-relocation and found it difficult to imagine a place on Earth where he would find peace. 'Disgust' was a word he used quite frequently by then, disgust at the situation in late 1939 and in general. English resilience could have a downside, or so he speculated; it would prolong the war and ruin Europe and its culture for good. In that sense, the period before the First World War now looked like a time *before* 'yesterday'. But all shades of the past retained a firm grip on him as he worked on his memoirs, which he by then called his '*Selbstdarstellung*' ('self-presentation'), as well as an essay on Cicero and the meaning of rhetoric.

'Where is the Where that would guarantee some safety and security at least for a decade or so'? he asked with an unmistakable undertone of desperation (Tb, 457). The thought of having to leave Rosemount, his new house on the hills of Bath, which he had begun to like, nauseated him; to be precise, the thought of 'leaving my work and house' behind 'to let me fall into uncertainty again' and into sheer 'bottomlessness' traumatised him (Tb, 462). To find some balance he read Dickens and discussed a translation of 'The Discovery of Eldorado', one of his *Decisive Moments in History* (having finished its final piece on Woodrow Wilson's 'failure', or 'Wilson versagt', during the peace negotiations in Versailles and Saint German in 1919) – all of that even though, to him, 'it has now become meaningless. But one pretends and continues 'as if nothing had happened' (Tb, 466).

The *Sternstunden*, or 'decisive moments in history', were on Zweig's mind even as he contemplated writing one on the outbreak of what turned into the Second World War (Tb, 417). History still seemed to him like an addition of such 'moments' but it was another concept that he introduced into his diary: the conception of 'bottomlessness', or '*das Bodenlose*', which was to bear a particular relevance to understanding the feelings of emigrés or exiled people. It is significant to find that later the highly reputed writer, communication theorist, media analyst, and art critic, Vilém Flusser, who as an eighteen-year-old emigrated from Prague to São Paulo via London, was to call his 'philosophical autobiography' *Bodenlos,* meaning 'bottomless'.[28] Flusser's own reflections on 'beleaguered England' read like a philosophical commentary on Zweig's observations. But the chapters on Brazil will be referred to later when we see Zweig arriving there for the second and last time in 1941, as they come across as testifying, in the manner of elective affinities, to Zweig's admittedly more controversial thoughts on his final destination.

At any rate, when Zweig (and Lotte!) were waiting in Bath with their packed suitcases for their next and, as it turned out, last transatlantic voyage, after agonising days – in connection with Zweig's obtaining visas and permits – 'running from Pontius to Pilate' as the German saying has it, they both remained doubtful as to whether the journey would really happen. Last-minute complications with the authorities had become the norm. But for once, 'good fortune' was on their side.

On board the *Alcântara* en route to Rio de Janeiro in August 1936
Heirs of Stefan Zweig

Autographs, Collections, and Other Approaches to World Literature

'"Now I will show you the only luxury I grant myself!" He then opened hidden behind a cupboard a safe and showed to me one of the most wondersome private autograph collections I have ever seen', said René Lévy, Zweig's guest in late summer 1933, adding: 'Much more psychological documents than appropriate for a museum'.[1] By this he meant Mozart's naughty letters to his cousin, Anna Maria, in Augsburg, which reminded the French journalist of Rabelais, except that he found Mozart even more lewd than this French Renaissance humanist known for his bawdy jokes.

Before the digital revolution the lines of our handwriting amounted to the graphics of life. Notes, texts written in one's own hand, have something reassuring or unsettling – depending on the aesthetic quality of one's handwriting. Stefan Zweig's handwriting was, most of the time, remarkably clear and steady. Whenever this was not the case, as with the diary he kept during his visit to Soviet Russia in 1928, it seemed worth a comment, so rarely did it happen.[2] These eminently legible handwritten manuscripts of Zweig's reflected his 'care for the letter', to use Hölderlin's famous phrase.

It is therefore not too surprising to find that, for the best parts of his life, collecting autographs was one of Zweig's passions. If there is a psychology behind this activity it might be found in the desire to gather material around oneself that relates to the tradition one wishes to be part of. Handwritten manuscripts epitomise a human connection; they personalise even if the essence of the work in question is transindividual. Zweig's large-scale written-material collection, then, served an intellectual and, to a certain extent, spiritual purpose; it reflected the beauty of the artistic production process itself. It testified to moments of inspiration and the labouring on an original idea. Autographs provided to Zweig traces of the 'demonic', but they were also visible extractions of invisible phenomena, which he was famously to call 'the secret of artistic creation'. He lectured on the subject first on 2 December 1938 in London and then between 9 January and 3 March 1939 in seventeen US cities, each time, to his surprise, in front of large audiences of up to 2,000 listeners.[3] The paradoxical point of this lecture, a seminal example of Zweig's rhetorical effectiveness, was that he suggested uncovering this very 'secret' only to leave it fully intact. It could be argued that this lecture reflected his insight into the meaning of autographs for determining the artistic process. But by that time he had dissolved his collection, which occurred between 1936 and 1937 in three stages, as Oliver Matuschek has shown:

1. In 1936 Zweig sold some 300 autographs through the Viennese antiquarian Heinrich Hinterberger to the Swiss collector, Martin Bodmer. These pieces are now kept in the Bibliotheca Bodmeriana in Cologny, near Geneva.
2. Zweig handed over some 100 autographs to the Theatre Collection of the National Library in Vienna in compensation for tax debts he had unknowingly accrued.
3. Autographs and private correspondence went to the National Library in Jerusalem in 1937. Some 200 pieces he took with him to London, most of which now belong to the Stefan Zweig Collection in the British Library in London.[4]

We cannot but speculate what the dissolution of this unique collection meant to Zweig psychologically. Quite surprisingly, in his letters he did not shed a tear when he reported that, with his move to London, he had to scale down his collection dramatically. This is even more astounding given that, in *The World of Yesterday*, he made the stunning comment that, through building up his autograph collection, he was conscious of having created something which was, as an entity, worthier of survival than his own literary work.

Zweig started collecting as a fifteen-year-old dilettante. His comments on the aims he later pursued with this collection are telling: 'I collect only handwritten documents which show the creative spirit in the act of creating. [...] I know not enough about an artist if I have only his finished work before me, and I subscribe to Goethe's dictum that in order to understand a great creative work fully, one should also have knowledge of its genesis.' What this means in real terms becomes clear when Zweig refers to one of his early role models, Honoré de Balzac, who continued to cast his spell on him until the very end of Zweig's life: 'A corrected proof of Balzac where almost every sentence is torn apart, every line is freshly ploughed, the blank margins are black with strokes, signs, and words, is for me the epitome of a human volcano.'[5]

Zweig saw his collection of autographs as a hub, alive with evidence of artistic creativity. In his lecture on the topic, the very climax of all his previous essayistic reflections on autographs, he suggested what one might call 'forensic hermeneutics' for the deciphering of signs that constitute the progression within a work of art. Interestingly, he compared this deciphering to 'criminology' and the artist to the perpetrator, who leaves 'fingerprints of his crime' – that is, the work of art. Thus, going through autographs meant for him being on the trail of the perpetrators.

The artist as culprit and 'hypnotised medium of a higher will' – this is the intriguing scale of Zweig's metaphorical approach to the 'genius', who produces works through which the 'divine act of creation' allegedly repeats itself. Artistic creativity derives, according to Zweig's 1938 lecture, from the interplay, if not struggle, 'between awareness and non-consciousness'. As such it is an 'act of transposition from the spiritual to the sensual world, from vision into reality'.[6] But Zweig considers another mode of transposition, too: that from the creator to the created, from the artist into the artefact, be it that the latter is a piece of music, a painting, or an invented character. This 'transposition' presupposes in the artist a state of 'ecstasy', whereby Zweig is quick to remind us of the word's original meaning: *being outside of oneself*. In the act of creation, or so he argues, the artist is not with himself but *in* the act of creation and its object.

Admittedly, this is not cutting-edge research on creativity in today's terms; true, even by the standards of 1938, Zweig's approach to the subject of artistic creativity seemed dated considering the extent of artistic revolutions that had taken place since 1900 alone. But the remnants of idolising the 'genius' in the tradition of the late eighteenth century, the Storm-and-Stress movement, and (early) Romanticism and the cult of the artist as hero are still present, incidentally, in James Joyce's posthumously published autobiographical novel *Stephen Hero* (1944). Of interest, however, is Zweig's emphasis on the material side of the creative process in the arts. He had hoped that, together with his extensive collection of auction catalogues and facsimiles, his autographs could one day become a major resource for researchers interested in comparative studies on creative processes or, to use George Steiner's phrase, the 'grammars of creation.'[7] In this context, Steiner defined 'grammar' as 'the articulate organization of perception, reflection and experience, the nerve-structure of consciousness when it communicates with itself and others.'[8] This is not too far off Zweig's mark, even though Steiner does not mention him but Hölderlin instead as having defined the function of art as 'the making present, the making contemporary of the unbounded.'[9] This, however, really does bring us into Zweigian territory.

But Zweig's conception of 'collecting' was not confined to his numerous (two dozen) essays on autographs, some of them even declaring such collections being a work of art in themselves, attributing to them a meaning and sheer 'beauty' of their own. It branched out into fiction, such as the short, yet significant, novella *The Invisible Collection*, and autobiography, for example in the twenty-second chapter of his Balzac biography on 'Balzac, the Collector', as well as into his plans for presenting collections of 'world literature'.

Even Zweig's advanced networking skills – *avant la lettre* – ought to be seen in this context. His ability to connect (with) people translated itself into his ambition to do the same as far as possible with the literatures. As mentioned before, the name for this collection was the *Bibliotheca Mundi*, conceived by Zweig as a direct *and* symbolic response to the First World War. The conception was 'large-scale'; the criteria were decidedly transnational. Zweig even spoke of an 'Artistic International', underlining the quasi-revolutionary impetus behind this project that was to be realised with Insel Verlag. His 'world library' was meant to be a 'total work of art' itself, with philosophy, music, and theology included. The collection was launched in 1920 with a few initial volumes but there was controversy between Zweig and his publisher, Kippenberg, over what was to be included and what not. Literature of 'universal vitality' was to be included, according to Zweig, although, surprisingly, not works by Gotthold Ephraim Lessing, *the* advocate of tolerance in German literature.[10] Anthologies of Russian and Swiss literature belonged to this project with the likelihood of more such collections of contributions to 'world literature'. But in 1924 Kippenberg of Insel Verlag had to stop the production of this series; it found too little resonance amongst readers and was therefore no longer financially viable. By-the-by, Hermann Hesse's not-dissimilar project remained in better shape, partly because it was located with Reclam's 'Universal Library' series, a kind of 'everyman' editorial undertaking. Hesse's recommendations for setting up a 'library of world literature', published in essay form in 1929, were also designed to be pointers towards 'discoveries through reading'. It continued to function as guiding principles for Reclam ever since.

Collecting narratives

One of Zweig's most intriguing short novellas centres on collecting, tantalisingly called *The Invisible Collection* of 1925. It is the story of a retired civil servant who, over the years, has invested all his funds in building up one of the finest collections of by now priceless prints and drawings. He lives in a provincial town and is described as a staunch German patriot who fought against the French in 1870 but was profoundly shocked by the 'slow advances' of the Imperial Army against France in 1914 – so much so that his eyesight was affected to the point of complete blindness. His wife and daughter, a spinster, did not even inform him of the end of Imperial Germany in 1918 out of fear that he might not survive such news. Instead, they read out to him 'edited versions' of newspaper articles. (It is as if Zweig had anticipated the plot of the 2003 film *Good Bye, Lenin!*) Important antiquarians know of his reputation as a collector, and one from Berlin in particular. During the period of hyperinflation in the early 1920s these antiquarians become increasingly short of precious collector items to sell, including autographs and prints, but one Berlin antiquarian remembers this highly reputed collector as one of his former customers. Now he wants to buy from him. He makes the journey full of expectations, only to find that this collector is now stone blind. Moreover, due to their hardship after the war and inflation, but unbeknown to him, his wife and daughter were forced to sell most of his precious items already. He cannot see that his folders are empty, and that the passepartouts in them frame nothing but blank sheets of paper. But the aged collector thinks that his precious possessions are still there and ritually during the afternoon he occupies himself with them, imagining what they had been. Wife and daughter beg the visiting antiquarian to play the game and pretend to marvel at what he sees – all but 'precious' originals. The old man is delighted to have, at last, a real expert appreciating his treasures, granting him the right to produce a catalogue of this collection and administer it when he is no longer. The antiquarian, who had hoped to stock up his goods by striking a favourable deal with this collector is now deeply touched by this delusional but 'happy' old man with his white hair and bushy eyebrows over dead eyes. Later on the antiquarian will see him from the street, believing that the blind man standing at his window resembles a pure, white, innocent cloud hovering over an otherwise corrupt and horrible world.[11] The narrator ascribes the phrase, 'collectors are happy people' to Goethe, who was himself one of the greatest collectors of his time. One could count some 2,000 autographs of the great and the good in his collection. Goethe *did* say, in a letter written from Carlsbad on 10 May 1812, that autographs provided him with the actual presence of a person 'in a magical manner'.[12] Sometimes such autographs would please him just as much as the portrait of the person in question. It is this very same 'magic attraction' that must have affected Zweig in a very similar manner.

With *The Invisible Collection* in mind, one cannot but be reminded of Jules-Joseph Colette, the would-be writer and father of famous Colette, who had his manuscripts bound, adorned with grandiose titles, and then put them on his shelves – except that these volumes contained nothing but blank pages. Thus, Jules Colette became the collector of his own inabilities, blind only to his talents.[13]

However, the striking feature of Zweig's novella is the extent to which this man has internalised collecting. It is his only joy in life – whether for real or as imagination. But Zweig also depicted the other side of collecting, namely in a chapter of his *Balzac* biography on the writer 'as collector'. The way in which Zweig describes Balzac in relation to this activity is nothing short of a caricature. In Balzac's case collecting was an act of speculating – that is, collecting bric-à-brac for the sake of making imaginary profits. When it came to collecting, if not hoarding of objects, he saw this epic writer walking 'the fine line between reason and folly'.[14] Although in more than one way his role model, Zweig's portrait of Balzac as a collector paints the exact opposite of himself in this capacity.

A brief word on Zweig's notebooks

Not many of Zweig's notebooks have survived but a mere few did, particularly of later years between 1936 and 1940, a time when Zweig summarised his thoughts on the mystery of the creative process. Some of these pages betray something of the early stages of this creative process in Zweig himself. For instance, when he was working on his legend *The Buried Candelabrum*, he wrote large sections in pencil followed by corrections in blue or turquoise ink. As he liked to use, at that time, spiral notebooks, he always left empty pages, making notes for changes or amendments on the blank left side. This was probably the basis for his dictations, by then, to Lotte.

Strangely, but characteristically, he often only used the first couple of pages of a notebook before turning it around and scribbling on the back pages, leaving the centre pages empty. It is as if Zweig wanted to frame the booklet's inner emptiness by approaching it from both sides. Interestingly, Friderike seemed to have adopted the same practice when she kept a diary for roughly one year during the First World War, from 1916 until mid-1917.[15]

Zweig's notebooks, purchased in Nice and Paris, give an indication of where he used them but rarely when. Place seemed to have mattered more than time, especially when he jotted down ideas for new projects. At some stage, he became interested in the 'tragedy of collectors' and their mania-like desire for completeness ('*Vollständigkeitswahn*'). At that time, around 1938, he seemed to have toyed with the idea of writing a music-related novella, the one subject matter he had not tackled, containing the bizarre phrase: 'Mozart: that was his black spot'. Franz Schubert's 'lost symphony', the so-called Gastein Symphony, intrigued him, combined with the question: 'What is happening to me?'[16] The latter does not have to refer to Zweig himself but could easily be applicable to one of his prospective protagonists.

What also concerned him, mainly in connection with his novella on the laying of the first transatlantic cable in 1858, is the issue of communication with technology. The thought of 'knowing in one minute what is happening' fascinated him. He copied a comment from *The Times* of 5 August 1858: 'Since the discovery of Columbus nothing has been done in [a] degree comparable to the vast enlargement which has thus been given to the sphere of human activity.' The 'overcoming of distance' is what Zweig connected with this event. His remark came shortly after completing *The Buried Candelabrum*, which implies the strength of spiritual communication over the centuries through an object – namely, the menorah buried in the sand outside Jerusalem. But he also noted down an ironic moment when, in 1850, a cable was laid through the English Channel and a fisherman thought he had caught a giant eel.

These notes reflect the parallelisms in Zweig's method of working, which was, perhaps, also a way of distracting himself from ever-frequent bouts of depression. In fact, on 21 June 1937 he told his friend, Felix Braun, that he would work 'most in phases of depression.' It was as if he wanted to create in himself 'high emotional pressure' through work to counteract those phases. This may account for the sheer multitude of projects he managed to advance often at the same time, for instance during the last two years of his life when work on his *Balzac, The World of Yesterday*, the novella *Chess*, his *Montaigne*, and the novel project *Clarissa* ran side by side with three of them (*Balzac, Montaigne*, and *Clarissa*) remaining unfinished by the time of his suicide.

What the sketchbook is for the painter, the notebook is for the writer and composer: a record of moments waiting to gain shape and, at best, comprehensive elaboration. In this respect even the sparseness of notes by Zweig of that period does not disappoint. We find him quoting Samuel 7:6: 'Why not build me a proper house to rest in.' Another note refers to Vienna 1938, suggesting a short story with one main motif: 'throwing away the Bravery Medaille'.[17] In fact, this is what the narrator in his novel *Beware of Pity* would do, non-literally speaking.

This is followed by renewed reflections on what it means to be Jewish: 'We are not a people. No religion any longer. No race. We are a community bound by common destiny, in which we are trapped [–] once this fate ceases to exist our community will, too.' Once again, he noted down the location of this reflection (49 Hallam Street, London) but did not date it, as if he wanted to tell himself that such thoughts are, in essence, timeless but that they can be located.

These notebooks even betray Zweig's (late) interest in contributing to crime fiction: not any crime, but what he calls a *'medizinischer Mordversuch'* ('medically attempted murder'). Tellingly, he speaks of the need to give a plot a certain *'emporgetrieben'* ('upward drive') for it to turn into fiction of this kind. This suggests that Zweig connected this genre with intensification. It is significant for the importance of this hazy conception that Zweig wanted to include the pre-First World War spy scandal surrounding Colonel Alfred Redl, who was in charge of the counterintelligence of the General Staff in the Austro-Hungarian Army but, in fact, was spying for Czarist Russia. Different from Alfred Dreyfus in France, Colonel Redl really was an arch-traitor that continues to spark the imagination of writers and film producers. Zweig did reflect on the case in *The World of Yesterday*; John Osborne based his play *A Patriot for Me* (1965) on Redl; and István Szabó produced a much-acclaimed film on *Colonel Redl* (1985) with Klaus Maria Brandauer in the title role.[18] But before Zweig took up this scandal for his own purpose there were two filmic renderings of it: first in 1925 by Hans Otto Löwenstein, and in 1931 by the producer Karl Anton.

In whatever shape and form, Zweig retained his dream of Austria 'as it was'. This very past was the pre-1914 Habsburg Empire, which remained fresh in his mind while his memory seemed to lose touch with Austria between 1921 and 1930. This became apparent when he was working on *Clarissa*, which he referred to, in a letter written to Friderike on 27 October 1941 from Petrópolis, as becoming a truly Austrian novel. But he would have had to read through ten years of Austrian newspapers to understand what the country had become during his absence.

Great expectations: Before arriving in Rio de Janeiro, August 1936
Heirs of Stefan Zweig

Zweig, the Transatlantic Explorer

Apart from Austria and Germany there was no other country over which Zweig agonised so much as England. As seen, his comments on England resembled an emotional rollercoaster. When he visited Brazil and Argentina in summer 1936, after barely three years of more direct experience with England and the English, he measured the experience against what England had to offer. With his South American venture already in mind, Zweig called London the 'best possible working place as long as one leaves it often enough to acquire new substance from elsewhere' (IV, 164). To the same addressee, the composer, collector of musical autographs, and friend of Ferruccio Busoni, Gisella Selden-Goth, he wrote a few months earlier in April that the English Channel separates the British Isles much more 'than one would assume a mere one hour of water could' (IV, 160). He told Rolland in a letter of May 1936 that it was not easy to live as a guest in England 'in view of the political stupidity there and the despicable hypocrisy' (RR/SZ, II, 628). Rolland, in turn, warned him in July that 'When you exchange Europe for Brazil you will jump out of the frying pan and into the fire' (RR/SZ, II, 633). But when Zweig left Southampton on 8 August 1936 he commented: 'colourless like everything English' (Tb, 393). When his steamer, the *Alcântara*, reached Vigo in Spain he mused: 'Two hours in Spain is still more intensive than one year in England' (Tb, 395). He sought no contact with the English fellow passengers but simply observed them. Being in the pool on deck, enjoying 'fancy balls', thereafter followed by some racing competition is the kind of thing 'the English take "sacredly seriously"'. He drew comfort from reading Henry Fielding's novel *Joseph Andrews* and Jane Austen's *Pride and Prejudice*. The latter he admired because of its composition and the 'richness of its characters', adding: 'What insight into what it means to be human and what hidden humour'. *Wuthering Heights*, however, he found positively 'unreadable' (Tb, 398). No reasons given.

But his main occupation on this voyage was working on yet another beginning to his prospective novel *Beware of Pity*, reading Edward Frederic Bensons's biography on Ferdinand Magellan, and probably also a monograph by Johann Georg Kohl on voyages of discovery at the time of Magellan in 1877.[1] Coincidence had it that he found these books in the cruise liner's library. He was soon fascinated by Magellan and contemplated writing another piece for his *Decisive Moments in History* collection, or even a novel on his Portuguese explorer. Furthermore, he conversed intensely with a botanist, who was commissioned to set up a centre for inheritance science in Brazil, chiefly about Gregor Mendel, the founding father of this science. Again, he considered writing about him.

During his brief stay on land in Vigo, Zweig admired – strangely enough for a dedicated pacifist – the young soldiers, but even more so the picturesque street scenes and the dignified gait of the women. In the shop window of a bookshop, he was bemused to see a copy of his *Mary Stuart*, together with writings by Hitler and the American industrialist Henry Ford's notorious book *The International Jew* (1920), which Hitler regarded an inspiration.

It was however the contact with emigrating Jews on board that pleased Zweig most. He noted that they had to travel third class but recognised in him the 'greeste Dichter' (semi-Yiddish for 'the greatest poet', which in proper Yiddish would be 'greste dikhter').[2] They had boarded in Lisbon, a city Zweig delighted in discovering for himself; 'a more colourful, more southern Genoa', as he called it.

The author as explorer

Colourless England, colourful Lisbon, and even more colourful Rio de Janeiro, where he arrived on 26 August 1936. He compared the entry into the harbour with New York. Whilst he detected something feminine in the landscape surrounding and backgrounding this city ('these undulating lines have something of the shape of a woman emerging from the waves, like Venus Anadyomene'[3]), in his eyes, New York's skyscrapers had something 'icy' about them. By contrast, Rio's enigmatic harbour seemed to be perpetually 'receiving' whilst New York was merely 'calling out'. The magic and sensuality of Rio clearly captivated Zweig. Part of this magic was to him the sharp social contrasts, which did not appal but excited him. With his Brazilian publisher Abrahão Koogan he ended up in Rio's so-called 'Mange' district, where along five long streets women of all races presented themselves in cubicles behind windows. It resembled to Zweig a 'huge department store of human flesh', which he did not deplore. Instead, he sensed something incredibly melancholic cast over these 'shop windows' like a veil – not dense enough, however, to cover the female nakedness. It did not excite or tantalise him; he found the scene rather harrowing. But in these streets and everywhere else in Brazil he discovered something almost too good to be true at a time of rampant state-official racism in Central Europe: the cohabitation of the races in Brazil and the complete absence of racial prejudice. This impressed Zweig most and it was to be one of the key motifs in his later book on Brazil. He reported back to Lotte – not about the red-light district of Rio but about the exalted reception that bordered on 'the grotesque' he received in São Paulo. For instance, he was taken to a renowned prison that prided itself on being the most modern in the world, where 'a music band consisting of fourteen murderers, four sex offenders and a number of thieves played for him the Austrian national anthem'. A three-time murderer acted as the prison's photographer. Then Zweig was taken to a snake farm. In spite, or because of, these absurdities, the country appealed to him at once.[4]

The landscape, at least outside of the rainforest but around Petrópolis, reminded him instantly of the Semmering mountain region near Vienna, or even of Switzerland, meaning, of course, that he *wanted* to be reminded of these regions with which he was so intimately familiar. Even though it became somewhat burdensome, Zweig enjoyed the attention he received everywhere he went in Brazil. It seemed to him that everyone had read everything he ever published. He was treated like a proper celebrity, which included a luncheon given by the foreign minister of Brazil in the presence of the two daughters of the dictator-president Getúlio Vargas and, finally, an audience with Vargas himself, who confirmed Zweig's popularity in Brazil.

Arguably, on this journey Zweig also felt a bit like an explorer, only the more so as disillusion about, and alienation from, Europe had set in by the time of his South American 'expedition'. At any rate, explorations were a feature and fixture in Zweig's works. Two out of five episodes in the first edition of *Decisive Moments* were devoted to such explorations – the discovery of 'Eldorado' being California, and the race to the South Pole between Scott and Amundsen – later enlarged editions included the discovery of the Pacific Ocean by Vasco Núñez de Balboa. But it was through his biographies on Ferdinand Magellan and Amerigo Vespucci that Zweig manifested his fundamental interest in explorers. As we have seen, he counted Freud amongst them as the explorer of the human psyche. To a quite certain extent, though, all of Zweig's biographies and the very best of his fiction benefitted from his interest in discovering the inner worlds of historical and imagined personalities. By the same token, even his *World of Yesterday* was intended to offer a rediscovery of time past and lost. Zweig turned into more of an explorer the more he felt the need to break free from his own constraints as defined by his origins and social class. Small wonder that when he, the world-renowned author, felt trapped and confined to a five-mile radius of movement in the deceiving idyll of Bath, he was reminded of his South American venture, perceiving it as a way out.

Remembering Johann August Suter

Evidently, the periods Zweig was interested in most were those of time thresholds – in the case of Erasmus, Castellio, and indeed Magellan, from the late Middle Ages to the Modern era. Like with all other biographies Zweig wrote, the one on Magellan was based on intensive research, which even included recently (1936) published material in Portuguese.[5]

Zweig's heroic explorers of all kinds felt 'demonically' driven, rushed, and propelled by a desire for newness, or indeed, Otherness. Time and again, perhaps even when he embarked on his *Magellan*, Zweig may well have been reminded of these feelings, which were epitomised by his description of the Swiss adventurer, or rather, desperado, Johann August Suter. This colourful character from the county of Basel – a trickster, fraud, in short, a petty criminal – 'tired of Europe', abandoned his wife and three children in 1834, and managed to join a passage from Le Havre to New York, where he established himself for about three years as a jack of all trades. He made enough money to mount an expedition to the West, leaving, as Zweig puts it, 'Fort Independence for the Unknown'. With the Pacific Ocean in sight he claimed a large territory, calling it New Helvetia and turning it to an immensely prosperous large-scale settlement where he became one of the world's richest men.

But the narrator of Zweig's version of the story repeatedly asks: 'The richest man? No – the most impoverished, pitiful, the most disappointed beggar on earth.' For it was gold that some of his workers found on Suter's territory, unleashing the famous gold rush by which Suter's land was overrun. The gold diggers in effect disowned Suter, who had no legal protection for his land until 1850 when California became part of the Unites States of America. The Law Courts, by then established in San Francisco, confirmed that Suter was the legal owner of the gold that was found on his land, but this only led to uproar and violent protest by the many intoxicated by a craving for gold. Suter's property was looted and destroyed. Legally speaking he remained in the right, but the authorities were too weak or too indolent to enforce the law. Suter would die as a pauper, having learnt to hate the precious metal that made him poor.

Somewhat surprisingly, Zweig did not expand this story into a major piece of non-fiction (or fiction). Perhaps he felt that the mere thought of a doomed expedition of this magnitude would have spoilt his own exploratory ambitions. At any rate, this snapshot of a historical failure assembles all possible downsides: expeditions can have fraudulent motivations; every explorer tempts fate; successful missions can be short-lived; and, most importantly, no explorer can help himself as he feels compelled to do what is necessary to take him into the unknown. The latter resembles the venture that, for Zweig, every literary 'exploration' entailed, most notably one major 'fruit' of the South American voyage: the decision to write a biography on Magellan, even though before he departed from Europe he wanted an end to his '*biografismo*', as he called it in a letter to Hans Carossa.[6]

Judaism, briefly re-examined

The layers of consciousness in a writer of Zweig's quality and multi-directional commitment generate a complex fabric. When reading his letters, diary entries, and literary as well as essayistic work at any given period in his life, one is struck by the simultaneity of Zweig's creative diversity. This very diversity consisted, however, of highly focused activities with (self-)distraction and concentration alternating often rapidly. It appears, though, that this journey to South America had a particularly cathartic and eminently inspiring effect on Zweig renewing his belief, at least for a while, in the regenerating forces within human culture. Thus, it is not surprising to find that we get some significant comments on fundamentals in terms of his outlook and plan for writing on his return journey from South America and in the months thereafter. Topics included, once again, his principal position towards Judaism, as expressed in a letter to Rabbi Alfred Wolf in Cincinatti, who had written an article on Zweig's attitude towards Judaism. In this letter, Zweig insisted that Judaism must retain its transnational quality and should not 'encrust itself' in Hebrew culture. It should remain a universal ideal, avoiding too much emphasis on its specificity. He pointed out that he had never denied his Jewish origins, but had not overemphasised them. He argued that since the destruction of the second temple in Jerusalem the world, as such, had become the temple for the Jews (IV, 178). This letter was written from Naples, still under the impression of the Brazilian culture where racial separation, let alone segregation, was unknown.

In correspondence with his Italian translator Lavinia Mazzucchetti, after she had expressed reservations against his Jewish legend *The Buried Candelabrum*, Zweig pointed out the strong symbolism that radiated from this one object 'travelling through [a] thousand years'. But he was also clear about his own reservations towards any dogmatic conception of Judaism, pointing out that Jews in the past, 'as a small Arab grouping', had lost their sense of measure by claiming that they were 'the divinely chosen centre of the universe'. He suggested that someone should write a new version of his 'dear Erasmus's' *In Praise of Folly*, claiming that it was always the '*Wahnmenschen*' ('possessed') that created the dangerously 'incommensurable'. Furthermore, he indicated that such 'folly' must have also been behind Magellan, whose action Zweig called 'a thousand times greater than that of Columbus' (IV, 169).

At any rate, to call Zweig's attitude towards Judaism even in 1936 'ambivalent' would not be a mistake. For instance, in a letter to his Jewish friend Raoul Auernheimer, written on his return passage from South America, Zweig gave the following reason for why he did not put himself too much into the foreground on the PEN International conference: he 'did not want that the few Jews that were present' would be prevented from appearing too prominently (IV, 166). This remark reminds one of an ironic comment made by Zweig in an interview with René Lévy in late summer 1933 for Henri Barbusse's weekly paper *Monde*, when he was asked what he made of the anti-Semitism amongst the Hitler supporters: 'All in all, [anti-Semitism] is the nicest compliment one can make Judaism by ascribing to it the future universal development of mystical forces and by claiming that five hundred thousand Jews could dominate and ruin sixty million Germans.' The following point was a less ironic one: 'The truth of the matter is that Jews occupy in the literary, artistic, and intellectual life, and worldwide, too, a scale of influence that exceeds their numbers. It is equally true that the Jews pushed themselves into the foreground of the political life at the beginning of the German revolution (1918/19). Perhaps a kind of counter-reaction is for some of them not all too regrettable.'[7] None of Zweig's words were so soon in urgent need of being eaten – but not so the rest of the interview, which sparkles with clear-cut analyses of the political situation in Germany in 1933.

The example of Magellan

Literary writing is projection. Perhaps this is especially the case when a writer of Zweig's ambition concerns, if not devotes, himself to a seafarer and explorer, with a figure whose brief was to transgress the limitations of the ordinary. Zweig, through his biographical work, connected himself often enough with extraordinary characters, suggesting an obvious implication: he who deals with the exceptional has something exceptional in him, too. Though one character trait in Zweig we have encountered frequently by now speaks against this identification with the extraordinariness of many of his literary 'objects': his almost self-effacing modesty and shying away from 'representation'. Except for Franz Anton Mesmer and to a certain extent Freud, this series of extraordinary personalities does not include (natural) scientists. Louis Pasteur he gladly left to Friderike.

At any rate, it is remarkable to find that after his large-scale biographical undertaking Zweig felt ready to embark on another equally ambitious project of a decidedly different kind. *Magellan* was to evidence what he explained in a letter of 10 December 1936 to Hans Carossa after his return to London: 'Travelling means to me to overcome inner inertia and contradict the laws of gravity that confines us to the narrowness' of ordinary existence, 'rewarding us with audaciousness'; travellers return from such journeys with 'affirming life more strongly' (III, 173).

Every so often, Zweig liked to examine, if not 'explore', how he came about writing a book. With his *Magellan*, too, he spends the entire introduction doing just that. Once again, he emphasises the intrinsic connection between life and work. Modifying the famous phrase by the Latin writer Terentianus Maurus, *habent sua fata libelli* (books have a fate of their own), just slightly, Zweig implies that every one of his books has a history. Narrating it must therefore be part of an author's personal history, or indeed autobiography. This is very much the message of the opening of his *Magellan*. As pointed out in the 'preliminaries' of this book, Zweig suggested a particular catchphrase for this biographical exploration: *navigare necesse est*. Navigating through space and time, as well as through lives, he identified as an essential task in any case – especially in connection with a seafarer's existence like Magellan's.

As for what it was that triggered writing his *Magellan*, Zweig mentions but one 'powerful sentiment – that of shame'.[8] He was thoroughly ashamed of himself, or so Zweig admits to his readers, once he realised his growing 'impatience' with this voyage; for he 'suddenly' realised just how privileged he was to travel in all this unspeakable luxury of a cruise liner, compared to the hardship explorers like Magellan, Columbus, or Vasco da Gama and their men had to endure when they encountered the unknown, 'lost in the infinite, ceaselessly in peril, exposed to all the vicissitudes of storm, to every kind of privation.'[9] Magellan's ambition and achievement – namely to have connected the Occident with the Orient by finding the sea link between the oceans, and thus having sailed around the world for the first time – seemed nothing short of implausible; 'Yet what can be better than a truth which seems utterly improbable? There is always something inconceivable about man's supreme deeds, for the simple reason that they greatly transcend average human powers, but it is by performing the incredible that man regains faith in his own self.'[10] Thus Zweig concludes his introduction, as so often, with a moral, and sets the scene and tone for his exploration of the life of this extraordinary explorer. Precisely the inclusion of wisdoms like these in Zweig's biographical writings distinguish him from today's approach to 'biographising'. They read like extrapolations from a wealth of human experience but, once again, testify to Zweig's interest in connecting historical situations with timeless insights into the course of life. But timelessness, assuming we subscribe to its existence, cannot become dated.

In his narrative of Magellan's life Zweig moves, again, back and forth from the general to the particular. Like with his previous biographies, it is a combination of painstaking research and a projection of what he wants to see in the historical personality in question. This amalgamation sometimes amounted to documentary fiction or imaginatively massaged documents. As ever interested in 'crucial moments' in his heroes' lives, he pays extended attention to Magellan's decision to renounce his allegiance to Portugal following King Emanuel's unfavourable, if not humiliating, treatment of his allegedly most experienced navigator, who was severely injured in combat (in Morocco in 1513). But then

> little gratitude did the kings of Spain and Portugal show to those bold conquistadors who added whole worlds to their dominions. Columbus was brought back to Seville in chains; Cortez fell into disgrace, Pizarro was murdered; Núñez de Balboa, the discoverer of the Pacific, was beheaded; Camoes, Portuguese warrior and poet, spent, like Cervantes, months and years in a jail which was little better than a dung heap. Amazing was the unthankfulness of the age of discovery.[11]

Magellan decided to go into voluntary exile and seek protection and commission from King Charles of Spain, later Emperor Charles V of the Holy Roman Empire of the German Nation – itself a multi-ethnic state entity if ever there was one.

At this point in Zweig's biography, one realises the significance he ascribed to Magellan against the backdrop of the 1930s. Emigration meant for Magellan – and perhaps not only for him, such is Zweig's implication – new orientation and perspectives. This explorer was ready to sacrifice himself for a greater good, in his case the connection between the Pacific and Atlantic Oceans, thus bringing together peoples and their cultures. Even though Magellan was in command of hundreds of sailors, Zweig portrays him as a 'tragic solitary' whose 'disposition compelled him to be so incessantly alone'; but one who was passionate, if not monomaniacal, about his idea to find the sea route around the world. But it is exactly this intentionality in what

Magellan did that remains controversial. Zweig wanted him to be on a 'hero's journey' even though the actual source material does not justify any such label. He had the order to reach the Maluku Islands on the Western route, subjugate them to the Spanish realm and return on the very same route. In the Indian Ocean it was not an option for him to sail under the Spanish banner as it was declared a Portuguese terrain in the Treaty of Tordesillas in 1494. It appears that the king of Spain had explicitly forbidden Magellan to trespass into those waters, however a monsoon wind made one of Magellan's ships, the *Victoria*, sail in the opposite direction.[12]

Ruthless determination met in Magellan the humanist, the military man, and the peace-lover. Zweig saw him undoubtedly as a kindred spirit to Erasmus and Castellio – an Erasmus-on-sea, so to speak. The 'demonic drive' in Magellan that clearly had continued to hold a special fascination over Zweig turned into the myth of this man, given that he went missing on an island in the Pacific. Already Alexander von Humboldt had declared Magellan a champion of progress that furthered the development of human mankind. Similarly, the Chilean historian Diego Barros Arana declared in what was the first biography on Magellan that he had died 'without heirs but his deeds and his glory … [were] both immortal'.[13] Zweig's *Magellan* was very much written in this tradition of transforming an accidental occurrence in history into something intentional. The life of the very seafarer whose destiny it was to prove, by default, that the earth is round had to be rounded off itself. It is puzzling and yet, at the same time, quite endearing to find that Zweig ignored in his Magellan biography that there is no such thing as a planned odyssey.

However, it is worth noting that the humanist message Zweig connected with this biography *did* reach his contemporaries, critical comments (of note, from Ludwig Marcuse, expressing reservations about the 'primacy of the heroic over any other cultural value') notwithstanding. The novelist and physician Ernst Weiss – a former friend of Kafka's and one of the many writers supported by Zweig – spoke in a 1938 review of the 'courage' this novel offered to its readers, 'the courage to live'; he added, 'What could be more precious than just that in times like these?'[14] Incidentally, Weiss committed suicide on 14 June 1940 when German troops entered Paris, where he was in exile. News one and three-quarter years later – that a German submarine had sunk two Brazilian ships in retaliation for the country's decision to break off diplomatic relations with the axis powers in Berlin, Rome, and Tokyo – may also have triggered Stefan and Lotte Zweig's decision to take their lives in the remoteness of their exile in Petrópolis.

Venturing through the United States (1938–9)

Fascination and bewilderment characterised Stefan Zweig's US-American experiences, his encounters with New York in particular. The 'rhythm' of this metropolis had excited him in 1911 when he encountered it for the first time. His enthusiasm for New York remained largely unchanged until the mid-1930s, when it eventually gave way to irritation. But nothing in his reflections on the US matched his diatribe against what he saw as the 'growing monotony' of the world because of its 'Americanisation'. He had published an article on this subject on 31 January 1925 in *Neue Freie Presse*. In today's terminology it would be called a diatribe against globalisation, in which he lambasted the growing standardisation and uniformity modelled on an American-style consumer society. As surprising as it is coming from Zweig, the European citizen of the world, this polemic is not inexplicable. To a certain extent it is quite like the 'culture' against 'civilisation' rhetoric practised most prominently by Thomas Mann in his *Reflections of a Nonpolitical Man* (1918). Zweig published his article at a time when the US-American influence in Europe reached its first peak, mainly due to the Dawes Plan of 1924 that aimed to resolve the German debt crisis that resulted from the Versailles Treaty. But, if anything, the mastermind behind this plan, Charles Gates Dawes, represented a highly cultivated type of a sophisticated banker, politician, diplomat, and musical composer, whose own 'worldliness' and foresight was nothing short of exemplary. Even though Zweig did not mention Dawes explicitly in his piece, it was US-backed global capitalism that provided the backdrop to this polemic against this trend to uniformity.

It was barely one week after Zweig's essay that the Austro-Hungarian writer and critic Felix Salten, the author of *Bambi* (published in 1923, it was intended as a parable for what he saw as the endangered Jewry of Europe, but went on to become a Disney icon), questioned the premises of Zweig's article, pointing out the merits of global plurality and technological achievements in the field of communication and travel alone.[15]

Some fifteen years later, Zweig's most elaborate lecture tour through the United States from December 1938 to the end of February 1939, including a concluding sneak visit to Canada, saw him performing amidst this very plurality at some fifteen places, among them Indianapolis, Chicago, Detroit, Cincinatti, Houston, New Orleans, San Antonio, Dallas, Denver, Salt Lake City, San Francisco, and Los Angeles. Such was the significance of this visit to him that Lotte, who accompanied him, kept a diary, which she typed up clearly for Zweig's later use.[16] This is evidenced by the fact that he used some of the material to extrapolate the substance for four short essays on 'Hotels', 'The Railway', 'The Negro Question' (from today's perspective, undoubtedly the most problematic), and, somewhat surprisingly, 'Detroit', a city which one would not necessarily connect him with.[17] He spoke about 'The Mystery of the Creative Process' and 'The Historiography of Tomorrow'; not the snazziest of topics, one would have thought, but they, or rather Zweig himself, had such an appeal that the lectures drew large audiences. He addressed the anxiety in Europe that war was imminent; the verbal terror of propaganda that would precede military confrontation; the resentment that had turned into open hatred, regardless of the political system; the reign of lying as the essence of propaganda; and the tendency of dangerous self-isolationism. He argued that tomorrow's historiography would have to take all these evils into account, to reflect them, but to point out that a genuinely cultural history would need to focus on what the nations owed to each other. But he conceded that it was more difficult to write engagingly about the 'soft humanism of Erasmus' than the 'amusing passions of

Casanova or the rise of Napoleon.'[18] The historiography of tomorrow should no longer contain, Zweig argued, heroism on the battlefield but instead, for instance, in the laboratory; he praised the fact that in the US the emphasis was on the rise of American civilisation, and not purely the nation – i.e. political history. He applauded news that a biography on Marie Curie had found millions of readers in the US, thus reflecting their interest in human creativity.

Already onboard ship, Zweig's ever-present concern with matters of creativity made him read John Livingston Lowes's *The Road to Xanadou* (1927), remarking in his notes that this was not only an important book about Coleridge but about the 'creative condition', intensified in this case through opium. In contrast, he was bemused by the 'strange habit' of American magazines to indicate the 'reading time' with bizarre precision, as time was increasingly of the essence: '6 minutes 7 seconds or 4 minutes 10 seconds'. He added, 'I do not know how they calculate this and why.' On arrival in New York, Zweig noted that the 'weather is as glorious as before' and 'people's faces are without restlessness and tension'. But soon he commented on racial issues, suggesting that different from legislation in the southern part of the US, racial cohabitation is blurred and leads to uncertainties: 'The negro in a hotel does not know whether he is welcome; does not know whether someone at the next table will get up and go.' He noted that 'the racial standpoint' was a mere intensification of the one of nationality with Hitler as its main exponent, adding, 'Negroes symbolise something of the Jewish fate.' This was a concern that would accompany him throughout this journey.[19]

Thanks to Lotte, this second voyage to the US is the most meticulously documented of all his journeys. The reasons for this meticulousness are not quite clear. It is possible that both Lotte and Stefan tried to ascertain potential future destinations should there be the need to leave England one day. Or did it simply reflect an increased curiosity in the US on their part, and an interest in keeping a record of what turned out to be Zweig's most extensive lecture tour to date?

Zweig's comments on racial segregation were prompted by what he referred to as the '*Negergrenze*' right through Kansas City – the so-called Troost Wall or Troost Divide, given that one part of the city belonged to the Federal State of Missouri and the other to Kansas.[20] Zweig compared the transgression of this inner-city racial border with going from the Netherlands or Switzerland to Germany there and then – with Kansas being Germany. But Zweig was quick to put a question mark behind his own former assumption that the situation of 'Afro-Americans' was directly comparable to those of the Jews under Hitlerism: 'The difference being that the tragedy begins with those [non-whites] who are educated' and still cannot participate in the 'so-called' culture of the white Americans, whilst the sophistication of Jews allowed them to come into their own – admittedly by 1938/9 a rather unrealistic notion.[21]

What follows is, from today's perspective, an openly racist perception of the Black American community in Kansas City. We get comments from Zweig like 'a Jew would find it dreadful to stay in a hotel run by, and designated to, negroes, given their awfully low standards'. He remarks at one point that what 'might also be interesting for Jews' is that 'total segregation' often means more 'safety and security' for the Black communities because 'they know exactly what they are allowed to do and what not'. It appears that Zweig (with Lotte or by himself is not clear) visited a 'negro hospital' and a 'negro university' (perhaps he meant the Lincoln High School in the Bowery district of Kansas City), the former mainly 'funded by Jewish philanthropists', although anonymously. He considers even a remigration of Black Americans back to Africa to be a possibility, suggesting that interracial relations, let alone the mixing of races, could never be as successful here as in Brazil – since 1936 Zweig's blue-eyed yardstick for racial community.[22]

Interestingly, in her daily account Lotte scarcely referred to the concept '*Negerfrage*' ('negro question') but did mention the segregating '*Farbgrenze*' ('colour border'; she did not use the word '*Negergrenze*' either) between the two parts of Kansas City. She also noted on their way to Texas appalling signs of apartheid, such as two different waiting rooms for Black and white train passengers. Furthermore, she speaks of their disappointment that their train did not have a restaurant car for breakfast but that 'a negro goes through the carriages selling coffee in paper cups with soggy sandwiches'. Standards were clearly slipping, even though Zweig would wax lyrical about the comfort of US trains. He was more critical about the lack of reliable timetables and the lower speed of the engine (compared to what he was used to from trains in Europe) but was impressed with the air-conditioning systems. All that occurred on 23 and 24 January 1939. It was in fact five days later, when Lotte and Stefan visited a 'negro hospital' together and indeed a 'negro university' in New Orleans, where and when she did record the 'strict segregation of the races' but refrained from commenting on it. On 30 January, on the train from Houston to San Antonio, they were caught up in European reality as the train radio in the club car relayed Hitler's speech in translation on the sixth anniversary of his coming to power, in which he spoke about the history of his 'movement'. Zweig continued his lecturing tour with reflections of 'history as a poetess'.[23]

Zweig's short impressionistic essays and the extensiveness of Lotte's diary might also suggest that he could have planned to write a more comprehensive book on America along the lines of his study on Brazil, which may well have set in with his reflections on one day in Detroit (18 January 1939). First, Lotte's account in her diary, which may also serve as a sample of a typical day on this lecture tour:

> 18.1[.1939] Detroit
> At 7.50 am arrived in Detroit [coming from Chicago, where they stayed in the Bismarck hotel – R. G.] Along long, sad street to the Statler Hotel. Once again, trouble because they wanted to give us an enormous suite for the day; breakfasting downstairs, telephoned with a lady from the Town Hall who had organised the viewing of the Ford Factory for us; changed the lecture slightly. Then by taxi to the Fisher Theatre, about a quarter of an hour drive, a modern beautiful cinema. After agreeing on Questions lecture on 'History', chaired by bookseller Hamer. Audience very impressed, questions mostly about the imminence of war. Asked to provide copies of the lecture for distribution. Luncheon in the same venue, at Z[weig's] table the bookseller, a rabbi and females. [Z.] was urged to give a short address at lunch. Thereafter a crush of women because of

signing books even though Z had signed already a lot of books after the lecture.

At 2 pm Mr Simonds picks us up, as we were told one of the five most important people at the Ford Factory and the one who has in fact build up 'Greenwich Village' there. In the car that takes us there is also Francis Jahl, one of the oldest associates of Edison. The car journey to the factory takes about half-an hour; we explored it partly by foot, partly by car and, eventually, by an old coach, or rather sleigh through Greenwich [that is, Greenfield – R. G.] Village that is snowed under. Entered Edison's house where Francis Jahl explains everything to us, in Lincoln's house and the school, which Edison attended, and into an old grocer's shop.

Eventually, after a peep into a kind of meeting dance, or sports hall we were taken back to Detroit followed by a short stay at Hamer's bookstore.

Limitless expanse of this city, which apparently houses three million people. Wrote a few letters back in the hotel, went back to an office in the Town Hall for which the key was deposited for me, dined in the hotel, whilst Z. had his fur coat mended and arranged; then a short walk and back to the Main Station. Left at 11.45 pm.[24]

Zweig's own essayistic account makes it plain that it was the Ford 'factory town' which fascinated him, even more so Thomas Edison's Menlo Park laboratory, which Henry Ford had reconstructed at Greenfield Village in the Detroit suburb of Dearborn. There, Zweig could study traces and instruments that testified to Edison's 'genius' and the process of creativity in technology. The living presence of Francis Jahl, Edison's associate, made the whole experience 'real' for him.

But what did Zweig make of the Detroit event? He was pleased that during his lecture the lights were dimmed, which spared him from 'seeing the all-too reverent faces of the audience'. He noted that dimming lights seems to be an American 'fashion in restaurants, dance halls, and bars'. He commented on the rabbi at lunch being a modern-minded one, without a beard (Zweig himself would periodically grow a beard, mainly when he felt depressed), who told him that he had read with his pupils Zweig's Jewish legend, *The Buried Candelabrum*, and gave sermons on his play *Jeremiah*. Like elsewhere in America, he met 'dispersed Austrians', in this instance a Baroness Hatvany, but also the daughter of Mark Twain, Mrs Gabrilowitsch.[25]

The Ford factory struck him as a 'world of its own', where a horse-drawn carriage looks like an oddity. He was impressed with the railway system within the factory compound consisting of some twenty locomotives: a whole fleet of ships that transported goods across Lake Michigan and along the extensive canal system. With delight, he noticed a radio station that connected the factory with *Brazilian* rubber plantations. He noticed the speed with which entire cars were being assembled ('in fifty-five minutes').[26]

Even though he wondered whether Henry Ford's habit of transporting whole houses from elsewhere in the country and reassembling them on his vast grounds was not slightly weird, he was grateful for being able to inspect Edison's house, which Ford had brought over from Newark with all its instruments, apparatuses, and chemicals. He even saw Edison's phonograph, which could still record and amplify sounds and was moved by the 'little lamp that after three years of experimenting provided the first electric light'. Zweig found himself enchanted by Francis Jahl's accent, a 'melange of Jiddish, Viennese and Hungarian, impossible to imitate'. Jahl interested Zweig because as a young man he had witnessed a 'world historical moment' when he saw for the first time a carbon filament glowing in a light bulb. With Jahl Zweig was in touch with what had mattered to him all along so much: '*Augenblicke*', moments in history that decided on the course of times. Zweig was struck by the fact that the house of this fiercely independent inventor Edison, who 'preferred to work not as part of a collective in a closed organisation', but as an individual, should be remembered here, amid a production system that had invented the assembly line.[27]

This is all very well, but something else is perhaps even more striking: the fact that Zweig seemed to have been completely unaware of Henry Ford's well-known rampant anti-Semitism and enthusiasm for Hitler. Ford was the leading voice amongst the US advocates of a

Jewish world conspiracy. His notorious publication in four volumes, *The International Jew*, which consisted of his articles in *The Dearborn Independent* in 1920, a paper he owned until 1927, also appeared in German in 1921. Hitler quoted Ford in *Mein Kampf* (1925) as their admiration for each other was distinctly mutual. All that was well known and it came as no surprise that Ford was awarded in 1938, only a few months before Zweig's visit to Detroit, the Grand Cross of the German Eagle, Hitler's Germany's highest decoration for foreign nationals.[28] Is it really possible that this was unknown to Zweig, or that nobody over lunch on 18 January 1939, not even the chief rabbi of Detroit, had mentioned this fact? The only thing Zweig could not have known was that Hitler had a framed photograph of Henry Ford on display in his study in the Chancellery.

With Lotte, in sickness and in health – until ...
Heirs of Stefan Zweig

Pity about Pity

When Zweig embarked on this second venture to the US, his work on his large-scale novel, *Beware of Pity*, lay behind him. Zweig would have been forgiven for entertaining the thought that he was the Balzac of Austria 'as it was' before 1914, together with Arthur Schnitzler, Robert Musil, Joseph Roth, and, to a certain extent, Alexander Lernet-Holenia, to mention but a few of his contemporaries in this extraordinary crop of literary and artistic talent in that particular period. But memory of this period was by now as dispersed as their representatives, if still alive at all. To a certain extent, Zweig must have experienced what was left of this former atmosphere when he visited Vienna back in March 1935. There, he enjoyed *Kaffeehaus* meetings with Alban Berg (who died later that year), Franz Werfel, Ernst Krenek, and Bruno Walter, thus almost simulating the past.

Zweig seemed to have been of the opinion that producing the 'great novel' was a precondition for lasting recognition, and *Beware of Pity* was to become just that: a comprehensive exploration of a particular emotion, that could capture the imagination of a large readership that wanted to immerse itself in times past during the increasingly unbearable times present.

At any rate, when Zweig's novel was published in 1938 by, for the first time, Gottfried Bermann Fischer in Stockholm, Hitler had reached the absolute peak of his popularity after the annexation of Austria and the Munich Agreement, which allowed him by consent of Great Britain, France, and Italy to incorporate parts of Czechoslovakia, the *Sudetenland*, into his Reich. It was also to be the year of the infamous pogroms against Jews on 9 November, the so-called *Reichskristallnacht*, making it plain that barbarity was in charge 'for good'.

Across the Atlantic, in Princeton, Thomas Mann was busy working on his cheery novel *Lotte in Weimar*, which Zweig would praise as a particularly fine achievement. It clearly struck a chord with him as he detected an equivalent to his main concern, namely, to help preserve cultural, or to be more precise Goethean, values, as derived from the past. Zweig could afford to be generous given that he now had his very own 'Lotte' – not as a fictitious character, but in real life.

But 1938 was also the year when Thomas Mann wrote his essay 'That Man is My Brother', later known under its German title 'Bruder Hitler', first published on 3 March 1939 in the US-American magazine *Esquire*. One does wonder whether Thomas Mann told Zweig anything about either when the latter visited him on 4 January 1939 for lunch in Princeton. Lotte only says in her diary of the 'American Journey' that 'Z.' was exhausted when he returned from there.[1] She assumed he had encountered traffic problems, but perhaps the luncheon with the revered master of German prose had been somewhat taxing and, just perhaps, conversation may have covered Mann's extraordinary approach to the subject of Hitler. Zweig never went as far as Thomas Mann did in suggesting that Hitler, as a failed artist, shared several characteristics with him, such as the art of cunning deception, inevitably coming up with deliberately incorrect claims as all literature operates with fictious, that is *per se* incorrect information. Nor did Zweig presume, as Thomas Mann speculated, that Hitler conquered Vienna because he wanted to control the city of Freud, literally and non-literally.[2] Even in his lucid penultimate chapter on the rise of Hitler ('Incipit Hitler') in *The World of Yesterday*, Zweig would not share Thomas Mann's view. In his ever-reliable diary Mann only noted Zweig's presence for lunch on that day. But in his letter to Zweig, which contained the invitation to lunch, Mann cryptically referred to his 'eagerness' to talk through 'the whole thing' with his prospective guest.[3] The commentary suggested that this 'whole thing' might have referred to the consequences of the *Anschluss* of Austria and the Munich Agreement of 29 September 1938, together with Mann's suggestion to produce '*Aufklärungsbroschüren*' for the Germans: brochures to enlighten the Germans about what was really happening to them, Europe, and the world. Mann had hoped that Zweig, together with Heinrich Mann, Erwin Schrödinger, Lotte Lehmann, Franz Werfel, and others, would contribute to this publication venture. The project had to be abandoned following the outbreak of the Second World War but, to a certain extent, Thomas Mann's essay 'That Man is My Brother', which provided such enlightenment about Hitler in an (enlarged) nutshell, could well have been part of 'the whole thing' they had intended to talk about at this luncheon in Princeton.

Novel of a lifetime

The mountainous text corpus of the novel *Beware of Pity*, as preserved in the German Literature Archive in Marbach, needs to be seen to be believed: the first stages of the project; the actual manuscript; typescript; and page proofs with Zweig's corrections, leather-bound by an English aristocratic friend to whom Zweig gave the entirety of this work and its traces, all kept in five boxes, containing seven volumes and three cassettes.[4] This corpus is a manifestation of literary achievement and the last that Zweig completed in Europe before his final transatlantic emigration. It is the kind of text corpus he would once have liked to acquire for his autograph collection himself. But by now the need to discharge material was stronger.

Just how highly Zweig rated the importance of this novel is reflected by the way he introduced it. It is the protagonist himself who, years after it all happened, tells his story to an acquaintance, the actual author of the novel. But this moment of hide-and-seek and of who is who does not deflect from the actual complex story but leads straight into it. If we look at the compositional method of this novel, we need to remind ourselves what this word originally means: the Greek *méthodos* means 'detour', or 'transcending path'. As such the reader is sent off on various 'detours', although the one crucial, striking event occurs early in the novel – a sudden insight into the condition of the main female protagonist, Edith. But some minor 'detours' first; the major ones are to follow suit.

The protagonist, named Hofmiller, a highly decorated knight commander in the Austro-Hungarian army in the First World War, recalls the story of when he was a twenty-five-year-old lieutenant in an Uhlan regiment somewhere in the sticks in the Hungarian plane in relative proximity to the Austrian heartland. Now, he is high up in the running of the National Theatre in Vienna and is tired of being reminded of his former military-celebrity status and being pigeon-holed as a war hero. Truth be told, he was in fact awarded the most prestigious military order, the *Maria Theresiaorden*, which was the only order of merit worldwide for acting out of line with a specific command, leading to military success. Failure, however, would have meant that the officer faced execution. It was an order for extraordinary bravery coupled with intelligent foresight. This is significant to know for the interpretation of this novel, as the young cavalry lieutenant Hofmiller possessed neither at the time of the story. In fact, his failure changed him to the extent that he became worthy of this – understandably – most rarely awarded order in the Austro-Hungarian army.

It is surprising to find that Zweig, the arch-pacifist, showed such intimate familiarity with the military, and that the non-horse-rider Zweig (dogs were more his thing) wrote with such great knowledge about horses and the world of cavalrymen.

Emotional volatility was one of Zweig's characteristics. Friderike already remarked on this very feature of 'St.' in her unpublished diary of 1916/17, from when they stayed in Hotel Nelböck in Salzburg in October 1916. It was during this stay that she discovered, on her lonely walks over the hills of Salzburg (in this instance the Kapuzinerberg), the villa that was to become their future domicile, whilst Zweig was busy working on his drama *Jeremiah*:

> Yesterday amidst an exuberant mood the demon was stirring in him and catapulted me, perhaps for good measure, out of the ecstasy caused by the happiness of our closely living together. Sometimes he feels especially in moments of well-being with me a certain fear that he might lose out in terms of adventures. He then paints the ghost

of infidelity before me. It then takes me a whole day to recuperate from it.[5]

Towards the end of their stay in Salzburg the situation had become worse, partly caused, or so it appears, by the daunting prospect of Zweig having to take up his duties in the War Archive again after this reprieve:

> Stefan is – I don't know why – perhaps because of the end of the vacation – erratic, easily irritable. Oh, dear God, nothing but nothing persists with him as far as his actions are concerned; nothing can calm him down, the calm one. When this happens something cold and indifferent emerges from his otherwise caring kindness and tenderness, something that does not even shy away from a bit of malice and revenge.

Friderike even spoke of Zweig's 'phantasms of liberty', suggesting that they were the cause of his erratic behaviour, resembling that of a caged animal.[6]

Was it that very 'coldness' that made Zweig exclude any reference to Friderike, and Lotte for that matter, in *The World of Yesterday* and most of his own diaries? Egotism and self-centeredness, normally camouflaged under the more palatable concept of 'subjectivity', as a source of artistic creativity was not a feature he had considered when examining the mysteries of artistic creation, but perhaps it should have been. For it clearly featured prominently in the psyche of this otherwise so thoroughly impressive advocate of humanism, too.

The crippling of emotions

Pity, or compassion, was not a topic or motif that had featured prominently in Zweig's works. But now they took centre stage. Zweig would have been familiar with Nietzsche's scathing verdict of this emotion but somehow it still comes as a surprise that Zweig's humanism had not embraced 'compassion' earlier. But his new protagonist, Hofmiller, learns about the pitfalls of pity the hard way.

The preface-like opening, or frame, of the novel insists on a moment of reciprocity, implying that those who tell lots of stories will be told some, too, and that those who have often tried to interpret people's fates will hear from many a person about their fate.[7] The novel's motto, a self-quotation, indicating the intrinsic connection between Zweig and this particular work, differentiates between two types of compassion. One is sentimental and weak – as captured by the title of the original, *Impatience of the Heart* – and results in an embarrassing captivation by the sorrow of others, which is not a real 'co-suffering' but an instinctive repudiation of alien suffering from one's own soul. The other form of compassion is non-sentimental and creative, which persists with the other to the point that it goes to the limit of and even transcends one's own capacity. The entire novel, then, focuses on the former 'false' conception of compassion.

In short, Zweig's novel tells the story of the relationship between a young officer (Hofmiller) and a young lady paralysed after an accident (Edith). It is the life on an estate owned by Edith's father, the overprotective and legendarily wealthy baron of Kekesvalva. When Hofmiller is graced with an invitation to a ball at the Kekesvalvas' he does not realise that Edith, who is sitting behind a table, is in fact bound to a wheelchair with a painful mechanical contraption that allows her only to get up and make one or two steps. When he becomes suddenly aware of her paraplegic state it is too late. She is confronted with Hofmiller's inept chivalry, but her fall also indicates her literally 'falling into' loving him. From then on, the story is permeated by a strange interplay of attraction and rejection, with Edith in her helpless frustration being torn between wooing and cursing Hofmiller whilst he does not know where he stands any more. He can only feel sympathy for Edith – compassion, pity, but not love. Yet, his attachment to Kekesvalva is ever-growing; he feels privileged by being in their company and earning the unconditional trust of the lord of the manor. But Kekesvalva, increasingly desperate for Hofmiller to commit himself to his daughter, has a (very) dark side to him too, which he discloses to Hofmiller by degrees. His original background is that of a Jewish jack of all trades, who managed to climb the social ladder through fraudulent activities. Most notably, he tricked the humble-minded heiress of Kekesvalva out of her possessions by making her sell the estate to him for a mere fraction of its real value. The narrator mobilises all the negative clichés about Jews but only to generate considerable 'sympathy' for this confident man, who has been shattered by the untimely death of his wife and then by his beloved daughter's condition. But it is the local medic, Doctor Condor, who pushes Hofmiller to accept Edith's advances as an 'emotional cure' for her, pointing out to him that if he refused her, it would kill her. But when Hofmiller finally agrees to be engaged to Edith and the celebrations in Kekesvalva are underway, he takes fright and 'escapes'. During the emotionally highly charged final sections (there are no actual chapters, thus intensifying the narrative stream) the reader realises that Edith will not survive this breaking of the engagement on Hofmiller's part. In fact, when unobserved for a moment, she throws herself with literally her last strength from the top of a tower, originally built for her to enjoy the view. When Hofmiller, who was transferred to a different regiment after his behaviour scandalises his previous one, decides, already far away from Kekesvalva, to change his mind and honour his engagement to Edith after all, the telephone lines and telegraph connections are blocked; for the day of Edith's suicide was also the day of the Archduke Franz Ferdinand's assassination in Sarajevo, 29 June 1914. This is the only date, Hofmiller, as narrator, discloses. Once news of Edith's suicide reaches him, he feels like a murderer, who wants to 'escape into the war like a criminal' (UdH, 451).

After their first fateful encounter, Edith concedes that she keeps dreaming about dance and the great ballerinas, be they Saharet, Pavlova, or Karsavina. But her dreams cannot but suffer rude awakenings. Repeatedly, she finds it difficult to control her emotions, and drastic mood swings are her daily bread whilst Hofmiller thinks of himself – in line with the Russian literary tradition – as a 'superfluous person' (UdH, 65) who cannot but hope for some excitement in his rather dreary life. He is keen to observe and preserve social conventions, as to him 'forms mean security' (UdH, 67). This anticipates the opening paragraphs of *The World of Yesterday*, which amount to praise for pre-world-war 'security'. Form is also related to aesthetic appreciation; consequently, Hofmiller notices early on that the tower of the baroque estate is out of keeping. Its 'geometrical forms looked more as if it belonged to harbour docks or an electric power plant' (UdH, 90). The reader gets the desired hint: it will be the tower where something unusual is going to happen.

There is little point in identifying autobiographical moments in this novel. Some might find it intriguing that in the episode when Hofmiller learns about Kekesvalva's fraudulent acquisition of the estate, the name 'Gollinger' crops up (UdH, 164). It might sound like a faint allusion to 'Gollhofer', who in 1937 bought Zweig's Salzburg estate – but on perfectly legal terms. When we read about Hofmiller's delight in horse-riding and the description of an extended ride into the countryside, we are tempted to see Zweig writing this with Rilke's famous *Cornet* epos in rhythmic prose in mind: a poetic composition that no one of Zweig's generation had failed to take note of. But approaches of this kind are ultimately futile. It is much more rewarding to consider the way in which the narrator describes his own appreciation of music (UdH, 206), or Edith's ability to see through her doctor's method of treatment (UdH, 266).

But if one had to single out an episode that displays Zweig's narrative mastery most, one could not do better than to refer to the very moment when Edith, through the tenderness of her caressing Hofmiller's hand, makes him understand that she loves him. It is the love of a disabled body, the tentative and then open eroticism that leaves an undeletable impression on Hofmiller's psyche.

Every so often, we have used the expression 'it is as if' during this biographical study, for it is precisely this mode that dominates Zweig's narratives. It features as the equivalent to the temporal 'as it was' that conditions the mode of remembrance in his fiction. Although in his fiction he inevitably delegated the act of remembering to (some of) his protagonists – like, in the case of *Beware of Pity*, to Hofmiller – his concern for the past, and for preserving the memory of it, became increasingly real.

'It is as if' is normally reserved for fairy tales but this expression captures the key emotions in this novel. Their romantic touch remains unfulfilled, or rather, these emotions are merely wishful thinking, particularly on Edith's part. But Zweig's novel is special because it raises the question of feelings and desires among disabled people, to an extent unmatched by other novels at the time. Hofmiller is embarrassed to admit that he had never thought about that side of their existence before experiencing Edith's passion for him.

Her dramatically restricted mobility, however, can be read as an expression of Zweig's own fear, namely that of being trapped by circumstances, whether personal or political. Small wonder that this novel shares some features with his novella *Fear*, in particular. Actual blackmail in the novella of 1920 (written in 1910) turns into the emotional blackmail that Hofmiller is subjected to. The question of who can trust whom applies to both texts. The message of this novel, if there is one, suggests that not only the mind but the body, too, can 'understand'. This is at least the conclusion Hofmiller draws from watching Edith. Her body tries to understand whether Hofmiller's hand on her is a sign of 'tenderness, love or merely of compassion' (UdH, 358).

Seeking truth about emotions and coming to some certainty about intentions emerge as main concerns in Zweig's novel. Edith is desperate to find out what Hofmiller really feels for her, and Hofmiller, with growing despair about his own situation, is longing for some clarity over the reasons for his attachment to the Kekesvalvar household. Whilst his military comrades back in the garrison act in the spirit of the Viennese proverb 'I say nothing, I only chat', Hofmiller wants to speak the truth but fails to do so out of pity for Edith. In that sense, Hofmiller is 'crippled', too – drastically limited in the way he is expected to behave towards her, with expectations in him going beyond what he seems capable of giving.

The only medical professional in this novel, Doctor Condor, is the one responsible for introducing the 'mysterious double-layeredness' of intellectual persuits (UdH, 156) when he becomes the second narrator in this novel, thus introducing a narrative within the narrative.

For he tells Hofmiller about the background of the 'baron' of Kekesvalva, *vulgo*: Leopold or 'Lämmel' Kanitz, a Jew from the borderlands between Hungary and Slovakia whose father was a poverty-stricken innkeeper. This story within the story has one major merit: It really does present 'truth' about one key character even though the doctor's own origins remain in the dark.

As said, pity deflects; pity weakens; pity dilutes – or such were, in a nutshell, Nietzsche's verdicts of compassion. It is a false emotion, or so he argued, for it is impossible for an outsider to feel what others feel. Therefore, or so Nietzsche judged, compassion is a mere illusion. Ultimately, Zweig's protagonist Hofmiller comes to the same conclusion.

Edith's condition, her severely restricted mobility, is as serious as it can be. But it also stands for a condition of Being that is determined by 'restricted' emotions – be it by convention, tradition, upbringing, or choice. With her erratic behaviour, she wants to burst all seams of 'propriety'; given all the appalling, humiliating constraints she suffers from, she nonetheless appears carefree. She is a born rebel who would take off any time, but her wings were clipped by fate.

There is something radical about this novel *Beware of Pity*, not so much in terms of narrative form but because of what Joan Acocella calls, in her introduction to a more recent translation, the 'first sustained fictional portrait of emotional blackmail based on guilt.'[8] It illustrates the futility of pity, presenting it by showing the reality of a neurosis (in Edith) and its formation (in Hofmiller).

The devaluation of compassion in this novel is striking. Not only does Hofmiller eventually reproach himself for harbouring this sentiment, denouncing himself as a 'fool of pity', he also confesses that he feels 'nauseated by words of pathos' (UdH, 452). By portraying his protagonist in that way, Zweig disowns one key characteristic of his entire œuvre: pathos, now disqualified as something pathetic.

In Zweig's own life, compassion was one of his characteristics. Yet eventually he found it difficult to engage with fellow exiles, whose demands on his support had reached proportions that brought him close to breaking point. Perhaps, therefore, Zweig applied the English title of his novel, *Beware of Pity*, to himself. It replaced in his letters one of his formerly preferred expressions: *'plaignez-moi'*, or 'pity me'.

Eva Altmann with Stefan Zweig and her aunt Lotte in Croton-on-Hudson
Heirs of Stefan Zweig

Clarissa, Montaigne, Balzac: A Fragmentary Trio

Even loose ends can form patterns, just as fragments contain notions of coherence. Fragments can even appear entirely complete, even more so than seemingly finished works of art. Franz Schubert's B-minor symphony *The Unfinished* comes to mind, or his C-major sonata, the so-called *Reliquie* – fragments only in the sense that they do not conform with the conventional form of the symphony or sonata. Otherwise, one would be hard pushed to imagine compositions more complete than these.

There are others, Mozart's *Requiem* of course, where death took the pen from the composer's hand, in this case after the first eight bars of the 'Lacrymosa' movement in the *Dies irae* sequence. In Stefan Zweig's case, the situation was different. In the final phase of his exile, after he decided to leave Europe for good, more of his works were left incomplete. Whilst before it was in essence only *The Post Office Girl* which he had left unfinished, after 1940 'circumstances' prevented him from putting finishing touches to his *Montaigne*, which was intended to be one large-scale essay, a hybrid of thematic monograph and short biography focusing on Zweig's third humanist after Erasmus and Castellio; *Clarissa*, one novel ('of an Austrian kind' as he informed Friderike on 27 October 1941); and *Balzac*, one further monumental biography devoted to his lifelong 'companion'. These incomplete texts need to be held against his book-length proclamation of Brazil as 'a country of the future', the final version of his story *Die spät bezahlte Schuld* (*The Debt*, drafted back in 1935 and first published on 29 June 1941 in *The Chicago Sunday Tribune*), the extraordinary achievement of *The World of Yesterday*, and his final novelistic masterpiece, *Chess*. This stunning array of works and projects came within a dramatically short period of time of barely three years, including two travels to the US and Paris, as well as twice moving house: first from London to Bath, then from Bath to Petrópolis via New York, Brazil, Argentina, and Uruguay (with an extended stay in Rio de Janeiro from mid-November 1940 until mid-January 1941) before going back to New Haven and Ossining in New York State, only to return to Brazil and Rio for a few weeks, then finally to what became his and Lotte's final destination in Petrópolis.

This account alone reads like that of a person 'lost in emigration'. But, to a certain extent, it mirrors Zweig's ever-present restlessness, now intensified under most challenging difficulties. Remarkably, Zweig himself – differently from Lotte, whose asthmatic disposition was of concern – continued to enjoy good physical health, even though the psychological strain on them both can only be imagined. But on Zweig's part, no psychosomatic ailments are known. At least they were able to travel in relative comfort, and compared to other émigrés the Zweigs were privileged as his reputation in exile remained only second to that of Thomas Mann.

It is the sheer parallelisms of these final projects that are nothing short of astounding, notwithstanding the evident cross-fertilisation between them. Their common denominator was 'memory': the force and burden of recollection, the compelling drive to preserve what was worth retaining, and the feeling of irretrievable loss in terms of values and tradition. With Joseph Roth and others no longer alive, and at the other end of the literary spectrum the great modernist (and declared adversary) Robert Musil, Zweig saw himself as the last 'genuine' representative of 'Austria as it once was' – namely, a hub of culture and sophistication. This perception of Austria was a myth that Zweig remained determined to perpetuate, but this did not prevent him from addressing its shortcomings and failings – most notably in *Clarissa*.

Clarissa, or on tangled paths

Memory, speak! – and mingle with all conceivable emotions. Be daring enough to get entangled by diverse directions and ways that somehow lead to some truth about life as it was; for nothing is less straight than a person's life and its circumstances, let alone its recollections. Such could have been the mottos for Zweig's other 'Austrian novel', *Clarissa*.

As we have seen, with his novel *Beware of Pity* Zweig explored a highly individualistic approach to the immediate pre-First World War atmosphere in an Austro-Hungarian setting, with the sole foci being Edith Kekesvalva's tragedy and Lieutenant Hofmiller's emotional ineptitude. With the *Clarissa* fragment, the thematic scope is considerably broader and explicitly political.

Emotional restraint and release, the problem of compassion and determination, uncertainty about circumstances, with all the inhibitions and anxieties that go with it, as well as unconditional care for a child that should not grow up as a stigmatised '*bâtard*' but as a boy with genuine prospects – these are a few of the themes that *Clarissa* offers. This is coupled with discussions on pacifism, a humane foundation of European identity, problems of loyalty, and the doubtful virtue of deception.

The ever-recurring problem of pacifism in relation to patriotic loyalism in times of crisis continued to reverberate in the intellectual scenes of the 1930s. One major document was a collection of essays edited by Julian Bell, *We Did not Fight* (1935). Its most prominent contributor was Bertrand Russell with his essay 'Some Psychological Difficulties in Wartime', in which he addressed the effect of the mass suggestion to which everyone was subjected during the first months and years of the war. Russell recalled: 'As much effort was required to avoid sharing this excitement as would have been needed to stand out against the extreme of hunger and sexual passion, and there was the same feeling of going against instinct.'[1]

Zweig's *Clarissa* fragment needs to be seen in this very context. The reconstruction of these plot elements, as far as can be deduced from what was found in Zweig's papers, give a clear indication of the psychological complexity he had envisaged for this novel.[2] In autobiographical terms, Zweig 'used' his novelistic draft to 'work through' the memory, if not trauma, of his relationship with Marcelle, his lover in Paris, who was pregnant by him but either lost or aborted their child.

We can refer to Zweig's entry into his diary of 10 August 1914, when he wrote that he was 'already planning quietly the book that would depict Marcelle's and his fate' (Tb, 87) in *'gesteigerter Form'* ('an intensified manner').[3] A quarter of a year before his and Lotte's decision to take their own lives, Zweig felt the need to come back to this emotionally charged episode in his life, which much like his first and second wives (or other of his female companions, for that matter) did not find a place in *The World of Yesterday*.

The 'intensified manner' of his recollection deserves some attention, as it gives us an indication of what the 'transformation from life into art' meant in Zweig's case. To begin with, the nationalities of the main protagonists are reversed – for Zweig easily done, as he refers to nationalities and patriotism as mere 'masks' when commenting on Marcelle in his diary. In the fragmentary novel of 1941 the female alias, Clarissa, is Austrian, not French, and the young pacifist and humanist she falls in love with – Léonard, partly modelled on Zweig himself – is French, a schoolteacher from Dijon. Clarissa is the daughter of a high-ranking officer and military statistician, who suffers because his work and findings of deficiencies in the supply system of the Austro-Hungarian army is only recognised when it is too late. Clarissa's mother having died giving birth to her, Clarissa's father tries to cope with the loss by becoming over-meticulous to the point of fastidious; he is obsessed with collecting data, even demanding from his daughter that she keep a daily account of her educational progress in her convent school. Even though she has adopted some of her father's characteristics, she finds working for a neurologist named Professor Silberstein a release. It is through him that she is able to attend an international congress in Lucerne organised by Léonard. The rest is the beginning of their 'history' at the threshold of the First World War. When she realises back in Vienna that she is pregnant by him, a Frenchman, she contemplates abortion. But Silberstein advises her to keep the baby, for it is the fruit of genuine love that must remain above all nationalist strife and chauvinist antagonism. In Silberstein, Clarissa finds the older equivalent to Léonard: a prudent pacifist who detests machinations of state affairs. The imperative here is not 'memory, speak!' but 'heart, prevail!'

Clarissa enters service as a nurse in a field hospital, where she meets Gottfried Brancoric, who displays less favourable characteristics of a pacifist, or rather conscientious objector. He appears weak and opportunistic, a dissembler who fakes trauma and psychosomatic disorder. Towards Clarissa he is subservient to the extreme, which annoys her, the officer's daughter, more than it flatters her – until she realises that a marriage of convenience with him could give legitimacy to her child. She wavers between compassion and disdain for him but accepts that he is the only way out of her dilemma. He agrees wholeheartedly to this fake marital arrangement, for it means that she will vouch for his being unfit for further military service. For the sake of her child, Clarissa will from now on 'live a lie'. The drafts indicate that Brancoric, once released from the military hospital, would have developed his deceptive abilities to a fine art, turning into a black marketeer and war profiteer until he ends up in a Turkish prison.

In more than one way, Clarissa is now on her own, with one purpose in life: the wellbeing of her child. She does not know whether Léonard has survived the war, and her own prospects are bleak. She is estranged from her father, who eventually hands over five letters written by Léonard to her – but it is too late. After Brancoric's return from Turkey he is destitute and needs her support, meaning that she is trapped in what was supposed to be an arrangement of convenience.

By default, Zweig's *Clarissa* looks 'modern', despite the draft's insistence on a recognisable plot and even clear-cut chronology. But – due to circumstances – there is a narrowing down of the narrative. The extensive draft concludes with but two sentences: '1921–1930 for Clarissa these were the dead years. She only had the child.'[4] One cannot be but reminded of the finale in Virginia Woolf's plot-abandoning novel *Mrs Dalloway* (1925), the namesake of Zweig's Clarissa:

It is Clarissa, he said.
For there she was.[5]

Having produced an extraordinary review of Joyce's *Ulysses*, it would not too difficult to imagine Zweig as, at least, an occasional reader of Woolf, even though there are no traces of his interest in the Bloomsbury Circle during his years in England. But was the young publisher and acquired friend, Desmond Flower, not likely to have at least mentioned, if only in passing, this circle, which was after all in Zweig's immediate vicinity in London? Regardless, for the reader 'it is Clarissa', too, at the end of Zweig's fragment; nothing else seems to matter. 'For there she was' – with her child, whose French father remained out of reach.

Even in its fragmentary form, this draft of a novel assembles some of the key motifs of Zweig's concern: the value and validity of pacifism; the prerogative of the heart; the force of deception; the futility of authority; dissolution of the function of the state; and the pitfalls of compassion. Apart from Silberstein, who regards the state as morally bankrupt, it is Léonard's socialist humaneness that impresses Clarissa most: his concern for the ordinary people and his plea for personal freedom coupled with his taking responsibility for others.[6] And there is Montaigne, his *Essais* being Léonard's favorite book, which he gives Clarissa as a parting present. He quotes to her Montaigne's belief: '*Il n'y a qu'une chose rester soy-même*', emphasising that the one thing that matters is to stay who one is, or rather what it is that remains with oneself.[7] Consequently, Clarissa reaches her real moment of crisis and inner turmoil when she feels to be losing herself, torn between lying about her pregnancy and her commitment to keep the yet-unborn child.[8] By the standards of the time, this child is the 'enemy' within her and, at the same time, the only 'reality' of her love for Léonard left. Assuming Clarissa does read Léonard's copy of Montaigne's essays, she would find the perfect chapter to explain Brancoric's behaviour: namely, the ninth section of the first book, called 'Des Menteurs' ('On Liars'). In it, Montaigne speaks about those '*qui dissent contre ce qu'ils sçavent*' ('who say something against their better judgement'), indulging in masquerading as different personae, thus disfiguring their essence and 'shell'.[9] By giving Montaigne's *Essais* to Clarissa, Léonard presents her with an intellectual labyrinth that matches her present and predicts her future entanglements. However, as a thinker who knew of no inhibition when it came to exploring his Self, Montaigne serves Clarissa as a pathfinder, too. He is to encourage her, or so we can interpret Léonard's intention connected with this gift, to find a way to herself, to access and explore her heart, body, and mind.

At any rate, it is with references to Montaigne throughout this fragmentary novel that Zweig connects this narrative with his second parallel project: an essayistic study on this first and foremost *homme de lettres* of early modernity.

A tower for a towering thinker

It was in the cellar of his new address in Brazil – R. Gonçalves Dias, 34, Valparaíso, Petrópolis – where Zweig found a two-volume edition of Montaigne's essays, left there by the previous occupants. It was evidently a case of serendipity. What was it, though, that attracted Zweig to Montaigne? He had not featured in previous texts, but Zweig was intimately familiar with the period of Montaigne's life (1533–92), the perennial conflict between Catholicism and Protestantism, between thought firmly anchored in religious belief and emancipated notions of the Self. Previously, Zweig would have encountered Montaigne through his preoccupation with Nietzsche and his admiration for this 'free spirit' with whom he connected his conception of 'moralistics'. He referred to these 'encounters' as 'lukewarm enjoyments'. Now, Zweig quickly saw in Montaigne the 'master and teacher of resignation and withdrawal'.[10] By the end of October 1941 Montaigne had already become 'the better Erasmus', as Zweig claimed in a letter to Friderike (SZ/FZ, 379). Nietzsche had recognised in Montaigne's essays verbal images of a particular form of thought, as Hugo Friedrich was to identify them, with reference to Montaigne's most engaged (both appreciative and critical) reader: Blaise Pascal.[11] Zweig may have found Montaigne's 'method' of intellectual appropriation appealing as it resembled, at least partly, his own: namely, to think 'with and through his favourite writers', in Montaigne's case the ancient Greek and Roman classical authors.[12] By January 1942, Zweig had also read André Gide's *Essai sur Montaigne* (1929), which emphasised the philosopher's sensual intellectualism. The other main biographical source Zweig used (extensively) was Marvin Lowenthal's edition of and commentary on *The Autobiography of Michel de Montaigne* (1935).

Montaigne famously liked to quote and to drag quotations out of their context, subjecting them to the movement of his essayistic reflections. To a certain extent, he spoke through his mostly unacknowledged quotations. They stood for an augmentation of perspectives, the sum of which he regarded as his '*soy-même*' (very self) together with the components of his persona he was so keen to explore. Perhaps for that reason, too, he was so demonstratively 'at ease with his limits, faults and errors'.[13] Charles Rosen argues that 'the coexistence of opposites and the refusal of a logical synthesis' were essential to this first 'modern' philosopher just as much as the absence of any 'sense of guilt'.[14] In the preface to his *Essais* Montaigne left his reader in no doubt about what they were to encounter on the following pages: '*Ainsi, lecteur, je suis moy-même la matière de mon livre*,' or 'I am myself the main subject matter'.[15] If Montaigne can be seen 'as the figure who first made self-exposure a legitimate and even fashionable activity' – one might call this 'activity' intellectual exhibitionism – we get closer, perhaps, to reasons for Zweig's interest in him.[16] Reading Montaigne seemed to have released 'hidden' ambitions in Zweig: namely, to be unconditionally honest with himself and to find a reliable friend whom he could trust unreservedly. To the latter he admitted quite frankly, but when it came to the former, he remained more reserved.

Zweig must have wondered how to write a (biographical) essay about the father of the modern essay. How to write something biographical about somebody who was a voyeur of himself and indulged in introspection, revealing everything about himself in his own essays, including details of the following kind: that he could hardly tell the cabbages from the lettuces in his garden and that he knew of no greater pain 'than that of a kidney stone blocking the urinary tract'.[17]

Zweig professes that when reading the *Essais* the printed-on paper disappears and someone who breathes becomes present in the 'half-dimmed' room – to Zweig, a stranger at first, but soon a friend, as the

400 years that lay between him and Montaigne evaporated: 'A friend has come to counsel me and to tell me about him.' He argues that the quiet sadness in his 'friend's voice' over the 'fragility of us humans, the inadequacy of our mind, the narrow-mindedness of our leaders, the absurdity and cruelty of our time, this very sadness' lived on in Shakespeare, Montaigne's disciple, and in 'his most favourite creatures Hamlet, Brutus and Prospero'.[18]

While Zweig was working on a man of letters who had found everything about humans within himself, he was rereading about a character who explored the outer world for the sake of his own development and *Bildung* (education), heaping one experience onto the next: Goethe's *Wilhelm Meister*. We remember Zweig reading this masterpiece of novelistic art for the first time when he was in Rome back in 1907. The subject matter of personal development and *Bildung* coincided with an experience of moving full circle – regardless of one's whereabouts. Or is it, then, an instance of self-criticism when Zweig quotes Montaigne's maxim: 'To be everywhere is to be nowhere'.[19]

However, Goethe is present in the sixth part of Zweig's *Montaigne* fragment, in which he claims that this French thinker had been searching for the '*Urmenschen*' ('primordial man') just as Goethe was later to identify the '*Urpflanze*' ('primordial plant') – that is to say 'the pure form' that had not yet been disfigured by prejudices, categories, or dependencies.[20] Given the proximity of the time of Zweig's reflections on Montaigne to his decision to take his own life, one would perhaps expect some more extensive comments by Zweig on the famous twentieth chapter of the *Essais* ('*Que philosopher, c'est apprendre à mourir*'), which Montaigne derived from Cicero's point that philosophising prepared one for dying. Not so – he only refers once to Montaigne's contemplating suicide, because of his suffering from pain caused by his kidney stones. Zweig quoted from Fortunat Strowski's biography *Montaigne: Sa vie publique et privée* (1938), which is interesting for one main reason: once again, Zweig used recently published material by an expert on the subject whom he knew personally, as he lived in Zweig's vicinity. Fortunat Joseph Strowski de Robkowa was the offspring of a Jewish family from Galicia who in 1939 took up a position at the newly established *Universidade do Brasil* in Rio de Janeiro.[21] In 1906 he produced the first critical edition of Montaigne's *Essais*.[22]

With Strowski he referred to one of the few biographers who took the public life of Montaigne seriously, even though Zweig emphasised the philosopher's desire to remain in his library tower, remote from public offices (tellingly, it was in his absence that he was elected mayor of Bordeaux) not only for intellectual reasons, but for those of health too. The tower of his château protected him, or so he thought, from being infected with pestilence. Zweig's fragmentary account of Montaigne does not indicate whether he would have made more of the philosopher's activities outside of the famous tower too, for instance in 1580–1 when he went to Paris to present King Henry III with a copy of his *Essais,* followed by his most extensive journey to Italy via Mulhouse, Basel, Lindau, Augsburg, Munich, Innsbruck, and the Tyrol, towards Verona, Padua, Venice, Ferrara (where he visited the poet Torquato Tasso in hospital), and finally Rome. There he hoped in vain to be appointed by Henry III as the French ambassador to the Vatican. It is also not clear whether Zweig was aware of Montaigne's critique of European colonial practices in the Americas. In his criticism he confined himself to the high cultures of Mexico and Peru and the way in which the Spaniards treated them, arguing that much more constructive interactions between Europe and those cultures could, and should, have taken place. He felt that the 'Brazilian Indians', however, had been 'far closer to nature' and should not have been subjected to the European conception of civilisation. Claude Lévi-Strauss singled out Montaigne's scepticism of the European colonial project, arguing that it derived from Montaigne's belief in the virtue of reason. Those colonial practices were simply against all reason, or so he claimed.[23] By then, Zweig would have realised that the protest against racism and colonialism had even reached children's literature. Claude Aveline had dedicated his children's book *Baba Diène et Morceau-de-Sucre* (1937) to him.

The first paragraph of Lévi-Strauss's essay on Montaigne provides an interesting reference to Lucien Febvre's comment that the discovery of the 'new world', even forty years after the first French translation of

Amerigo Vespucci's travelogue to the Americas, had not caused a major stir, let alone an intellectual revolution.[24] But there is the interesting phenomenon that Zweig, in spring 1941, produced a short biography of Vespucci with the intriguing subtitle *The History of a Historical Error*. Strictly speaking, this is not a biography nor, as often suggested, an appendix to his book on Brazil. Rather, it approaches the problem of identity by presenting alternative, complementary information about Vespucci and the reasons why the fourth continent was named after him. The concluding chapter ('Who was Vespucci') connects this study more with his exploration of Montaigne and his lecture-based essay on 'History as a Poetess', since the implication of this finale is that history herself had generated this error.[25]

Time and again, Zweig managed to go through complex source materials and condense and appropriate them for his own purposes. With the trance-like self-assurance of a sleepwalker, he identified what was necessary for him in terms of material and argument.

What intrigued him about Vespucci is the question of whether he 'was a hero or a swindler', meaning a master of deception and pretence. For it seems clear from the sources available to Zweig at the time that Vespucci never made this very first voyage to the Americas. To be precise, others attributed authorship of two key texts (*Mundus Novus* and *Quattuor Americi Navigationes*) to Vespucci, as well as the discovery of America before Columbus. Thus, he was a trickster by default. Others turned him into one. For our purposes, it is not necessary to assemble more details. What matters is Zweig's method, as it reflects, once again, his principal concern: to demonstrate that 'history herself is a distinguished dramatist' and that the 'will of fate is always right.'[26] This meant he could afford to tell his readers about Vespucci without turning him into the heroic protagonist of Zweig's story. It is, after all, a different kind of 'biography' – that of an abstract phenomenon with very concrete consequences, namely the 'portrait' of a 'historical error'. That 'America' is still called 'America' is therefore a mere matter of convenience in the face of better knowledge.

Balzac, or the physiognomy of time

For his sixtieth birthday on 28 November 1941, his Brazilian publisher, Abrahão Koogan, presented him with a complete edition of Honoré de Balzac's works and a terrier called 'Plucky' for trouble-free company. Both presents were particularly welcome as Zweig had to leave his extensive collection of papers and notes on Balzac – some 600 pages of manuscript, 2,000 pages of notes, and 40 books with markings – behind in Bath, and the dog-lover Zweig may have found at least some temporary consolation in this new four-legged companion.

However, the third part of this trilogy of fragments, Zweig's biography of Balzac, which he himself regarded as his *chef d'œuvre*, had been the project of his lifetime. It is likely that Zweig came across Balzac when he was working on his dissertation on Hippolyte Taine, who had written an essay on Balzac. Already in 1906 Zweig had published 'Anmerkungen zu Balzac' ('Notes on Balzac') which referred to the writer's identification with Napoleon and Balzac's embodiment of 'genius'. By 1908, when his landmark essay on Balzac appeared in Maximilian Harden's magazine *Die Zukunft* (later re-published in his 1919 collection *Three Masters*) Zweig seemed to have recognised in this French novelist his (unattainable) role model. In the same year Hugo von Hofmannsthal referred to Balzac as the Shakespeare of the novel, given his 'most extensive, substantial and creative fantasy'.[27]

Zweig marvelled at Balzac's seemingly inexhaustible energy, as well as the richness of his works saturated with sheer 'life'. Arguably, Zweig kept writing on his biography on Balzac long before he had decided to properly embark on this project. This was certainly true in 1912 and 1917, when he reflected on the lesser-known pieces by this eminent novelist – especially his 'Treatise on Elegant Living', which appeared in German translation two years before the First World War. It illustrates Balzac's preoccupation with clothes, echoed by Thomas Carlyle only three years after its initial publication in his satirical novel *Sartor Resartus* (*The Re-Tailored Tailor*) and later captured in Gottfried Keller's 1874 novella *Clothes Make the Man*. In our time Zweig's approach to Balzac has been vindicated, as one sees him more and more as a 'pathologist of ordinary life and its culture'.[28] Zweig argued in 1912 that Balzac was interested in providing his readers with the 'inner life of average existences' and, in so doing, providing us with perfect examples of 'how to be light without being superficial.'[29]

Balzac's encyclopaedic writings – which included reflections on journalists, walking, lost illusions, and the fate of Père Goriot, not to speak of the notorious Regency dandy Beau Brummel, all as elements of the 'human comedy' – were of genuine appeal to Zweig, as they combined narratives with essayistic excursions and, at the end of the *Comédie Humaine*, analytical studies of the social conditions of his time. To a certain extent, *The World of Yesterday* was a condensed version of the Austrian 'Human Comedy' around 1900 and its tragic aftermath. In this respect, too, it was but consequential that work on Zweig's 'memories of a European' and his biography on Balzac progressed almost side by side.

Already in his early writing on Balzac, Zweig recognised the novelist's fairness towards the '*juste milieu*' ('happy medium'), calling him a 'dialectician, who was able to appreciate the individual points of view of his protagonists, be it the scrooge or the spendthrift, the worker or the dreamer, the forceful or weak character'.[30] For Zweig, Balzac embodied the type of writer who was able to pretend at least that he was after a system, or systematic exploration of the phenomena of life. This was in complete contrast to what he had encountered with Montaigne, whose refusal to systematise his thoughts made him a direct forerunner of Nietzsche.

But with his attempt on writing a comprehensive biography on Balzac, he demonstrated, even in its fragmentary form, that any separation between 'life' and 'work' would not make any sense. He claimed that the more we learn about Balzac's life, the deeper we dive into his works – and vice versa. Zweig portrays Balzac as a writer who lived for his work and whose writings provided him with an ever-renewing energy.

Illusion and realism on Balzac's part and the way he conducted his life and shaped his texts is one pair of intriguing contrasts that Zweig pursues in his biography on this role model. But what makes this biography, even in its incompleteness, so eminently appealing is the way in which Zweig appoints the reader to be a witness of Balzac's *Lebensroman* (novel of his life) through his numerous novelistic projects.[31] In Zweig's biography this concept is the title of its third part.

It was literally *en train* between Toronto and New York in February 1939 when Zweig took the decision to start working on his comprehensive biography on Balzac, as he informed Romain Rolland in a letter written from that very train (RR/SZ, II, 696). In this letter he referred to himself as a 'Balzacian' whilst calling Rolland a 'Beethovian'. He wanted it to be something that would stand the test of time: a biography and critique of Balzac, not the apology of a mere admirer. His *Balzac* was to be a document that demonstrated Zweig's *critical* engagement with the master from whom he had learnt so much throughout his life – except the idolising of the 'moment' and 'suddenness', which was not a characteristic of Balzac's fiction. At the same time, Zweig found plenty to criticise: as we have seen already, Balzac's obsession with collecting objects almost indiscriminately; his illusionism and tendency to take things for real that he had only imagined, including his social status; his squandering of money, resulting in huge debts he could barely meet. But there was even more to admire, most importantly his 'will', which Zweig called 'demonically magnificent'.[32] Where Zweig refers to this quality he comes, clearly unintentionally, dangerously close to the term 'the triumph of the will' and with it to Leni Riefenstahl's notorious filmic documentation of the Nuremberg Party Rally of the Hitlerists in 1935.

Zweig's *Balzac* is in more than one way an extrapolation, and further elaboration, of his previous essays, with his early 'Notes on Balzac' being the most remarkable in terms of providing a nucleus for his later insights into Balzac's 'method'.

To start with, it offers reasoning behind Zweig's view that anything written about Balzac, eventually even his large-scale biography, cannot be but fragmentary. Inevitably, or so he argues, these fragments will have something 'detached – they are mere notes, impressions' given that one could hardly 'be exhaustive about someone so inexhaustible as Balzac.'[33] Tellingly, Zweig points out that Balzac's epics consisted of 'thousands of [self-contained] fragments' and therefore, some of his shorter novellas, like *Une passion dans le désert* and *Les Cent Contes drolatiques*, could be rated as more complete than entire novels. The latter was said mostly on his own behalf, given that the novella was to become his favourite form of expression in prose. But with his reference to the fragmentary in Balzac's œuvre Zweig goes one step further, claiming the characters in his novels, too, were but fragments.[34] Balzac's characters are, or so Zweig argues, the result of compressing first the entire world to the size of Paris, and second Parisian society into several principal types: intellectuals, poets, aristocrats, journalists. Balzac, the materialist, is another feature of Zweig's early essay and later biographic writing. But he also portrays the author of the *Illusions perdues* as someone who would attribute 'to any alley a human physiognomy'.[35] Moreover, he comes up with a revealing observation which he drew from his study of Balzac's manuscripts: at the beginning of a text the diligent artist is at work, reflected by relatively meticulous handwriting. But towards its finalisation a work of art can turn into a colportage, as the state of a manuscript betrays Balzac's hurry to finish it. His handwriting becomes untidy and erratic, with the pages littered with blots. His 'volcanic energy' appears to have got the better of him and he was forced to cash in his work as his debtors queued up for him.[36]

Just how Zweig missed having his Balzac papers at hand in Petrópolis, as they would have given him at least the hope of being able to finish work on his biography. Eventually his young friend back in Bath, Richard Friedenthal, put them together and dispatched them to Brazil, where they finally arrived in mid-November 1941, as Zweig reported to his publisher in New York (IV, 322). He spoke of the *Balzac* manuscript as a 'rough draft' that would need to be reworked and restructured from the very beginning. But this he put on halt for the sake of his own novelistic work – on *Clarissa* and the first draft of the novella *Chess*.

In harmony until the end
Heirs of Stefan Zweig

Austria in Brazil: Arriving at the Final Address

When Stefan and Lotte Zweig, by now British citizens, left Liverpool for Brazil via New York on 25 June 1940 on a passenger liner named *Scythia*, the symbolism of this name will not have escaped them. Being a Scythian means to be constantly on the move, derived from the name of an Eastern Iranian nomadic tribe.[1] Their visas, finally obtained, included permanent residency in Brazil. An intensive period of gathering impressions and exploring options was to follow once they reached Rio de Janeiro on 21 August after roughly a one-month stay in New York and surrounding areas. Writing a book about his new host country was Zweig's prime concern as well as finding a proper place of residence. Only after one and a half months in Rio, Zweig embarked on what was to be his final lecture tour through parts of Brazil, Argentina, and Uruguay – only to find himself back in Rio, where they stayed from mid-November until mid-January 1941. This was followed by more journeying through Brazil before they returned to New York in spring.

As ever Zweig worked relentlessly, as did, consequently, Lotte, mainly producing typescripts of her husband's texts. By the time they moved to Petrópolis, his book on Brazil was completed; so was *The World of Yesterday*, retyped several times by Lotte. With it, Zweig's memories of Austria and a world bygone had arrived at what he termed 'a country of the future' to quote the full title of his monograph on Brazil. Remembrance turned for once into prophecy, or rather both merged in Zweig's mind. In terms of landscape this merger had already taken place since, like in Bath, he saw some of Austrian pastoral settings in these hilly surroundings of Petrópolis. The bungalow-type small villa that the Zweigs rented could not pass for a new version of the Kapuzinerberg estate in Salzburg, but at least it was on a hill. Zweig clearly liked what he saw; whether Lotte did, too, is another matter. It remains a mystery why they chose a place which involved climbing dozens of stairs, given Lotte's asthmatic condition.

At first both were clearly happy living in 'primitive' Petrópolis. They were often the only white people, especially in the local open-air Café Elegante, with a black housemaid serving dishes wearing no shoes. Lotte would teach her to make *Semmelknödel* (Bavarian dumplings), as she reported proudly to her brother and sister-in-law on 24 November 1941. After only three weeks in Petrópolis, Zweig spoke glowingly of 'the inborn civilisation and humanity I admire so much here in this country'. But on 10 November 1941 Zweig came to the conclusion: 'All my efforts to learn Portuguese are in vain and I cannot adapt myself to America – much less to Brazil and the Spanish countries.'[2]

Nonetheless, it was there where Zweig celebrated his sixtieth birthday on 28 November 1941, and he did so with the last poem he wrote, basically dedicated to himself. It is a remarkably, if not surprisingly serene poem with which he greets the gratifying transition to old age. In its conciliatory melodic tone and sense of resignation it seems to reflect all dissonances and tensions, all inner conflict and traumata. To a certain extent it anticipates the *Four Last Songs* by Richard Strauss, or rather, had Strauss known this poem he could have used it, too, together with those by Hermann Hesse and Joseph von Eichendorff:

A Sixty-year-old's Vote of Thanks

The roundelay of hours gently hovers
Over by now greying hair.
For only when the cup is tilting
Does the golden bottom clear.

Foreshadowing of night's close-by:
It does no longer worry – it lightens me!

Pure delight in watching the world
Only knows who does desire no more,

And does not ask what he achieved,
Nor laments what he has missed.
To whom ageing only is the light
Beginning of his parting.

Never glows the view more freely
Than in the glimmer of waning light,
Never does one love life more dearly
Than in the shadow of renunciation.[3]

Nothing in this poem points towards a depressant's frame of mind. It is strikingly measured, calm, truly composed. The German original rhymes rather casually; nothing sounds in any way forced or trite. Any trace of rhetorical pathos has disappeared. It reads like the poem of a sage who has finally made peace with himself and the world; its raging and disastrous turmoil seem forgotten. These verses were written in a rare moment in Zweig's life with a view towards a sphere *sub specie aeternitatis*.

Relatively cheerful 'Xmas and New Year' greetings from 'Stefan, Lotte, and Plucky, the dog' on a card with the silhouette of Rio made of butterfly wings reached Stefanie and Alfred Zweig in New York in December 1941.[4] Life in Petrópolis was pure bliss, or so it seemed. Ben Huebsch, his New York publisher, learnt in the aforementioned letter, which also addressed the problem of working on the biography on Balzac, that

> We live here the most withdrawn life one can imagine. The nature is miraculously beautiful and varied, the little house with its terrace is magically situated and quiet, every walk reveals the most beautiful things and life is incredibly cheap and without needs not to speak of an atmosphere of absolute peace. (IV, 323)

In the same letter, however, he uses the word 'monotonous' to describe this existence in this otherwise 'blissful loneliness' and mentions this as a reason for his working on four projects at the same time. Zweig clearly needed several attempts to find an adequate expression that would characterise this sort of life. At the end of this letter to Huebsch he found it: '*angenehm verschollen*', a strange expression meaning 'pleasantly lost' – to the world that otherwise caused him '*Bedrückungen*', oppressions that can easily turn into depressions. Most importantly, though, he had managed to dispatch the final version of *The World of Yesterday* to Huebsch in New York and to Bermann Fischer in Stockholm one week before his sixtieth birthday. He referred to the birthday itself with the expression 'the black day', at least brightened up slightly by Plucky the dog (IV, 328). What was brewing in him became clear in statements like one to Victor Wittkowski on 13 December 1941: 'The generation for which I was able to speak has no heirs' (IV, 332). This he said six days after the Japanese attack on Pearl Harbour, which destroyed 19 battle ships and 188 fighter planes. Joachim Maass, a fellow emigré and correspondent of Zweig since 1929, received a letter written on Christmas Day 1941 which offers the following self-characterisation: 'I always feel like a virtuoso who is supposed to play in an auditorium with bad and distorting acoustics' (IV, 333). Zweig felt, as he said in the same letter, that 'the provisional had become permanent and the feeling of uncertainty the norm'. Furthermore, he emphasised that anything theoretical was alien to him and that he could only think and write in terms of figurations and symbols. One such 'symbol' derived from the profanity of getting old, as he had to learn how to function with 'false teeth' and to 'crack with them the hard nuts that fate would bang against one's skull' (IV, 334). Incidentally, Elias Canetti reported in the second volume of his memoirs, *The Play of the Eyes*, that Zweig had all his teeth extracted in Vienna when he visited his hometown for the penultimate time in 1936. He suggested that this was a symbolic act of sorts.

But even at the end of January 1942 – that is, one month before his and Lotte's suicide – Zweig contemplated founding a German,

Austrian, French, and Spanish *Yearbook of Emigration*. As he explained in a letter to Bruno Kreitner it was intended to be an anthology for the respective literary cultures in exile, which would consist of extracts of their works produced in 1941 and thereafter – that is, for as long as their exile lasted (IV, 337). In all those letters though, one reference is missing: that of his second wife Lotte, with one exception. On the day of their suicide, in his final letter to Friderike, he speaks of 'poor Lette', even misspelling her name.

Brazil – the biography of a wishful country

What had impressed Zweig with Irwin Edman's book *A Candle in the Dark* was the author's sympathetic view of the world, his *'mitfühlender Weltblick'*. It was this very view that Zweig wanted to adopt when he wrote his book on Brazil, in a sense an extended version of his short travelogue on Brazil of 1936. In Brazil he wanted to see 'a country of the future'. In the introduction to his 'biography' of a country that happened to provide him with the venue of his final destination, he was blunt about his intention: his wish had become increasingly 'passionate' to escape 'suicidal Europe' for a while and experience a 'peaceful *and* creative country'.[5] But perhaps the best introduction to his relationship with Brazil was written when the book had already appeared; it can be found in his letter to Felix Braun, written on his birthday in 1941. The letter heading gives the Petrópolis address, stating: 'until the end of March [1942]', the time until which he had rented this small villa from Marguerida Banfield. This letter is so significant that it should be quoted in full:

> My dear Felix,
>
> As you can see I am again in South America. The United States are no good for my work except for the magnificent libraries and the presence of some of friends. But life there is demanding, alien and hard; I feel more at home in the Latin sphere. I live here in a small

Brazilian place in the mountains for the next couple of months, and we have rented a tiny bungalow for this period, have a negress for the service, everything is delightfully primitive, donkeys pass by at our window laden with bananas, palm trees and primeval forest surround us and at night an indescribable starred sky. What is missing are books and friends. The little Wittkowski is in Rio, incurably literary minded, but nice; but nobody for a real conversation like Werfel, Broch, Beer-Hofmann in New York, and the continuously speaking in foreign languages is secretly tiring the brain – I am always in fear that I might lose my own mother tongue. I have completed my autobiography, worked on a few novellas, for Balzac I am missing my notes of ten years and the books. Will I ever be able to start with it? *I cannot find any identity with my Self, belonging to nowhere, nomadic and unfree with it* – my work, my books are over there [in Europe], and for years I have been living out of suitcases and packages; one cannot think of returning for a long time and even then it would not be a proper home any more. The others have burnt the ships behind them, have Americanised themselves, and even gave up their language – I am too old for all of that. Well – one has to bear it and the unspeakably beautiful landscape, the generosity, naivety and childlikeness of the people here help a lot toward it.

I thank you both for your good wishes: please allow me to respond with a poem ['A Sixty-year-old's Vote of Thanks' – R. G.]. I think of you so often! You would like it here [not in the USA – R. G.], the primitive life here is like it once was in Italy very attractive, unfortunately even here a feeling of selfhood and nationalism begins to take shape – the world disease. Strange to think that I should find myself in my sixtieth year in a small Brazilian place – in Vienna one thought it absurd when one sought 'solitude' in Salzburg! At any rate, the main part of the way is done; it is getting cool and dark, sometimes one feels a shiver, but like a far away good light in such darkness is then a letter like yours!

Heartfelt thanks to you
Stefan[6]

The short lease of just about half a year in Rua Gonçalves Dias happened to be a period of roughly the same length for which the Zweigs had stayed in their Bath property. In Bath – only in dark moments described by Zweig as the most tedious of places – like in Petrópolis, it was the landscape that consoled him, for a while at least providing him with memories of Salzburg and Bad Ischl. True, he declared Petrópolis an idyll but he felt distinctly out of place there.

Although Zweig offers several disclaimers at the beginning of his *Brazil* book, including all of the parts of the country he had not seen, he had in fact made extensive excursions and gained impressions of the vast topography of this land of a future that, in his eyes, Europe had wilfully foregone. He saw Pernambuco, Ouro Preto, and even Bahia in the north-east of Brazil where the 'nordestinos', mostly descendants of African slaves, lived in appalling poverty. After all, it was not before 1888 that Brazil had abolished slavery. The letter to Felix Braun, although not his book, confirms that Zweig was certainly aware of growing nationalism in Brazil.

No work by Zweig has received more critical comments than this biography, or rather morphology, of Brazil – and in some ways for good measure.[7] This is especially the case in respect of the practice and legacy of slavery in Brazil and Zweig's emphasis on Brazilian identity being a new version of Europeanness, in particular the Portuguese influence. He rather categorically undervalues the presence of the African cultural heritage and that of the indigenous population. In other sections, however, Zweig is keen to present Brazil as a counter-model to European fascism and racism, suggesting a harmonic model of ethnic hybridity which he singles out as a recipe for the future of mankind. As Jeroen Dewulf has pointed out, Zweig's excursions into the depths of the Brazilian landscape and social makeup was also a form of 'self-discovery'.[8] Even though the book consists of a series of individually conceived essays and presents a morphology of Brazil in the shape of a large-scale patchwork, it nonetheless generates the impression of a coherent, yet shamelessly idealising approach to the immensity of this subject. Still, Zweig's achievement remains considerable given the shortness of time he had allocated to this work. Incidentally, no evidence points to this book having been commissioned by the Vargas regime in exchange for permanent residency in Brazil (or other privileges) for the Zweigs. This textual composition, its style and structure, is through-and-through genuine Zweig and deserves to be recognised as such. In writing it Zweig seemed to have tried to create for himself and others a basis for identifying a new conception of society.

It is simply unclear whether Zweig was, or could have been, aware of the details of Getúlio Vargas's immigration policy. It was decidedly restrictive towards Jewish immigrants, or at least rather selective, for visas were only issued to those Jews of Europe whom the government officials believed would benefit the Brazilian economy. Rough estimates suggest that between 1933 and 1945 some 16,000–19,000 German-speaking immigrants with Jewish roots succeeded in entering the country.

As ever with Zweig, it is the very writing style in his account of things Brazilian that appeals, his verbal images and comparisons; for instance when he compares Rio de Janeiro with São Paulo. He suggests that one ought to be a painter to depict Rio but a statistician or economist to capture the energy in the latter city and its dynamic development. The social downside of this craze for speed and business – the deprivation of the slums – he largely ignores. He only bemoans the fact that, different from Rio, nobody in São Paulo seems to have the time to enjoy life and the luxury goods they keep producing.

In his chapter on the country's history Zweig made intriguingly little of another Austrian who, despite her death at only twenty-nine years of age, scored a spectacular success with the people of Brazil back in 1822. It was Maria Leopoldina of Austria, daughter of the Habsburg Emperor Francis II and great-niece of Marie Antoinette, and, as wife to Dom Pedro I, the first empress of Brazil. She was accomplished in the natural sciences, botany in particular, with more pronounced political skills than her philandering husband. Long after her death in 1826 she continued to be revered as the 'mother of the Brazilian nation' as it was her who signed the charter that declared Brazil's independence from Portugal. Moreover, she tried to persuade her father to lobby Brazilian interests with the Portuguese and make Lisbon recognise Brazil diplomatically. This finally happened in 1825. It was as if she died having accomplished this remarkable outcome. Her argument towards her imperial father was far-sighted enough: it would be in the interest of Europe to have, in an independent state of Brazil, a strong transatlantic partner.[9]

Under normal circumstances this would have been ideal material for Zweig to work on. But these circumstances were anything but normal and the time pressure Zweig subjected himself to for completing this book was immense. Thus he, the Austrian exile, mentioned Maria Leopoldina only in passing and only with reference to the triumphant reception when she, as archduchess of Austria, reached Rio de Janeiro on 5 November 1817 to be received by Dom Pedro as his bride. However, Zweig was keen to emphasise that 'royalty' and the Americas did not go together for long. Might it be that Zweig, in the back of his mind, compared the grand reception he and Lotte were given when entering Brazil with the one for the archduchess some 120 years earlier? Was it that he felt compelled to make, through his book, a literary contribution to celebrate Brazil's cultural identity, regardless of the rose-tinted glasses through which he portrayed the country, especially its social condition? To a certain extent, Zweig's book on Brazil reads like an extended commentary on this puzzlingly diverse nation's declaration of lasting independence.

In this Brazilian morphology Rio de Janeiro comes across as the capital of contrasts. It was the city's artistry that fascinated Zweig, and with it the harmony it displayed to the visitor. Except for the first three more systematically argued chapters on history, the economy (the only less typical subject matter by Zweig's standards), and his 'View onto the Brazilian Culture', the majority of the chapters are decidedly impressionistic. Among them, as a short centrepiece, are his reflections 'on a few things that might have disappeared by tomorrow'. Even in this account of a country for the future, Zweig was preoccupied with putative loss. Some of these 'unique things' were features that made Rio 'so colourful and picturesque'. In Zweig's view, strangely if not scandalously, the *favelas* too, which he called 'negro villages', belonged to such 'things', as they were pieces of the city's mosaic, or kaleidoscope, and represented 'a piece of nature in the midst of civilisation'.[10] In the following he almost beautifies the *favelas* with their *mocambos*, primitive huts 'that do not require architects'.[11] When reading these sections one cannot but shake one's head in disbelief. Nothing would be easier than ignore such lapses in Zweig's humanism, but to gain some insight into his way of thinking remarks of this kind are important to acknowledge. The same applies to his writings about Rio's red-light district, whose likely disappearance before long he lamented with equally aestheticising comments. Today's reader of this book breathes a sigh of relief when it reaches at last one genuinely endearing and uncontroversial object whose continued existence was under threat, the *bondes*, the old trams of Rio, with a rough charm of their own.

Undoubtedly, Zweig saw what he wanted to see, whether in Bahia or in Belém when flying towards the mouth of the *Rio Amazonas* – be it ever-encroaching landscape, or the *Instituto do Cacau*. There is something dreamlike in the way Zweig wrote about what he saw. What interested him throughout were the traces of the Europeans here in Brazil, their achievements, as interpreted by him as investments into the future. It is as if he wanted to regard Brazil as a purified version of Europe. It is rather more the 'good European' in Zweig that had made him write this book. Perhaps only during these final months in Brazil did Zweig put into practice the European cosmopolitanism in him with remnants of what he had experienced half a lifetime before in India.

For a last time he was back in Rio, the ever-colourful 'kaleidoscope' in his book, now engulfed in the magic reality of the carnival. It was 16 and 17 February 1942 when his Brazilian publisher Koogan invited him and Lotte, together with a befriended couple, to dive into this Dionysian experience. The publisher meant well and thought that such distraction would do his prime author the world of good. But self-abandonment was no longer an option for the Zweigs once news reached them that Singapore had fallen into the hands of the Japanese. News was to follow that a German submarine had sunk two Brazilian battleships in retaliation to Vargas's decision not to join forces with the axis of Berlin, Rome, and Tokyo. In the evening of 21 February Zweig played chess with Ernst Feder. The following day, the Zweigs were no more.

In a letter written on 5 March 1942, Feder gave a heart-rending and at the same time concise account of their last meetings to Lotte's brother, Manfred Altmann. He emphasised the states of depression he had found Zweig in, of which Zweig himself was acutely aware, referring at times to his 'black liver' – an age-old symbol for melancholy. On their last meeting Zweig gave Feder a copy of Bainville's biography of Napoleon and handed back the Montaigne edition that Feder had lent him, whilst Lotte returned an Austrian cookery book to Feder's wife. We also learn from this letter that Zweig may have consulted (twice) a psychiatrist in Rio.

When the Zweigs joined the Feders for tea in their house on 14 February 1942 together with three other guests, Zweig asked Feder at the end whether he thought that they would one day really be able to return to Europe. Feder replied in the emphatic affirmative and felt that, for once, Zweig's depression subsided, at least for a short while. Tellingly, Feder never saw Zweig laughing, only smiling, during those final meetings – we don't know whether wryly or mildly, or both.

The meaning of 'Yesterday'

The past – no temporal space is more knowingly unknown. We keep pretending that we are at best familiar with what is absent, missing, or irretrievably lost.

'Remember!', the narrator of *Chess* says to Dr B., 'at the same time running my finger over the scar on his hand', reminding him that he vowed only to play one more chess match lest it destroy him, given his traumatic memories. The scar that becomes redder as a sign of his inner agitation is a physical reminder of that time of torture, in line with Nietzsche's thought that we only remember what hurts.

But when we remember and try to assess what these memories mean to us, we put shadows on a pair of scales, so to speak, weighing them up whereby we constantly redefine the weights we are using. We have learnt from Freud and his conception of '*Nachträglichkeit*' or 'afterwardness' that 'the meaning of a life comes into being retrospectively'.[12] In that sense, the future, or at least the present, can give 'birth to the past'. Once again, Friedrich Schlegel's notion of the historian as the backward-oriented prophet rings true, especially when reading and rereading *The World of Yesterday*.

In his preface to this stunning act of recollection Zweig indicates that *Yesterday* should be taken for a plural, and he does speak of his 'yesterdays': '*So verschieden ist mein Heute von jedem meiner Gestern*', or 'my today is so different from each of my yesterdays'. This suggests that, to him, the extent of these differences between his 'today' and any of these pasts indicated that he had lived several lives 'completely different from one another.'[13]

In this process of remembering and finding orientation in his various pasts, which were from our point of view interrelated after all, Zweig attributes to the mind a filtering function. 'Our memory', he argues, 'does not retain one thing by coincidence' whilst coincidentally losing the other. Instead, he saw memory as a 'knowingly structuring and prudently eliminating force' (WY, 14). This conviction made him believe that we should not mourn what we fail to remember, for we must have felt that it was worth losing. This said, a strong sense of melancholy and loss prevails in *The World of Yesterday*. But this melancholy does indeed come across as 'powerful', as the writer Daniel Kehlmann confirms by quoting a colleague of his talking about Zweig's most well-known book in New York in 2019.[14] Zweig's account of his world 'keeps a tightly closed lid on personal feelings, preferring to articulate his life as affected by larger events.' But he is severe about the shortcomings of the 'optimistic liberal' outlook he had known as a youth.[15]

The motto Zweig chose for his 'memoires' is suitably telling. It is Shakespeare's King Cymbeline who says, anticipating the tone of Prospero's voice in *The Tempest*, 'I thank you. Let's withdraw; / And meet the time as it seeks us.' – whereby Zweig only quotes the second line. Time is in charge but by taking up its challenge and meeting her where she wants to confront us, we may have the chance to offer a 'check' to her as if she were the king on a chessboard. After all, Zweig confirmed that in his youth chess was about the only game, or sport, that he and his friends accepted, otherwise their 'fanaticism about art' prevailed (WY, 74).

A trilogy of shorter reflections on the meaning of history and, by implication, memory, preceded his work on *The World of Yesterday*: the text for his 'Historiography of Tomorrow' US lecture tour in 1938–9; the lecture 'History as a Poetess', written for the seventeenth PEN International Congress in Stockholm in September 1939, which had to be cancelled due to the outbreak of the Second World War; and the lecture 'The Vienna of Yesterday', held in the Parisian Théâtre Marigny on 26 April 1940, shortly before Hitler declared war on France, and thus Zweig's last appearance in Europe. By summer 1941 he had managed to bring his memoirs to a close, at least as a final draft. It was written, as Zweig mentioned to several correspondents, with a mixture of imagination, 'artificial optimism', and states of depression. 'I told you', he wrote to his US publisher Ben Huebsch in July 1941, 'that depressions are helpful to my work' (IV, 309). He was, however, unsure about the title for his autobiography. 'My Three Lives', 'Our Generation', 'Europe was my life', 'Tested Generation', 'A Life for Europe', 'Life of a European', or simply 'We' were considered. He was only adamant to drop 'the title and idea of "Three lives"' (IV, 310).[16]

Zweig took the manuscript with him to Petrópolis where he worked on the final version, admitting in September 1941 to his Spanish translator and agent in Argentina, Alfredo Cahn, that it was nothing short of a miracle for him to complete this manuscript given that the endless meandering from one hotel to another had had a decidedly 'de-concentrating' effect on him (IV, 317). Most of the first draft was written in Ossining, New York in a rented modest, rather grim bungalow, a mile uphill from Sing Sing Correctional Facility – in dramatic contrast to the habitually picturesque settings for Zweig's work. Perhaps it was precisely this atmospheric contrast he needed to accomplish this sustained act of recollecting a past as diverse as it possibly could have been.

To a certain extent *The World of Yesterday* is more the autobiography of an era than of Zweig himself. It seems that he had lent his hand and pen to the time for it to write about itself through him. It is therefore only in the first chapters that Zweig's persona takes centre stage; it is there where he pays justice to his parents and upbringing, and to a lesser extent to his brother Alfred. Most importantly Zweig gives an account of what Jewishness meant to him there and then – a form of culture and cultivation that transcended materialism. Judaism to him was the equivalent to sophistication and permanent striving to enhance one's intellectual and artistic faculties. These chapters also offer generous accounts of his contemporaries, most notably the young Hugo von Hofmannsthal and his aestheticism; it is with some embarrassment that the reader of these lines of admiration be reminded of Hofmannsthal's disdain for Zweig.

Much can, and has, been said about Zweig's so-called 'omissions' in *The World of Yesterday*, as if they were the main points of this, to date, most widely received of his books. Of course, Zweig's account was selective. He wrote about those phenomena and people, tendencies, and actual developments that mattered to him most and contributed to the formation of his Self. Naturally, there are some glaring absences – most notably that of Robert Musil,[17] not to speak of Friderike and Lotte – but there is an abundance of presences in terms of people and contexts, from which the reader benefits to this very day.[18]

With this account of the past, Zweig wanted to tame what seemed to have haunted him all along – the presence of the 'yesterdays' in his life.[19] One senses a certain tremor in Zweig's ever-shaky English – touching in its shakiness – when he reported to Huebsch from Ossining the completion of the first draft of his manuscript:

> Dear friend Huebsch, this is to notify that in an [sic] terrific effort I have come through my autobiography – about 400 pages, all of which have been prepared before in only a rough form. Now don't believe that I am eager to publish it immediately – I am only glad that by working from morning till the night I could still make such

a tour de force! But I wanted finished it [sic] before I take a decision when I shall lieve [sic!] and so I have done the impossible (IV, 310).

He was in such haste and agitation that he did not date the letter, and the ambiguity of the last sentence could not be greater. Does 'lieve', meaning 'leave' of course, refer to leaving Ossining or Earth? Be it as it may, Zweig had undoubtedly realised that he had achieved something extraordinary under adverse, if not existentially precarious, circumstances.

Arguably, *The World of Yesterday* can be read as an antidote to Hitler's *Mein Kampf*, in the sense that it provides an account of humane development far removed from any ideology.[20] Zweig's self-denomination reads as follows: 'an Austrian, a Jew, a writer, a Humanist, and a pacifist', in that order (WY, 9). As a fellow Austrian, he perceived Hitler as his categorical opponent. In his memoir he points out that the panorama from his baroque domicile in Salzburg on the Kapuzinerberg included the Salzberg near Berchtesgaden where Hitler was about to take up residence (WY, 310). In *The World of Yesterday*, Hitler is mentioned more often than any other person, including Romain Rolland and Balzac; in the chapter 'Incipit Hitler' he explicitly laments this fact: 'for years now we are forced to have this name in our mind every day, almost every second in any given context' (WY, 382). But as said earlier, Zweig would not have considered regarding Hitler as his 'brother', in a non-literal sense of the word, as Thomas Mann did. Zweig insisted on presenting an alternative form of development that owed more to Goethe's conception of individual progression, as epitomised by his novelistic protagonist Wilhelm Meister. But Zweig acknowledged that few of his peers, including himself, had taken Hitler seriously early enough, let alone read his book from cover to cover, ridiculing 'the bombast of his stilted prose' instead of occupying themselves with his intellectually flawed but propagandistically effective programme. We will never know what possession of the (autographed) thirteen pages of Hitler's notes for a speech given in Berlin in 1928 on foreign policy matters really meant for Zweig. He acquired it for 1,000 Reichsmark in August 1933, six months after Hitler had come to power. Was it that with this autograph, too, Zweig wanted to study the process of creation, in this case its rhetorical dimension, the emergence of an idea on paper, or was this an expression of Zweig wanting to have at least some symbolic possession of this despicable creature whose claim to 'possess' Germany turned him into an embodiment of evil?[21] But at the time of Zweig's acquisition of these notes such thoughts would have been premature, certainly on Zweig's part. With these notes he wanted to have a document that allowed him to come closer to a charismatic phenomenon and its main creativity to date: oratory or the manipulation with words.

Zweig's 'memories of a European', written in the Americas, was a response to his early reflections on times past, for instance in autumn 1912 when he referred to himself as an 'anticipated echo' of things, suggesting that he drew too much on the past (Tb, 12). He even claimed that his life 'was dancing between memories and expectations' (Tb, 23). Already then he had construed a strange connection between memory of the past and Shakespeare, which seemed to have come to the fore with the motto for *The World of Yesterday* when he said in September that 'strangely Shacespeare [sic!] always *irritates* rather than encourages me' (Tb, 12, my emphasis). The German word is '*reizen*', suggesting a neat ambiguity as it can mean both 'irritate' and 'challenge'. Cymbeline's quotation may indeed have done both. Meeting time where time is looking for us may have triggered these truly European memoirs written in a cosmopolitan context. But it also summarised neatly what he had achieved with *The World of Yesterday*: time had found him there as he had found himself after numerous detours, as one of his chapters phrased it (WY, 179–96). Perhaps because he had done just that he was in no hurry to see his account of those routes of memory published. It seemed, however, that he was sure of one thing: his legacy, the only 'security' that was left to him. It was not for nothing that he opened his recollections with a chapter on 'the world of security'. Interestingly, Thomas Mann also emphasised this very value when in Princeton in 1939 he gave an account of his time. But this 'golden age of security' only glittered and tragically collapsed, as Zweig was quick to acknowledge. After all, the route to self-awareness goes through plenty of self-deceptions.

With his friend Ernst Fuchs (the 'Chess-Fuchs') in Ostend, 1936
Heirs of Stefan Zweig

Chess with Time, or Yesterday's Checkmate

Not carnivalistic frolicking in Rio, but playing chess was Zweig's ultimate distraction. This had been the case for the best parts of his life. Already in his Salzburg years, Emil Fuchs had been his favourite chess partner. Even in Ostend in June 1936, two months before his first Brazilian and Argentinian venture, a photograph shows him together with Emil Fuchs documenting their passion for the 'royal game'. This was when he met Joseph Roth for the last time in person together with Irmgard Keun, Egon Erwin Kisch, and not to forget Lotte Altmann. But now, at the end of his life, chess came back – not with a vengeance but with a subtle plot, stylistic mastery, and narrative sovereignty. Whilst he admitted in May 1940 to have written 'the history of his life' – that is, *The World of Yesterday* – out of sheer despair, as a 'testimony' which he now rated more desirable than a work of art, his final accomplishment was, once again, decidedly and distinctly artistic. To a large extent, *Chess* contains the essence of *The World of Yesterday*, reducing it to the comments of one of the main protagonists, a certain 'Dr B.', and his humane conservatism. It is not even broken by his suffering during his detention in solitary confinement and mental torture by the Gestapo in a re-functionalised former hotel.[1] At the same time, through chess Zweig was 'upping the game' with his own time, transferring it to a symbolic level whilst being mostly realistic when it came to the actual manoeuvres on the board with its squares and figures.

Chess meant to Stefan Zweig what card games like Skat and Taroc meant to Richard Strauss. (A study on the favourite pastimes and games of the great and the good still needs to be written.) Like other one-to-one games, chess resembles a silent dialogue with figures and their moves mirroring, or representing, the players' thoughts. But more than with other such games, the chess player needs to be able to anticipate the opponent's next move. To assess this, the players will try to enter the other's mind. Such acts of mutual intellectual penetration give this game something more than what otherwise might look relatively mechanical.

Reflections on the meaning of chess are as plentiful as literary renderings of this extraordinarily taxing game, ranging from *Alice's Adventures in Wonderland* by Lewis Carroll and T. S. Eliot's 'A Game of Chess' as part of *The Waste Land* to Vladimir Nabokov's novel *The Luzhin Defense* and Ninette de Valois's ballet *Checkmate*, based on Carroll's masterpiece.[2] But it was Benjamin Franklin's essay on *The Morals of Chess*, with its claim that chess would lead to 'foresight, circumspection and caution' in people, that must have rang true to Zweig.[3]

Females are absent from Zweig's novella, as chess had long been perceived as a notoriously male game (*The Queen's Gambit* corrected this impression in 2020 with Beth Harmon, played by Anya Taylor-Joy, who has aptly been called 'this Joan of Arc of the sixty-four squares'[4]). But before we get too worked up about this non-feminist approach from Zweig, who only refers to the first narrator's shadowy wife fleetingly as a decoy (their game of chess serves as a bait for the world champion onboard their ship), we need to take note of the fact that Lotte was an accomplished chess player, too. In fact, on one of the very rare occasions when he referred to her, namely in a letter to Friderike at the end of September 1941, he explicitly mentioned that they were re-enacting together the great games in the history of chess. Zweig's major source for them was S. G. Tartakower's *Die hypermoderne Schachpartie* (*The Hypermodern Game of Chess*, 1924), which he had bought soon after their arrival in Petrópolis.[5] This information is significant as it means that at least some of the games described in *Chess* were also the result of Lotte's involvement (and not only of Ernesto Feder's advice and practice).

The title of this chapter owes its paradoxical implication to a note by Paul Celan: 'Check to time – but how does time react to it?'[6] This is indeed the question. Is 'time' indifferent to such playful challenge, or can a game of chess leave a mark on time? On a practical level it can be argued, like Brian Murdoch, that 'chess as play helps human beings overcome the twin tyrannies of fate and time [...] We may remember that the purpose of the novellas that form Boccaccio's *Decameron* was to pass time during a period of refuge from the plague'.[7] But we feel that with Zweig something else was at stake. In his novella, 'time' is forced to play chess with the author, his narrating protagonists, and fundamentally different characters onboard a ship on its voyage into an unknown future. This passenger liner represents, in a long-standing tradition, the world in a nutshell, just as much as the games of chess played between the monosyllabic, automaton-like, and rather dictatorial world champion Mirko Czentovic, the uncouth oil magnate McConnor, and Dr B. represent an attempt to encapsulate history, display the machinations of politics, and expose a world that seems to consist of nothing but 'black and white' judgements and figurations. It is a competitive world and only when the players reach a checkmate do they achieve some proper balance. But any checkmate challenges the demand for 'revenge'. All of these constellations and configurations are played through in this novella.

The narrated game and the game of narration

In a game of chess, the two players appoint themselves masters of their sixteen figures with the sole purpose of outmanoeuvring the other in a process of sophisticated combatting. They are two 'sovereigns' fighting for supremacy. A particular variant of this principle is simultaneous chess, also practiced onboard Zweig's liner on its way from New York to Buenos Aires, the very journey he had made shortly before embarking on this novella. There is even the variant of an entire group of passengers coming together, discussing each move they should make to cause difficulties for the master player. The group instructs McConnor to carry out the moves they have contemplated but, ultimately, it is a voice from the background that takes over – the one of Dr B. His whispering intervention prevents a wrong move that would have cost

McConnor and the group, or collective, he plays for the triumph of a checkmate against the world champion, Czentovic. That is to say, the 'message' here is that not even a humanely minded collective is enough to stand up against a technocrat of power. Another individual, in this case Dr B., must emerge from the group to provide a proper challenge.

Arguably, Czentovic, with his cold-blooded calculating manner, stands for the gruesome spirit of the age; McConnor represents the oligarch with little reflective ability; and Dr B. displays humane reason, but not without a streak of monomania. During his detention in solitary confinement, he kept his sanity by learning from a book on chess many famous games by heart. This enabled him to play so-called 'blind games', too, and to instantly recognise particular moves. Dr B. is, so to speak, a genius by default, whilst Czentovic's ingenious playing of the game is innate. But his special gift has made him, to borrow Herbert Marcuse's famous denomination for people with 'false consciousness', a one-dimensional person, and 'Soon the secret was leaking out that, in private life, this grandmaster of chess couldn't write a sentence in any language without making spelling mistakes, and as one of his piqued colleagues remarked with irate derision, "his ignorance was universal in all fields"'.[8] It is with utter irony that the author of *Chess* should have given the final words of this novella to the monosyllabic Czentovic. At last, he credits his opponent, Dr B., stating that 'for an amateur, that gentleman really is uncommonly gifted,' after Dr B. breaks the game off after a delusionary move.

It was a mistake that resulted from a fit of 'pseudodementia' known as Ganser syndrome.[9] In the confined atmosphere of the ship Dr B. re-experiences the traumatic situation of his solitary confinement, with Czentovic possibly reminding him of his Gestapo interrogators. In this situation he suddenly believes himself to be playing a different game than the actual one, one of the 150 matches he had learnt by heart in his cell-like hotel room. Finding this book with all these matches listed and the moves presented as mere figures and letters had helped Dr B. to survive the mental torture he was subjected to. But, at the end, this 'poisoning with chess', as the narrator puts it, drove him to a different kind of insanity. The point is, however, that Dr B.

is willing to expose himself experimentally to this dangerous situation on the ship by playing against Czentovic.[10] By doing this, however, Dr B. meets his nemesis, and he commits mental suicide.

'Madness is lingering at the door of our mind', as Hippolyte Taine put it in his study on reason, quoted by the young Zweig in his dissertation.[11] It is possible, as James Vigus assumes, that Zweig was also familiar with Jacques Mieses's short introduction to *Das Blindspielen* (*Playing Blind*, 1918), which, at the time, was considered dangerous as it would lead to mental instability.[12] Research has even identified the chess champions José Raul Capablanca and Efim Bogoljubow and their manner and style of playing chess as the models on which Zweig based Dr B. and Czentovic.[13] As illuminating and helpful as such findings are, the question remains open as to what it is that the novella *Chess* actually signifies, if anything other than a final indulgence on Zweig's part in turning his favourite game into a piece of literature. Given its position in Zweig's life one cannot but attribute to it a testament-like significance. But what is it that this 'last literary will' contains – in real and symbolic terms?

Time and nothingness

Speculations, assumptions, jumped-at conclusions have been rife as to the 'true identity' of Mirko Czentovic and Dr B., ranging in Czentovic's case from Hitler to the Sarajevo assassin Gavrilo Princip, whilst – more predictably – Dr B., and the narrator especially, have been identified with Stefan Zweig himself.[14] But Czentovic and Dr B. have also been seen as one person presented in the shape of two opposing figures, the result of 'self-division' and artful schizophrenia.[15] Yet, Zweig's novella offers more than a mere identification game. It is almost inconceivable how he managed to produce a perfect work of verbal art under such psychotically charged circumstances and in so short a time. It is not for nothing that 'time' and 'spaces' play a significant part in this text, and recent interpretations of *Chess*, most notably by Ruth Klüger and Daniela Strigl, have taken this more and more into account. There is the narrator's obsessive attention to detail — from the pattern of the wallpaper in Dr B.'s hotel room confinement, to the scar on his hand, let alone the focus on hands in Zweig's works altogether. Furthermore, there is the presence of — often shabby — rooms in Zweig's stories and essays. These rooms are occupied by solitude, loneliness, and desolation, furnished with despair. But they are also breeding grounds for illusions and dreams — in other words, self-deception. Strigl argues that such details are 'pitted against [the] nothingness' that surrounds Zweig's personae, Dr B. in particular.[16] Klüger singles out the 'torture of solitude' that dominates Dr B.'s psyche.[17] Whilst Strigl insists on the artistic achievement to which *Chess* owes its lasting appeal, Klüger offers some illuminating contexts, not least with a reference to Lessing's drama *Nathan the Wise*, which features a game of chess between the Sultan Saladin and his sister Sittah shortly before the arrival of Nathan. He is knowledgeable about chess, too, and this knowledge somehow feeds into the proverbial conversation between the Sultan and Nathan about the equality of the three monotheistic religions.[18] Klüger also refers to an 1856 painting by Moritz Daniel Oppenheim showing Moses Mendelssohn and Johann Caspar Lavater playing chess with Lessing as an onlooker, or at standby, ready to play at any time. Klüger correctly implies that the game of chess, with its enacting of rationality, stands for enlightenment and Jewish emancipation.[19] But the fact that Dr B. had turned into a chain-player of chess — in other words, an addict, like Czentovic — infected by chess-mania, or succumbed to 'chess-poisoning', demonstrates, or so Klüger argues, 'the horrific dialectics of Enlightenment.'[20]

Time and space are of the essence in this novella, especially when, for hours, Dr B. played in both physical confinement and in the confinement of his mind, against himself — the most absurd of actions imaginable, as he tells the narrator. He had to play 'with two brains, so to speak, White's brain and Black's brain. But even this splitting of myself wasn't the most dangerous part of my abstruse experiment; that was the fact that in devising the games independently I suddenly lost the ground under my feet and fell into an abyss.'[21] It is this feeling of '*Bodenlosigkeit*', being exposed to a bottomless ground — which we have already encountered with reference to Vilém Flusser, Zweig's unbeknown fellow exile in Brazil – that conditioned Dr B.'s situation in the Viennese Hotel Metropol, the Gestapo headquarters. Every minute counts in this story, even when (and especially when), ten minutes or one hour or four months (of Dr B.'s confinement) feel like a lifetime. Dr B. comments on the torture of waiting, and one is reminded of the dread of waiting that Zweig wrote about when he was waiting in London for his and Lotte's naturalisation and thereafter for their visa to Brazil:

> It is easy to say: four months – two syllables. Your lips can articulate such a sound in a quarter of a second: four months! But no one can describe, assess, demonstrate to himself or anyone else how long a given period lasts in a timeless, spaceless void, and you can't explain to anyone how it gnaws away at you and destroys you, nothing, nothing, nothing around you, only the same table and bed and washbasin and wallpaper, and always that silence, always the same jailer handing in food without looking at you, always the same thoughts circling around the same object in the void until you go mad.[22]

There is something unmistakably sensual about this reference to what the 'lips can articulate' in terms of something as abstract as a denomination of time; and there is something evidently paradoxical about an 'object in the void' unless we perceive the void itself as an object. But this reflection also shows that Dr B.'s growing insanity was not only due to his playing chess with himself in his mind but also due to the exposure of a daily routine in solitary confinement. Even though the former is the result of the latter, they are two different, albeit related, experiences – but in terms of effect, they potentiated each other in Dr B.'s mind.

The principal qualities of time in *Chess* are determined by accelerating and decelerating the speed of play; mainly by Czentovic, whose own career was, however, 'meteoric'.[23] He is in fact in charge of time and delays and speeds up his moves as he pleases, yet within a given space of time defined by himself, namely the 'confinement' of 'ten minutes' for each move. At first, the narrator goes out of his way to portray Czentovic as a 'hopelessly grotesque and almost comic figure', who even gave his name 'to a philosophy of chess' ghost-written by someone else. But he cannot see his own ridiculousness 'like all such dogged characters'.[24] Later, though, this characteristic does not seem relevant any longer. It is as if Czentovic can metamorphosise himself, at least to a certain degree; his former ridiculousness has turned into cold-blooded rigidity.

Once again, we cannot but wonder how Zweig was able to accomplish this masterly text – extraordinary in the sense that it presents us with the essence of Zweig's narrative artistry and thematic concerns, namely what it means to have lost pre-1914 values (Dr B., with his connections to members of the Habsburg royal family, belongs to these values); uncertainty about the future; the conflict between humaneness and cold indifference; the difficulty of retaining one's individuality; and the arrogance of those who pretend to be in charge of fate.

It has been suggested that the novella is structured in the manner of a chess match itself, thus underlining the artistic quality of this story; and this is arguably the case if we consider the various phases of the narration as phases in this game.[25] But if so, we can confidently add that it shows us, for the last time, Zweig playing a game of chess on paper, against himself and against the past, in the relative confinement of his small, rented villa on a hill in Petrópolis.

The man of words and the world
Lebrecht Music & Arts/Alamy Stock Photo

Notes on Zweig's Legacy

When Zweig wrote to Alma and Franz Werfel that he would, if at all, feel the mere shimmer of dawns, but never again their warmth after this abyss-like night of mankind – meaning the Second World War, which was to him identical to the end of culture as one knew it – he had found an image that would be in the centre of the final paragraph of his suicide note, the '*declaracão*', written in German. In fact, the image of the morning red had occurred already in a letter to his friend Felix Braun of March 1938 after Hitler's annexation of Austria: 'For us there will be no dawn anymore, the night will last endlessly long and only the firelight of a war might illuminate it devilishly' (IV, 218). It would not have come as a surprise if Zweig had quoted Joseph von Eichendorff's poem 'Im Abendrot' ('In the Sunset'). As mentioned earlier, five years later Richard Strauss was to choose these verses as the final piece of his *Four Last Songs*. Listening to 'Im Abendrot', like reading the final paragraphs of Zweig's farewell to the Europe of his past, can almost be too much to bear, as it makes one's innermost strings quietly but irrepressibly resonate.

It appears that Zweig thought he had come full circle at sixty, and miraculously so given the horrors of time he had witnessed – though not always first-hand. The final paragraph of his 'declaration' greeted all of his friends, wishing that they may 'still see the dawn after a long night! I, the all-too impatient one, lead the way' (IV, 345).

Equally telling as this 'declaration' was a strophe from Luís de Camões's epic poem *Os Lusíadas* that was found amongst Zweig's papers, pinned to a wall in their small bungalow with its large terrace, where Zweig liked to work most (writing *en plein air* was as close as he would get to painters). He had translated the strophe into German. In English it would sound like this:

> Woe, how much plight and danger on the sea!
> How close death is in thousandfold appearances!
> On earth, how much warfare! How much of honour
> Is invidious business! If only one pleat of world's
> Shape would be for Man a safe place
> To peacefully keep his little bit of being.
> Instead, the heavens tempestuously compete.
> And against whom? The poorest worm on earth![1]

It seems that Zweig was looking for this 'safe place' all his life, once he realised that he had to leave this state of 'golden security' behind as it vanished in the depths of history. He succeeded in escaping the worst of the First World War, Austrofascism, Hitlerism, and the reality of the Second World War. In doing so he safeguarded the legacy of his own work and the memory of what the world had once been before it was invaded by uncertainty, accompanied by unspeakable brutality. Zweig, ideally, wanted to keep himself to himself and yet advocated worldliness and cosmopolitanism. Earlier than many he felt estranged and expelled from Europe but retained his illusion of his European mission. He was read worldwide in countless translations, with huge print runs of his books, yet he remained conscious that, by his own standards, he would not reach the highest levels of literary sophistication. He was aware that the sheer imaginative and innovative faculties of his idols in world literature, more past than present, were unattainable. But he saw his calling in making his readership cherish the spirit of artistic creation.

Some immediate reactions

Throughout his life Zweig stayed a reluctant, or rather highly selective, modernist, steeped in tradition from which he did not want to break away. His 'modernism' – a word he characteristically used sparsely – was rooted in applying Freud's psychoanalysis to literature. Amongst writers of his time, Zweig was perhaps the one and only genuine Freud disciple. But we find no reference in his works to, say, Virginia Woolf,

Stravinsky, or Picasso. He attended a Schönberg premiere but does not tell us what he made of his music. Joan Acocella is close to the mark when she says, in her introductory essay to *Beware of Pity*, 'that the frontier of modern art, in his mind, appears to have been Rilke and Richard Strauss'.[2] Zweig did not explicitly reject formal experimentation in the arts, but simply ignored it.

Where and when does a 'legacy' or aftermath begin? In Stefan Zweig's case, when the news of his and his wife's death reached the war-shaken (literary) world. This immediate reaction is best described by the word 'bewilderment'. Some were irritated by Zweig's alleged 'betrayal' of the fight against Hitler(ism); inwardly, they might have been disappointed, if not angered, by Zweig's final 'escape'. Thomas Mann, for one, barely concealed his condemnation of his colleague (and temporary rival). His statement, written for the exile periodical *Aufbau* and published in New York on 27 February 1942 much to Friderike's dismay, could not have been clearer:

> The death of Stefan Zweig rips up a gap in the rows of the European literary emigration. His world fame was well-earned, and it is tragic that the emotional and mental resilience of this highly gifted man collapsed under the heavy pressure of this time. What I admired most about him was his ability to enliven historical periods and figures – psychologically and artistically. This form of artistic comprehension derived from a deep and gentle humanism, a benevolence that has helped many to continue to live. It is therefore only the more sorrowful to realize that he himself was not robust enough to survive this time of darkness and see daylight.[3]

When, on the tenth anniversary of Zweig's death, Thomas Mann was asked to comment, he had changed his mind and modified his position somewhat. His most revealing thought on Zweig comes at the end of his piece:

> I should like to say one more thing: There were times when his radical, his unconditional pacifism tortured me. He seemed to be

prepared to allow the reign of evil if only, by doing so, what he hated most, warfare, could be avoided. The problem is unsolvable. But since we have seen that even a just war causes nothing but evil, I think differently about his attitude of then – at least I am trying to think differently about it.

Thomas Mann's prediction made in this context, that Zweig's literary fame would before long turn into a 'legend', became, to a certain extent, true.[4]

However, Thomas Mann's son, Klaus, and Franz Werfel had more to say on the subject. Klaus Mann, writing in the periodical *Free World* in April 1942 and disregarding previous tensions with Zweig, commented:

> How trite and arrogant are our judgements, considering the overpowering reality which is death – the unspeakable drama which is suicide. Was he 'right' to throw away his life? Was he a defeatist? Does his voluntary death affect the validity of his works? And so how? The last one of these questions is the only one that makes sense.

Then follows Klaus Mann's crucial point:

> No doubt the tragic end of the author is apt to influence our views as regards these brilliant biographies, masterly essays, skilful novelettes. Zweig's desperate action in Petrópolis, Brazil, seems to have added a new note of gravity to the fluent elegance of his prose. The lights as well as the shadows become more distinct in the rich and colourful texture. With wistful admiration we watch the display of his craftmanship. We relish his daintiness, but not without apprehension. His own death reminds us of the enemy, who wants to destroy all this.[5]

Klaus Mann, who was to take his own life seven years later, displays a profound understanding of Zweig as a fellow 'intellectual, humanist, and unselfish servant of the spirit.' In characterising their common features he applies discreetly the title of Roman Rolland's courageous pacifist manifesto of 1915, *Au-dessus de la mêlée* (*Above the Battle*), to the just-deceased author of *Beware of Pity*: 'Hesitant, out of conscientiousness; seemingly aloof, but actually partaking in every human effort; profoundly versed in all abysmal secrets of the human soul and, therefore, au dessus de la mêlée.'[6]

Franz Werfel spoke in Los Angeles in 1942 at a memorial service for Stefan Zweig, pointing out the following and thus defining some of his fellow writer's legacy:

> There is no other writer who had helped others with similar magnanimity and generosity. [...] None of all émigrés was lesser an émigré than this genuine cosmopolitan, who was at home in the countries of exile long before such exile existed. [...] Stefan Zweig was a man without anger. Hence, he was one of the very few genuine pacifists. War meant hell on earth for him [...] and, admittedly, he fled war [...].

This was a point also made by Robert Neumann, who argued that 'he spent his life on the run.' Zweig, Werfel argued, did not see mere numbers of casualties in war, but identified himself with the poor creatures in death and agony: 'Stefan Zweig did not believe in victory. He was looking for peace. He was looking for it in the non-being.'[7]

Radio news of Zweig's death was 'like a piercing into the heart' for Romain Rolland, as noted in his diary on 24 February 1942. It prompted him to write a lengthy reflection on the ups and downs of their, at times, intensive friendship. He remarked on Zweig's 'anxiety', which had underscored his entire existence – even though he liked to give the impression of self-confidence and self-assurance when in public. Rolland emphasised that point, even during the time of their estrangement over the French writer's support for Soviet Russia. But even during his cooling-off period, Zweig kept some connection to him alive. Rolland mused that it must have been very hard for the 'great European', spoilt by immense success as a writer, to die far away from his friends and the 'old world, whose glamorous image he had been, noble and slightly old-fashioned.'[8]

But perhaps the most surprising reaction came from the young Ilse Aichinger one year after the war, in the form of a fictitious letter to Zweig dated 3 April 1946 in the daily *Wiener Kurier*, intended as a 'vote of thanks' offered 'on behalf of the young generation'.[9] Born in 1921, Aichinger, together with Ingeborg Bachmann and others in the context of 'Young Austria' after 1945, represented this very 'dawn' of a new morning that Zweig had addressed in his final 'declaration'. She refers to it in the first paragraph of her letter as the 'trembling red of the morning'. The title 'Bitte – Stefan Zweig!' refers to the request addressed to the librarian of a small old lending library: anything by Zweig, after his works had been banned from public libraries. To find nourishment for their 'resisting hearts' these young girls wanted to read what was suppressed. Aichinger refers to Zweig's *Mary Stuart*, *Marie Antoinette*, and *Fouché*, which she and her friends had lapped up. 'With you, Stefan Zweig, our hearts moved centuries back where we found in the womb of time what cannot perish: attitude. The glowing demeanour of the Scottish and the inextinguishable smile of the French Queen', as well as the 'observing silence' of this difficult and impenetrable chief of police. Zweig's rendering of history was 'like warming torches' in the coldness of the present. Zweig's sense of rhetorical pathos flows into Aichinger's letter like never again in her later works. It is a multiple vote of thanks for all signs of humaneness that his banned books provided, read surreptitiously as a tonic for inner resistance against barbarity. Aichinger's letter reads like a short anticipatory equivalent to José Ortega y Gasset's 'In Search of Goethe from Within: Letter to a German'[10] of 1948 and can be seen in the context of numerous attempts after 1945 to ask what was still left, if anything, of European humanism. Like others, Lernet-Holenia and Mann singled out Zweig's *Erasmus of Rotterdam* as his lasting legacy but the emphasis on what remains of Zweig's immense works and worldwide reputation has shifted since.

Indicators of legacy – matters of optics

Zweig's legacy can, and has been, discussed in terms of the editions of his works and correspondence, his biographies, his presence in the film world, and his contribution to historiography.[11] But the neat separation of his historical/biographical works and his fiction, let alone between life and work, is only helpful up to a point. As far as Zweig's contribution to historiography is concerned, it seems considerably more interesting to ask whether his approach to writing history might not be one of his lasting achievements. There is something exemplary about the way that Zweig presents historical phenomena and makes them appeal to a broader audience – namely, to bring fact and measured fiction together to re-enliven history. It needed Hayden V. White's landmark study on *Metahistory* to remind us of the narrative foundations of any form of writing about history.[12] White's understanding of writing history, which 'not only makes us know something about the historical process but know how it knows it', demonstrated by implication the validity of what Zweig had done in his historical biographies and essays.[13] He reimagined 'things past' that he felt worth being reimagined, thus providing a lasting future for them.

It is therefore quite telling that the young Ilse Aichinger singled out Zweig's historical biographies as models of orientation in times of unspeakable oppression. Reading them helped her and her peers survive, as they provided these young people with perspectives and specific optics to look at past occurrences and compare them with the present; thus to remain open towards a future that seemed, for many, prematurely ruined and already buried in rubble.

In literary terms, we can refer – again with Hayden V. White – to the specific 'content of form' that Zweig's novellas and indeed his novels offer to readers.[14] Zweig wrote novellas that can be called 'exemplary' in the vein of Cervantes, but in the sense that they emancipated sensuality by setting free the psyche of his (predominantly female) protagonists. They are narrated case studies of suffering or failing individuals whose own personal histories are pitched against the grander scheme of things in the context of their times.

But of equal significance is the way in which Zweig addressed the 'content of emotions', devoting individual literary texts to the exploration of one specific sentiment, psychological condition, or emotional attitude – from 'Fear' to 'Pity', 'Obsession', 'Compassion', or 'Empathy'.

Cinematographic dimensions

What is it in the biography of a writer that makes him single out one such emotion? This question itself has become part of Zweig's legacy. In his most accomplished literary texts, be it *Fear, Letter from an Unknown Woman, Beware of Pity*, or indeed *Chess*, these emotions and conditions turn into actual protagonists. And it is consequential that cinematic renderings of his stories have enjoyed such lasting resonances, perhaps none more than Andrew Birkin's rendering of *Burning Secret* (1988) with Faye Dunaway and Klaus Maria Brandauer.

In connection with filmic renderings of Zweig's life and works, we associate him today mainly with Wes Anderson's film *The Grand Budapest Hotel* (2014) with Jude Law, Tom Wilkinson, and Ralph Fiennes, and Maria Schrader's *Vor der Morgenröte* (2016) with Josef Hader and Barbara Sukowa. It seems that we need to be presented with images in order to see essences.

The motion pictures and the media began to interest Stefan Zweig quite intently, like most of his fellow writers, with the prospect of writing film scripts or seeing their fiction turned into films appearing exceedingly lucrative. This became particularly true for (prominent) writers in exile, ideally with connections in Hollywood. Often, such great expectations were bitterly disappointed – not in Stefan Zweig's case though. Filmic versions of Zweig's fiction accompany his work since 1911, when for the first time one of his novellas, *Burning Secret*, found its way onto the screen. Research on this phenomenon has become ubiquitous.[15] However, the intriguing question is if, how, and when Zweig was influenced by these cinematographic realisations of his work, or whether the style of his writing was influenced by filmic considerations.

Whilst Anderson's take on Zweig is a free-floating filmic fantasy with Zweigian motifs, Schrader's biographically orientated film focuses on Zweig's final phase of life as the exiled pacifist and European in the US and South America. We first encounter Zweig at the PEN International Conference in Buenos Aires in September 1936, when he declines to make a statement against the National-Socialist dictatorship in Germany.

It is surprising, though, that given the sensitive subject matter – emotional blackmail – *Beware of Pity* has been turned into a film only once (in 1946). But it featured in a stage adaptation by Simon McBurney, a production by the Schaubühne Berlin at the Barbican in London in February 2017.[16] I mention this as a particular feature of Zweig's aftermath because it matches his own profound concern in other contexts with the 'optics, the visible, and what one can feel'. Originally, he connected these qualities with political demands and the European idea, which he applied to next to all that he wrote. This is a neat paradox, too: the very writer in whose works the visual arts hardly feature called for 'Europe' to make its 'supranationalism' more visible through symbols and other optical features.[17] One could call this Zweig's preoccupation with making abstract thought sensually transparent and thus tangible and intelligible.

Zweig was a writer with, and of, 'many qualities' – one of them was a caring interest in the Other. He turned it into vocal appeals of what we might term his 'practical intellectualism'. It found its expression in what he had lived through, with empathy for the suffering of people with an intensity that matched those exposed to the idiocy of trench warfare, caught between ideological frontiers, or driven into the soup kitchens of London's shelters. He found words for these situations when many of his fellow writers pondered over the 'crisis of language'; for he regarded it as the overriding task of a writer-as-artist to give expression to what others might find too difficult to express. In this regard, his play *The Lamb of the Poor* (1929) deserves renewed attention. At the same time, Zweig was acutely and painfully aware of the shortcomings of 'simply writing books' in response to the traumata of what happens around us. The way we live our lives, how we conduct our daily affairs, develop our inner attitude, and translate it into our actual conduct was to Zweig of equal, if not higher, significance. The conflict between artistic production and taking up responsibility for a greater good – in short, the antagonism between aesthetics and ethics – mattered to Zweig more than to many of his contemporaries, with the notable exception of Romain Rolland – that is, before he turned a blind eye to the horrors of Stalinism.

Anticipating legacy

Rolland was right in noting in his diary that it was in early June 1915 when he noticed in one of Zweig's letters a turning point in his friend's attitude, revealing a new conception of Zweig's practical 'politics' borne from a fusion of art and ethics. Looking alone at these few letters exchanged between Zweig and Rolland in late spring 1915 we have the essence of this other noble legacy of Zweig's: his networking abilities. But 'networking' here is understood in terms of deepening cultural ties and working on linking and connecting in an intellectual and material sense of the word: creating a fabric of meaning between cultures, as opposed to some superficial scheming for networking's sake.

In the second year of the First World War, when the abundance of horrors from the frontlines had become only too apparent and early enthusiasm for this war was already drowned in blood, Zweig and Rolland shared their despair and hopes, mediated by the Dutch poet and psychiatrist Frederik van Eeden's poem 'To my friends in East and West' (RR/SZ, I, 186–7). Rolland confirmed that the poem was intended for both Rolland and Zweig, enclosing it in a letter of 2 June 1915. Eeden came to admire Zweig's conception of the 'demonic', as Rolland informed him some ten years later (RR/SZ, II, 145). Eeden's conception of 'lucid dreams', which he derived from Hindu notions of the Self and Jakob Böhme's mysticism, brought him in contact with Hermann Hesse and Sigmund Freud, whose first advocate he became in the Netherlands. It was the woe of mankind that he regarded as his path; this foundation of applied ethics he shared with Rolland, Albert Schweitzer, and indeed Stefan Zweig. In spring 1915 this conception was needed more than ever. In their letters, the socialist writer Alfons Petzold featured too, whose experience of hardship of all kinds turned him to produce autobiographical texts at a relatively early stage in his short life. Rolland rated them highly. Zweig, in turn, met in Vienna a friend of the highly regarded musicologist Jules Écorcheville, himself a friend of Rolland's, who had perished in the trenches in February of that year (1915). This was the kind of 'network' Zweig and Rolland maintained despite, and to a certain extent because of, the darkness of the time. But it was Zweig's letter of 7 June 1915 that Rolland singled out in particular, and for good measure. It sets in with a quotation from Laotse: 'The softest thing on earth overcomes the hardest thing on earth.' This, or so Zweig wrote, made him think of Rolland. Zweig felt that, from day to day, he was surer of himself but not necessarily happier. Too many of his burdensome memories were weighing upon him, for instance the fact that on 21 May 1915 Émile Verhaeren's birthday had passed and Zweig was prevented by 'circumstances' to send him any greetings, let alone hold Europe-wide celebrations of his works. This realisation triggered in Zweig the following reflections, which were to impress Rolland profoundly:

1. 'On that day I felt just how much there is lying on the bottom of the ocean called 'memory' that cannot, or [can] no longer, be lifted by any power of love.'
2. 'There is no religion and no belief that could dry up the tears of a mother over her only child.'
3. 'The thirst for words tortures me.'
4. 'After the war there ought to be an assembly of people who had remained loyal towards each other. Anonymous forces underground must work to change the attitude of nations from beneath.'
5. 'Whatever it is that one touches upon there is connection and relation, a binding together and things ripped apart, thus pain everywhere and pledges [for the future].'

As ever, Zweig laments his 'impatience' with people and situations and tells himself to exercise patience. He emphasises that he was willing to 'give himself' over to accomplish the task of renewing the collective consciousness. This was his notion of 'ethics'. Of equal importance, though, was for him to send Rolland the piano score of Gustav Mahler's *The Song of the Earth* (1908/9). He hoped it would tell Rolland 'something' (RR/SZ, I, 188–90).

This gift could not have been more symbolic, as it indicated Mahler's transcultural identification with the spirit of death in life and life in death, as conveyed by Chinese poetry (Li Bai in particular, the wandering poet of the Tang dynasty). In the lonely 'eternal wanderer' who sings the opening 'Drinking Song of Earth's Misery', set by Mahler in the fateful A-minor key, Mahler recognised the lot of being a Jew, too. This symphonic 'song'-movement suddenly breaks off without a resolution, as if to say: there cannot be a harmonious ending to such a topic. Interestingly, this was when Zweig began to gather his thoughts for his drama *Jeremiah* and with it his stance on the meaning of Judaism.

But the reference to Li Bai is also symbolic in another respect, as it points to the reception of Zweig in China to an extent nothing short of stunning.[18] Zweig's works have become an integral part of *Weltliteratur*, even though he is less present and popular in Germany because his works fall between 'easy' appreciation for readers and literary snobbery from critics and academics. The verdict there is often that it is too light and slightly *kitschig* for serious literature and too high-brow and demanding for light-hearted *Unterhaltungsliteratur* (entertaining literature). By contrast, in France works by Zweig are included in the prestigious Bibliothèque de la Pléiade; his dramas are regularly performed on Parisian stages; and *Le Monde*, in its impressive *Hors-Série* documentary *Une Vie, Une Œuvre*, devoted an entire issue of over 100 pages to Zweig in 2022. But it was not too long ago when, in England, the application for a blue plaque to be displayed at 49 Hallam Street in London was rejected on the following grounds:

> The Panel acknowledged his popularity as a writer but noted that his profile has never been as high in Britain as elsewhere. It was felt

that a critical consensus does not appear to exist at the moment regarding Zweig's reputation as a writer and that, as a consequence, it was not possible to be certain of his lasting contribution.

That was back in 2012. Protests against this decision by the Blue Plaque Panel were led by Dame A. S. Byatt and others and, remarkably, reached the *Evening Standard* at the time. It is just possible that this negative decision was at least partly influenced by an infamous article that appeared in the *London Review of Books* on 28 January 2010 under the title 'Vermicular Dither'. In it, Michael Hofmann, a fine writer and excellent translator himself, mainly of works by Joseph Roth, accuses Zweig of 'insincerity', with particular reference to his final 'declaration'. Inexplicably, he compares Zweig's letter written before he and Lotte took their lives to speeches given by Hollywood film stars when receiving an Oscar. Hofmann concludes by saying Zweig was 'the Pepsi of Austrian writing'. Never had criticism of Zweig sunk any lower. Since then, however, attitudes towards Zweig have changed quite significantly, not least thanks to the extraordinary accomplishment and critical resonance of Anthea Bell's translations. It now appears that even a blue plaque for Zweig is about to arrive at 49 Hallam Street after all.

A final note

In an interview given to the weekly newspaper *Aufbau*, published by the German–Jewish Club in New York, Stefan Zweig argued as follows on 19 July 1940:

> Freedom – haven't we all forgotten what this means? We were free with the same naturalness with which we wear ties and ride a tram. There is a deep sorrow in the fact that we had to lose that [freedom]. Only now do we appreciate freedom's price. It's more valuable – but not valuable enough that the world won't pay for it. After the war we will be better off than before, because only then will we have properly recognised human values.[19]

It is a freedom Zweig had gained by losing it – a freedom from belongings and traditional ties; the tragically earned freedom of an exile; and the freedom of speech lost in Europe and regained in the Americas. This arch-European ended up being a modern, cosmopolitan preservationalist, a Magellan-like explorer, and Amerigo of the mind; an Erasmus on the Cunard liner the RMS *Scythia*, with the Statue of Liberty and the Corcovado Mountain before his eyes and the Kapuzinerberg in Salzburg in his heart. With that, yet not as the lonely wanderer of *The Song of the Earth* but with Lotte in Petrópolis at his side, Zweig was ready for his ultimate freedom of movement.

A final farewell: Visiting Paul Valéry
Heirs of Stefan Zweig

Words of Thanks

Stefan Zweig's life was destined to become literature. He could not but write about what he had read. In doing so the magic want of his pen brought words to life. When realising this creative circle as embodied by this extraordinary writer, I felt compelled to dive ever deeper into his world, to which he himself had provided the master-key in the shape of *The World of Yesterday*. But it was not before I realised that his approach to remembrance contained issues of striking relevance for today, and most likely for tomorrow, that I considered writing this biography – particularly with an Anglophone readership in mind. At first, I thought that this could be accomplished on the basis of a number of pieces that I had written on Stefan Zweig over the years, but I soon realised that with this undertaking I would have to start afresh.

The definite decision to embark on this biography was triggered by Jeremy Adler, who quite unexpectedly suggested to me just that. Therefore, my first expression of gratitude must go to him, whose long-lasting friendship means more to me than I can say. More votes of thanks are due, mainly to the Stefan Zweig Centre in Salzburg and its director, Martina Wörgötter; the Literaturarchiv Salzburg with Manfred Mittermayer; Birger Vanwesenbeeck of the Fredonia Archive; Oliver Matuschek for his stupendous works on Stefan Zweig; Eva Alberman and her son Daniel (London) for their unfailing helpfulness; Michael Leaman for first critical comments on the project; the late Anthea Bell for numerous conversations about 'translating Zweig'; the International Zweig Society with its president Hildemar Holl for encouraging deliberations; Pardaad Chamsaz (British Library, London); but most and foremost to Barbara Schwepcke and Harry Hall of

Haus Publishing for having taken this project on board, and especially to their outstandingly competent editor, Ed Doxey.

Like all such works, *In The Future of Yesterday* was daring to write and thus risk-ridden. If it generates more critical debate about Stefan Zweig's works and his worldwide legacy it will have been worth responding to this challenge.

Notes

Preliminaries, or How to Approach Stefan Zweig: A Writer from the Past for Our Time

1. Virginia Woolf, *Orlando: A Biography* [1928] (London/Toronto/Sydney/New York, 1982), 200.
2. Ibid., 186–7.
3. T. S. Eliot, *Collected Poems 1909–1962* (London, 1983), 189.
4. Stefan Zweig, *Tagebücher*, ed. by Knut Beck (Frankfurt am Main, 1984), 11. All references to diaries in the text are quoted from this edition as follows: Tb and page (here: Tb, 11).
5. Roy Foster, 'A stay against confusion: Seamus Heaney and the Ireland of his time', *TLS*, 5812–13 (22/29 Aug. 2014) 15–17, 15.
6. Erich Ebermayer, *Eh' ich's vergesse ...: Erinnerungen an Gerhart Hauptmann, Thomas Mann, Klaus Mann, Gustaf Gründgens, Emil Jannings und Stefan Zweig*, ed. and prefaced by Dirk Heißerer (Munich, 2005), 278.
7. 'Erich Maria Remarque – Talk with Friedrich Luft (1960)' [online video], *Text und Bühne* (2 Jan. 2018), <youtu.be/aOzROBGLkpE> (accessed 30 Dec. 2022).
8. For example: Monika Ritzer, *Friedrich Hebbel* (Göttingen, 2019).
9. Cf. Alberto Dines, *Morten o Paraíso, a Tragédia de Stefan Zweig* [1981] (Rio de Janeiro, 2004).
10. Cf. Günter Blamberger, 'Wie vermeidet man "Lieblose Legenden"? Zur Kunst des Biographierens' in G. B., *Von der Faszination ästhetischer Ideen und der Macht poetischen Denkens* (Leiden/Boston/Paderborn, 2021), 97–110.
11. Stefan Zweig, *Die schlaflose Welt: Aufsätze und Vorträge aus den Jahren 1909–1941*, ed. by Knut Beck (Frankfurt am Main, 2006), 90–103, 92.
12. Ibid., 101.
13. Ibid., 102.
14. Ibid., 103.
15. Ibid., 102.
16. See for an exemplary discussion of this topic: Mathias Mayer, *King Lear – Die Tragödie des Zuschauers: Ästhetik und Ethik der Empathie* (Göttingen, 2022), 36–44 and 161–72.
17. In her major biography on the proverbially incorruptible German philosopher Karl

Jaspers, Suzanne Kirkbright aptly chose the subtitle *Navigations in Truth* (New Haven, CT/London, 2004).

18 Stefan Zweig and Friderike Zweig, *'Wenn einen Augenblick die Wolken weichen': Briefwechsel 1912–1942*, ed. by Jeffrey B. Berlin and Gert Kerschbaumer (Frankfurt am Main, 2006), 228. All references to Zweig and Friderike's correspondence in the text are quoted from this edition as follows: SZ/FZ and page (here: SZ/FZ, 228).

19 A milestone in research on Stefan Zweig was the publication of *The Stefan Zweig Handbook*, with extensive research reports by its many contributors: Arturo Larcati, Klemens Renoldner, and Martina Wörgötter (eds.), *Stefan-Zweig-Handbuch* (Berlin/Boston, 2018). Contributions will be referenced by contributor, title of article, and the signet *SZH*.

Portrait of a Writer as a Young Man, or Early (Poetic) Orientations in Vienna and Elsewhere

1 In biographical terms, a most recent example is Claire Tomalin, *The Young H. G. Wells: Changing the World* (London, 2022).

2 Cf. Rüdiger Görner, *Kokoschka: The Untimely Modernist*, transl. from the German by Debra Marmor and Herbert Danner (London, 2020).

3 Jill Lloyd and Ingrid Pfeiffer (eds.) in collaboration with Raymond Coffer, *Richard Gerstl: Retrospective* [catalogue for the exhibition in New York] (Munich, 2017).

4 Arnold Schönberg, *Das bilderische Werk* [German and English] (Klagenfurt, 1991).

5 William Boyd, 'Viennese Waltz', *The Saturday Guardian* (4 Feb. 2012) 2–4, 2.

6 Ludwig Wittgenstein, *Tractatus Logico-Philosophicus*, transl. by D. F. Pears and B. F. McGuinness, introduction by Bertrand Russell (London and New York, 1997), 74: 'What we cannot speak about we must pass over in silence.'

7 See for instance Carl Schorske, *Fin de Siècle Vienna: Politics and Culture* (New York, 1980); Moritz Csáky, Astrid Kury, and Ulrich Tragatschnigg (eds.), *Kultur – Identität – Differenz: Wien und Zentraleuropa in der Moderne* (Innsbruck, 2004); Peter Gay, *Schnitzler's Century: The Making of Middle-Class Culture 1815–1914* (New York, 2002).

8 Hilde Spiel, *Vienna's Golden Autumn 1866–1938* (London, 1987).

9 Hugo Wittmann, 'Wien darf nicht New York werden!' [1910] in Arnold Klaffenböck (ed.), *Sehnsucht nach Alt-Wien: Texte zur Stadt, die niemals war*, preface by Wolfgang Kos (Vienna, 2005), 113–17.

10 Ibid., 103–6, 103.

11 Ibid., 113.

12 Ibid., 119–22, 119.

13 Cf. 'Gewalttätige Rhetorik und rigorose Praxis: Adolf Loos im architekturästhetischen Diskurs der frühen Moderne', *Slowakische Zeitschrift für Germanistik*, 9/2 (2017) 33–48, 39.

14 William Boyd, 'Virtual Vienna', *TLS* (29 May 2020), 17. Cf. Brigitte Hamann,

Vienna: A Dictator's Apprenticeship (Oxford, 1999); William A. Jenks, *Vienna and the Young Hitler* (New York, 1960).
15 George Steiner, 'On the edge of hunger: Hitler's Vienna years and the formation of his anti-semitism' [review of Brigitte Hamann's study, *Hitler's Wien*], *TLS* (31 Jan. 1997), 3–4, 3.
16 Zweig, *Die schlaflose Welt*, 7–8.
17 Ibid., 13.
18 Ibid., 15.
19 Ibid., 15–16.
20 Klaffenböck (ed.), *Sehnsucht nach Alt-Wien*, 89–91, 89.
21 Ibid., 89
22 Ibid., 90.
23 Stefan Zweig, *Briefe 1897–1914* [vol. I], ed. by Knut Beck, Jeffrey B. Berlin, and Natascha Weschenbach-Feggeler (Frankfurt am Main, 1995), 15. All references to Zweig's letters in the text are quoted from the Fischer editions, vols. I–IV, as follows: number of volume and page (here: I, 15).
24 Cf. Michael Navratil, '"Den Schauer des Mythos neu schaffen": Die kreative Rezeption von Nietzsches "Geburt der Tragödie" in der Wiener Moderne', *Sprachkunst*, 42/2 (2011), 245–69.
25 Oliver Matuschek, *Three Lives: A Biography of Stefan Zweig*, transl. from German by Allan Blunden (London, 2011), 61. For further reference cf. Natascha Weschenbach, *Stefan Zweig und Hippolyte Taine: Stefan Zweigs Dissertation über Die Philosophie des Hippolyte Taine*, Studia Imacologica vol. 2 (Leiden, Boston, Paderborn, Singapore, 1992).
26 Cf. Glenn H. Roe, 'Contre Taine and Renan: Charles Péguy and the Metaphysics of Modern History', *French Forum*, 34/2 (2009), 17–37.
27 Ernest Renan, *What is a Nation? And Other Political Writings*, transl. and ed. by M. F. N. Giglioni (New York, 2018), 56.
28 Dubravaka Stojanovis, 'What is a nation? The Balkanization of historical memory', *TLS* (13 Sep. 2019), 29.
29 Cf. Donald A. Prater, 'Stefan Zweig and Hermann Hesse', *Modern Austrian Literature*, 14/3–4 (1981), 11–38.
30 Cf. Rüdiger Görner, 'Eines Freundes Freund zu sein: Zum Motiv der Freundschaft bei Stefan Zweig', *Sinn und Form*, 69/5 (2017), 647–55.
31 Collected in: Stefan Zweig, *Rhythmen: Nachdichtungen ausgewählter Lyrik von Emile Verhaeren, Charles Baudelaire und Paul Verlaine*, ed. by Knut Beck (Frankfurt am Main, 1983); and Stefan Zweig, *Emile Verhaeren* (Frankfurt am Main, 1984).
32 Cf. Donald A. Prater (ed.), *Rainer Maria Rilke und Stefan Zweig in Briefen und Dokumenten* (Frankfurt am Main 1987).
33 Stefan Zweig, *Die Welt von Gestern: Erinnerungen eines Europäers*, ed. by Oliver Matuschek (Frankfurt am Main, 2017), 143.
34 Cf. the exemplary achievement by Piet Defraeye, Helga Mitterbauer, and Chris

Reyns-Chikuma (eds.), *Brussels 1900 Vienna: Networks in Literature, Visual and Performing Arts, and other Cultural Practices* (Leiden/Boston, 2022). The pioneering work was done in 1987 when a major conference in Brussels examined 'Bruxelles–Vienne: Reflets croisés 1890–1938'.
35 For a detailed analysis of this role see in particular Norbert Bachleitner, 'Stefan Zweig as a Mediator and Translator of Emile Verhaeren's Poetry' in *Brussels 1900 Vienna*, 140–67.
36 Ibid., 141.
37 Quote from Bachleitner, ibid., 144.
38 Stefan Zweig, *Silberne Saiten*, ed. by Knut Beck, sixth edn. (Frankfurt am Main, 2008), 68. ('*Aus schweren Nächten ... In meine Nächte zittert manche Träne / Kein Traum schließt meine wunden Augen zu ... / Oh, wie ich mich nach Deinen Lippen sehne / Nach ihrem glockenreinen weichen "Du"!*')
39 Ibid., 232.
40 Matuschek, *Three Lives*, 78.
41 Cf. Monika Meister, '*Tersites* (1907)' in *SZH*, 112–18.
42 Cf. the second chapter 'Verwirrung der Gefühle' in Ulrich Weinzierl, *Stefan Zweigs brennendes Geheimnis* (Vienna, 2015), 83–165.
43 Ibid., 98.
44 Ibid., 98.

The Virtue of Restlessness
1 Cf. Will Stone's introduction to his translation of a selection of Zweig's prose on travelling in Stefan Zweig, *Journeys* (London, 2010), vii and viii. For a more comprehensive collection see Stefan Zweig, *Auf Reisen*, ed. by Knut Beck, third edn. (Frankfurt am Main, 2008).
2 L. Aennaeus Seneca, *Ad Lucilium epistulae morales LXX–CXXIV*, ed. by Manfred Rosenbach (Darmstadt, 1999), 186 ('*otium sine litteris mors est et hominis vivi sepultura*').
3 Franz Hessel, *Ermunterung zum Genuß*, ed. by Karin Grund and Bernd Witte (Berlin, 1981), 60–1.
4 Zweig, *Journeys*, 4, 24.
5 Ibid., 7, 18.
6 Ibid., 31.
7 Ibid., 31
8 Karl Philipp Moritz, 'Reisen eines Deutschen in England im Jahre 1782', in Moritz, *Werke: Reisen, Schriften zur kunst und Mythologie Vol. II*, ed. by Horst Günther, second edn. (Frankfurt am Main 1993), 57.
9 Stefan Zweig, 'Der Genius Englands', in *Neue Freie Presse Wien: Morgenblatt* (25 Jan. 1924), 23–4. See also Margit Dirscherl, '"Eine seltsame Umkehr": Stefan Zweigs Feuilleton "Der Genius Englands"' in Rüdiger Görner and Klemens

Renoldner (eds.), *Zweigs England: Schriftenreihe des Stefan Zweig Centre Salzburg, Vol. 5* (Würzburg, 2014), 129–39.
10 Rainer Maria Rilke, *Werke IV: Frühe Erzählungen und Dramen*, ed. by Ernst Zinn (Frankfurt am Main, 1987), 553.
11 Cf. The chapter 'Why Don't You Go to India?' in Matuschek, *Three Lives*, 85–97. See also: Walther Rathenau, *Schriften und Reden*, ed. with an afterword by Hans Werner Richter (Frankfurt am Main, 1986). See also: Lothar Gall, *Walther Rathenau: Portrait einer Epoche* (Munich, 2009).
12 Quoted in Gall, *Rathenau*, 68.
13 Matuschek, *Three Lives*, 88–90.
14 Zweig, *Silberne Saiten*, 149.
15 Its grotesque culmination would be reached in the shape of Subhas Bose's affiliation with National Socialism. See for instance: Romain Hayes, *Subhas Chandra Bose in Nazi Germany: Politics, Intelligence and Propaganda 1941–1943* (Oxford, 2011).
16 Stefan Zweig, *Auf Reisen*, 111–20, 113. All references to *Auf Reisen* in the text are quoted from this edition as follows: AR and page (here: AR, 113).
17 See Knut Beck's comment, ibid., 283. Beck refers to Haushofer's German nationalist tendencies.
18 Jens Malte Fischer, *Gustav Mahler: Der fremde Vertraute* (Vienna, 2003), 836–9; Matuschek, *Three Lives*, 94–6.
19 Zweig, *Die Schlaflose Welt*, 17–24.
20 Ibid., 25–9 ('*Heimfahrt nach Österreich*', 'Homeward-bound back to Austria').
21 Friedrich Schiller, *Sämtliche Werke, Vol. IV: Historische Schriften*, ed. by Gerhard Fricke and Herbert G. Göpfert, sixth edn. (Munich, 1980), 316–61. Schiller published this text first in his periodical *Die Horen* in March and April 1795.
22 Cf. Laura Spinney, *Pale Rider: The Spanish Flu of 1918 and How it Changed the World* (New York, 2017), 166–70. See also Alex de Waal, 'Die Influenza von 1918: Geschichten über Seuchen und die evolutionär-ökologische Erzählung', *Lettre International* (Autumn 2021), 31–4. As de Waal points out, Franz Kafka, too, succumbed to this pandemic in October 1918.
23 Claudio Magris, *Danube*, with an introduction by Richard Flanagan (London, 2016).

Early Days for Fiction
1 Schiller, *Sämtliche Werke, Vol. I: Gedichte, Dramen I*, 429 ('*Und der mächtigste von allen / Herrschern ist der Augenblick. [...] Schnell, wie es der Geist geboren, / Will das Werk geboren sein. [...] So ist jede schöne Gabe / Flüchtig wie des Blitzes Schein, / Schnell in ihrem düstern Grabe / Schließt die Nacht sie wieder ein.*')
2 Stefan Zweig, *The Governess and Other Stories*, transl. from the German by Anthea Bell (London, 2011), 224.
3 Ibid., 228.
4 Ibid., 229.

5   Ibid., 229.
6   Knut Beck, 'Afterword' in Stefan Zweig, *Phantastische Nacht*, ed. by Knut Beck, twenty-first edition (Frankfurt am Main, 2011), 248.
7   Zweig, *The Governess and Other Stories*, 152–5.
8   He calls Zweig's way of composing prose with a slight ironic twinkle 'so perfected, so rounded and so clean'. Joseph Roth and Stefan Zweig, *Jede Freundschaft ist mir verderblich: Briefwechsel 1927–1938*, ed. by Madeleine Rietra and Rainer Joachim Siegel, with an afterword by Heinz Lunzer (Göttingen, 2011), 7. All references to Roth and Zweig's correspondence in the text are quoted from this edition as follows: JR/SZ and page (here: JR/SZ, 7).
9   Zweig, *The Governess*, 79.
10 Ibid., 98.
11 Cf. Marlen Mairhofer, '*Die spät bezahlte Schuld* (1942)' in *SZH*, 295–300.
12 W. H. Auden, *Collected Poems*, ed. by Edward Mendelson (London, 1991), 181.
13 Stefan Zweig, *Amok and Other Stories*, transl. from the German by Anthea Bell (London, 2006), 88.
14 Ibid., 90.
15 Ibid., 90.
16 Ibid., 92.
17 Stefan Zweig, *Der Amokläufer: Erzählungen*, ed. by Knut Beck, thirteenth edition (Frankfurt am Main, 2004), 67–73.
18 Zweig, *Die schlaflose Welt*, 112–21, 112.
19 Stefan Zweig, *Twilight and Moonbeam Alley*, transl. from the German by Anthea Bell (London, 2005), 9–66; German original in: Zweig, *Der Amokläufer*, 7–53.
20 Zweig, *Twilight and Moonbeam Alley*, 20.
21 Ibid., 66.
22 Cf. Ulrike Vedder, '*Erstes Erlebnis* (1911)' in *SZH*, 188–97, particularly 195.
23 Stefan Zweig, *Burning Secret*, transl. by Anthea Bell (London, 2008), 14.
24 Ibid., 31.
25 Ibid., 17.
26 Cf. Zweig's diary entry of 18 Dec. 1912 in Tb, 35.
27 Zweig, *Burning Secret*, 13.

Keeping Up with 'Life'
1   Weinzierl, *Stefan Zweigs brennendes Geheimnis*, 9.
2   'Die Liebe ist die Gefahr des Einsamsten, die Liebe zu Allem, wenn es nur lebt! Zum Lachen ist wahrlich meine Narrheit und meine Bescheidenheit in der Liebe!', in Friedrich Nietzsche, *Also sprach Zarathustra* in *Sämtliche Werke: Kritische Studienausgabe Bd. 4*, ed. by Giorgio Colli and Mazzino Montinari (Munich, 1988), 196.
3   Cf. Weinzierl, *Stefan Zweigs brennendes Geheimnis*.
4   Quoted in Wilhelm W. Hemecker (ed.), *Haschisch: Mit dreizehn Zeichnungen von*

    Alfred Kubin (Graz, 2002), 9. Zweig's review appeared in *Das Literarische Echo*, 5 (1902/3), 747.
5. Klaus Mann, *Der Wendepunkt: Ein Lebensbericht*, second edn. (Berlin/Weimar, 1979), 393.
6. Zweig, *Rhythmen*, 169.
7. *The Memoirs of Ethel Smyth*, abridged and introduced by Ronald Crichton (New York, 1987), 293.
8. Romain Rolland and Stefan Zweig, *Briefwechsel 1910–1940, Vol. 1: 1910–1923*, transl. by Eva and Gerhard Schewe and Christel Gersch, ed. by Waltraud Schwarze with an introduction by Wolfgang Klein (Berlin, 1987), 46. All references to Zweig and Rolland's correspondence in the text are quoted from these editions as follows: RR/SZ, number of volume, and page (here: RR/SZ, I, 46).
9. Cf. Peter Sprengel, *Gerhart Hauptmann: Bürgerlichkeit und großer Traum, Eine Biographie* (Munich, 2012), 437.
10. Zweig, *Twilight and Moonbeam Alley*, 71–96, 96.
11. Cf. Michel Reffet, '*Marceline Desbordes-Valmore. Das Lebensbild einer Dichterin* (1920)' in *SZH*, 455–60.

Jeremiah in the First World War
1. Zweig, *Schlaflose Welt*, 39 and Zweig, *Tagebücher*, 89.
2. Romain Rolland, *Über den Gräbern: Aus den Tagebüchern 1914–1919*, ed. by Hans Peter Buohler with an afterword by Julia Encke (Munich, 2015), 112–16.
3. For detailed discussion of the various aspects and influences that conditioned Zweig's relationship with Judaism, see, in particular, Mark H. Gelber, *Stefan Zweig: Judentum und Zionismus* (Innsbruck, 2013). Cf. the thoughtful review of this book by Margit Dirscherl in *Modern Language Review*, 110/4 (2015), 1164–6.
4. Cf. Rüdiger Görner, 'The Drama of Prophecy: On Stefan Zweig and 'Jeremiah', *Jewish Quarterly*, 44 (2011), 44–6.
5. It is worth noting that Jean-Paul Sartre produced his version of Euripides's tragedy in 1964 as a manifestation against colonialism of any sort. Sartre's message was clear: wars do not know winners, only losers.
6. For further discussion of the Jeremiah motif in Zweig and its context cf. Rüdiger Görner, 'The Figure of Jeremiah in the Work of Stefan Zweig and Rainer Maria Rilke', in Louis Stulman and Edward Silver, *The Oxford Handbook of Jeremiah* (Oxford, 2021), 553–65.
7. Ernst Hardt, *König Salomo: Ein Drama in drei Akten* (Leipzig, 1915).
8. There is a plethora of literature on the Balfour Declaration. For a historical account see for example: Michael J. Cohen, *The Origins and Evolution of the Arab–Zionist Conflict* (Berkeley, 1989).
9. I quote from 'the final edition' of the work, dedicated to 'Meiner Frau, Ostern 1917': Stefan Zweig, *Jeremias: Eine dramatische Dichtung in neun Bildern* (Leipzig, 1928), 15.

10 Ibid., 85.
11 Ibid., 88.
12 Ibid., 185.
13 Ibid., 188.
14 Ibid., 95.
15 This point was made by Lionel B. Steiman, 'The Eclipse of Humanism: Zweig between the Wars', *Modern Austrian Literature*, 14/3–4 (1981), 147–93. Cf. Eva Plank, '*Jeremias* (1917)' in *SZH*, 128–34.
16 Quoted in Plank, *Jeremias*, 130.
17 Thomas Mann and Stefan Zweig, *Briefwechsel, Dokumente und Schnittpunkte*, ed. by Katrin Bedenig and Franz Zeder (Frankfurt am Main, 2016), 21–2.
18 Rosa Mayreder, *Tagebücher 1873–1937*, ed. and with an introduction by Harriet Anderson (Frankfurt am Main, 1988), 178.
19 'Der Krüppel' in Zweig, *Silberne Saiten*, 175–6.
20 Cf. The important article by Arturo Larcati, 'Das Motiv des Besiegten' in *SZH*, 722–32.
21 Zweig, *Silberne Saiten*, 177–9.
22 Cf. for instance Bernard Sergent, *Homosexuality in Greek Myth* (Boston, 1986); Kenneth J. Dover, *Greek Homosexuality* (Cambridge, MA, 1989), 118.
23 Zweig, *Die schlaflose Welt*, 136–40.
24 Ibid., 52–67.
25 Stefan Zweig, 'Compulsion' in Stefan Zweig, *Wondrak and Other Stories*, transl. by Anthea Bell (London, 2009), 31–81, 41. All references to *Wondrak and Other Stories* in the text are quoted from this edition as follows: WOS and page (here: WOS, 41).
26 Cf. Iris Himmelmayr, 'Das Trauma des Ersten Weltkriegs: Einige Beobachtungen zu Stefan Zweigs Prosa' in Klemens Renoldner (ed.), *Stefan Zweig – Abschied von Europa* (Vienna, 2014), 67–77.
27 Stefan Zweig, *Drei Meister: Balzac, Dickens, Dostojewski* (Frankfurt am Main, 1981), 5.
28 Rainer Maria Rilke, *Auguste Rodin* (Leipzig, 1930), 6.
29 Ibid., 7.
30 Stefan Zweig, *Roman Rolland*, ed. by Knut Beck, second edn. (Frankfurt am Main, 1987), 51.
31 Ibid., 54.
32 Ibid., 37.

Tracing Demons, or How to Approach Greatness
1 Jules Michelet, *Histoire du XIXe siècle, Vol. 2* (Paris, 1875), III.
2 Osip Mandelstam, *Über Dichtung*, ed. by Pawel Nerler (Leipzig/Weimar, 1991), 59.
3 George Steiner, *Martin Heidegger* (Chicago, 1991), vii–viii.

4 Quoted in Bernd Hamacher, '*Amok* (1922)' in *SZH*, 199. Letter to Kippenberg of 12 Mar. 1921 (Archiv Insel Verlag, DLA, Marbach).
5 Oliver Matuschek (ed.), *Stefan Zweig 'Ich wünschte, dass ich Ihnen ein wenig fehlte': Briefe an Lotte Zweig 1934–1940* (Frankfurt am Main, 2013), 210–14.
6 Cf. Rüdiger Görner, *Hölderlin and the Consequences: An Essay on the German 'Poet of Poets'* (London/Berlin, 2021).
7 Cf. Ashwin J. Manthripragada, *Constituting a Self through an Indian Other: A Study of Select Works by Stefan Zweig and Hermann Hesse* [thesis] (Berkeley, 2014). Cf. Christine Berthold and Arturo Larcati, '*Die Augen des ewigen Bruders* (1921)' in *SZH*, 309–13.
8 Quoted in Berthold and Larcati, '*Die Augen des ewigen Bruders*', 310.
9 *The Bhagavad Gita*, transl. by Juan Mascaro (Harmondsworth, 1980), 56.
10 Ibid., 62.
11 Stefan Zweig, *'Ich habe das Bedürfnis nach Freunden': Erzählungen, Essays und unbekannte Texte*, ed. by Klemens Renoldner (Vienna, Graz, Klagenfurt, 2013), 85–120, 86.
12 Renoldner, Fritz (eds.), *Zweig: Erzählungen, Essays und unbekannte Texte*, 92.
13 Ibid., 104.
14 Zweig, *Der Amokläufer*, 100, 126. Cf. Stefan Zweig, *Amok and Other Stories*, transl. by Anthea Bell, 38, 65. Bell's otherwise elegant translations of Zweig do have the tendency, though, to embellish 'problematic' expressions.
15 Zweig, *Amok and Other Stories*, 24. All references to *Amok and Other Stories* in the text are quoted from this edition as follows: AOS and page (here: AOS, 24).
16 Zweig, *Phantastische Nacht*, 158.
17 T. S. Eliot, *Collected Poems 1909–1962*, 76 (v. 341–2 and v. 357–8).
18 Ibid., 164.
19 Zweig, *Phantastische Nacht*, 189.
20 Ibid., 216.
21 Ibid., 216.
22 Stefan Zweig, *Meisternovellen*, second edn. (Frankfurt am Main, 2002), 191.
23 Ibid.
24 Zweig, *Silberne Saiten*, 225–31.
25 See for example: Alexander J. Sakulku, 'The Imposter Phenomenon', *International Journal of Behavioral Science*, 6 (2011), 73–92.
26 Friedrich Nietzsche, *Thus Spoke Zarathustra*, transl. with an introduction by R. J. Hollingdale (London, 2003), 333.
27 Zweig, *Silberne Saiten*, 226 and 227.
28 Thomas Mann, *Aufsätze, Reden, Essays, Vol. 2: 1919–1925*, ed. by Harry Matter (Berlin and Weimar, 1986), 159 (lecture version of Mann's essay of 1921, which he delivered first in Lübeck in September of that year and, consecutively, at various occasions, including in Salzburg).

29 Stefan Zweig, *Der Kampf mit dem Dämon: Hölderlin, Kleist, Nietzsche* (Frankfurt am Main, 1981), 7.
30 Anthony Heilbut, *Thomas Mann: Eros & Literature* (London, 1997), 449.
31 Zweig, *Der Kampf mit dem Dämon*, 9.
32 Cf. Rüdiger Görner, 'Beethoven, Hegel & Hölderlin at 250: Thoughts on the presence of triadic structures in their works', in *Archiv für das Studium der neueren Sprachen und Literaturen*, 259 (2022), 29–39.
33 Zweig, *Der Kampf mit dem Dämon*, 9.
34 Ibid., 17–19.
35 Ibid., 91.
36 Ibid., 131.
37 Ibid., 178, 181, 183.
38 Cf. Burkhard Stenzel, '"… gerade gerne in Weimar": Stefan Zweig und die Klassikerstadt: verborgene Verbindungen – werkgeschichtliche Wirkungen', *Weimar-Jena: Die große Stadt*, 6/2 (2013), 100–13.

Towards European Transnationalism
1 Zweig, *Erzählungen, Essays und unbekannte Texte*, 420.
2 Ibid., 465.
3 Stefan Zweig, 'Ehrfurcht vor Georg Brandes' in Zweig, *Die schlaflose Welt*, 163–5.
4 Cf. K. M. Asadowski, 'Die Briefe Stefan Zweigs an den Verlag Wremja', *Neue Deutsche Literatur*, 26/12 (1978), 119–31.
5 Stefan Zweig, *Adam Lux: Zehn Bilder aus dem Leben eines deutschen Revolutionärs*, with essays and materials by Franz Dumont and Erwin Rotermund (Obernburg, 2003).
6 For a recent reappraisal of Toussaint Louverture, see: Sudhir Hazareesingh, *Black Spartacus: The Epic Life of Toussaint Louverture* (London, 2019).
7 'Neuerwerbungen aus der Sammlung Inge und Erich Fitzbauer', Literaturarchiv Salzburg, www.stefanzweig.digital/archive/objects/context:szd/methods/sdef:Context/get?mode=miscellaneous (accessed 8 May 2022).

The Torch of Eros, or The Confusion of a Reluctant Modernist
1 Erwin Rieger, *Stefan Zweig: der Mann und das Werk* (Berlin, 1928).
2 Cf. Evelyne Polt-Heinzl, '*Rausch der Verwandlung* (erstmals 1982)' in *SZH*, 376–83.
3 For a comprehensive discussion of the various interpretations of these three novellas, see: Marlen Mairhofer, '*Verwirrung der Gefühle* (1927)' in *SZH*, 207–17. Mairhofer points out that the majority of interpretations focus on the title story *Confusion* itself and claims, quite correctly, that the highly positive popular reception of the stories, including their frequent filmic renderings, is in stark contrast to the often-critical comments by literary scholars.
4 For detailed survey of the structure and content, cf. Werner Michler, '*Sternstunden der Menschheit* (1927)' in *SZH*, 323–9.

5   All quotations from: Stefan Zweig, 'Anmerkungen zu Joyces Ulysses', *Neue Rundschau*, 39/10 (1928), 477–9.
6   The first English translation was accomplished by Eden and Cedar Paul under the title 'Four-and-Twenty Hours in a Woman's Life' in Stefan Zweig, *Conflicts: Three Tales* (New York, 1927), 3–110.
7   The most recent re-edition is noteworthy because of the comprehensive afterword by Karl-Heinz Ott: Constance de Salm, *24 Stunden im Leben einer empfindsamen Frau: Roman*, transl. from the French by Claudia Steinitz (Hamburg, 2008), 5.
8   For comment see especially: Barbara Neymeyr, 'Aporien der Hasard-Leidenschaft im kulturanthropologischen Kontext: Die Inszenierungen des Glücksspiels in Stefan Zweigs *Vierundzwanzig Stunden aus dem Leben einer Frau* und in Arthur Schnitzlers *Spiel im Morgengrauen*' in *Hasard: Der Spieler in der deutschsprachigen Literaturgeschichte*, ed. by Louis Gerrekens and Achim Küpper (Würzburg, 2012), 141–68.
9   For a critical edition of this novella, incorporating all known changes made by Zweig and a comprehensive documentation of its reception, see: Elisabeth Erdem and Klemens Renoldner (eds.), *Stefan Zweig: Verwirrung der Gefühle* (Stuttgart, 2017). The English translation by Anthea Bell (London, rev. 2009) is based on Knut Beck's edition of 2002.
10 Ibid., 133.
11 Ibid., 176.
12 Stefan Zweig, *Confusion: The Private Papers of the Privy Councillor R. von D.*, transl. by Anthea Bell (London, rev. 2009), 147.
13 Ibid., 152.
14 Ibid., 30.
15 Stefan Zweig, *The Governess and Other Stories*, 189.
16 Stefan Zweig, *Journey into the Past*, transl. and with an afterword by Anthea Bell, foreword by Paul Bailey (London, 2009), 21. All references to *Journey into the Past* in the text are quoted from this edition as follows: JiP and page (here: JiP, 21).

Political Ridge Walks
1   Quoted in Thomas Migge, 'Dank dem Diktator', *Deutschlandfunk* (14 Jun. 2006). Report about Fabio Rugge's find in the Italian State Archive at www.deutschlandfunk.de/dank-dem-diktator-100.html (accessed 19 May 2022).
2   Cf. P. C. Roy Chaudhuri, *C. F. Andrews: His Life and Times* (Ann Arbor, MI, 1971).
3   Klaus Mann, *Der Wendepunkt: Ein Lebensbericht*, second edn. with an afterword by Friedrich Albrecht (Berlin/Weimar, 1979), 321.
4   Stefan Zweig Collection, The British Library (MS 158). Cf. Jean H. Leventhal, 'A Public Memorial to a True European: Stefan Zweig's Autograph Collection and the British Library', *Modern Austrian Literature*, 33/2 (2000), 23–36.

Life Amidst Crises: Stefan Zweig at and around Fifty

1. Henry James, *The Diary of a Man of Fifty* [1879], foreword by David Lodge (London, 2008), 14.
2. Stefan Zweig, *Marie Antoinette*, transl. by Eden and Cedar Paul (London, 2010), 13.
3. Oliver Matuschek, *Das Salzburg des Stefan Zweig*, with photographs by Angelika Fische (Berlin, 2008), 28.
4. Joseph Roth and Stefan Zweig, *Jede Freundschaft mit mir ist verderblich: Briefwechsel 1927–1938*, ed. by Madeleine Rietra and Rainer-Joachim Siegel with an afterword by Heinz Lunzer (Göttingen, 2011), 316.
5. Matuschek, *Das Salzburg des Stefan Zweig*, 25.
6. Ibid., 20.
7. Ibid., 20.
8. Gisela Prossnitz, '"Salzburg: Perhaps Art's Last Existing Sanctuary from the Political World" – The Salzburg Festival in the Thirties' in Kenneth Segar and John Warren (eds.), *Austria in the Thirties: Culture and Politics* (Riverside, CA, 1991), 234–52, 240.
9. Ibid., 240.
10. Cf. Rüdiger Görner, 'Eines Freundes Freund zu sein: Zum Motiv der Freundschaft bei Stefan Zweig', *Sinn und Form*, 69/5 (2017).
11. His biographer, Roman Roček, generously granted him 'nine lives' in *Die neun Leben des Alexander Lernet-Holenia* (Vienna, 1999) as opposed to Zweig's mere three lives, according to Matuschek.
12. Cf. Rüdiger Görner, 'Schwieriges Erbe: Lernet-Holenias Verhältnis zu Rilke', *Sprachkunst* XXXI (2000), 307–21.
13. Alexander Lernet-Holenia, *Baron Bagge*, transl. by Richard and Clara Winston, with a foreword by Patti Smith, three letters between Zweig and Lernet-Holenia, and a note by Arturo Larcati (London, 2022), 69. Letters and note by Larcati transl. by Krishna Winston.
14. Cf. Birgit Peter, '*Quiproquo* (1928)' in *SZH*, 149–54, 151.
15. Cf. Ibid., 152.
16. Lernet-Holenia, *Baron Bagge*, 73.
17. Ibid., 76.
18. Larcati, 'A Note [on Baron Bagge]' in ibid., 76.
19. For a most recent biography on Roth see Keiron Pim, *Endless Flight: The life of Joseph Roth* (London, 2022). As George Prochnik points out in his review of this biography ('A stranger in every town: Joseph Roth and his skill at identifying "fleeting moments with universal implications"', *TLS* (7 Oct. 2022), 3–5), Pim's treatment of this friendship is rather unbalanced. Prochnik points at an interesting difference between Roth and Zweig in terms of their respective fiction: 'That Roth was the more arresting writer of the two, Zweig himself would have been the first to acknowledge [...] But the two men were doing different things – Roth did little with his female characters – and Zweig's literary engagement with the drama of

women's interior lives imparted a meaningful sense of recognition to his large female readership.'

The Uprooting of an Austrian, or Fascist Trauma and Early Exile

1. Zweig, *Joseph Fouché*, 106.
2. See: Görner, *Kokoschka*, 162–94.
3. Anton Staudinger, '"Austria" – The Ideology of Austrofascism' in Segar and Warren, *Austria in the Thirties*, 12.
4. Ibid., 17.
5. See: Gordon Brook-Shephard, *Dollfuss* (London, 1961); and the memoirs of Dollfuss's daughter: Eva Dollfuss, *Mein Vater: Hitlers erstes Opfer* (Vienna/Munich, 1994). For a more critical and scholarly profound assessment see: Florian Wenninger, Lucile Dreidemy, *Das Dollfuss/Schuschnigg-Regime 1933–1938: Vermessung eines Forschungsfeldes* (Vienna, 2013).
6. John Drinkwater, *Abraham Lincoln* [play] (London, 1918).
7. Cf. Stefan Zweig, *Briefe an Lotte Zweig 1934–1940*, 28.
8. The reason for this meeting is unknown and the minutes are lost.
9. Cf. Christian Klein, '*Castellio gegen Calvin oder Ein Gewissen gegen die Gewalt* (1936)' in *SZH*, 424–32, 424, and 430.
10. Stefan Zweig, *Castellio gegen Calvin oder Ein Gewissen gegen die Gewalt*, fourteenth edn. (Frankfurt am Main, 2006), 54.
11. Christian von Zimmermann, *Biographische Anthropologie: Menschenbilder in lebensgeschichtlicher Darstellung 1830–1940* (Berlin/New York, 2006), 324.
12. Zweig, *Castellio Gegen Calvin*, 7.
13. Thomas Mann and Stefan Zweig, *Briefwechsel, Dokumente und Schnittpunkte*, ed. by Katrin Bedenig and Franz Zeder, *Thomas Mann-Studien*, 51 (Frankfurt am Main, 2016), 89 (thereafter: TM/SZ, 89).
14. Thomas Mann, *Tagebücher 1935–1936*, ed. by Peter de Mendelssohn (Frankfurt am Main, 2003), 306–7 (entries for 24–27 May 1936).
15. TM/SZ, 68.
16. Diary entry of 24 Apr. 1935, in Mann, *Tagebücher*, 89.
17. Zweig, *Castellio gegen Calvin*, 157.

How to Become an Alien and Experiencing England

1. Zweig, *Briefe an Lotte Zweig*, 41 and 111.
2. TM/SZ, 68 (letter of 2 Nov. 1933).
3. Ibid., 70 (diary entry of 4 Nov. 1933).
4. Ibid., 71 (letter of 10 Nov. 1933).
5. Richard Dove, '"Meilenweit von Politik": Stefan Zweig's exile in Britain' in Görner and Renoldner, *Zweigs England*, 11–20.
6. Cf. Margit Dirscherl, '"Eine seltsame Umkehr": Stefan Zweigs Feuilleton "Der Genius Englands"' in ibid., 129–39.

7   All quotations from: Stefan Zweig, 'Der Genius Englands', *Neue Freie Presse* [Special Issue: England and Austria] (25 Jan. 1924), 23–4. For further comment see: Dirscherl, 'Eine seltsame Umkehr'.
8   Quoted in Dove, 'Meilenweit von Politik', 12.
9   Quoted in ibid., 18.
10 Zweig, *Briefe an Lotte Zweig*, 46.
11 Daria Santini, *The Exiles: Actors, Artists and Writers Who Fled the Nazis for London* (London, 2019), 209. Santini gives a full and excellent account in Chapter 5, 'The London Life of two literary exiles', 179–210.
12 Quoted in ibid.
13 Ibid., 15.
14 Ibid., 15.
15 Ibid., 15.
16 Zweig, *Briefe an Lotte Zweig*, 225.
17 Dove, 'Meilenweit von Politik', 19.
18 For discussion of current debates of the refugee's problem, in Germany in particular, and the media usage of charged concepts see: Uwe Becker, *Deutschland und seine Flüchtlinge: Das Wechselbad der Diskurse im langen Sommer der Flucht 2015* (Bielefeld, 2022).
19 Ibid., 17.
20 Ibid., 462.
21 For a comprehensive overview on the different positions held see: 'Phony War', *Encyclopedia Britannica*, www.britannica.com/event/Phony-War (accessed 29 Sep. 2022).
22 Stefan Zweig, *Über Sigmund Freud: Porträt, Briefwechsel, Gedenkworte*, ed. by Knut Beck (Frankfurt am Main, 1989), 249–52, 251.
23 At an earlier stage, in autumn 1935, Freud even tried to interest Zweig in the 'problem Shakespeare – Oxford', meaning the hypothesis that the 'real' Shakespeare was in fact the seventeenth earl of Oxford, Edward de Vere. Might Zweig not write about this mysterious earl? In the end, he did not. Freud will have read at the time Frank Harris's study *The Man Shakespeare and his Tragic Life Story* (1909; German transl. 1928), which claimed to have evidence for Shakespeare's 'real identity'. Interestingly, Thomas Mann was to concern himself with this problem in Feb. 1943 and found it intriguing but not sufficiently plausible; Zweig clearly did not either.
24 Zweig, *Über Sigmund Freud*, 189.
25 Richard Friedenthal, *Die Welt in der Nußschale: Roman*, second edn. (Munich, 1986). Cf. Rüdiger Görner, '*Between Yesterday and Tomorrow: London in the Eyes of Richard Friedenthal (1896–1979)*' in Ritchie Robertson and Michael White (eds.), *Fontane and Cultural Mediation: Translation and Reception in Nineteenth-Century German Literature* (Cambridge/Leeds, 2015), 134–41.
26 Irwin Edman, *Ein Schimmer Licht im Dunkel*, transl. by Stefan Zweig and Richard Friedenthal (Stockholm, 1940), 8.

27 The text was discovered by Klemens Renoldner in the Reed Library of the University of New York in Fredonia. Published together with a comment by Renate Lunzer, 'Zweig als politischer Berater: Zum Memorandum für Beverley Baxter über Triest', *zweigheft*, 20 (2019), 9–12 (for Zweig's memorandum) and 13–16 (for Lunzer's comment).
28 Vilém Flusser, *Bodenlos: Eine philosophische Autobiographie*, with an afterword by Milton Vargas (Bensheim and Düsseldorf, 1992). Cf. Matthew D. Goodwin, 'The Brazilian Exile of Vilém Flusser and Stefan Zweig', *Flusser Studies*, 7 (2008), 1–9.

Autographs, Collections, and Other Approaches to World Literature
1 René Lévy, 'In Salzburg bei Stefan Zweig', *zweigheft*, 21 (2019), 14.
2 Cf. Lina Maria Zangerl and Manfred Mittermayer, '"Theater Spaziergang Kreml": Stefan Zweigs Notizbuch der Russlandreise 1928' in Bernhard Fetz, Arnhilt Inguglia-Höfle, and Arturo Larcati (eds.), *Stefan Zweig: Weltautor* (Vienna, 2022), 140–8.
3 Cf. Mathias Mayer, 'Der künstlerische Prozess' in *SZH*, 661–5.
4 Oliver Matuschek, 'Autographensammlung' in *SZH*, 618–23, 620–1; Cf. in particular: Oliver Matuschek (ed.), *Ich kenne den Zauber der Schrift: Katalog und Geschichte der Autographensammlung Stefan Zweig*, with annotated copies of Zweig's essays on collecting manuscripts (Vienna, 2005).
5 All quotes from: Albi Rosenthal, 'Autograph Collecting from Goethe to Stefan Zweig', with a foreword by Julia Rosenthal, in Görner and Renoldner (eds.), *Zweigs England*, 169–92, 178.
6 All quotations from: Stefan Zweig, *Das Geheimnis des künstlerischen Schaffens*, second edn., ed. by Knut Beck (Frankfurt am Main, 2007), 348–71.
7 Cf. Matuschek, 'Autographensammlung' in *SZH*, 619; George Steiner, *The Grammars of Creation* (London, 2001).
8 Steiner, *Grammars*, 5.
9 Ibid., 102.
10 See: Arturo Larcati, 'Stefan Zweigs international Netzwerke, das Projekt einer Bibliothea Mundi und sein Konzept der Weltliteratur' in Fetz et al (eds.), *Stefan Zweig: Weltautor*, 257–69.
11 Stefan Zweig, 'Die unsichtbare Sammlung: Eine Episode aus der deutschen Inflation' in S. Z., *Meisternovellen*, second edn. (Frankfurt am Main, 2002), 408–25.
12 Johann Wolfgang Goethe, *Sämtliche Werke, Briefe, Tagebücher und Gespräche* [40 Vols.], Part II, Vol. 7(34), ed. by Rose Unterberger (Frankfurt am Main, 1994), 58.
13 Michèle Roberts, 'Chic lit: The enduring fascination of Colette', *TLS* (17 Jun. 2022), 5.
14 Stefan Zweig, *Balzac*, fifteenth edn., posthumously ed. by Richard Friedenthal and newly ed. by Knut Beck (Frankfurt am Main 2008), 460.

15 This diary is kept in the Literaturarchiv Salzburg (FZ-LAS/L1) like Zweig's notebooks (SZ-AAP/W 41–45).
16 Ibid.
17 Ibid.
18 Richard Grenier, 'Colonel Redl: The Man Behind the Screen Myth', *The New York Times* (13 Oct. 1985).

Zweig, the Transatlantic Explorer

1 Cf. The informative source-orientated piece by Maria de Fátima Gil, '*Magellan. Der Mann und seine Tat* (1938)' in *SZH*, 432–42, esp. 432–3.
2 Daniela Strigl, '*Joseph Fouché. Bildnis eines politischen Menschen* (1929)' in *SZH*, 395.
3 Ibid., 399.
4 Zweig, *Briefe an Lotte*, 162–3.
5 Cf. Gil, '*Magellan*' in *SZH*, 433.
6 Quoted in Knut Beck's afterword to Stefan Zweig, *Magellan: Der Mann und seine Tat*, twenty-fourth edn. (Frankfurt am Main, 2011), 303. The first edition was published by Reichner, Vienna in 1938.
7 René Lévy, 'In Salzburg bei Stefan Zweig', *zweigheft*, 21 (2019), 9–15, 13. See also Jacques Le Rider, 'Ein Pilger aus Paris besucht im Sommer 1933 ein Haus auf dem Kapuzinerberg', ibid., 16–20. Somewhat surprisingly, Le Rider fails to reflect on Zweig's stance on the position of the Jews. For a concise and comprehensive account of Zweig's position towards Judaism see: Mark H. Gelber, 'Judentum und jüdische Identität' in *SZH*, 755–8.
8 Stefan Zweig, *Magellan*, transl. by Eden and Cedar Paul (London, 2011), 7.
9 Ibid., 13.
10 Ibid., 15.
11 Ibid., 69.
12 Cf. Christian Jostmann, 'Magellan: Held der Geschichte und Held einer literarischen Biographie' in Fetz et al (eds.), *Stefan Zweig: Weltautor*, 208–29, esp. 211–13.
13 Jostmann, 'Magellan', 213.
14 Gil, '*Magellan*' in *SZH*, 436.
15 Felix Salten, 'Die Monotonisierung der Welt?', *zweigheft*, 09 (2013), 19–26. Now fully documented in: Felix Salten and Stefan Zweig, *"Ihre Briefe bewahre ich alle": Die Korrespondenz von 1903 bis 1939*, ed. by Marcel Atze and Arturo Larcati (Göttingen, 2023), 214–25.
16 Literaturarchiv Salzburg, Stefan Zweig Archive. File without signature.
17 All published under the title 'Bilder aus America [Pictures from America]' in Zweig, *Auf Reisen*, 367–86.
18 Stefan Zweig, *Die schlaflose Welt*, 244.

19 Stefan Zweig's notebooks, Literaturarchiv Salzburg, Working notes 2, SZ-AAP/W 40.
20 'Dissecting the Troost Divide and Racial Segregation in Kansas City', *The Martin City & South KC Telegraph* (30 Jun. 2020). By 1920, 75 per cent of the population on the east side of Kansas City were African–American.
21 Zweig's notebooks, Literaturarchiv Salzburg.
22 Ibid.
23 Ibid.
24 Ibid.
25 Ibid.
26 Ibid.
27 Ibid.
28 Samuel Warde, 'Henry Ford pioneered modern industry, made America an economic power, and was a fervent anti-semite', *All That's Interesting*, allthatsinteresting.com/henry-ford-nazi (accessed 30 Oct. 2022).

Pity about Pity

1 Lotte Zweig, *Amerikareise* [typescript diaries, 1938/1939], Literaturarchiv Salzburg (35 S), 7.
2 For a succinct interpretation of this essay see: 'Politisch Inkorrekt: Thomas Manns Essay *Bruder Hitler*' in Jochen Hörisch, *Poesie und Politik: Szenen einer riskanten Beziehung* (Munich, 2022), 127–44.
3 TM/SZ, 96 (letter dated 28 Dec. 1938).
4 Deutsches Literaturarchiv Marbach (HS.2007.0124.00001).
5 Friderike Zweig, wartime diary, Literaturarchiv Salzburg, FZ-LAS/L1. Friderike Zweig gave this fragmentary diary to her 'loyal friend and supporter of Stefan's', Harry Zohn, in Stanford, October 1961. Entry dated 26 Oct. 1916.
6 Ibid. (5 Nov. 1916).
7 Stefan Zweig, *Ungeduld des Herzens* [1939], thirty-second edn. (Frankfurt am Main, 2004), 5. All references to *Ungeduld des Herzens* in the text are quoted from this edition as follows: UdH and page (here: UdH, 5).
8 Joan Acocella, 'Beware of Pity', first published in *The New York Review of Books* (13 Jul. 2006), 17–19.

Clarissa, Montaigne, Balzac: A Fragmentary Trio

1 Bertrand Russell, 'Some Psychological Difficulties in Wartime' in Julian Bell (ed.), *We Did Not Fight: 1914–1918 Experiences of War Resisters* (London, 1935), 329. For further comment see: Peter Edgerly Firchow, *The Death of the German Cousin: Variations on a Literary Stereotype, 1890–1920* (London/Toronto, 1986), 157–60.
2 Stefan Zweig, *Clarissa*, a draft, published by the estate and edited by Knut Beck, third edn. (Frankfurt am Main, 2009). The editor, Knut Beck, has given a comprehensive account of how he accomplished this reconstruction, incl. samples

of his text transcriptions, in: ibid., 189–213. For a more detailed discussion see: Arnim Eidherr and Tina Ornezeder, 'Clarissa (erstmals 1990)' in *SZH*, 383–9. To date, a critical edition of Zweig's actual draft is not available.
3. For further discussion of his relationship with Marcelle, see Weinzierl, *Stefan Zweigs brennendes Geheimnis*, 35–7.
4. Zweig, *Clarissa*, 185.
5. Virginia Woolf, *Mrs Dalloway*, ed. and with an introduction and notes by David Bradshaw (Oxford, 2000), 165.
6. Zweig, *Clarissa*, 73.
7. Ibid., 73.
8. Ibid., 138.
9. Michael de Montaigne, *Essais: Livre I*, chronology and introduction by Alexandre Micha (Paris, 1969), 73.
10. Stefan Zweig, *Montaigne*, ninth edn., ed. by Knut Beck (Frankfurt am Main, 2017), 95.
11. Cf. Karlheinz Stierle, 'Souverän seiner Lektüren: Hugo Friedrichs Buch über Montaigne', *Frankfurter Allgemeine Zeitung* (18 Feb. 1989).
12. Tobias Gregory, 'Did he want the job? Review of Philippe Desan's *Montaigne: A Life*', *London Review of Books*, 40/5 (8 Mar. 2018), 17–19, 19.
13. Ibid., 17
14. Charles Rosen, 'The Genius of Montaigne', *The New York Review of Books* (14 Feb. 2008), 48–53, 53.
15. Montaigne, *Essais*, 35.
16. Mark Lilla, 'The Hidden Lesson of Montaigne: review of Sarah Bakewell's *How to Live: A Life of Montaigne in One Question and Twenty Attempts at an Answer*', *The New York Review of Books* (24 Mar. 2011), 19–21, 19.
17. Ibid., 17.
18. Zweig, *Montaigne*, 16–17.
19. Ibid., 17.
20. Ibid., 60.
21. Darién J. Davis; Oliver Marshall (eds.), *Stefan and Lotte Zweig's South American Letters: New York, Argentina and Brazil 1940–1942* (New York/London, 2010), 203.
22. Maurice Levaillant, 'Un Montaigniste souriant: Fortunat Strowski (1866–1952)', *Bulletin de la Société des Amis de Montaigne* (1953–1954), 73–87.
23. Claude Lévi-Strauss, 'Kein Erstaunen vor den Wilden: Montaignes skeptische Betrachtungen über die Entdeckung der Neuen Welt', *Frankfurter Allgemeine Zeitung* (20 Jun. 1992).
24. Ibid.
25. Cf. Tobias Krüger, '*Amerigo: Die Geschichte eines historischen Irrtums* (erstmals 1944)' in *SZH*, 438–42.
26. Stefan Zweig, *Amerigo: Die Geschichte eines historischen Irrtums*, seventeenth edn. (Frankfurt am Main, 2018), 88, 110.

27 Hugo von Hofmannsthal, 'Balzac', in H. v. H., *Gesammelte Werke in zehn Einzelbänden: Reden und Aufsätze I (1891–1913)*, ed. by Bernd Schoeller and Rudolf Hirsch (Frankfurt am Main, 1979), 382–97, 382.
28 Edgar Pankow (ed.), *Honoré de Balzac: Pathologie des Soziallebens*, transl. by Christiana Goldmann (Leipzig, 2002), esp. 7–13.
29 Stefan Zweig, 'Balzacs Codices vom eleganten Leben' in S. Z., *Begegnungen mit Büchern: Aufsätze und Einleitungen aus den Jahren 1902–1939*, ed. by Knut Beck (Frankfurt am Main, 1983), 179–84, quotes 183 and 184.
30 Ibid., 181.
31 Stefan Zweig, *Balzac: Eine Biographie*, edited from Zweig's unpublished papers, with an afterword by Richard Friedenthal, verified and complemented by Knut Beck with a note on 'Stefan Zweig's Road to Balzac', fifteenth edn. (Frankfurt am Main, 2008), 289.
32 Ibid., 288.
33 Zweig, 'Anmerkungen zu Balzac' in Zweig, *Begegnungen mit Büchern*, 169–78, 169.
34 Ibid., 171.
35 Ibid., 172.
36 Ibid., 170.

Austria in Brazil: Arriving at the Final Address
1 Cf. for instance William James Johnson, 'The Scythian: His Rise and Fall', *Journal of the History of Ideas*, 20/2 (1959), 250–7.
2 Quoted with permission of Eva and Daniel Alberman (London, Stefan Zweig Private Archive).
3 Zweig, *Silberne Saiten*, 232.
4 Made available as a facsimile with a commentary by Oliver Matuschek, *Grüße aus Brasilien: Eine Postkarte von Stefan and Lotte Zweig*, Literaturarchiv Salzburg (Salzburg, 2016).
5 Stefan Zweig, *Brasilien: Ein Land der Zukunft* (Frankfurt, 2009), 10 (my emphasis).
6 Erich Fitzbauer (ed.), *Stefan Zweig: Spiegelungen einer schöpferischen Persönlichkeit* (Vienna, 1959), 92–3 (my emphasis).
7 The best summary of this criticism is by Jeroen Dewulf, '*Brasilien. Ein Land der Zukunft* (1941)' in *SZH*, 330–9. It includes a comprehensive survey of relevant commentaries. An animated and well-researched read is Alberto Dines, *Tod im Paradies: Die Tragödie des Stefan Zweig* (Frankfurt am Main, 2006).
8 Dewulf, 'Brasilien', 331.
9 Cf. Roderick J. Barman, *Brazil: The Forging of a Nation, 1798–1852* (Stanford, CA, 1988).
10 Zweig, *Brasilien*, 203.
11 Ibid.

12 Matthias Kettner, 'Das Konzept der Nachträglichkeit in Freuds Erinnerungstheorie', *Psyche*, 53/4 (1999), 309–42, 312.
13 I translate from the new commented edition by Oliver Matuschek: Stefan Zweig, *Die Welt von Gestern: Erinnerungen eines Europäers* (Frankfurt am Main, 2017), 10. All references to *The World of Yesterday* in the text are quoted from this edition as follows: WY and page (here: WY, 10).
14 Daniel Kehlmann, '"Die Welt von Gestern" in New York' in Fetz et al (eds.), *Stefan Zweig: Weltautor*, 307–9, 307.
15 Patrick Wright, 'Enemy alien: On Stefan Zweig', *Guardian* (2 Feb. 2008), 21.
16 Oliver Matuschek was right in choosing this very title for his biography, as it captures perfectly what Zweig perceived as the plurality of his past(s).
17 See the helpful summary on their relationship by Norbert Christian Wolf, 'Der Großschriftsteller und sein Hauptbuch: Stefan Zweig als weltumspannender Literaturindustrieller' in Fetz et al., *Stefan Zweig: Weltautor*, 17–31.
18 Research on Zweig's memoirs is plentiful and succinctly summarised by Ulrich Weinzierl and Helmut Galle in their contributions to the *SZH*, 340–355 (Weinzierl, 'Autobiografie als Epochendarstellung') and 356–65 (Galle, '*Die Welt von Gestern* als Autobiografie, Memoirenwerk und Zeugnis').
19 'Gewesene Zukunft: Die Optik des Nachsehens in *Die Welt von Gestern*' in Rüdiger Görner, *Stefan Zweig: Formen einer Sprachkunst* (Vienna, 2012), 31–43, 43.
20 Cf. Rüdiger Görner, 'Wie man wird, was man erinnert: Überlegungen zu Stefan Zweigs Die Welt von Gestern' in Renoldner (ed.), *Stefan Zweig: Abschied von Europa*, 91–103, esp. 92.
21 Oliver Matuscheck, 'Stefan Zweig als Zeitzeuge in Geschichte und Gegenwart' in O. M. (ed.), *Die drei Leben des Stefan Zweig* [booklet for the exhibition at the Deutsche Historische Museum in Berlin] (Berlin, 2008), 47–8.

Chess with Time, or Yesterday's Checkmate
1 A breakthrough in research on Zweig's last completed text came with a new edition, commentary, and documentation on *Chess*: Stefan Zweig, *Schachnovelle: Kommentierte Ausgabe*, ed. by Klemens Reboldner (Stuttgart, 2013). This was followed by a landmark conference on the occasion of the seventy-fifth anniversary of the novella on 8 December 2017 in Munich's Literaturhaus, organised by Margit Dirscherl and Laura Schütz. Contributions were documented in Margit Dirscherl and Laura Schütz (eds.), *Schachnovelle: Stefan Zweigs letztes Werk neu gelesen* (Würzburg, 2019).
2 Cf. Rüdiger Görner, 'Schach dem Autor oder: Rochaden trotz Remis. Das königliche Spiel in der literarischen Republik' in Dirscherl and Schütz (eds.), *Schachnovelle*, 103–112. This range can and must be extended, as Daniel Johnson shows in his highly informative piece on 'Knights and ladies: Sexism, obsession and chess', *TLS* (4 Dec., 2020), 16.
3 Görner, 'Schach dem Autor', 109.

4 Johnson, 'Knights and ladies', 16. In their productively multi-faceted documentation of research on Zweig's last novella, Dirscherl and Schütz include in *Schachnovelle* three studies dedicated to the question as to 'why the females are disappearing' in Zweig's *Chess*, most prominently Annette Keck, 'Viele Männer und eine Erscheinung: Zur Geschlechterdifferenz in Stefan Zweigs Schachnovelle', 61–72. See also the important contribution on Zweig's actual and likely source material by James Vigus, 'Die Schachnovelle im Hinblick auf die Geschichte des Schachs', 85–102, esp. 87. For detailed analysis of the origins, plot, and reception of Zweig's novella, see also: Klemens Renoldner and Norbert Christian Wolf, '*Schachnovelle* (1942)' in *SZH*, 233–45.
5 Stefan Zweig, *Schachnovelle*, ed. by Brian Murdoch (London, 1986), 11 (substantial introduction, 1–41).
6 Paul Celan, *Mikrolithen sind, Steinchen: Die Prosa aus dem Nachlaß*, ed. by Bertrand Badiou and Barbara Wiedemann (Frankfurt am Main, 2005), 101 ('*Der Zeit wird Schach geboten – aber wie reagiert die Zeit darauf?*').
7 Zweig, *Schachnovelle*, 33.
8 Stefan Zweig, *Chess*, transl. by Anthea Bell (London, 2006), 2.
9 Cf. Sven Hanuschek, '"In dieser kalten Form des Wahnsinns": Psychopathologische Aspekte in der Schachnovelle' in Dirscherl/Schütz (eds.), *Schachnovelle*, 73–80, esp. 78–9.
10 Ibid., 75.
11 Cf. Vigus, 'Die Schachnovelle im Hinblick auf die Geschichte des Schachs', ibid., 97.
12 Ibid., 97.
13 Ibid., 100.
14 Cf. Oliver Jahraus, 'Das Schachspiel als politische Metapher und Stefan Zweigs Schachnovelle' in Dirscherl/Schütz (eds.), *Schachnovelle*, 33–45, esp. 42–3. Jahraus offers a whole range of illuminating political connotations implied in this novella, most importantly the significance of the pawn. Ibid., 41.
15 Görner, *Stefan Zweig: Formen einer Sprachkunst*, 126.
16 Daniela Strigl, 'Warum die Schachnovelle so gut ist: Ästhetische Bemerkungen' in Dirscherl and Schütz (eds.), *Schachnovelle*, 21–31.
17 Ruth Klüger, 'Selbstverhängte Einzelhaft: Die Schachnovelle und ihre Vorgänger' in Renoldner (ed.), *Stefan Zweig: Abschied von Europa*, 105–22, 106.
18 Ibid., 121.
19 Ibid., 121.
20 Klüger, 'Selbstverhängte Einzelhaft', 121.
21 Zweig, *Chess*, 54.
22 Ibid., 42.
23 Ibid., 2.
24 Ibid., 9.
25 Strigl, 'Warum die Schachnovelle so gut ist', 30.

Notes on Zweig's Legacy
1. German original in: Zweig, *Spiegelungen*, 102.
2. Acocella, 'Beware of Pity', 19.
3. TM/SZ, 395.
4. Ibid., 401.
5. Klaus Mann, 'Victims of Fascism: Stefan Zweig' in ibid., 276.
6. Ibid., 275.
7. All quotations in: Franz Werfel, *Leben heißt, sich mitteilen: Betrachtungen, Reden, Aphorismen*, ed. by Knut Beck (Frankfurt am Main, 1975), 400–8.
8. Romain Rolland, 'Er war mir ein guter Freund' from the *Journal de Vézelay 1938–1944, zweigheft*, 09 (2013), 27–31.
9. Ilse Aichinger, 'Bitte – Stefan Zweig!', *Wiener Kurier*, 2/79 (3 Apr. 1946). For comment see: Gabriela Rovagnati, '"So wurden Sie Brennmaterial für unsere Herzen": L'omaggio di Ilse Aichinger a Stefan Zweig' in Fausto Cercignani (ed.), 'Ilse Aichinger' [1996], *Studia austriaca*, 20 (2012), 31–40.
10. Ortega y Gasset, *The Dehumanization of Art*, transl. by Helene Weyl (Princeton, 1968), 150–64.
11. Cf. the exemplary and comprehensive survey of Zweig's reception during and after his lifetime in *SZH*, 783–906.
12. Hayden V. White, *Metahistory: The Historical Imagination in Nineteenth-Century Europe* (Baltimore, 1973).
13. Ibid., 277.
14. Hayden V. White, *The Content of the Form: Narrative Discourse and Historical Representation* (Baltimore, 1987).
15. A succinct survey is offered by Manfred Mittermayer, 'Verfilmungen von Stefan Zweigs Texten' in *SZH*, 864–75.
16. Cf. Jasper Rees, 'The Private Life of Stefan Zweig in England', theartsdesk.com (9 Feb. 2017).
17. Stefan Zweig, *Einigung Europas* [speech], ed. from Stefan Zweig's unpublished papers by Klemens Renoldner (Salzburg/Paris, n. d.), 12.
18. See the meticulously researched study by Arnilt Johanna Hoefle, *China's Stefan Zweig: The Dynamics of Cross Cultural Reception* (Honolulu, 2018). See also: Birger Vanwesenbeeck and Mark H. Gelber (eds.), *Stefan Zweig and World Literature: Twenty-First Century Perspectives* (Rochester, NY, 2014).
19. 'Gespräch mit Stephan Zweig. Drei Leben', *Aufbau*, VI/29 (19 Jul. 1940), archive.org/details/aufbau5619391940germ/page/n285/mode/1up (accessed 20 Feb. 2023).

Bibliography

Zweig's works
Zweig, Stefan, *Tagebücher*, ed. by Knut Beck (Frankfurt am Main, 1984).
—————, *Die schlaflose Welt: Aufsätze und Vorträge aus den Jahren 1909–1941*, ed. by Knut Beck (Frankfurt am Main, 2006).
————— and Zweig, Friderike, *'Wenn einen Augenblick die Wolken weichen': Briefwechsel 1912–1942*, ed. by Jeffrey B. Berlin and Gert Kerschbaumer (Frankfurt am Main, 2006).
—————, *Briefe 1897–1914* [vol. I], ed. by Knut Beck, Jeffrey B. Berlin, and Natascha Weschenbach-Feggeler (Frankfurt am Main, 1995).
—————, *Briefe 1914–1919* [vol. II], ed. by Knut Beck, Jeffrey B. Berlin, and Natascha Weschenbach-Feggeler (Frankfurt am Main, 1998).
—————, *Briefe 1920–1931* [vol. III], ed. by Knut Beck and Jeffrey B. Berlin (Frankfurt am Main, 2000).
—————, *Briefe 1932–1942* [vol. IV], ed. by Knut Beck and Jeffrey B. Berlin (Frankfurt am Main, 2005).
—————, *Rhythmen: Nachdichtungen ausgewählter Lyrik von Emile Verhaeren, Charles Baudelaire und Paul Verlaine*, ed. by Knut Beck (Frankfurt am Main, 1983).
—————, *Emile Verhaeren* (Frankfurt am Main, 1984).
—————, *Silberne Saiten: Gedichte*, ed. by Knut Beck, sixth edn. (Frankfurt am Main, 2008).
—————, *Journeys (Modern Voices)*, transl. and introduced by Will Stone (London, 2010).
—————, *Auf Reisen*, ed. by Knut Beck, third edn. (Frankfurt am Main, 2008).
—————, *The Governess and Other Stories*, transl. from the German by Anthea Bell (London, 2011).
—————, *Phantastische Nacht*, ed. by Knut Beck, twenty-first edn. (Frankfurt am Main, 2011).
————— and Roth, Joseph, *'Jede Freundschaft ist mir verderblich': Briefwechsel 1927–1938*, ed. by Madeleine Rietra and Rainer Joachim Siegel, with an afterword by Heinz Lunzer (Göttingen, 2011).
—————, *Amok and Other Stories*, transl. from the German by Anthea Bell (London, 2006).

———, *Der Amokläufer: Erzählungen*, ed. by Knut Beck, thirteenth edn. (Frankfurt am Main, 2004).
———, *Twilight and Moonbeam Alley*, transl. from the German by Anthea Bell (London, 2005).
———, *Burning Secret*, transl. by Anthea Bell (London, 2008).
——— and Rolland, Romain, *Briefwechsel 1910–1940* [two vols.], transl. by Eva and Gerhard Schewe and Christel Gersch, ed. by Waltraud Schwarze, with an introduction by Wolfgang Klein (Berlin, 1987).
———, *Jeremias: Eine dramatische Dichtung in neun Bildern* (Leipzig, 1928).
——— and Mann, Thomas, *Briefwechsel, Dokumente und Schnittpunkte*, ed. by Katrin Bedenig and Franz Zeder (Frankfurt am Main, 2016).
——— and Salten, Felix, *"Ihre Briefe bewahre ich alle": Die Korrespondenz von 1903 bis 1939*, ed. by Marcel Atze and Arturo Larcati (Göttingen, 2023).
———, *Wondrak and Other Stories*, transl. by Anthea Bell (London, 2009).
———, *Drei Meister: Balzac, Dickens, Dostojewski* (Frankfurt am Main, 1981).
———, *Romain Rolland*, ed. by Knut Beck, second edn. (Frankfurt am Main, 1987).
———, *Meisternovellen*, second edn. (Frankfurt am Main, 2002).
———, *Der Kampf mit dem Dämon: Hölderlin, Kleist, Nietzsche* (Frankfurt am Main, 1981).
———, *'Ich habe das Bedürfnis nach Freunden': Erzählungen, Essays und unbekannte Texte*, ed. by Klemens Renoldner (Vienna/Graz/Klagenfurt, 2013).
———, *Die schlaflose Welt*, ed. by Knut Beck (Frankfurt/Main, 1983).
———, *Adam Lux: Zehn Bilder aus dem Leben eines deutschen Revolutionärs*, with essays from Franz Dumont and Erwin Rotermund (Obernburg, 2003).
———, *Confusion: The Private Papers of the Privy Councillor R von D*, transl. from the German by Anthea Bell (London, rev. 2009).
———, *Journey into the Past*, transl. from the German and with an afterword by Anthea Bell, foreword by Paul Bailey (London, 2009).
———, *Marie Antoinette*, transl. from the German by Eden and Cedar Paul (London, 2010).
———, *Joseph Fouché: Bildnis eines politischen Menschen* (Frankfurt/Main, 1988)
———, *'Ich wünschte, dass ich Ihnen ein wenig fehlte': Briefe an Lotte Zweig 1934–1940*, ed. by Oliver Matuschek (Frankfurt am Main, 2013).
———, *Castellio gegen Calvin oder Ein Gewissen gegen die Gewalt*, fourteenth edn. (Frankfurt am Main, 2006).
———, 'Der Genius Englands', *Neue Freie Presse Wien: Morgenblatt* [Special Issue: England and Austria], (25 Jan. 1924), 23–4.
———, *Über Sigmund Freud: Porträt, Briefwechsel, Gedenkworte*, ed. by Knut Beck (Frankfurt am Main, 1989).
———, *Das Geheimnis des künstlerischen Schaffens: Essays*, ed. by Knut Beck, second edn. (Frankfurt am Main, 2007).

_____, *Meisternovellen*, second edn. (Frankfurt am Main, 2002).
_____, *Balzac*, posthumously ed. by Richard Friedenthal, newly ed. by Knut Beck, fifteenth edn. (Frankfurt am Main, 2008).
_____, *Magellan: Der Mann und seine Tat*, with an afterword by Knut Beck, twenty-fourth edn. (Frankfurt am Main, 2011).
_____, *Ungeduld des Herzens*, thirty-second edn. (Frankfurt am Main, 2004).
_____, *Clarissa: Ein Romanentwurf*, published by the estate and ed. by Knut Beck, third edn. (Frankfurt am Main, 2009).
_____, *Montaigne*, ed. by Knut Beck, ninth edn. (Frankfurt am Main, 2017).
_____, *Amerigo: Die Geschichte eines historischen Irrtums*, seventeenth edn. (Frankfurt am Main, 2018).
_____, *Begegnungen mit Büchern: Aufsätze und Einleitungen aus den Jahren 1902–1939*, ed. by Knut Beck (Frankfurt am Main, 1983).
_____, *Balzac: Eine Biographie*, published by the estate with an afterword by Richard Friedenthal, reviewed and with a follow-up note by Knut Beck, fifteenth edn. (Frankfurt am Main, 2008).
_____, *Brasilien: Ein Land der Zukunft* (Frankfurt, 2009).
_____, *Die Welt von Gestern: Erinnerungen eines Europäers*, ed. by Oliver Matuschek (Frankfurt am Main, 2017).
_____, *Schachnovelle*, commented edn., ed. by Klemens Renoldner (Stuttgart, 2013).
_____, *Schachnovelle*, ed. by Brian Murdoch (London, 1986).
_____, *Chess: A Novella*, transl. by Anthea Bell (London, 2006).
_____, *Einigung Europas* [speech], from the estate, published by Klemens Renoldner (Salzburg/Paris, n. d.).

Archives

Friderike's wartime diaries, Literaturarchiv Salzburg (FZ-LAS/L1).
Lotte's *Amerikareise* diaries [typescript], Literaturarchiv Salzburg (35 S).
Zweig's notebooks, Literaturarchiv Salzburg (SZ-AAP/W 40–45).
Deutsches Literaturarchiv Marbach (HS.2007.0124.00001).
Eva and Daniel Alberman (Stefan Zweig Private Archive, London).
The British Library Zweig Collection (MS 158).

Secondary sources

Acocella, Joan, 'Beware of Pity', first published in *The New York Review of Books* (13 Jul. 2006), 17–19.
Asadowski, K. M., 'Die Briefe Stefan Zweigs an den Verlag Wremja', *Neue Deutsche Literatur*, 26/12 (Berlin, 1978), 119–31.
Auden, W. H., *Collected Poems*, ed. by Edward Mendelson (London, 1991).
Becker, Uwe, *Deutschland und seine Flüchtlinge: Das Wechselbad der Diskurse im langen Sommer der Flucht 2015* (Bielefeld, 2022).

Blamberger, Günter, 'Wie vermeidet man "Lieblose Legenden"? Zur Kunst des Biographierens' in Blamberger, *Von der Faszination ästhetischer Ideen und der Macht poetischen Denkens* (Leiden/Boston/Paderborn, 2021), 97–110.
Boyd, William, 'Viennese Waltz', *The Saturday Guardian* (4 Feb. 2012), 2–4.
_____, 'Virtual Vienna', *Times Literary Supplement* (29 May 2020).
Brook-Shephard, Gordon, *Dollfuss* (London, 1961).
Celan, Paul, *Mikrolithen sinds, Steinchen: Die Prosa aus dem Nachlaß*, ed. by Bertrand Badiou and Wiedemann, Barbara (Frankfurt am Main, 2005).
Chaudhuri, P. C. Roy, *C. F. Andrews: His Life and Times* (Mumbai, 1971).
Cohen, Michael J., *The Origins and Evolution of the Arab-Zionist Conflict* (Berkeley, 1989).
Csáky, Moritz, Kury, Astrid, and Tragatschnigg, Ulrich (eds.), *Kultur – Identität – Differenz: Wien und Zentraleuropa in der Moderne* (Innsbruck, 2004).
Davis, Darién J. and Marshall, Oliver (eds.), *Stefan and Lotte Zweig's South American Letters: New York, Argentina and Brazil 1940–1942* (New York/London, 2010).
Defraeye, Piet, Mitterbauer, Helga, and Reyns-Chikuma, Chris (eds.), *Brussels 1900 Vienna: Networks in Literature, Visual and Performing Arts, and other Cultural Practices* (Leiden/Boston, 2022).
Dines, Alberto, *Morten o Paraíso: a Tragédia de Stefan Zweig* [1981] (Rio de Janeiro, 2004).
_____, *Tod im Paradies: Die Tragödie des Stefan Zweig*, transl. from the Portuguese by Marlen Eckl (Frankfurt am Main, 2006).
Dirscherl, Margit, 'Stefan Zweig: Judentum und Zionismus bei Mark H. Gelber', *Modern Language Review*, 110/4 (2015), 1164–6.
_____ and Schütz, Laura (eds.), *Schachnovelle: Stefan Zweigs letztes Werk neu gelesen*, vol. 11 of a series of publications by the Stefan Zweig Centre, Salzburg (Würzburg, 2019).
Dollfuss, Eva, *Mein Vater – Hitlers erstes Opfer* (Vienna/Munich, 1994).
Dover, Kenneth J., *Greek Homosexuality* (Cambridge, MA, 1989).
Drinkwater, John, *Abraham Lincoln: A Play* (London, 1918).
Ebermayer, Erich, *Eh' ich's vergesse ...: Erinnerungen an Gerhart Hauptmann, Thomas Mann, Klaus Mann, Gustaf Gründgens, Emil Jannings und Stefan Zweig*, ed. and prefaced by Dirk Heißerer (Munich, 2005).
Edman, Irwin, *Ein Schimmer Licht im Dunkel*, transl. by Stefan Zweig and Richard Friedenthal (Stockholm, 1940).
Eliot, T. S., *Collected Poems 1909–1962* (London, 1983).
Erdem, Elisabeth and Renoldner, Klemens (eds.), *Stefan Zweig: Verwirrung der Gefühle* (Stuttgart, 2017), English translation by Anthea Bell (London, 2002/rev. 2009), based on Knut Beck's edition of 2002.
Fetz, Bernhard, Inguglia-Höfle, Arnhilt, and Larcati, Arturo (eds.), *Stefan Zweig: Weltautor* (Vienna, 2022).

Fitzbauer, Erich (ed.), *Stefan Zweig: Spiegelungen einer schöpferischen Persönlichkeit* (Vienna, 1959).
Flusser, Vilém, *Bodenlos: Eine philosophische Autobiographie*, with an afterword by Milton Vargas (Bensheim/Düsseldorf, 1992).
Foster, Roy, 'A stay against confusion. Seamus Heaney and the Ireland of his time', *Times Literary Supplement* (22 and 29 Aug. 2014), 15–17.
Friedenthal, Richard, *Die Welt in der Nußschale* [novel], second edn. (Munich, 1986).
Gall, Lothar, *Walther Rathenau: Portrait einer Epoche* (Munich, 2009).
Gasset, Ortega y, *The Dehumanization of Art*, transl. by Helene Weyl (Princeton, NJ, 1968).
Gay, Peter, *Schnitzler's Century: The Making of Middle-Class Culture 1815–1914* (New York, 2002).
Gelber, Mark H., *Stefan Zweig: Judentum und Zionismus* (Innsbruck, 2013).
Goodwin, Matthew D., 'The Brazilian Exile of Vilém Flusser and Stefan Zweig', *Flusser Studies*, 7 (2008), 1–9.
Görner, Rüdiger, *Kokoschka: The Untimely Modernist*, transl. from the German by Debra Marmor and Herbert Danner (London, 2020).
_____, 'Eines Freundes Freund zu sein: Zum Motiv der Freundschaft bei Stefan Zweig', *Sinn und Form*, 69/5 (2017), 647–55.
_____, 'The Drama of Prophecy: On Stefan Zweig and "Jeremiah"', *Jewish Quarterly*, 44 (2011), 44–6.
_____, 'The Figure of Jeremiah in the Work of Stefan Zweig and Rainer Maria Rilke' in Louis Stulman and Edward Silver, *The Oxford Handbook of Jeremiah* (Oxford, 2021), 553–65.
_____, *Hölderlin and the Consequences: An Essay on the German 'Poet of Poets'* (London/Berlin, 2021).
_____, 'Beethoven, Hegel & Hölderlin at 250: Thoughts on the presence of triadic structures in their works', *Archiv für das Studium der neueren Sprachen und Literaturen*, 259 (2022), 29–39.
_____, 'Schwieriges Erbe: Lernet-Holenias Verhältnis zu Rilke', *Sprachkunst*, XXXI (2000), 307–21.
_____, 'Between Yesterday and Tomorrow: London in the Eyes of Richard Friedenthal (1896–1979)' in *Fontane and Cultural Mediation: Translation and Reception in Nineteenth-Century German Literature* [essays in honour of Helen Chambers], ed. by Ritchie Robertson and Michael White (Cambridge/Leeds, 2015), 134–41.
_____, *Stefan Zweig: Formen einer Sprachkunst* (Vienna, 2012).
_____ and Renoldner, Klemens (eds.), *Zweigs England* (Würzburg, 2014).
Gregory, Tobias, 'Did he want the job?' [Review of Philippe Desan, *Montaigne: A Life*, transl. by Steven Kendall and Lisa Neal (Princeton, NJ, 2017)], *London Review of Books* (8 Mar. 2018), 17–19.
Hamann, Brigitte, *Vienna: A Dictator's Apprenticeship* (Oxford, 1999).

Hardt, Ernst, *König Salomo: Ein Drama in drei Akten* (Leipzig, 1915).
Harris, Frank, *The Man Shakespeare and his Tragic Life Story* (London, 1909; German trans. 1928).
Hayes, Romain, *Subhas Chandra Bose in Nazi Germany: Politics, Intelligence and Propaganda 1941–1943* (Oxford, 2011).
Hazareesingh, Sudhir, *Black Spartacus: The Epic Life of Toussaint Louverture* (London, 2019).
Heilbut, Anthony, *Thomas Mann: Eros & Literature* (London, 1997).
Hemecker, Wilhelm W. (ed.), *Haschisch: Erzählungen*, with thirteen drawings by Alfred Kubin (Graz, 2002).
Hessel, Franz, *Ermunterung zum Genuß: Kleine Prosa*, ed. by Karin Grund and Bernd Witte (Berlin, 1981).
Hoefle, Arnhilt Johanna, *China's Stefan Zweig: The Dynamics of Cross-Cultural Reception* (Honolulu, 2018).
Hofmannsthal, Hugo von, 'Balzac' in *Gesammelte Werke in zehn Einzelbänden: Reden und Aufsätze I (1891–1913)*, ed. by Bernd Schoeller and Rudolf Hirsch (Frankfurt am Main, 1979).
Hörisch, Jochen, *Poesie und Politik: Szenen einer riskanten Beziehung* (Munich, 2022).
Jenks, William A., *Vienna and the Young Hitler* (New York, 1960).
James, Henry, *The Diary of a Man of Fifty* [1887], foreword by David Lodge (London, 2008).
Johnson, Daniel, 'Knights and ladies: Sexism, obsession and chess', *Times Literary Supplement* (4 Dec. 2020).
Johnson, William James, 'The Scythian: His Rise and Fall', *Journal of the History of Ideas*, 20/2 (1959) 250–7.
Kirkbright, Suzanne, *Karl Jaspers: A Biography – Navigations in Truth* (New Haven, CT/London, 2004).
Larcati, Arturo, Renoldner, Klemens, and Wörgötter, Martina (eds.), *Stefan-Zweig-Handbuch* (Berlin/Boston, 2018).
Le Rider, Jacques, 'Ein Pilger aus Paris besucht im Sommer 1933 ein Haus auf dem Kapuzinerberg', *zweiheft*, 21 (2019), 16–20.
Lernet-Holenia, Alexander, *Baron Bagge*, transl. by Richard and Clara Winston, with a foreword by Patti Smith, three letters between Zweig and Lernet-Holenia, and a note by Arturo Larcati (London, 2022).
Levaillant, Maurice, 'Un Montaigniste souriant: Fortunat Strowski (1866–1952)', *Bulletin de la Société des Amis de Montaigne* (1953–1954), 73–87.
Leventhal, Jean H., 'A Public Memorial to a True European: Stefan Zweig's Autograph Collection and the British Library', *Modern Austrian Literature*, 33/2 (2000), 23–36.
Lévi-Strauss, Claude, 'Kein Erstaunen vor den Wilden: Montaignes skeptische Betrachtungen über die Entdeckung der Neuen Welt', *Frankfurter Allgemeine Zeitung* (20 Jun. 1992).
Lévy, René, 'René Lévy in Salzburg bei Stefan Zweig', *zweiheft*, 21 (2019), 11–17.

Lilla, Mark, 'The Hidden Lesson of Montaigne' [Review of Sarah Bakewell, *How to Live, or, A Life of Montaigne in One Question and Twenty Attempts at an Answer*], *The New York Review of Books* (24 Mar. 2011), 19–21.
Lloyd, Jill and Pfeiffer, Ingrid (eds.) in collaboration with Raymond Coffer, *Richard Gerstl: Retrospective* [catalogue for the exhibition in New York], (Munich, 2017).
Lunzer, Renate, 'Zweig als politischer Berater: Zum Memorandum für Beverley Baxter über Triest', *zweigheft*, 20 (2019), 9–12.
Magris, Claudio, *Danube*, with an introduction by Richard Flanagan (London, 2016).
Malte Fischer, Jens, *Gustav Mahler: Der fremde Vertraute* (Vienna, 2003).
Mandelstam, Osip, *Über Dichtung*, ed. by Pawel Nerler (Leipzig/Weimar, 1991).
Mann, Klaus, *Der Wendepunkt: Ein Lebensbericht*, second edn. (Berlin/Weimar, 1979).
_____, 'Victim of Fascism: Stefan Zweig', *Free World*, II/3 (1942), 274–6.
Mann, Thomas, *Aufsätze, Reden, Essays Vol. 2: 1919–1925*, ed. by Harry Matter (Berlin and Weimar, 1986).
_____, *Tagebücher 1935–1936*, ed. by Peter de Mendelssohn (Frankfurt am Main, 2003).
Manthripragada, Ashwin J., *Constituting a Self through an Indian Other: A Study of Select Works by Stefan Zweig and Hermann Hesse* [thesis] (Berkeley, 2014).
Matuschek, Oliver, *Three Lives: A Biography of Stefan Zweig*, transl. from the German by Allan Blunden (London, 2011).
_____, 'Stefan Zweig als Zeitzeuge in Geschichte und Gegenwart' in Oliver Matuschek (ed.), *Die drei Leben des Stefan Zweig* [booklet for the exhibition at the Deutsche Historische Museum in Berlin] (Berlin, 2008).
_____, *Das Salzburg des Stefan Zweig*, with photographs by Angelika Fische (Berlin, 2008).
_____ (ed.), *'Ich kenne den Zauber der Schrift': Katalog und Geschichte der Autographensammlung Stefan Zweig*, with annotated reprints of Zweig's essays on collecting manuscripts (Vienna, 2005).
_____, *Grüße aus Brasilien: Eine Postkarte von Stefan and Lotte Zweig* (Salzburg, 2016).
Mayer, Mathias, *King Lear – Die Tragödie des Zuschauers: Ästhetik und Ethik der Empathie* (Göttingen, 2022).
Mayreder, Rosa, *Tagebücher 1873–1937*, ed. and with an introduction by Harriet Anderson (Frankfurt am Main, 1988).
Michelet, Jules, *Histoire du XIXe siècle*, vol. 2 (Paris, 1875).
Montaigne, Michel de, *Essais: Livre I*, chronology and introduction by Alexandre Micha (Paris, 1969).
Moritz, Karl Philipp, 'Reisen eines Deutschen in England im Jahre 1782' in Moritz, *Werke: Reisen, Schriften zur Mythologie*, vol. 2, ed. by Horst Günther, second edn. (Frankfurt am Main, 1993).
Navratil, Michael, '"Den Schauer des Mythos neu schaffen": Die kreative Rezeption von

Nietzsches "Geburt der Tragödie" in der Wiener Moderne', *Sprachkunst*, XLII/2 (2011) 245–69.

Nietzsche, Friedrich, 'Also sprach Zarathustra' in *Sämtliche Werke: Kritische Studienausgabe*, vol. 4, ed. by Giorgio Colli and Mazzino Montinari (Munich, 1988).

_____, *Thus Spoke Zarathustra*, transl. with an introduction by R. J. Hollingdale (London, 2003).

Pankow, Edgar (ed.), *Honoré de Balzac: Pathologie des Soziallebens*, transl. by Christiana Goldmann (Leipzig, 2002).

Pim, Keiron, *Endless Flight: The Life of Joseph Roth* (London, 2022).

Prater, Donald A., 'Stefan Zweig and Hermann Hesse', *Modern Austrian Literature*, 14/3–4 (1981), 11–38.

_____ (ed.), *Rainer Maria Rilke und Stefan Zweig in Briefen und Dokumenten* (Frankfurt am Main, 1987).

Prochnik, George, 'A stranger in every town: Joseph Roth and his skill at identifying "fleeting moments with universal implications"', *Times Literary Supplement* (7 Oct. 2022), 3–5.

Rathenau, Walther, *Schriften und Reden*, ed. with an afterword by Hans Werner Richter (Frankfurt am Main, 1986).

Renan, Ernest, *What is a Nation? And Other Political Writings*, transl. and ed. by M. F. N. Giglioni (New York, 2018).

Renoldner, Klemens (ed.), *Stefan Zweig: Abschied von Europa* (Vienna, 2014).

Rieger, Erwin, *Stefan Zweig: Der Mann und das Werk* (Berlin, 1928).

Rilke, Rainer Maria, *Auguste Rodin* (Leipzig, 1930).

_____, *Werke IV: Frühe Erzählungen und Dramen*, ed. by Ernst Zinn (Frankfurt am Main, 1987)

Ritzer, Monika, *Friedrich Hebbel* (Göttingen, 2019).

Roberts, Michèle, 'Chic lit: The enduring fascination of Colette', *Times Literary Supplement* (17 Jun. 2022), 5–6.

Roček, Roman, *Die neun Leben des Alexander Lernet-Holenia* (Vienna, 1999).

Roe, Glenn H., 'Contre Taine and Renan: Charles Péguy and the Metaphysics of Modern History', *French Forum*, 34/2 (2009), 17–37.

Rolland, Romain, *Über den Gräbern: Aus den Tagebüchern 1914–1919*, ed. by Hans Peter Buohler and with an afterword by Julia Encke (Munich, 2015).

_____, 'Er war mir ein guter Freund' [from *Journal de Vézelay 1938–1944*], *zweigheft*, 9 (2013), 27–31.

Rosen, Charles, 'The Genius of Montaigne', *The New York Review of Books* (14 Feb. 2008), 48–53.

Rovagnati, Gabriela, '"So wurden Sie Brennmaterial für unsere Herzen": L'omaggio di Ilse Aichinger a Stefan Zweig' in Fausto Cercignani (ed.), 'Ilse Aichinger', *Studia austriaca*, 20 (1996, electronic edn. 2012), 31–40.

Sakulku, Alexander J., 'The Imposter Phenomenon', *International Journal of Behavioral Science*, 6 (2011), 73–92.
Salten, Felix, 'Die Monotonisierung der Welt?', *zweigheft*, 9 (reprint 2013), 19–26.
Santini, Daria, *The Exiles: Actors, Artists and Writers Who Fled the Nazis for London* (London, 2019).
Schiller, Friedrich, *Sämtliche Werke, Vol. IV: Historische Schriften*, ed. by Gerhard Fricke and Herbert G. Göpfert, sixth edn. (Munich, 1980).
_____, *Sämtliche Werke, Vol. I: Gedichte, Dramen* I, eighth edn. (Munich, 1987)
Schönberg, Arnold, *Das bilderische Werk* (Klagenfurt, 1991).
Schorske, Carl, *Fin de Siècle Vienna: Politics and Culture* (New York, 1980).
Segar, Kenneth and Warren, John (eds.), *Austria in the Thirties: Culture and Politics* (Riverside, CA, 1991).
Seneca, Aennaeus L., *Ad Lucilium epistulae Morales* LXX-CXXIV, ed. by Manfred Rosenbach (Darmstadt, 1999).
Sergent, Bernard, *Homosexuality in Greek Myth* (Boston, 1986).
Spiel, Hilde, *Vienna's Golden Autumn 1866–1938* (London, 1987).
Spinney, Laura, *Pale Rider: The Spanish Flu of 1918 and How it Changed the World* (New York, 2017).
Sprengel, Peter, *Gerhart Hauptmann: Bürgerlichkeit und großer Traum* [biography], (Munich, 2012).
Steiman, Lionel B., 'The Eclipse of Humanism: Zweig between the Wars', *Modern Austrian Literature*, 14/3–4 (1981), 147–93.
Steiner, George, 'On the edge of hunger: Hitler's Vienna years and the formation of his anti-semitism' [review of Brigitte Hamann's study, *Hitlers Wien*], *Times Literary Supplement* (31 Jan. 1997), 3–4.
_____, *Martin Heidegger* (Chicago, 1991).
_____, *Grammars of Creation* (Yale, 2002).
Stenzel, Burkhard, '"... gerade gerne in Weimar": Stefan Zweig und die Klassikerstadt: verborgene Verbindungen – werkgeschichtliche Wirkungen', *Weimar-Jena: Die große Stadt*, 6/2 (2013), 100–13.
Stierle, Karlheinz, 'Souverän seiner Lektüren: Hugo Friedrichs Buch über Montaigne', *Frankfurter Allgemeine Zeitung (Bilder und Zeiten)* (18 Feb. 1989).
Stojanovis, Dubravaka, 'What is a nation? The Balkanization of historical memory', *Times Literary Supplement* (13 Sep. 2019).
The Bhagavad Gita, transl. by Juan Mascaro (Harmondsworth, 1980).
Smyth, Ethel, *The Memoirs of Ethel Smyth*, abridged and introduced by Ronald Crichton (New York, 1987).
Tomalin, Claire, *The Young H. G. Wells: Changing the World* (London, 2022).
Waal de, Alex, 'Die Influenza von 1918: Geschichten über Seuchen und die evolutionär-ökologische Erzählung', *Lettre International* (Autumn 2021), 31–4.
Weinzierl, Ulrich, *Stefan Zweigs brennendes Geheimnis* (Vienna, 2015).

Wenninger, Florian and Dreidemy, Lucile, *Das Dollfuss/Schuschnigg-Regime 1933–1938: Vermessung eines Forschungsfeldes* (Vienna, 2013).

Werfel, Franz, *Leben heißt, sich mitteilen: Betrachtungen, Reden, Aphorismen* [collected works in individual volumes], ed. by Knut Beck (Frankfurt am Main, 1975).

Weschenbach, Natascha, 'Stefan Zweig und Hippolyte Taine: Stefan Zweigs Dissertation über Die Philosophie des Hippolyte Taine', *Studia Imacologica*, 2 (Leiden/Boston/Paderborn/Singapore, 1992).

White, Hayden V., *Metahistory: The Historical Imagination in Nineteenth-Century Europe* (Baltimore, 1973).

_____, *The Content of the Form: Narrative Discourse and Historical Representation* (Baltimore, 1987).

Wittgenstein, Ludwig, *Tractatus Logico-Philosophicus*, transl. by D. F. Pears and B. F. McGuinness, with an introduction by Bertrand Russell (London/New York, 1997).

Wittmann, Hugo, 'Wien darf nicht New York werden!' [1910] in Arnold Klaffenböck (ed.), *Sehnsucht nach Alt-Wien: Texte zur Stadt, die niemals war*, with a preface by Wolfgang Kos (Vienna, 2005), 113–17.

Woolf, Virginia, *Orlando: A Biography* [1928] (London/Toronto/Sydney/New York, 1982).

_____, *Mrs Dalloway*, ed. with an introduction and notes by David Bradshaw (Oxford, 2000).

Wright, Patrick, 'Enemy alien: On Stefan Zweig', *The Guardian* (2 Feb. 2008).

Zimmermann, Christian von, *Biographische Anthropologie: Menschenbilder in lebensgeschichtlicher Darstellung 1830–1940* (Berlin/New York, 2006).

Online sources

'Erich Maria Remarque – Talk with Friedrich Luft (1960)' [online video], *Text und Bühne* (2 Jan. 2018), youtu.be/aOzROBGLkpE (accessed 30 Dec. 2022).

'Gustav Klimt und due Kunstschau 1908', belvedere.at, web.archive.org/web/20101223021432/http://www.belvedere.at/jart/prj3/belvedere/main.jart?rel=de&content-id=1173990963641&reserve-mode=active (accessed 8 Aug. 2024).

'Neuerwerbungen aus der Sammlung Inge und Erich Fitzbauer', Literaturarchiv Salzburg, www.stefanzweig.digital/archive/objects/context:szd/methods/sdef:Context/get?mode=miscellaneous (accessed 8 May 2022).

'Phony War', *Encyclopedia Britannica*, www.britannica.com/event/Phony-War (accessed 29 Sep. 2022).

'Dissecting the Troost Divide and Racial Segregation in Kansas City', *The Martin City & South KC Telegraph*, martincitytelegraph.com/2020/06/30/dissecting-the-troost-divide-and-racial-segregation-in-kansas-city/ (accessed 30 Oct. 2022).

'Gespräch mit Stephan Zweig: Drei Leben', *Aufbau*, VI/29 (19 Jul. 1940), archive.org/details/aufbau5619391940germ/page/n285/mode/1up? (accessed on 20 Feb. 2023).

Grenier, Richard, 'Colonel Redl: The Man Behind the Screen Myth', *The New York*

Times (13 Oct. 1985), www.nytimes.com/1985/10/13/movies/colonel-redl-the-man-behind-the-screen-myth.html (accessed 31 Oct. 2022).

Migge, Thomas, 'Dank dem Diktator', *Deutschlandfunk* (14 Jun. 2006). Report about Fabio Rugge's find in the Italian State Archive, at www.deutschlandfunk.de/dank-dem-diktator-100.html (accessed 19 May 2022).

Rees, Jasper, 'The Private Life of Stefan Zweig in England', *theartsdesk.com* (9 Feb. 2017), theartsdesk.com/books-theatre/private-life-stefan-zweig-england (accessed 11 Jun. 2024).

Warde, Samuel, 'Henry Ford pioneered modern industry, made America an economic power, and was a fervent Anti-Semite', allthatsinteresting.com/henry-ford-nazi (accessed on 30 Oct. 2022).